Thomas Edwards, William Edward Buckley

Cephalus and Procris

Thomas Edwards, William Edward Buckley

Cephalus and Procris

ISBN/EAN: 9783337380168

Printed in Europe, USA, Canada, Australia, Japan

Cover: Foto ©Thomas Meinert / pixelio.de

More available books at **www.hansebooks.com**

CEPHALUS AND PROCRIS.

NARCISSUS.

BY

THOMAS EDWARDS.

FROM THE UNIQUE COPY
IN THE CATHEDRAL LIBRARY, PETERBOROUGH.

EDITED BY

REV. W. E. BUCKLEY, M.A.,
RECTOR OF MIDDLETON-CHENEY, NORTHAMPTONSHIRE;
FORMERLY FELLOW OF BRASENOSE COLLEGE, OXFORD.

WITH AN APPENDIX FROM DIVERS SOURCES.

PRINTED FOR THE

Roxburghe Club.

LONDON:
NICHOLS AND SONS, 25, PARLIAMENT STREET.

MDCCCLXXXII.
E.V.

CEPHALUS AND PROCRIS.
NARCISSUS.

Roxburghe Club.

The Roxburghe Club.

MDCCCLXXXII.

THE DUKE OF BUCCLEUCH AND QUEENSBERRY, K.G.

PRESIDENT.

MARQUIS OF LOTHIAN.
MARQUIS OF BATH.
EARL OF CRAWFORD.
EARL OF CARNARVON.
EARL OF POWIS, *V.P.*
EARL BEAUCHAMP.
EARL OF CAWDOR.
LORD ZOUCHE.
LORD HOUGHTON.
LORD COLERIDGE.
RIGHT HON. ALEX. JAMES BERESFORD HOPE.
SIR WILLIAM REYNELL ANSON, BART.
SIR EDWARD HULSE, BART.
ARTHUR JAMES BALFOUR, ESQ.
HENRY BRADSHAW, ESQ.
HENRY ARTHUR BRIGHT, ESQ.
REV. WILLIAM EDWARD BUCKLEY.

FRANCIS HENRY DICKINSON, ESQ.
GEORGE BRISCOE EYRE, ESQ.
THOMAS GAISFORD, ESQ.
HENRY HUCKS GIBBS, ESQ. *Treasurer.*
ALBAN GEORGE HENRY GIBBS, ESQ.
RALPH NEVILLE GRENVILLE, ESQ.
ROBERT STAYNER HOLFORD, ESQ.
JOHN MALCOLM, ESQ.
JOHN COLE NICHOLL, ESQ.
EDWARD JAMES STANLEY, ESQ.
SIMON WATSON TAYLOR, ESQ.
REV. WILLIAM HEPWORTH THOMPSON, D.D.
GEORGE TOMLINE, ESQ.
REV. EDWARD TINDAL TURNER.
VICTOR WILLIAM BATES VAN DE WEYER, ESQ.
W. ALDIS WRIGHT, ESQ.

CONTENTS.

	PAGE
Title, general, to the whole Volume.	
Preface of the Editor - - - - -	i
Title, Original, of Cephalus and Procris, Narcissus	1
Dedication to Master Thomas Argall, Esquire -	3
Preface of the Poet Thomas Edwards -	4
Cephalus and Procris, The Poem	6
L'Envoy to Cephalus and Procris	30
Title, Original, of Narcissus -	- 35
Narcissus, The Poem -	37
L'Envoy to Narcissus	61
Appendix -	- 65
Italiæ Urbes Potissimæ, with Vilvain's Translation	- 67
Lines from Bodleian, Tanner MSS. 306, fol. 175	72
If all the Goddes would now agree.	
Lines from Bodleian, Tanner MSS. 306, fol. 175	- 74
The musses nyne that cradle rockte.	
Lines from Bodleian, Ashmole MSS. 38, p. 176	- 76
Various Readings from Parvum Theatrum Urbium -	- 77
Cephalus and Procris, from Golding's Translation of Ovid, 1567	- 81
Narcissus, from the same - - - - -	90
Cephalus and Procris, from " A Petite Pallace of Pettie his Pleasure, 1608 "	99
Narcissus, from Chaucer, Romaunt of the Rose -	- 121
Narcissus, from Gower, Confessio Amantis -	- 125
The Fable of Ovid Tretyng of Narcissus, in Englysh Mytre, 1560	- 129
The Moralization of the Fable, from the same - -	139

Contents.

	PAGE
Metamorphosis Ovidiana Moraliter a Mag. Thoma Waleys	173
Narcissus	175
Echo	176
The same in French, from " La Bible des Poetes "	177
The same in French Burlesque, " L'Ovide Bouffon 1665," reference to	177
The same in Spanish, 1609	178
Cephalus and Procris	179
The same in French, from " La Bible des Poetes "	181
The same in Spanish, 1609	181
Boccacio, "De Procri Cephali Conjuge," from " De Claris Mulieribus, Ulmæ, 1473	182
The same in Spanish, 1494	184
The same, translated by H. H. Gibbs, Esq.	186
The Tale of Cephalus and Procris, from Poems written by W. Shakespeare, 1640, by Thomas Heywood	*Not paged.*
Introduction to Cephalus and Procris	*Not paged.*
Notes to Cephalus and Procris	189
Introduction to Narcissus	265
Notes to Narcissus	283

Roxburghe Club.

1812. PRESIDENT.

1. GEORGE JOHN, EARL SPENCER.

1812.	2.	WILLIAM SPENCER, DUKE OF DEVONSHIRE.
1812.	3.	GEORGE SPENCER CHURCHILL, MARQUIS OF BLANDFORD.
		1817. DUKE OF MARLBOROUGH.
1812.	4.	GEORGE GRANVILLE LEVESON GOWER, EARL GOWER.
		1833. MARQUIS OF STAFFORD.
		1833. DUKE OF SUTHERLAND.
1812.	5.	GEORGE HOWARD, VISCOUNT MORPETH.
		1825. EARL OF CARLISLE.
1812.	6.	JOHN CHARLES SPENCER, VISCOUNT ALTHORP.
		1834. EARL SPENCER.
1812.	7.	SIR MARK MASTERMAN SYKES, BART.
1812.	8.	SIR SAMUEL EGERTON BRYDGES, BART.
1812.	9.	WILLIAM BENTHAM, ESQ.
1812.	10.	WILLIAM BOLLAND, ESQ.
		1829. SIR WILLIAM BOLLAND. KNT.
1812.	11.	JAMES BOSWELL, ESQ.
1812.	12.	REV. WILLIAM HOLWELL CARR.
1812.	13.	JOHN DENT. ESQ.
1812.	14.	REV. THOMAS FROGNALL DIBDIN.
1812.	15.	REV. HENRY DRURY.

1812.	16.	FRANCIS FREELING, ESQ.
		1828. SIR FRANCIS FREELING, BART.
1812.	17.	GEORGE HENRY FREELING, ESQ.
		1836. SIR GEORGE HENRY FREELING, BART.
1812.	18.	JOSEPH HASLEWOOD, ESQ.
1812.	19.	RICHARD HEBER, ESQ.
1812.	20.	REV. THOMAS CUTHBERT HEBER.
1812.	21.	GEORGE ISTED, ESQ.
1812.	22.	ROBERT LANG, ESQ.
1812.	23.	JOSEPH LITTLEDALE, ESQ.
		1824. SIR JOSEPH LITTLEDALE, KNT.
1812.	24.	JAMES HEYWOOD MARKLAND, ESQ.
1812.	25.	JOHN DELAFIELD PHELPS, ESQ.
1812.	26.	THOMAS PONTON, ESQ.
1812.	27.	PEREGRINE TOWNELEY, ESQ.
1812.	28.	EDWARD VERNON UTTERSON, ESQ.
1812.	29.	ROGER WILBRAHAM, ESQ.
1812.	30.	REV. JAMES WILLIAM DODD.
1812.	31.	EDWARD LITTLEDALE, ESQ.

1816.	32.	GEORGE HIBBERT, ESQ.
1819.	33.	SIR ALEXANDER BOSWELL, BART.
1822.	34.	GEORGE WATSON TAYLOR, ESQ.
1822.	35.	JOHN ARTHUR LLOYD, ESQ.
1822.	36.	VENERABLE ARCHDEACON WRANGHAM.
1823.	37.	THE AUTHOR OF WAVERLEY.
		1827. SIR WALTER SCOTT, BART.
1827.	38.	HON. AND REV. GEORGE NEVILLE GRENVILLE.
		1846. DEAN OF WINDSOR.
1828.	39.	EDWARD HERBERT, VISCOUNT CLIVE.
		1839. EARL OF POWIS.
1830.	40.	JOHN FREDERICK, EARL OF CAWDOR.
1831.	41.	REV. EDWARD CRAVEN HAWTREY, D.D.
1834.	42.	SIR STEPHEN RICHARD GLYNNE, BART.
1834.	43.	BENJAMIN BARNARD, ESQ.
1834.	44.	VENERABLE ARCHDEACON BUTLER, D.D.
		1836. SAMUEL, LORD BISHOP OF LICHFIELD.

1835. PRESIDENT.
EDWARD HERBERT, VISCOUNT CLIVE.
1839. EARL OF POWIS.

1835.	45.	WALTER FRANCIS, DUKE OF BUCCLEUCH AND QUEENSBERRY.
1836.	46.	RIGHT HONOURABLE LORD FRANCIS EGERTON.
		1846. EARL OF ELLESMERE.
1836.	47.	ARCHIBALD ACHESON, VISCOUNT ACHESON.
		1849. EARL OF GOSFORD.
1836.	48.	BERIAH BOTFIELD, ESQ.
1836.	49.	HENRY HALLAM, ESQ.
1837.	50.	PHILIP HENRY STANHOPE, VISCOUNT MAHON.
		1855. EARL STANHOPE.
1838.	51.	GEORGE JOHN, LORD VERNON.
1838.	52.	REV. PHILIP BLISS, D.C.L.
1839.	53.	RIGHT HONOURABLE SIR JAMES PARKE, KNT.
		1856. LORD WENSLEYDALE.
1839.	54.	REV. BULKELEY BANDINEL, D.D.
1839.	55.	WILLIAM HENRY MILLER, ESQ.
1839.	56.	EVELYN PHILIP SHIRLEY, ESQ.
1840.	57.	EDWARD JAMES HERBERT, VISCOUNT CLIVE.
		1848. EARL OF POWIS.
1841.	58.	DAVID DUNDAS, ESQ.
		1847. SIR DAVID DUNDAS, KNT.
1842.	59.	JOHN EARL BROWNLOW.
1842.	60.	HONOURABLE HUGH CHOLMONDELEY.
		1855. LORD DELAMERE.
1844.	61.	SIR ROBERT HARRY INGLIS, BART.
1844.	62.	ALEXANDER JAMES BERESFORD HOPE, ESQ.
1844.	63.	REV. HENRY WELLESLEY.
1845.	64.	ANDREW RUTHERFURD, ESQ.
		1851. LORD RUTHERFURD.
1846.	65.	HON. ROBERT CURZON, JUN.
1846.	66.	GEORGE TOMLINE, ESQ.
1846.	67.	WILLIAM STIRLING, ESQ.
		1866. SIR WILLIAM STIRLING MAXWELL, BART.
1847.	68.	FRANCIS HENRY DICKINSON, ESQ.

1848. PRESIDENT.

WALTER FRANCIS, DUKE OF BUCCLEUCH AND QUEENSBERRY, K.G.

1848.	69.	NATHANIEL BLAND, ESQ.
1848.	70.	REV. WILLIAM EDWARD BUCKLEY.
1849.	71.	REV. JOHN STUART HIPPISLEY HORNER.
1849.	72.	HIS EXCELLENCY MONSIEUR VAN DE WEYER.
1849.	73.	MELVILLE PORTAL, ESQ.
1851.	74.	ROBERT STAYNER HOLFORD, ESQ.
	75.	PAUL BUTLER, ESQ.
	76.	EDWARD HULSE, ESQ.

1855. SIR EDWARD HULSE, BART.

1853.	77.	CHARLES TOWNELEY, ESQ.
1854.	78.	WILLIAM ALEX. ANTH. ARCH. DUKE OF HAMILTON AND BRANDON.
	79.	HENRY HOWARD MOLYNEUX, EARL OF CARNARVON.
1855.	80.	SIR JOHN BENN WALSH, BART.

1868. LORD ORMATHWAITE.

	81.	ADRIAN JOHN HOPE, ESQ.
	82.	RALPH NEVILLE GRENVILLE, ESQ.
1856.	83.	SIR JOHN SIMEON, BART.
	84.	SIR JAMES SHAW WILLES, KNT.
1857.	85.	GEORGE GRANVILLE FRANCIS, EARL OF ELLESMERE.
	86.	WILLIAM SCHOMBERG ROBERT, MARQUIS OF LOTHIAN.
	87.	FREDERICK TEMPLE, LORD DUFFERIN.

1872. EARL OF DUFFERIN.

1858.	88.	SIMON WATSON TAYLOR, ESQ.
	89.	THOMAS GAISFORD, ESQ.
1861.	90.	JOHN FREDERICK VAUGHAN, EARL CAWDOR.
1863.	91.	GRANVILLE LEVESON GOWER, ESQ.
	92.	HENRY HUCKS GIBBS, ESQ.
1864.	93.	RICHARD MONCKTON, LORD HOUGHTON.
	94.	CHRISTOPHER SYKES, ESQ.
	95.	REV. HENRY OCTAVIUS COXE.
	96.	REV. WILLIAM GEORGE CLARK.
	97.	REV. CHARLES HENRY HARTSHORNE.
	98.	JOHN COLE NICHOLL, ESQ.
	99.	GEORGE BRISCOE EYRE, ESQ.
	100.	JOHN BENJAMIN HEATH, ESQ.
1866.	101.	HENRY HUTH, ESQ.
	102.	HENRY BRADSHAW, ESQ.
1867.	103.	FREDERICK, EARL BEAUCHAMP.
	104.	KIRKMAN DANIEL HODGSON, ESQ.
1868.	105.	CHARLES WYNNE FINCH, ESQ.

1870.	106.	HENRY SALUSBURY MILMAN, ESQ.
	107.	EDWARD JAMES STANLEY, ESQ.
1871.	108.	REV. EDWARD TINDAL TURNER.
1872.	109.	SCHOMBERG HENRY, MARQUIS OF LOTHIAN.
1875.	110.	JOHN ALEXANDER, MARQUIS OF BATH.
	111.	JOHN DUKE, LORD COLERIDGE.
	112.	VICTOR WILLIAM BATES VAN DE WEYER, ESQ.
	113.	HENRY ARTHUR BRIGHT, ESQ.
	114.	ALBAN GEORGE HENRY GIBBS, ESQ.
1876.	115.	REV. WILLIAM HEPWORTH THOMPSON, D.D.
1877.	116.	JOHN LUDOVIC LINDSAY, LORD LINDSAY.
		1880. EARL OF CRAWFORD.
1879.	117.	ROBERT NATHANIEL CECIL GEORGE, LORD ZOUCHE.
	118.	ROBERT AMADEUS HEATH, BARON HEATH.
	119.	ARTHUR JAMES BALFOUR, ESQ.
	120.	JOHN MALCOLM, ESQ.
	121.	WILLIAM ALDIS WRIGHT, ESQ.
	122.	SIR WILLIAM REYNELL ANSON, BART.
1880.	123.	FREDERIC OUVRY, ESQ.

Roxburghe Club.

CATALOGUE OF THE BOOKS

PRESENTED TO

AND PRINTED BY THE CLUB.

LONDON:

MDCCCLXXXII.

CATALOGUE.

Certaine Bokes of VIRGILES Aeneis, turned into English Meter. By the Right Honorable Lorde, HENRY EARLE OF SURREY.
        WILLIAM BOLLAND, ESQ. 1814.
Caltha Poetarum; or, The Bumble Bee. By T. CUTWODE, ESQ.
        RICHARD HEBER, ESQ. 1815.
The Three First Books of OVID de Tristibus, Translated into English. By THOMAS CHURCHYARDE.
        EARL SPENCER, PRESIDENT. 1816.
Poems. By RICHARD BARNFIELD.
        JAMES BOSWELL, ESQ. 1816.
DOLARNEY's Primerose or the First part of the Passionate Hermit.
        SIR FRANCIS FREELING, BART. 1816.
La Contenance de la Table.
        GEORGE HENRY FREELING, ESQ. 1816.
Newes from Scotland, declaring the Damnable Life of Doctor Fian, a notable Sorcerer, who was burned at Edenbrough in Ianuarie last 1591.
        GEORGE HENRY FREELING, ESQ. 1816.
A proper new Interlude of the World and the Child, otherwise called Mundus et Infans.
        VISCOUNT ALTHORP. 1817.
HAGTHORPE Revived; or Select Specimens of a Forgotten Poet.
        SIR SAMUEL EGERTON BRYDGES, BART. 1817

Istoria novellamente ritrovata di due nobili Amanti, &c. da LUIGI PORTO.
REV. WILLIAM HOLWELL CARR. 1817.

The Funeralles of King Edward the Sixt.
REV. JAMES WILLIAM DODD. 1817

A Roxburghe Garland, 12mo.
JAMES BOSWELL, ESQ. 1817.

Cock Lorell's Boat, a Fragment from the original in the British Museum.
REV. HENRY DRURY. 1817.

Le Livre du Faucon.
ROBERT LANG, ESQ. 1817.

The Glutton's Feaver. By THOMAS BANCROFT.
JOHN DELAFIELD PHELPS, ESQ. 1817.

The Chorle and the Birde.
SIR MARK MASTERMAN SYKES, BART. 1818.

Daiphantus, or the Passions of Love. By ANTONY SCOLOKER.
ROGER WILBRAHAM, ESQ. 1818.

The Complaint of a Lover's Life.
Controversy between a Lover and a Jay.
REV. THOMAS FROGNALL DIBDIN, VICE PRESIDENT. 1818.

Balades and other Poems. By JOHN GOWER. Printed from the original Manuscript in the Library of the Marquis of Stafford, at Trentham.
EARL GOWER. 1818.

Diana; or the excellent conceitful Sonnets of H. C., supposed to have been printed either in 1592 or 1594.
EDWARD LITTLEDALE, ESQ. 1818.

Chester Mysteries. De Deluvio Noe. De Occisione Innocentium.
JAMES HEYWOOD MARKLAND, ESQ. 1818.

Ceremonial at the Marriage of Mary Queen of Scotts with the Dauphin of France.
          WILLIAM BENTHAM, ESQ. 1818.

The Solempnities and Triumphes doon and made at the Spousells and Marriage of the King's Daughter the Ladye Marye to the Prynce of Castile, Archduke of Austrige.
          JOHN DENT, ESQ. 1818.

The Life of St. Ursula.
Guiscard and Sigismund.
          DUKE OF DEVONSHIRE. 1818.

Le Morte Arthur. The Adventures of Sir Launcelot Du Lake.
          THOMAS PONTON, ESQ. 1819.

Six Bookes of Metamorphoseos in whyche ben conteyned the Fables of OVYDE. Translated out of Frensshe into Englysshe by WILLIAM CAXTON. Printed from a Manuscript in the Library of Mr. Secretary Pepys, in the College of St. Mary Magdalen, in the University of Cambridge.
          GEORGE HIBBERT, ESQ. 1819.

Chevelere Assigne.
          EDWARD VERNON UTTERSON, ESQ. 1820.

Two Interludes: Jack Jugler and Thersytes.
          JOSEPH HASLEWOOD, ESQ. 1820.

The New Notborune Mayd. The Boke of Mayd Emlyn.
          GEORGE ISTED, ESQ. 1820.

The Book of Life; a Bibliographical Melody.
   Dedicated to the Roxburghe Club by RICHARD THOMSON.
          8vo. 1820.

Magnyfycence: an Interlude. By JOHN SKELTON, Poet Laureat to Henry VIII.
          JOSEPH LITTLEDALE, ESQ. 1821.

Judicium, a Pageant. Extracted from the Towneley Manuscript of Ancient Mysteries.
PEREGRINE EDWARD TOWNELEY, ESQ. 1822.

An Elegiacal Poem, on the Death of Thomas Lord Grey, of Wilton. By ROBERT MARSTON. From a Manuscript in the Library of The Right Honourable Thomas Grenville.
VISCOUNT MORPETH. 1822.

Selections from the Works of THOMAS RAVENSCROFT; a Musical Composer of the time of King James the First.
DUKE OF MARLBOROUGH. 1822.

LÆLII PEREGRINI Oratio in Obitum Torquati Tassi. Editio secunda.
SIR SAMUEL EGERTON BRYDGES, BART. 1822.

The Hors, the Shepe, and the Ghoos.
SIR MARK MASTERMAN SYKES, BART. 1822.

The Metrical Life of Saint Robert of Knaresborough.
REV. HENRY DRURY. 1824.

Informacōn for Pylgrymes unto the Holy Londe. From a rare Tract in the Library of the Faculty of Advocates, Edinburgh.
GEORGE HENRY FREELING, ESQ. 1824.

The Cuck-Queanes and Cuckolds Errants or the Bearing Down the Inne, a Comœdie. The Faery Pastorall or Forrest of Elues. By W—— P——, Esq.
JOHN ARTHUR LLOYD, ESQ. 1824.

The Garden Plot, an Allegorical Poem, inscribed to Queen Elizabeth. By HENRY GOLDINGHAM. From an unpublished Manuscript of the Harleian Collection in the British Museum. To which are added some account of the Author; also a reprint of his Masques performed before the Queen at Norwich on Thursday, August 21, 1578.
VENERABLE ARCHDEACON WRANGHAM. 1825.

La Rotta de Francciosi a Terroana novamente facta.
La Rotta de Scocesi.
EARL SPENCER, PRESIDENT. 1825.

Nouvelle Edition d'un Poeme sur la Journée de Guinegate.
Presented by the MARQUIS DE FORTIA. 1825.

Zuléima, par C. PICHLER. 12mo.
Presented by H. DE CHATEAUGIRON. 1825.

Poems, written in English, by CHARLES DUKE OF ORLEANS, during his Captivity in England after the Battle of Azincourt.
GEORGE WATSON TAYLOR, ESQ. 1827.

Proceedings in the Court Martial held upon John, Master of Sinclair, Captain-Lieutenant in Preston's Regiment, for the Murder of Ensign Schaw of the same Regiment, and Captain Schaw, of the Royals, 17 October, 1708; with Correspondence respecting that Transaction.
SIR WALTER SCOTT, BART. 1828.

The Ancient English Romance of Havelok the Dane; accompanied by the French Text: with an Introduction, Notes, and a Glossary. By FREDERIC MADDEN, ESQ.
PRINTED FOR THE CLUB. 1828.

GAUFRIDI ARTHURII MONEMUTHENSIS Archidiaconi, postea vero Episcopi Asaphensis, de Vita et Vaticiniis Merlini Calidonii, Carmen Heroicum.
HON. and REV. G. NEVILLE GRENVILLE. 1830.

The Ancient English Romance of William and the Werwolf; edited from an unique copy in King's College Library, Cambridge; with an Introduction and Glossary. By FREDERIC MADDEN Esq.
EARL CAWDOR. 1832.

The Private Diary of WILLIAM, first EARL COWPER, Lord Chancellor of England.
REV. EDWARD CRAVEN HAWTREY. 1833.

The Lyvys of Seyntes; translated into Englys be a Doctour of Dyuynite clepyd OSBERN BOKENAM, frer Austyn of the Convent of Stocklare.
VISCOUNT CLIVE, PRESIDENT. 1835.

A Little Boke of Ballads.
Dedicated to the Club by E. V. UTTERSON, ESQ. 1836.

The Love of Wales to their Soueraigne Prince, expressed in a true Relation of the Solemnity held at Ludlow, in the Countie of Salop, upon the fourth of November last past, Anno Domini 1616, being the day of the Creation of the high and mighty Charles, Prince of Wales, and Earle of Chester, in his Maiesties Palace of White-Hall.
Presented by the HONOURABLE R. H. CLIVE. 1837.

Sidneiana, being a collection of Fragments relative to Sir Philip Sidney, Knight, and his immediate Connexions.
BISHOP OF LICHFIELD. 1837.

The Owl and the Nightingale, a Poem of the Twelfth Century. Now first printed from Manuscripts in the Cottonian Library, and at Jesus' College, Oxford; with an Introduction and Glossary. Edited by JOSEPHUS STEVENSON, ESQ.
SIR STEPHEN RICHARD GLYNNE, BART. 1838.

The Old English Version of the Gesta Romanorum: edited for the first time from Manuscripts in the British Museum and University Library, Cambridge, with an Introduction and Notes, by SIR FREDERIC MADDEN, K.H.
PRINTED FOR THE CLUB. 1838.

Illustrations of Ancient State and Chivalry, from MSS. preserved in the Ashmolean Museum, with an Appendix.
        BENJAMIN BARNARD, ESQ. 1840.

Manners and Household Expenses of England in the Thirteenth and Fifteenth Centuries, illustrated by original Records. I. Household Roll of Eleanor Countess of Leicester, A.D. 1265. II. Accounts of the Executors of Eleanor Queen Consort of Edward I. A.D. 1291. III. Accounts and Memoranda of Sir John Howard, first Duke of Norfolk, A.D. 1462 to A.D. 1471.
        BERIAH BOTFIELD, ESQ. 1841.

The Black Prince, an Historical Poem, written in French, by CHANDOS HERALD; with a Translation and Notes by the Rev. HENRY OCTAVIUS COXE, M.A.
        PRINTED FOR THE CLUB. 1842.

The Decline of the last Stuarts. Extracts from the Despatches of British Envoys to the Secretary of State.
        PRINTED FOR THE CLUB. 1843.

Vox Populi Vox Dei, a Complaynt of the Comons against Taxes. Presented according to the Direction of the late
        RIGHT HON. SIR JOSEPH LITTLEDALE, KNT. 1843.

Household Books of John Duke of Norfolk and Thomas Earl of Surrey; temp. 1481—1490. From the original Manuscripts in the Library of the Society of Antiquaries, London. Edited by J. PAYNE COLLIER, ESQ., F.S.A.
        PRINTED FOR THE CLUB. 1844.

Three Collections of English Poetry of the latter part of the Sixteenth Century.
    Presented by the DUKE OF NORTHUMBERLAND, K.G. 1845.

Historical Papers, Part I. Castra Regia, a Treatise on the Succession to the Crown of England, addressed to Queen Elizabeth by ROGER EDWARDS, ESQ., in 1568. Novissima Straffordii, Some account of the Proceedings against, and Demeanor of, Thomas Wentworth, Earl of Strafford, both before and during his Trial, as well as at his Execution; written in Latin by ABRAHAM WRIGHT, Vicar of Okeham, in Rutlandshire. The same (endeauord) in English by JAMES WRIGHT, Barrister at Law.

REV. PHILIP BLISS, D.C.L., and REV. BULKELEY BANDINEL. 1846.

Correspondence of SIR HENRY UNTON, KNT., Ambassador from Queen Elizabeth to Henry IV. King of France, in the years MDXCI. and MDXCII. From the originals and authentic copies in the State Paper Office, the British Museum, and the Bodleian Library. Edited by the REV. JOSEPH STEVENSON, M.A. PRINTED FOR THE CLUB. 1847.

La Vraie Cronicque d'Escoce. Pretensions des Anglois à la Couronne de France. Diplome de Jacques VI. Roi de la Grande Bretagne. Drawn from the Burgundian Library by Major Robert Anstruther.

PRINTED FOR THE CLUB. 1847.

The Sherley Brothers, an Historical Memoir of the Lives of Sir Thomas Sherley, Sir Anthony Sherley, and Sir Robert Sherley, Knights, by one of the same House. Edited and Presented by
EVELYN PHILIP SHIRLEY, ESQ. 1848.

The Alliterative Romance of Alexander. From the unique Manuscript in the Ashmolean Museum. Edited by the REV. JOSEPH STEVENSON, M.A.

PRINTED FOR THE CLUB. 1849.

Letters and Dispatches from Sir Henry Wotton to James the
First and his Ministers, in the years MDCXVII—XX.
Printed from the originals in the Library of Eton College.
George Tomline, Esq. 1850.

Poema quod dicitur Vox Clamantis, necnon Chronica Tripartita,
auctore Johanne Gower, nunc primum edidit H. O. Coxe,
M.A. Printed for the Club. 1850.

Five Old Plays. Edited from Copies, either unique or of great
rarity, by J. Payne Collier, Esq., F.S.A.
Printed for the Club. 1851.

The Romaunce of the Sowdone of Babylone and of Ferumbras
his Sone who conquerede Rome.
The Duke of Buccleuch, President. 1854.

The Ayenbite of Inwyt. From the Autograph MS. in the British
Museum. Edited by the Rev. Joseph Stevenson, M.A.
Printed for the Club. 1855.

John de Garlande, de Triumphis Ecclesiæ Libri Octo. A Latin
Poem of the Thirteenth Century. Edited, from the unique
Manuscript in the British Museum, by Thomas Wright, Esq.,
M.A., F.S.A., Hon. M.R.S.L., &c. &c.
Earl of Powis. 1856.

Poems by Michael Drayton. From the earliest and rarest Editions, or from Copies entirely unique. Edited, with Notes and
Illustrations, and a new Memoir of the Author, by J. Payne
Collier, Esq., F.S.A. Printed for the Club. 1856.

Literary Remains of King Edward the Sixth. In Two Volumes.
Edited from his Autograph Manuscripts, with Historical Notes
and a Biographical Memoir, by John Gough Nichols, F.S.A.
Printed for the Club. 1857.

The Itineraries of WILLIAM WEY, Fellow of Eton College, to Jerusalem, A.D. 1458 and A.D. 1462; and to Saint James of Compostella, A.D. 1456. From the Original MS. in the Bodleian Library. PRINTED FOR THE CLUB. 1857.

The Boke of Noblesse; Addressed to King Edward the Fourth on his Invasion of France in 1475. With an Introduction by JOHN GOUGH NICHOLS, F.S.A.
LORD DELAMERE. 1860.

Songs and Ballads, with other Short Poems, chiefly of the Reign of Philip and Mary. Edited, from a Manuscript in the Ashmolean Museum, by THOMAS WRIGHT, ESQ., M.A., F.S A., &c. &c.
ROBERT S. HOLFORD, ESQ. 1860.

De Regimine Principum, a Poem by THOMAS OCCLEVE, written in the Reign of Henry IV. Edited for the first time by THOMAS WRIGHT, ESQ., M.A., F.S.A., &c. &c.
PRINTED FOR THE CLUB. 1860.

The History of the Holy Graal; partly in English Verse by Henry Lonelich, Skynner, and wholly in French Prose by Sires Robiers de Borron. In two volumes. Edited, from MSS. in the Library of Corpus Christi College, Cambridge, and the British Museum, by FREDERICK J. FURNIVALL, ESQ., M.A., Trinity Hall, Cambridge.
PRINTED FOR THE CLUB. 1861 AND 1863.

Roberd of Brunne's Handlyng Synne, written A.D. 1203; with the French Treatise on which it is founded, Le Manuel des Pechie3 by William of Waddington. From MSS. in the British Museum and Bodleian Libraries. Edited by FREDERICK J. FURNIVALL, ESQ., M.A.
PRINTED FOR THE CLUB. 1862.

The Old English Version of Partonope of Blois. Edited for the first time from MSS. in University College Library and the Bodleian at Oxford, by the REV. W. E. BUCKLEY, M.A., Rector of Middleton Cheney, and formerly Fellow of Brasenose College.   PRINTED FOR THE CLUB. 1862.

Philosophaster, Comœdia; Poemata, auctore Roberto Burtono, S. Th. B., Democrito Juniore, Ex Æde Christi Oxon.
REV. WILLIAM EDWARD BUCKLEY. 1862.

La Queste del Saint Graal. In the French Prose of Maistres Gautiers Map, or Walter Map. Edited by FREDERICK J. FURNIVALL, Esq., M.A., Trinity Hall, Cambridge.
PRINTED FOR THE CLUB. 1864.

A Royal Historie of the excellent Knight Generides.
HENRY HUCKS GIBBS, ESQ. 1865.

The Copy-Book of Sir Amias Poulet's Letters, written during his Embassy in France, A.D. 1577.
PRINTED FOR THE CLUB. 1866.

The Bokes of Nurture and Kervynge.
HON. ROBERT CURZON. 1867.

A Map of the Holy Land, illustrating Wey's Itineraries.
PRINTED FOR THE CLUB. 1867.

Historia Quatuor Regum Angliæ, authore Johanne Herdo.
SIMON WATSON TAYLOR, ESQ. 1868.

Letters of Patrick Ruthven, Earl of Forth and Brentford, 1615—1662.   DUKE OF BUCCLEUCH, PRESIDENT. 1868.

The Pilgrimage of the Lyf of the Manhode, from the French of Guillaume de Deguileville.   PRINTED FOR THE CLUB. 1869.

Correspondence of Colonel N. Hooke, 1703—1707. Vol. I.
PRINTED FOR THE CLUB. 1870—1.

Liber Regalis; seu ordo Consecrandi Regem et Reginam.
EARL BEAUCHAMP. 1870.

Le Mystère de Saint Louis, Roi de France.
PRINTED FOR THE CLUB. 1871.

Correspondence of Colonel N. Hooke, 1703—1707. Vol. II.
PRINTED FOR THE CLUB. 1871.

The History of the Most Noble Knight Plasidas, and other Pieces; from the Pepysian Library. PRINTED FOR THE CLUB. 1873.

Florian and Florete, a Metrical Romance.
MARQUIS OF LOTHIAN. 1873.

A Fragment of Partonope of Blois, from a Manuscript at Vale Royal. PRINTED FOR THE CLUB. 1873.

The Legend of Sir Nicholas Throckmorton.
PAUL BUTLER, ESQ. 1874.

Correspondence of the First Earl of Ancram and the Third Earl of Lothian. 1616—1687. 2 Vols.
MARQUIS OF LOTHIAN. 1875.

The History of Grisild the Second.
JOHN BENJAMIN HEATH, ESQ. 1875.

The Complete Poems of Richard Barnfield.
PRINTED FOR THE CLUB. 1876.

The Apocalypse of St. John, from an Anglo-Saxon Manuscript.
PRINTED FOR THE CLUB. 1876.

Poems from Sir Kenelm Digby's Papers.
HENRY ARTHUR BRIGHT, ESQ. 1877.

Cephalus and Procris, by THOMAS EDWARDS.
PRINTED FOR THE CLUB. 1880—2.

Sir John Harington on the Succession to the Crown, 1602.
PRINTED FOR THE CLUB. 1880.
An Inquisition of the Manors of Glastonbury Abbey. 1589.
MARQUIS OF BATH. 1882.
The Lamport Garland. PRINTED FOR THE CLUB. 1882.

PREFACE.

Among the literary treasures brought to light in 1867 at Lamport Hall, Northamptonshire, the seat of Sir C. E. Isham, Bart., by Mr. C. Edmonds, who had been called in to report upon the state of the library, was a fragment of "Cephalus and Procris," by Thomas Edwards, consisting of the first sheet only, from which he was enabled to communicate to Mr. Hazlitt for insertion in the Handbook of Popular Literature, then on the eve of publication, the notice which is printed among "The Additions" at p. 690 of that work. Subsequently in 1871 Mr. Hazlitt, in his edition of Warton's History of English Poetry, sect. 58, vol. iv. p. 298, added to the mention made of this work in a note, that "No perfect copy is known." This remark, true at the time, was not long to remain so, and it is a matter of no little satisfaction to myself to have been instrumental in supplying the means for correcting it, as I had the good fortune, some seven years after, to discover that a perfect copy was in the Cathedral Library at Peterborough. This most precious volume was entrusted to me, as well as the Lamport fragment, for the purpose of preparing the present reprint, which I have endeavoured to make in all respects an exact reproduction of the

a

ii Preface.

original. In one instance only have I ventured to make a correction by substituting "*forlorne*" instead of the manifest typographical error "*forlotne*" in the fourth line of the last stanza on p. 56. The punctuation has in all cases been scrupulously preserved, so that the present volume may be regarded as almost equivalent to a facsimile.

II. The fate of the Author and his work is remarkable. Although he mentions several of his contemporaries with the most kind and just appreciation of their merits, it does not appear that any one of them thought his name worthy of record: and his work, with one or two exceptions, may be said to have been left unregarded from the time of its publication. If the writers of his own age were indifferent, their successors were, as might be expected, ignorant even of his existence, and thus neither the works of any of our poetical antiquaries, biographers, or critics, nor those of our professed bibliographers, until Hazlitt, contain any notice whatever of him or his work. It may seem somewhat strange that our late colleague and treasurer, Mr. Beriah Botfield, should not have discovered this volume, and mentioned it in his "Notes on the Cathedral Libraries of England," privately printed in 1849, in which pp. 369 to 384 are devoted to the description of the Library at Peterborough. The omission, however, may perhaps be thus accounted for. There are in the Library many volumes in quarto of miscellaneous tracts bound together without any attempt at classification, or separation even of prose from poetry, and when Mr. Botfield made his notes this volume of poems was no doubt bound with others, and thus escaped his observation, whereas it, and some few others

Preface. iii

of the same size, have been bound, evidently at no distant date, as separate volumes, and thus they now more readily attract the eye.

The articles contained in these volumes were apparently not entered separately in the Catalogue, on which Mr. Botfield mainly relied for his knowledge of the contents of the Library, as he intimates on p. viii. of his preface, "I have in every instance carefully perused the Catalogue, and minutely examined every volume which I have ventured to describe. This I have done at various times and different intervals. * * * No one can be more sensible than myself of the imperfections and omissions of a work compiled under such circumstances, and I shall feel deeply indebted to any one who will undertake to correct the one or to supply the other." How numerous the omissions are may be estimated from the few lines devoted to English Poetry at p. 377. "Of English Poesy the chaplet to be woven is but small; the curious reader may however cull such flowers as the works of Chaucer and of Milton; Heywood's Spider and the Flie, 1536; Churchyard's Challenge; and the Vision of Pierce Plowman, may yield."

With all its imperfections, Mr. Botfield's volume has done good service by calling attention to our Cathedral Libraries, wherein there are doubtless many treasures both of printed books and manuscripts to reward more thorough research.

III. The earliest reference to this work or, if not to this, to one on the same subject, is an entry in the Register of the Stationers' Company, which Herbert in his Typographical Antiquities (vol. ii. p. 1189) briefly records in his account of John Wolfe, under the

a 2

iv   *Preface.*

year 1593, as "Procris and Cephalus." The publication, however, of these Registers by Mr. Arber enables me to quote the entry at full length:

⎡ G. Cawood.   ⎫ W. Norton.
⎢ T. Woodcock. ⎬ G. Bishop.   22 October—14 November] *Anno* 1593.
⎣ T. Stirrop. ⎭
                              Annoque Regni Regin[a]*e Elizabeth*[æ] 35to.

22° die ©ctobris.

John Wolff. Entred for his Copie vnder the handes of Master MURGETROD and the Wardens a booke entytuled PROCRIS and CEPHALVS *devided into foure partes* . . . .vj^d

Arber Transcript, ii. 639, being p. 302a of the original Register B.

It will be observed that the printed book is entitled "Cephalus and Procris. Narcissus," and that the former poem is not divided into four parts, but is continuous throughout. If then this entry be held to relate to the work of Thomas Edwards, it must be supposed that he had some valid reasons for shortening the former poem and altering the order of the two names on the title; as well as for including the second poem, Narcissus, in the same volume. Most authorities[*] consider that there was another poem with the

---

[*] Ritson, Bibliographica Poetica, 1802, p. 170. "Anthony Chute. It appears from a passage in Nash's 'Have with you to Saffron Walden,' 1596, that he had, likewise, written 'Procris and Cephalus.' " Collier, Bibliographical Account of Early English Literature, 1865, ii. 18. " Some pages on Nash abuses Barnabe Barnes and Anthony Chute, and imputes to the latter a work called ' Procris and Cephalus,' which was entered by Wolfe on the books of the Stationers' Company in 1593, but, if printed, no copy of it is now known." Warton, History of English Poetry, iv. 243, note, ed. 1824. "There is likewise, which may be referred hither, 'a booke intitled Procris and Cephalus, divided into four parts,' licenced Oct. 22, 1593, to J. Wolfe, perhaps a play,

Preface.

title "Procris and Cephalus," by Anthony Chute, and rely for this view on the following passage from Thomas Nash's "Have with you to Saffron Walden, or Gabriell Harvey's Hunt is up," printed at London by John Danter in 1596, small quarto, which occurs on sign. O 2, fol. 103, the pages however not being numbered.

" In plaine truth and in verity, some pleasures he did *Wolfe* in my knowledge. For first and formost he did for him that eloquent *post-script* for the Plague Bills, where he talkes of the series the classes & the premisses, and presenting them with an exacter methode hereafter, if it please God the Plague continue. By the style I tooke it napping, and smelt it to be a pig of his *Sus Minervam* the Sow his Muse as soone as euer I read it, and since the Printer hath confest it to mee. The vermilion *wrinckle de crinkledum* hop'd (belike) that the Plague would proceed, that he might haue an occupation of it. The second thing wherein he made *Wolfe* so much beholding to him, was, that if there were euer a paltrie *Scriuano*, betwixt a Lawiers Clark & a Poet, or smattring pert Boy, whose buttocks were not yet coole since he came from the grammer, or one that houers betwixt two crutches of a Scholler and a Traueller, when neither will helpe him to goe

and probably ridiculed in the Midsummer Night's Dream under the title *Shefalus and Procris*. Reg. Stat. B. fol. 302a. [Procris and Cephalus, by A. Chute, is mentioned with his poem of Shore's Wife in Nash's "Have with you to Saffron Walden," 1596, where he alludes to a number of Pamphlagonian things more, PARK.] Lowndes and Hazlitt, under A. Chute, repeat this in their Bibliographical Manuals, though Mr. Hazlitt in his edition of Warton ascribes it to Thomas Edwards, and suppresses the latter part of Warton's note, vol. iv. 298.

vpright in the worlds opinion, & shuld stumble him in there with a Pamphlet to sell, let him or anie of them but haue conioynd with him in rayling against mee, and feed his humor of vaine-glorie, were their stuffe by ten millions more *Tramontani* or *Transalpine* barbarous than ballctry, he would haue prest it vpon *Wolfe* whether he would or no, and giu'n it immortall allowance aboue *Spencer*. So did he by that Philistine Poem of *Parthenophill* and *Parthenope*, which to compare worse than it selfe, it would plunge all the wits of *France Spain* or *Italy*. And when hee saw it would not sell, hee cald all the world asses a hundred times ouer, with the stampingest cursing and tearing he could vtter it, for that he hauing giu'n it his passe or good word, they obstinately contemnd and mislik'd it. So did he by *Chutes Shores Wife*, and his *Procris and Cephalus*, and a number of *Pamphlagonian* things more, that it would rust & yron spot paper to haue but one sillable of their names breathed ouer it."

The ordinary interpretation of this passage, which would make Anthony Chute the author of "Procris and Cephalus," is controverted by Mr. E. Arber in the following letter which he was good enough to write to me in reply to my inquiry.

"I think your query admits of a satisfactory solution.

Nash does not say that *Procris and Cephalus* was by Chute at all, but the *his* refers to the *he* (*i. e.* Wolfe), thus,

So did he [Wolfe] by Chute's *Shores Wife*, and his [Wolfe's] *Procris and Cephalus*. [Author not named.]

Had Nash attributed the latter work to Chute the construction would have been

Preface. vii

So did he [Wolfe] by Chute's *Shores Wife and Procris and Cephalus* leaving out the *his*.
Therefore we are left to the testimony of the Registers.
No leaf is left out in vol. ii. for you will see that the last entry on p. 672 and the first on p. 273 are both 10 March, 1595.
The Registers do not attribute *Procris and Cephalus* to Chute.
The only difficulty lies in the distance of time between the registration on 22° die Octobris, 1593, and the publication in 1595, *i. e.* after 25 March, 1595.
Wolfe as the Beadle of the Company would have the utmost freedom of access to the Registers.
Either, then, you have a second edition, or Wolfe registered the book at the very earliest opportunity under the title as at first intended, which was afterwards changed while the printing was in progress.
I incline to the latter hypothesis: until demonstrative evidence to the contrary turns up, I should believe in one *Procris and Cephalus*.
The going back of the Register to p. 293 arises from the book entries having exceeded the space which the Clerk had provided for them in the volume.

EDWARD ARBER."

In whatever way the words of Nash are to be parsed, it seems more improbable that two poems on the same subject should have been written at the same time, that only one entry should be found in the Registers of the Stationers' Company, and that one should have utterly perished, than that there was one poem, one entry, and a change in the wording of the title. Nash, too, was probably writing hastily, and from memory, even if his words must be understood to make Chute the author.

There is one other reference to " Cephalus and Procris " by a contemporary writer, viz. W. C., supposed to be William Clerke, whose work bears the title "Polimanteia," &c., Cambridge, 1595.

Preface.

Sweet Master Campio.

Britton, Percie, Willobie, Fraunce, Master Davis of L. I. Drayton. Learned M. Plat.

Ballad makers.

A work howsoever not respected yet excellently done by Th. Kidd.

But by the greedy Printers so made prostitute that they are contemned.

Nor Poetrie be tearmed Ryme.

"I know *Cambridge* howsoever now old, thou haſt ſome young, bid them be chaſt, yet ſuffer them to be wittie; let them be ſoundly learned, yet ſuffer them to be gentlemanlike qualified; Oxford thou haſt many, and they are able to ſing ſweetly when it pleaſe thee. And thou youngeſt of all three, either in Hexameter Engliſh, thou art curious (but that thou learnedſt of my daughter *Cambridge*) or in any other kinde thou art ſo wiſely merrie, as my ſelfe (though olde) am often delighted with thy muſicke, tune thy ſweet ſtrings, & ſing what pleaſe thee. Now me thinks I begin to ſmile, to ſee how theſe ſmaller lights (who not altogether vnworthily were ſet vp to expel darknes) bluſhinglie hide themſelues at the Suns appeare. Then ſhould not tragickie *Garnier* haue his Cornelia ſtand naked vpon euery poſte; then ſhould not Times complaint delude with ſo good a title: then ſhould not the Paradiſe of daintie deuiſes bee a packet of balde rimes: then ſhould not *Zepheria, Cephalus* and *Procris* (workes I diſpraiſe not) like watermē pluck euery paſſinger by the ſleeue: then euery braineles toy ſhould not vſurpe the name of Poetrie; then ſhould not the muſes in their tinſell habit be ſo baſely handled by euery rough ſwaine; then ſhould not loues humour ſo tyranniſe ouer the chaſt virgines: thē ſhould honor be mournd for in better tearms."

Preface.

"England to her three Daughters, Cambridge, Oxford, Innes of Court, and to all her Inhabitants," pp. 15, 16; in Dr. Grosart's Reprint, pp. 38, 39 : in the British Bibliographer, 1810, vol. i. p. 282. This is printed with, and forms the second part of, the "Polimanteia."

From the date of this work, 1595, it might be inferred that the writer could hardly be alluding to the poem by Thomas Edwards which was published in the same year, 1595 ; but against this supposition must be set the fact that the writer refers to the poem by its correct title, "Cephalus and Procris," and that poems at that period were often current in manuscript for some time before they were printed. On this point Mr. Ingleby, in the General Introduction to "Shakspere Allusion Books," New Shakspere Society, Series iv. London, 1874, p. xxvi. speaks authoritatively, "One must remember how commonly in the Elizabethan age works circulated in manuscript years before they found their way into print."

Altogether there seems little reason to doubt that the author of Polimanteia had seen, and was referring to, the poem which we have by Thomas Edwards.

Warton, in his History of English Poetry, section 58, where he is treating of the translations of the Classic Poets and their influence on the writers of the Elizabethan age, mentions in a note the "Procris and Cephalus of the Register of 1595" [should be 1593] as perhaps a play, and ridiculed by Shakspere in the Midsummer Night's Dream, Act v. 1, 200, 201.

x *Preface.*

"PYRAMUS. Not Shafalus to Procrus was so true.
THISBE. As Shafalus to Procrus, I to you."

Ritson more cautiously says, "This is, probably, the poem alluded to in Midsummer Night's Dream." Bibliographia Poetica, 170—note to Anthony Chute.

Mr. Corser, however, in his notice of Anthony Chute's "Shores Wife," while agreeing with others in the belief that Chute had written a "Procris and Cephalus," corrects the above-quoted opinions, and states, as is most likely the case, that "Shakspere only alludes to the tale, and not to any particular work on the subject." Collectanea Anglo-Poetica, iv. 395, Chetham Society Series, No. 77.

The date of the composition of the Midsummer Night's Dream is too uncertain to make it safe to base an argument upon it in regard to this point. It was first printed in 1600, it is spoken of by Meres in 1598, Mr. Furnivall dates it in 1595, and Malone in 1594. The earlier dates make it almost incredible that there could be any allusion to a work published in 1595; and though some hit at it might have been subsequently introduced into the play, it is not very likely that the dramatist would have sought to make a point by referring to a work which seems to have met with but scant notice from the world of readers at the time of its publication.

IV. All my researches about the author, Thomas Edwards, have been fruitless in positive information. Contemporary authors, even the Satirists, seem to have ignored his existence; and, though there were several persons bearing both his names who were living about the end of the sixteenth and the beginning of the seventeenth century, I have met with no evidence by which it is possible for a certainty to identify him with any of them.

1. Thomas Edwards, an Englishman, wrote fifty-four hexameter lines in Latin on the Cities of Italy, printed by Adrianus Romanus in his Parvum Theatrum Urbium, Frankfort, 1595, and reprinted in this volume, whom Mr. Hazlitt, in his Collections and Notes, 1876, p. 139, assumes to be the same as the author of Cephalus and Procris, and it is possible that he may be, but in default of further evidence Mr. Hazlitt's opinion must be regarded as a mere assumption.

2. A Thomas Edwards, of All Souls' College, Oxford, is mentioned in Wood's Fasti Oxonienses under the year 1590 (vol. i. 252, ed. Bliss), as proceeding to the degree of Doctor of Law. "He was afterwards Chancellor to the Bishop of London, and a great benefactor to Bodley's Library, and to that of Ch. Ch." "He appears in the Old Benefaction book of the Bodleian only as the donor of 10*l*., with which forty-seven books were purchased, the date of his gift being 1611; but nothing further is recorded about him." (Letter from the Rev. W. D. Macray, Assistant-Librarian.) With reference to the Library at Ch. Ch. the Very Rev. the Dean, Dr. Liddell, was kind enough to inform me, that "the only book given to the Library by Dr. Edwards is thus entered, 'Ornatissimus et dignissimus Vir Dñus Thomas Edwards, LL. Doctor, Cancellarius Episcopi Lond. D.D. Missale man.script.

fol. A.D. 1615.' Donation Book, p. 25. The Book of Poems (*i. e.* Cephalus and Procris) does not appear in our Catalogue." It is shown by the All Souls' Registers that "Thomas Edwards, L. (*i. e.* Legist), Berks, was admitted Fellow for 1577." He took his B.A. degree 26 March, 1582; B.C.L. Nov. 19, 1584; and D.C.L. Dec. 17, 1590. Beyond the entry in the All Souls' archives of his having given a legal opinion on a College matter in 1615 there is nothing recorded about him, and no mention of authorship. (Information from Professor Burrows of All Souls.)

Whether he was the same person as a Thomas Edwards presented to the Rectory of Langenhoe, in Essex, Oct. 1, 1618, temp. Bp. Bancroft, is not certain. See Newcourt, Repertorium, Lond. 1708-10, folio, ii. 364.

3. Newcourt, *ibid.* i. 916, mentions a Thomas Edwards, who seems a different person from the above, as licensed to St. Botolph, Aldgate, July 1, 1629.

4. A Thomas Edwards took the degree LL.B. at Cambridge, in 1562, no college named.

5. "Thomas Edwards, Coll. Regin. Cant. adm. in matric. Acad. Cant. Jun. 15, 1575, A.B. 1578-9, A.M. 1582, Reg. Acad. Cant." BAKER. (Note in Fasti Oxon. i. 413, ed. Bliss.) The Rev. G. Phillips, D.D., the venerable President of Queen's College, Cambridge, very courteously examined the College Books for me with the following result: "The only entry I can find in the College Book, called The Old Parchment Register, respecting Thomas Edwards, is the following, '1575, Thomas Edwards,

Preface. xiii

Hunting. 9 Apr.' This occurs in the list of sizars. The Tutor was Mr. Fegon, B.A. The Deputy-Registrar has informed me that the record in the Matriculation Book is quite correct, as stated by Baker." In the Visitation of Huntingdonshire, printed by the Camden Society in 1849, a short pedigree of the Edwards family is given at p. 113, but without any record of a Thomas Edwards. A Henry Edwards is mentioned in the same vol. p. 1, Anno 1613, as one of the Bayliffs of Huntingdon.

6. There was another Thomas Edwards of Queen's College, Cambridge, B.A. 1622, who is probably identical with the Mr. Thomas Edwards late of Queen's College, Cambridge, who on Feb. 11, 1627, was committed to safe custody for words in a sermon preached at St. Andrew's, Cambridge, about Midsummer last, and on April 6, 1628, explained his meaning. (Cambridge Transactions during the Puritan Period, by J. Heywood and T. Wright, London, 1854, 8vo. ii. pp. 361-363.)

This is, I suppose, the same Thomas Edwards mentioned by Wood, Fasti Oxon. i. 413, ed. Bliss, as incorporated a Master of Arts on July 16, 1623, and of whom and his works he there gives an account. In the Rawlinson MSS. at the Bodleian, in MS. 280, fol. 47, 48, there is a transcript of the proceedings against Thomas Edwards, in most beautiful writing, from the original records, certified by the Registrary of the University of Cambridge. He would be of too late a date to have been the author of Cephalus and Procris.

7. In the Visitation of Cornwall, 1620, p. 65, is a pedigree of the

family of Edwardes of Lelant, in com. Corn., the head of which was a Thomas Edwards, whose eldest son Henry was then aged 20. He signs his name Edwardes.

8. Among the admissions of Members of the Inner Temple in 1647 is a Thomas, son and heir of Thomas Edwards, London. (See List of Members of Inner Temple, by W. H. Cooke, Esq., Q.C. 1877. 8vo.)

9. In the Westminster Abbey Registers, printed by the late Colonel Chester (whose death is so great a loss), is an entry among the burials:

"1624, April 21. Mr. Thomas Edwards: in the broad Aisle, on the south side," on which is this note, "His will dated 12 April, was proved in the Court of the Dean and Chapter 1 June, 1624, by his relict Jane and by Griffith Pritchard, M.A. He is described as of the City of Westminster, Gent. He left his estate in England and Wales to his wife and daughters Grace, Frances, and Catherine, and mentioned his sons-in-law Reynold Conway, and Robert ap Hugh, Gent."

10. In the Appendix to the Fifth Report of the Royal Commission on Historial Manuscripts, London, 1876, folio, p. 65, there is recorded in the year 1642 a Petition of Thomas Edwards, scaler at the Great Seal of England, who states, that he has for twenty-four years carefully performed the painful and laborious duties of his place, having only 4*d*. per diem for his certain fee, and 20*s*. per annum for livery, while the casual fees anciently belonging to his place are for the most part kept from him, "particularly the great

Preface.

seal when it is repudiated, appears by records in the Tower to belong to the Spigurnell,* or sealer, as his fee," but petitioner could never enjoy this, nor many other privileges; prays for an examination of his place, and that he may have such fees and privileges as shall be found due to him, and meet to maintain him and three or four servants, and particularly that he may enjoy the old Great Seal, if it appears to be his due. The Petition is to the House of Lords.

V. DEDICATION. The Poems are dedicated to "the Right Worshipfull Master Thomas Argall Esquire," a form of expression common at the time of their publication, as may be seen by the following examples:

A Posie of Gilloflowers, by Humfrey Gifford, Gent. Lond. 1580. "To the Worshipfull his very good Maister Edward Cope of Edon Esquier."

Webbe, W. A Discourse of English Poetrie. Lond. 1586. "To the right worshipfull, learned, and most gentle Gentleman, my verie good Master, Ma. Edward Suliard, Esquire."

Arisbas, by John Dickenson. Lond. 1594. "To the Right Worshipfull Maister Edward Dyer Esquire."

Fidessa More Chaste then Kinde, by B. Griffin, Gent. Lond. 1596. "To the most kind and vertuous gentleman M. William Essex of Lamebourne in the countie of Barke Esquire."

---

* Spigurnel, [so called from *Galfridus Spigurnel*, who was appointed to that office by King Henry III.] he that hath the office of sealing the King's Writs. Bailey, Dict. in v.

xvi   *Preface.*

The Triumphe over Death, by Robert Southwell. Lond. 1596. "To the Worshipful M. Richard Sackvile, Edward Sackvile, Cecilia Sackvile, and Anne Sackvile, The hopeful issues of the Hon. Gentleman, Master Robert Sackvile, Esq."

Either *Master* or *Esquire* by itself would now be deemed sufficient. The use of the word Master as a title of respect will be best illustrated by an extract from a contemporary work, "The Commonwelth of England, and Maner of Government Thereof, by Sir Thomas Smith, London, 1589, and 1594, quarto." Chap. 20. Of Gentlemen. "As for Gentlemen they be made good cheape in England. For whosoever studieth the lawes of the realme, who studieth in the Universities, who possesseth liberall Sciences; and to be short, who can live idly and without manuall labour, and wil beare the port, charge, and countenance of a Gentleman, hee shall bee called *master*, for that is the title which men geve to esquires and other gentlemen, and shall be taken for a Gentleman." p. 37

How general the practice was Shakespere proves, who applies the term to nearly all classes, from "master marquess" to "master tapster," (viz., to the constable, doctor, guest, Jew, lieutenant, marquess, mayor, parson, porter, schoolmaster, secretary, sheriff, steward, tapster, and young-man), and ridicules it, perhaps, in Much Ado about Nothing, where Conrade says, "I am a gentleman, Sir, and my name is Conrade;" to which Dogberry replies, "Write down master gentleman Conrade," iv. 2, 15-17. While Verges, too, exclaims, "Here, here comes master Signior Leonato," v. 1, 266.

It seems to have been from an early period applied to members of the legal profession, *e.g.* in Wilkins's Concilia, ii. 405, anno 1422, "præsente mag. Johanne Stafford, legum doctore," and again, p. 410, "mag. Thomas Bronns, utriusque juris doctor, archidiaconus Stowe in ecclesia Lincoln., mag. Thomas Bekynton, LL. doctor, decanus curiæ Cant. etc. mag. David Pryce in legibus licentiatus, mag. Johannes Lyndefeld archid. Cicestr. in legibus licentiatus, et Johannes Estcourt in legibus bacalarius." 4 Rot. Parl. 9 Henr. V. anno 1422, "In quorum omnium et singulorum testimonium atque fidem præsentes literas seu præsens publicum instrumentum per *Magistros* Ricardum Petworth et Willielmum Fremon, Notarios Publicos feci subscribi," etc. p. 144. And the same two persons are again mentioned as Notaries on p. 145. Again in 1475, in the enumeration of the army of Edward IV. prepared for invasion of France, Rymer, ii. 848, "*Magistro* Johanni Coke, Doctori Legum." The term Master was also applied to Jacob Fryse, Physician of the King, and William Hobbs, Physician and Surgeon of the King.

Edmondson (Heraldry, London, 1780, folio, vol. ii. 3 C 2) enumerates four families named Argall, with their respective bearings, viz.

Argall, or Argnall. Or, a lion rampant regardant ar. (*sic*).

Argall, Dr. [Much-Baddow and Lowhall, in Essex]. Per fesse, ar. and vert, a pale counterchanged, three lions' heads erased gu. Crest, a sphinx with wings expanded proper. Another crest, an arm embowed in armour proper, supporting a battle-axe.

Argall or Argell. Party per fesse three pales counterchanged or and sa. as many lions erased gu.

Argall [Lancashire]. Or, a pale vert counterchanged per fesse; on the first and fourth quarter, a lion's head erased gu.; on the second and third, an acorn slipped or.

c

The second of these families, whose arms are given also by Papworth, Ordinary of British Armorials, 1874, p. 1011:

On a Pale betw. or within Lions,
    Per fess arg. and vert a pale counterchanged three lions' heads erased gu. ARGALL, East Sutton. ARGALL, London, V. ARGALL, Much Baddow and Low Hall, Essex. (V is the reference to Glover's Ordinary, Cotton MS. Tiberius, D. 10, Harl. MSS. 1392 and 1459.)

is no doubt the family of which the Thomas Argall of the Dedication was a member, and which was originally from Cornwall. At least, the Rev. J. Banister, in his Glossary of Cornish Names, Truro, 1869, 8vo. claims and explains it. "ARGALL, ARGLE, ARGOLL? on the ridge, promontory, or point (*col*); or, in front (*arag*) of the moor (*hal*); or, = w. *argel*, a concealing, hiding." p. 4. To these explanations I may add that it may be a variation of Artegal, and if so it would bear a different meaning, for which a reference must be made to the History of Christian Names by Miss Yonge, London, 1863, vol. ii. 126, in the chapter on the names of Cymric Romance. "Ardghal, or Ardal, of high valour, is an Erse name, and was long used, though it has now been suppressed by the supposed Anglicism, Arnold, eagle-power. It explains the name Arthgallo, who, in Geoffrey of Monmouth's *Legendary History* (Book iii. chap. 17), is the persecuting brother, whom Elidure's untiring love and generosity finally won from his cruel courses to justice and mercy. *Artegal and Elidure* was one of the best of the ante-Shakesperian dramas; and Artegal was selected by Spenser as one of the best and noblest of his knights errant." He

Preface. xix

is the hero of the fifth Booke of the Faerie Queene contayning the Legend of Artegall or of Justice.

"The champion of true Justice Artegall." v. i. 3.
"For Artegall in justice was upbrought." v. i. 5.

Whatever the origin of the name Argall may be, it is found early in connection with the legal profession and the administration of justice, in Rymer's Fœdera, ed. 2, vol. xiv. p. 348, A.D. 1529: "Transcriptum Bullæ qua declaratur Censuras contra Regis Personam esse præter Mentem Papæ et nullius Roboris: et ego Thomas Argall Wintoniensis Diœcesis Publicus sacra Auctoritate Apostolica Notarius ... hoc præsens Transumptum manu mea propria fideliter scriptum in publicam formam redegi." See also ibid. pp. 455, 465, 470, 478, A.D. 1533, and Wilkins, Concil. iii. 755, A.D. 1532: "Hoc instrumentum retro scriptum erat subscriptum manibus trium notariorum, viz. M. Willielmi Potkyn, M. Johannis Hering, et Thomæ Argall," and ibid. p. 759, A.D. 1533, "et ego, Thomas Argall, Wintoniensis diœcesis, publicus auctoritate notarius," etc.

This Thomas Argall in the year 1540, on Wednesday, July 11, was officially present at the proceedings for the divorce between K. Henry VIII. and the Lady Anne of Cleves. Strype records that "the King's commissional letters were presented to the Convocation by the Archbishop of Canterbury, and read by Anthony Hussey, Notary Public, in the presence also of Thomas Argal, Notary Public." Ecclesiastical Memorials, i. 558, ed. Oxon. 1822. The original document is in Wilkins' Concilia, i. 851, wherein the names are spelt Husey, Argall. In the year

c 2

Preface.

1549 he attended on April 30 the Archbishop's Court at Lambeth, for handing over to the secular power Johanna Bocher, alias Johanna de Kente, who refused to abjure her heretical opinions, "præsentibus Thoma Huse, armigero, Thoma Argell, generoso, Willelmo Walker et Johanni Gregory, notariis publicis." And again on May 11 he was present when Michael Thombe, bocher, recanted "in præsentia magistorum Thomæ Argall et Willelmi Walker, notariorum publicorum." Wilkins' Concilia, iv. pp. 43 and 42. In the Genealogist, by G. W. Marshall, Lond. 1880, vol. iv., at p. 5, to the will of Sir James Wylford, Knt., proved in P. C. C. 26th November, 1550, are appended as witnesses, "John Sydenham, Constance Simpson, Thomas Argall," and others. The last occasion on which I have met with his name is at the trial of Bishop Gardiner in 1550, 1551, as recorded by John Fox in his first edition, pp. 770, *seqq.* reprinted in the octavo ed. of 1838, vol. vi. There at p. 94 "Thomas Argall and William Say were the notaries and actuaries in that matter assigned Dec. 15, 1550," who were present, one or both, at the several Sessions, for which see pp. 100, 104, 121, 135, 137, 138, 258, 261, 266. At this last reference we find, "Upon the reading and giving of which sentence, the promoters willed William Say and Thomas Argall to make a public instrument, and the witnesses then and there present to bear testimony thereunto." This was on Saturday, 14th of February, 1551.*

* If the date in the following extract be correct, there must have been another Thomas Argall living at this time: "December 23, 1559, Letters of Administration

Preface. xxi

This constant employment in great state trials, as well as the ordinary practice of his profession, must have brought him considerable wealth, as the Manor of East Sutton, Kent, 180 acres, which had been granted to certain parties, was by them alienated to him in the 37th Henry VIII. 1546; and having procured his lands in the county of Kent to be disgavelled by the Act 2nd and 3rd Edward VI. he died possessed of the manor in the 6th year of that reign, 1553. (Hasted's Kent, ii. 418, iii. 97, i. cxliv.)

He was the son of a John Argall, of London, Gentleman, whose wife's name is not recorded, and married Margaret Talkarne, daughter of John Talkarne, of the family of Talcarne, of Talcarne, in Cornwall, who lived there four generations before 1620. (C. S. Gilbert, History of Cornwall, ii. 273, 4.) She married secondly to Sir Giles Allington, of Horshed, in the county of Cambridge, knight. By this marriage he had issue five sons and a daughter; viz. Richard, Lawrence, John, Rowland, Gaberell, and Ann. The eldest son Richard Argall, of East Sutton, in com. Kent, sonne and heir, was specially admitted as a Student of the Inner Temple in the year 1552, February 2, as "Richard Argall, London,"* and was elected M.P. for Maldon in 1563. He is apparently the person mentioned in the Diary of H. Machyn, printed by the Camden Society 1848 : "Argalle, Master, a morner

granted to Thomas Skott, brother of Brian Skott, late of the City of London, Gentleman, deceased, of the goods, &c., of his late brother in the Province of Canterbury. Thomas Argall, Officer of Court." See Memorials of the Family of Scott, of Scots Hall, in the county of Kent, by James Renat Scott, F.S.A. Lond. 1876, 4to. Correspondence, p. lxvii.

* See "Members Admitted to the Inner Temple 1547—1660, by W. H. Cooke, Esq. Q.C." privately printed, 8vo. p. 13.

at the funeral of Master Husse, sqwyre, and a grett merchant-venturer, and of Muskovia, and haburdasher." This was on June 5, 1560, at St. Martin's, Ludgate (p. 237). Again on July 16, 1563, he was present at St. Stephen's-by-London-Stone at the funeral of "Master Berre,* sqwyre and draper, and merchant of the Stapull, Ser Wylliam Chester cheyff morner, and Master Argall next," p. 311. Again on June 6, 1575, he was one of the 41 Gentlemen Mourners in gowns at the solemn funeral of Archbishop Parker. (Strype's Life of Parker, ii. 432.)

He is probably the Mr. Argoll, or Argoell, mentioned in "The Spending of the Money of Robert Nowell, of Reade Hall, Lancashire, brother of Dean Alexander Nowell," privately printed from the Townley MSS. by Dr. Grosart in 1877. At p. 66 are the following entries :—

"to Mr Orwell, clearke to Mr Argoell . . . . x^s

" to Mr Orwell for the ffee of the pbatt, the othe, was paparators regestringe † of the will & to Mr Doctor hadons servante called Edward for his paynes & to Mr Argoell clearkes for their paynes in the whole } xxxvj^s viij^d

" To M^r harisonn the xxxth of Maye A^o 1572 for his ffee, for examyning o^r brothe^{rs} ynvintorie, and for Mr Argoll his fee. } x^s "

* Lawrence Argall, second son of Thomas, which Lawrence was among the exiles at Geneva in 1556 (see Livre des Anglois à Genève, compiled by Sir E. Brydges, and printed in 1831 by J. S. Burn, and reprinted in his History of Parish Registers, 1862); married the daughter of [Thomas] Bery, of Oxfordshire. Harleian MSS. 1541, fol. 137. Perhaps of the same family with this Berre. Laur. Argall signs the Inventory of John Hovenden, of Cranbrook, Jan. 15, 1579. See Miscellanea Genealogica et Heraldica, New Series, 1874, vol. i. p. 109.

† Should this be read "the otbe[r, viz. fee] was pro aparators," *i. e.* apparitors, who are "the lowest officers of the Ecclesiastical Court: summoners"? "They

Preface. xxiii

Richard Argall married Mary, daughter to Sir Reynold (or Reginald) Scott, of Scott's Hall, in com. Kent, knight, date not recorded, and had by her five sons and six daughters. The following monumental inscription is in East Sutton Church: "Richd Argall, of East Sutton, in the county of Kent, Esq., deceased anno Dm^{ni} 1588, leaving 5 sons and 6 daughters living. Mary, his second wife, one of the daughters of Sir Reginald Scott, of Scots Hall, married the second time to Lawrence Washington, Esq., died in anno 1605. Thomas Argall, eldest son of the said Richard and Mary, died in anno 1605, whose souls," &c. From " Memorials of the Family of Scott, of Scots Hall, in the county of Kent, by James Renat Scott, F.S.A. London, 1876, 4to. p. 185, note c." According to a pedigree contained in Harleian MSS. No. 6065, fol. 112, "Thomas and Sir Rainold, the eldest and second sons, died without issue in 1605 and 1611 respectively. John, the third son, of Colchester in Essex, thus became, as described in the pedigree, "sonne and heire"; Richard, the fourth, and Samuel, the fifth, sons, being entered similarly as the second and third.

John sold the estate of East Sutton to his brother-in-law Sir Edward Filmer, Knt., in the eighth year of K. James I., and is described afterwards as of Colchester, Essex, in which county the Argall family continued for several generations, as shown by

swallowed all the Roman hierarchy from the Pope to the *apparitor*." *Ayliffe, Parergon Juris Canonici.* "Many heretofore have been by *apparitors* both of inferior courts, and of the courts of the Archbishop's Prerogative, much distracted and diversly called and summoned for probate of wills," &c. *Ecclesiastical Constitutions and Canons,* section 92, quoted in Latham's Johnson's Dictionary.

pedigrees in the Harleian Collection of MSS. in the British Museum, and by numerous extracts from Parish Registers in my own possession. He was executor of the will of Sir John Scott, of Nettlested, proved January 17, 1618. Memorials of Scott Family, p. 217.

Richard, the fourth, but second surviving son, was "an excellent divine poet," and author of several works, enumerated by Wood, Ath. Oxon. i. 760.

Samuel, the fifth, but third survivor, was Governor of Virginia, and is repeatedly mentioned in public documents relating to that colony.

Of the six daughters, Elizabeth, married to Sir Edward Filmer, Knt., of East Sutton (he having bought the estate from his brother-in-law, John Argall, of Colchester), from which marriage descends the present family of Filmer, of East Sutton, now Baronets.

Margaret, m. to Edm. Randolph, of Aylesford, in Kent. Esq.

Mary, m. to Raynold Kempe, of Wye, in Kent, Esq.

Catherin, m. to Raynold Bathurst, of Horton, in Kent, Esq.

Jayne, m. to Pawle Flettewood, of Roose, in com. Lancaster, Esquier.

Sara, 6th daughter.

Thomas, the eldest son of Richard Argall, and his brother Reginald, are mentioned as witnesses to a letter written by Sir John Scott to Lord Willoughby of Eresby, by way of remonstrance against the haughty language and overbearing conduct of his

Lordship, from whom he had received the honour of knighthood while serving in the Netherlands, c. 1587-8, or in France, c. 1590. The letter is not dated, but must have been after the time just mentioned, when possibly Thomas Argall may have been about thirty years of age. . I have been able to discover no other mention of him. The volume of Poems was dedicated to him in 1595, and he died in 1605. There is no evidence to show that he carried on the family business as a notary, but he may have done so, and Thomas Edwards, the author of the Poems, may have been one of his clerks; at all events, he seems to have been in some way dependent on, or indebted to, him. The matrimonial alliances contracted by the several members of the family are with persons of good name and position, and help to prove that Thomas Argall was of such standing in society as to warrant Edwards in dedicating his volume to him, apart from any considerations on the score of literary ability, of which his uncle John Argall,* of Halesworth,

* "John Argall, third son of Thomas Argall, by Margaret his wife, daughter of John Talkarne, of the county of Cornwall, was born in London, entered a student in Ch. Ch. in the latter end of Q. Mary, took the degrees in arts, that of Master being completed in 1565, and was senior of the act celebrated the 18th of Feb. the same year. Afterwards he studied the supream faculty, was admitted to the reading of the sentences, and at length became parson of a market-town in Suffolk, called Halesworth. He was always esteemed a noted disputant during his stay in the University, was a great actor in plays at Ch. Ch. (particularly when the Queen was entertained there 1566), and when at ripe years a tolerable theologist and preacher. But so much was he devoted to his studies, that being withal unmindful of the things of this world, he lived and died like a philosopher. He hath written and published, *De Vera penitentia*, Lond. 1604, oct. [Bodl. 8vo. A. 20, Th.] [A copy in MS., on paper, among the royal collection, 8 B, ix., Casley's *Catalogue*, p. 145.] *Introductio ad artem Dialecticam*, Lond. 1605, oct. [Bodl. 8vo. A. 43, Art.] In which book (very facete and pleasant)

and Richard Argall,* his own brother, have left specimens of no mean quality.

Among the Harleian MSS. in the British Museum, the following, No. 1541, fol. 137; No. 6065, fol. 112; No. 1137, fol. 114b;

the author saith of himself in the *Post Prædicamenta* under *Simul tempore*, that whereas the great God had raised many of his cronies and contemporaries to high dignities in the Church, as Dr. Tho. Bilson to the See of Winton, Mart. Heton to Ely, Hen. Robinson to Carlisle, Tob. Mathews to Durham, &c., yet he, an unworthy and poor old man, was still detained in the chains of poverty for his great and innumerable sins, that he might repent with the prodigal son, and at length by God's favour obtain salvation. What other things he hath written I know not, nor anything else of him, only that he was reputed by the neighbouring ministers of Halesworth a great scholar, and that being at a feast at Cheston (a mile distant from that town), he died suddenly at the table. Afterwards his body being carried to Halesworth, it was buried in the church there 8 Octob., in sixteen hundred and six. Johannis Argalli Epistola Monitoria ad R. Jacobum I., cum in regem Angliæ inauguratus est. MS. in bibl. Reg. 7, A xii. 7." A Wood, Ath. Oxon. i. 760, ed. Bliss.

* " Now I am got into the name of Argall, I must let the reader know, that in my searches I find one Rich. Argall to be noted in the reign of K. James I. for an excellent divine poet, having been much encouraged in his studies by Dr. Jo. King, bishop of London, but in what house educated in Oxon, where he spent some time in study, I cannot now tell you. He wrote and published (1) *The Song of Songs, which was Solomon's metaphrased in English Heroicks, by way of Dialogue*, Lond. 1621, qu., dedic. to Henry King, Archd. of Colchester, son to the Bishop of London. (2.) *The Bride's Ornament; Poetical Essays upon a Divine Subject ;* in two books, Lond. 1621, qu. The first dedic. to Jo. Argall, Esq., the other to Philip, brother to Henry King. (3.) *Funeral Elegy consecrated to the memory of his ever honoured Lord King late B. of London, &c.* 1621.

He also wrote a book of *Meditations of Knowledge, Zeal, Temperance, Bounty, and Joy.* And another containing *Meditations of Prudence, Obedience, Meekness, God's Word, and Prayer.* Which two books of meditations were intended by the author for the press, at the same time with the former poetry; but the ever lamented loss of his most honoured lord (which did change all his joys into sorrows, and songs to lamentations) did defer their publication; and whether they were afterwards published I know not." A. Wood, Ath. Oxon. i. 761, ed. Bliss.

PEDIGREE OF THE ARGALL FAMILY.

John Argall, of London, = Wife's name not known.
gentleman.

Richard Argall = **Joane,** dau. and coheir of Robert Martyn of Graveney Court of Nayolon in Graveney. Hasted, iii. 16.

had property at Goodneston, Kent, in 1653. Hasted's Kent, ii. 816, iii. 148.

Thomas Argall, of London, Esq. = **Margaret,** dau. of John Talkarne, of Taliaerne, Cornwall. She mar. 2ndly to Sir Giles Allington, of Horseheed, Cambridge, knt.

Notary Public, bought Manor of East Sutton, Kent, died 1563.

Thomas Argall, 1550, Dec. 23, signed letters of administration of Thomas Skott, as "Officer of Court." 1564 had lands at Chatham, Kent. Hasted, iii. 148.

Lawrence Argall, 2nd sonne m. Joan dau. of Thomas Bery, of Oxfordshire. Exile at Geneva in 1556. Signed Inventory of John Hovenden, of Cranbrook, Jan. 1579.

Richard Argall, of East Sutton, = 1. Wife's name not known.
Esq. sonne and heire. Ad- = 2. **Mary,** dau. of Sir Reynold
mitted at Inner Temple, 1553. Scott, of Scot's Hall, Kent.
M.P. for Maldon 1563. Died She m. 2ndly Lawrence
1588. Washington, Esq. and died in 1605.

John Argall, 3rd son. | B.A. 1562.
Of Ch. Ch. Oxford, | M.A. 1565.
Rector of Halesworth, | B.D. 1652.
Suffolk, d. 1606. (A. |
Wood, Athenæ. |
Oxon.) |

Rowland. Gaberell. Ann, m. Thomas Sisley, of Essex. 2ndly to Augustyne Steward of London.

THOMAS ARGALL, eldest son.

1588. Succeeded his father.
1590. Witness to letter of Sir John Scott to Lord Willoughby.
1595. Had CEPHALUS and PROCRIS dedicated to him.
1605. o. s. p. Monument in East Sutton Church.

Reginald, or Reynold succeeded his brother Thomas.
1600 Purchased advowson of Walthamstow, Essex.
1606. Knighted at Hampton Court Aug. 17.
1611. Dec. 20, o. s. p.

John Argall, heir of his brother Sir Reginald. Sold Walthamstow to Dr H. King, Bp. of Chichester in .... Sold East Sutton to his brother-in-law Sir E. Filmer, knt. Described as of Co'chester, J.P. for Essex. Bur. at Great Baddow, Essex, March 9, 1642.

Sara, d. of Edward Grammt, D.D. Bur. at Great Baddow, April 12, 1648.

Richard Argall, called "2 sonne," 1622, June 26, knighted at Rochester of his two brothers. In 1627 dedicated his poems to "John Argall of Colchester."

Samuel Argall, called "3 sonne," 1622, June 26, knighted at Rochester, Governor of Virginia.

Six daughters, viz.:
Elizabeth, m. to Sir E. Filmer, knt of East Sutton, Kent.
Margaret, m. to Edmund Randolph of Aylesford, Kent, Esq.
Mary, m. to Raynold Kemp of Wye, Kent, Esq.
Catherin, m. to Raynold Bathurst of Horton, Kent, Esq.
Jayne, m. to Pawle Fletewood of Roos, Lancashire, Esq.
Sara.

Sarah, m. 1641 July 29, by licence to Edmund Humphry, gentleman. She d. and was bur. 1641, May 30.

Richard, 2nd son of Emmanuel Coll. Camb. Rector of Eythrope Roothing, Snorcham, and Rivenhall, Essex, d. 1670, bur. at Much Baddow.

Mary, eldest dau. of Wm. Brainston, of Halstead, Essex, gent.

Samuel, 3rd son, apparently the Samuel Argall who took the degree of M.D. at Padua in 1648, and was incorporated at Oxford, 1651. Physician in Ordinary to Catherine Queen of Charles II.

Elizabeth, dau. of Sir Thomas Palmer of Wingham, in Kent.

Charles, 4th son. Bapt. 1627, Jan. 6.

John, 6th son. Bapt. 1638. Jan. 27.

Thomas Argall, son and heir, aged 23 in 1634. "Adventured his life and fortune in the King's cause and endured the siege of Colchester, &c." Friend of Chief Justice Bramston. Bur. at Great Baddow, Dec. 9, 1669. (Life of Bramston, pp. 159, 162.)

Alice

Mary, m. to Thomas Tendring of Boreham, or Burkham, in com. Essex.

Thomas Argall, = **Ann** Entered inner Temple, Nov. 1663. Called to bar, 1662. Mentioned in Life of Bramston, 1672, p. 159.

Richard, bur. Dec. 17, 1661.
William, bur. June 13, 1643.
Charles, bapt. Sept. 2, 1648. Mar. Jane, by whom he had issue Jane, bur. July 31, 1683. Ann, bur. Nov. 8, 1683. His wife bur. Oct. 8, 1683.
Richard, bapt. Mar. 24, 1650 or 1651. Bur. Dec. 6, 1659.
Samuel, bapt. July 26, 1663.

Elizabeth, bapt. Sept. 3, 1680.

Thomas, bur. June 13, 1651.

Ally, bur. Nov. 16, 1686.

Sarah, bapt. Aug. 13, 1644, bur. Oct. 6, 1646.
Maria, bapt. Jan. 21, 1646.
Ann, bur. Jan. 30, 1646.
Sarah, bapt. Oct. 23, 1654.
Elizabeth, bapt. Mar. 6, 1658.

William Argall, bapt. July 8, 1682, bur. April 22, 1684.

Jane, bapt. Jan. 15, 1684.

Mary, bapt. Oct. 16, 1686.

Mary, m. to Captain Blackman.
? **Elizabeth,** b. Aug. 20, 1643.

A child, bur. Oct. 9, 1669.

Preface. xxvii

No. 1083, fol. 71b; No. 1432, fol. 110b; No. 1542, fol. 94b, contain pedigrees more or less complete of the Argall family, about which Hasted's Kent, Morant's Essex, Newcourt's Repertorium, the Memorials of the Family of Scott, of Scots Hall, the Autobiography of Sir John Bramston, and the Poems of Bishop H. King, edited by the Ven. Archdeacon Hannah, supply divers particulars.

In the annexed pedigree some few statements rest only on probabilities. There is no evidence that Richard Argall, of Goodneston, was son of John Argall, nor that the Thomas Argall described as "Officer of Court," and living A.D. 1564, was the son of the above-mentioned Richard. Again, there is no positive proof that Thomas, the eldest son of Richard Argall, of East Sutton, is to be identified with the Thomas Argall of the Dedication of Edward's Poems—though, as he was then (in 1595) the head of the family, it seems all but certain that they are one and the same person. Lastly, the Thomas Argall mentioned in the Life of Bramston does not appear to have been recorded in the Parish Register of Great Baddow, from which the names of the rest of that generation have been extracted. The following particulars as to several members of the family have been collected (1). In the "Herald and Genealogist," 1867, vol. i. 429, " Margaret Tolkerne, d^r of John Tolkerne, of London, Esq., wife of Thomas Argall, afterwards re-married to Sir Giles Allington." MS. Addit. Brit. Mus. 16,279. This statement, however, is not incompatible with that of Antony Wood, that John Talcarne was of Cornwall. See also

d 2

Collectanea Topographica, vol. iv. p. 35, in an extract relating to the church of Horseheath, co. Cambridge, from Cole's MSS.:

"On the large rim over the pillars is this inscription in capitals: Sir Gyles Alington, Knighte, sonne & heyre of Sir Gyles Alington Knighte died 22nd Augt 1586, aged 86 . . . . . And thirdly he married Margaret, daughter of John Tallakarne, Esquier, before wife of Thomas Argall, Esquier, and had by her no issue."

(2). In the Calendar of State Papers, Domestic, 1547—1580, p. 691, Dec. 1580, are these entries:

> 67. Answers by Lawrence Argoll to such objections as may be urged against his suit for registration of Wills by the Proctors of the Arches, and others.
>
> 68. Statement of the number of Wills proved in the Prerogative Court communibus annis, from January 1575 to the last of December 1580, in support of Argoll's suit.

(3). Gabriel Argall, Trin. Aul. Cambridge, incorporated M.A. 1573, Oxon. (Register of University of Cambridge.)

(4). Richard Argall of East Sutton is not altogether unknown in the annals of literature. In fact Watt in his Bibliotheca Britannica, vol. i. 42a, ascribes to him "The Accedens of Armory. London 1568, 4to." This, however, is a mistake. The book is the composition of Gerard Leigh, but after the preface follows an address to the reader by *Richard Argoll of the Inner Temple*. He probably wrote some of the latter passages of the book, in the opinion of Mr. Nichols, Herald and Genealogist, 1863, vol. i. p. 108. "In this part of the volume there are some curious passages full of bombast, attributable to his Templar friend Richard Argall." Leigh thus blazons the Argall coat. "Because the bearer hereof

Preface. xxix

not only embraceth the Arte, but all other good sciences (as a thing given to him naturally, besides all gentlemanly behaviour), I will give him a precious blazonne. The field is parted per fesse Perle and Emerode, a pale counterchanged of the first, three lions' heads erased Rubie. Consider that the Moone and Venus are the fielde, and how Mars keepeth the same, who will never flee," fol. 86, 1st ed. 1562; fol. 49, ed. 1576. This coat in ordinary blason is, Per fess argent and vert, a pale counterchanged three lions' heads erased, gules. Again at p. 115 Leigh writes "Item I gyve to Mr. Richard Argall my picture of the Wyndmylle, and my shylde of Lyons bones."

(5). The first-mentioned Samuel Argall was rather a prominent personage in the early history of Virginia, as we find from Beverley's History of that colony, printed at London 1722, octavo. For "*anno* 1612 two Ships more arrived with supplies: And Capt. *Argall*, who commanded one of them, being sent in her to *Patowmeck* to buy Corn, he there met with *Pocahontas*, the excellent Daughter of *Powhatan*, and having prevail'd with her to come Aboard to a Treat, he detain'd her Prisoner, and carried her to *James* Town, designing to make Peace with her Father by her Release: But on the contrary, that Prince resented the Affront very highly; and, although he loved his Daughter with all imaginable Tenderness, yet he would not be brought to Terms by that unhandsome Treachery; till about two Years after a Marriage being proposed between Mr. *John Rolfe*, an *English* Gentleman, and this Lady; which *Powhatan* taking to be a sincere Token of Friendship, he vouchsafed to consent to it, and to conclude a Peace, tho' he would not come to the Wedding." (p. 25.)

"In the year 1617 Captain Samuel Argall was sent to Virginia as Governor, and made the Colony flourish and increase wonderfully, and kept them in great Plenty and Quiet." (p. 32.)

The next year he undertook a coasting voyage northward, and obliged the French to desert two Settlements which they had made on the north of *New England*, and at *Port Royal*, and in 1619 returned to England. (pp. 33-35.)

Beverley was probably indebted for these particulars to Purchas's Pilgrimes, in the fourth volume of which great work they will be found at pp. 1758, 1764, 1768, 1773, 1805, 1808. In the British Museum, Bibl. Cotton. Otho. E. viii. No. 299, there is a document of three pages, injured by fire at the top of each leaf, containing the answer of Captain Argoll to a charge of having taken a French ship. His name ought to be added to the long list of adventurous Englishmen whose boldness contributed to the extension of our Colonial Empire. It is evident that K. James I. was not unmindful of his services, for, being at Rochester in 1622, "he there knighted, on the 26th of June, Sir Samuel Argall of Essex." (Nichols's Progresses of K. James I. vol. iii. 770.)

(6). Richard Argall, 2nd son of John and Sara Argall, was of Emanuel College, Cambridge, B.A. 1635, and M.A. 1638. Chief Justice Bramston in his Autobiography (Camden Society, xxxii. 1845, p. 23) writes thus: "Mary, eldest d^r of William Bramston of Halstead married to Mr Richard Argall of Badow Esq. He

Preface. xxxi

was bred up in Emanuel College. A wittie man he was, a good scholler, and tooke Orders, and was Rector of Eythrope Roothing in Essex, and after the King's return Sir William Wyseman gave him Rivenhall too in 1662. There he dyed, leaving a widow and one daughter Mary, which he married to Captain Blackman, as he thought richly, but he proved a cross ill-natured man." He preached the funeral Sermon of C. J. Bramston his wife's uncle, and died in 1670. The following entry is in the Register of Rivenhall. "Mem. That I had institution into the Rectory of Rivenhall from the reverend father in God Gilbert L^d Bp. of London, uppon the 3rd day of October 1662, and that I had Induction from John Hansley Archdeacon of Colchester October 4th 1662 and was put into actual possession thereof accordingly Rich. Milward D.D. Rect. de Braxted Magn. the 13th day of the same Octob. R. Argall." "Richard Argall, Rector of this Parish dyed Feby 23rd and was buried at Much Baddow the 26th Feby 16$\frac{69}{70}$ Richard Strutt Rect."

(7). Samuel Argall, third son of John and Sara Argall, was born at Great Baddow, and is, I conjecture, the child entered in the Register there, "1621, July 4. Samuel, son of John and Ann Argall, Baptized." The mother's name *Ann* is probably a mistake for *Sara*. He was for five years at Chelmsford School, under Mr. Peake, and was entered Pensioner 19 April, 1639, at St. John's, under Wrench as Tutor. He was M.D. at Padua in 1648.

Of this Samuel Argall, Antony Wood in his Fasti Oxonienses (ii. 167, ed. Bliss) has left this record : "1651, Mar. 11. SAM.

xxxii *Preface.*

ARGALL, doct. of phys. of the said Univ. (Padua) was also then incorporated. He was an Essex man born, and took that degree at Padua in 1648." He was afterwards "of *Low Hall*, in the parish of *Walthamstow* in *Essex*, Dr. in Physick, Candidate and Honorary Fellow of the College of Physicians in London, and Physician in Ordinary to her Majesty." (This was Catherine, Queen of Charles II.) Guillim, Heraldry, p. 275, ed. 1679; p. 397, ed. 1724. He married Elizabeth, dr. of Sir Thomas Palmer, Baronet, of Wingham (Wotton, Baronetage, i. 442), and had issue. Four of his children were buried at Great Baddow, but whether any survived I do not know.

After 1686 there appear to be no entries of the Argalls in the Registers at Great Baddow, and the Rev. A. W. Bullen, Vicar of the parish, writes: "I never heard of the family before, though I have lived here all my life, and cannot discover in what house they lived. They were evidently persons of some note, as many entries are made in large characters, vouchsafed only to the Lords of the Manor and a few besides."*

VI. In making choice of such subjects for his Muse as *Cephalus and Procris*, and *Narcissus*, Thomas Edwards was acting in perfect harmony with the spirit of his age. Classical knowledge was now widely diffused. For a century and a half the press had been issuing editions of the Greek and Roman authors in their original tongues, and most of the chief writers had been translated into

---

* Argall is a local name in Cornwall. There is a cave at Argall, near Falmouth, in which luminous moss is found. Journals of Caroline Fox, Lond. 1882, i. 135.

Preface. xxxiii

the several leading languages of Europe. The aid of art had been called in to illustrate such as were fitted for pictorial effect, and the publication of the version of Ovid's Metamorphoses, called the "Bible des Poetes," printed by Verard at Paris in 1493, had been followed by other works of a similar character. Beside this general taste, it may be inferred that the success attending Marlowe's Hero and Leander, and the two poems of Shakspere, would encourage a young writer to aim at distinction in the same field. The whole of this subject has been most thoroughly investigated and dealt with by Warton in his History of English Poetry, sections lvii. to lxi. In a note to section lix., as already stated, he refers to *Cephalus and Procris* as entered on the Stationers' Book, but in ignorance of the real nature of the work. Mr. Hazlitt, however, in his edition, while making good the omission, has gone out of his way to express an opinion on very insufficient grounds, by saying, "It is a dull poem. No perfect copy is known." At the time of writing this note Mr. Hazlitt could not have read more than the first sheet, supposing he had seen the whole of the Lamport fragment; but probably he had read only the few lines sent by Mr. C. Edmonds, which are printed in the Additions to the Handbook of Popular Literature, p. 690.

Whatever may be the faults of Edwards's poem I cannot admit that dulness is one of them. It has variety of person, scene, and incident, and its references to contemporary poets, however much out of place, carry the reader on to the end. No doubt he sometimes fails to convey his meaning clearly—his rhymes are

e

xxxiv   *Preface.*

often faulty, and his punctuation is valueless. At the same time there are lines of considerable beauty, and compound words which are most expressive. But faults and beauties alike must be left for each reader to discover for himself. My object in the few remarks here made has been simply to guard against what I conceive to be an erroneous opinion, and to leave it open for all to weigh his merits and demerits impartially, and as he is now first presented to their view to bespeak for him a fair field and no favour. In the notes I have endeavoured to explain difficulties, to illustrate words and phrases, and thus to save readers the trouble of having to refer to many books, and must ask for myself the same indulgence which I have requested for my author.

VII. I have now to express my acknowledgments to all who have kindly assisted me in this work. To the Dean and Chapter of Peterborough especially for the loan of the unique Original, and to Sir C. E. Isham, Bart. for the opportunity of collating the fragment in his possession.

At Oxford to the Very Rev. H. G. Liddell, Dean of Ch. Ch.; Professor Burrows of All Souls; the Rev. W. D. Macray of the Bodleian—and at Cambridge to the Rev. G. Phillips, President of Queen's; Professor Mayor of St. John's, and the Rev. H. R. Luard, Registrary, who examined records in their custody to afford me information. Several of the Clergy, now Incumbents of Parishes with which the Argall family had been connected, most kindly searched for and transcribed such entries as were likely to be of service.—I beg to thank the Rev. G. W. Lockhart Ross of

Preface.

Sutton Valence, V. J. Stanton of Halesworth, F. Spurrell of Faulkbourn, P. F. Britton of Cadeleigh, R. E. Formby of Latchington, and especially the Rev. A. W. Bullen of Great Baddow, who at the request of the late Ven. Archdeacon Ady sent most copious extracts from his Register.

It is a matter of deep regret that death should have placed both the Ven. Archdeacon and another friend, our late colleague the Rev. H. O. Coxe, M.A., Bodleian Librarian, beyond the reach of words, but I must here record my sense of gratitude to each of them for their assistance, and especially to Mr. Coxe for the warm interest he evidenced for the publication of these poems, and for many valuable suggestions, which were a continual encouragement amid the difficulties of editorial work. My best thanks are also due to our treasurer, Mr. H. H. Gibbs, by whose intervention Mr. Furnivall obtained the opinions of so many eminent scholars on the difficult problem of identifying the author alluded to in the Envoy to Narcissus. To all those gentlemen I tender my respectful acknowledgments—as also to my nephew, Mr. E. F. Buckley, of Lincoln's Inn; and to Mr. C. Edmonds, editor of the Isham Reprints and the Lamport Garland, for some valuable references and researches.

Nor should I omit my thanks to Mr. Gravell, of Messrs. Nichols and Sons' Office, for the great pains he has taken to ensure accuracy while the Work was at press.

W. E. BUCKLEY.

Middleton Cheney,
   December, 1882.

CEPHALVS
& PROCRIS.

NARCISSVS.
Aurora musæ amica.

LONDON
Imprinted by *Iohn Wolfe.*
1 5 9 5.

To the Right worshipfull Master
Thomas Argall Esquire.

DEere Sir the titles refyant to your ftate,
Meritorious due: becaufe my penne is ftateleffe,
I not fet downe, nor will I ftraine it foorth,
To tilt againft the Sunne, with feeming fpeeches,
Suffizeth all are ready and awaite,
With their hartes-foule, and Artes perfwafiue miftreffe,
To tell the louely honor, and the worth,
Of your deferuing praife, Heroicke graces:
   What were it then for me to praife the light?
   When none, but one, commendes darke fhady night.

Then as the day is made to fhame the finner,
To ftaine obfcuritie, inur'd fuppofes,
And mainetaine Artes ineftimable treafure,
To blind-fold Enuie, barbarifme fcorning,
O with thy fauour, light a young beginner,
From margining reproach, Satyricke glofes,
And gentle Sir, at your beft pleafing leyfure,
Shine on thefe cloudy lines, that want adorning,
   That I may walke, where neuer path was feene,
   In fhadie groues, twifting the mirtle greene.
Thomas Edwards.

To the Honorable Gentlemen & true fauourites of Poetrie.

 *Vdiciall and courteous, leaſt I be thought in this my boldeneſſe, to Imitate* Irus, *that car'd not to whome he bar'd his nakedneſſe, ſo hee might be clothed. Thus much vnder your fauours I proteſt, that in writing of theſe twoo imperfect Poemes, I haue ouergonne my ſelfe, in reſpect of what I wiſh to be perfourmed: but for that diuers of my friendes haue ſlak't that feare in me, & (as it were) heau'd me onwards to touch the lap of your accompliſhed vertues. I haue thus boldly, what in a yeare bene ſtudiouſly a dooing now in one day (as our cuſtome is) ſet to the view of your Heroicke cenſures.*

Baſe neceſſitie, which ſchollers hate as ignorance, hath beene Englanddes ſhame, and made many liue in baſtardy a long time: Now is the ſap of ſweete ſcience budding, and the true honor of Cynthia *vnder our climate girt in a robe of bright tralucent lawne: Deckt glorouſly with bayes, and vnder her faire raigne, honoured with euerlaſting renowne, fame and Maieſty.*

O what is Honor without the complementes of Fame? or the liuing ſparkes in any heroicke gentleman? not ſowzed by the adamantine Goate-bleeding impreſſion of ſome Artiſt.

Well could Homer *paint on* Vlyſſes *ſhield, for that* Vlyſſes *fauour made* Homer *paint.*

Thriſe happy Amintas *that bode his penne to ſteepe in the muſes golden type of all bounty: whoſe golden penne bode all knightes ſtoope, to thy* O *thrice honoured and honorable vertues.*

The teares of the muſes haue bene teared from Helicon. *Moſt haue endeuoured to appeaſe* Iupiter, *ſome to applauſe* Mercury, *all to honor the deities.* Iupiter *hath beene found pleaſant,* Mercury

cury *plaufiue, all plyant; but few knowne to diſtill* Ambroſia *from heauen to feaſt men that are mortall on earth.*

How many when they toſſe their pens to eternize ſome of their fauourites, that although it be neuer ſo exquiſite for the Poeme, or excellent for memoriall: that either begin or end not with the deſcription of blacke and ougly night, as who would ſay, my thoughts are obſcur'd and my ſoule darkened with the terrour of obliuion.

For me this reſtes, to wiſh that ſuch were eyther dum & could not ſpeake, or deafe and could not heare, ſo not to tune their ſtately verſe to enchant others, or ope their eares to the hurt of thēſelues.

But why temporize I thus, on the intemperature of this our clymate? wherein liue to themſelues, Schollers and Emperours; eſteeming bountie as an ornament to dazell the eie, and telling to themſelues wonders of themſelues, wherein they quench honor with fames winges, and burne maieſtie with the title of ingratitude, and ſome there are (I know) that hold fortune at hazard, & trip it of in buskin, till I feare me they will haue nothe but skin.

Silly one, how thou tatleſt of others want? is it not an ordinary guiſe, for ſome to ſet their neighbours houſe on fire, to warme themſelues? beleue me courteous gentlemen, I walke not in clouds, nor can I ſhro'dly morralize on any, as to deſcribe a banquet becauſe I am hungry, or to ſhew how coldly ſchollers are recompenſt, becauſe I am poore, onely I am vrg'd as it were to paraphraſe on their doinges with my penne, becauſe I honour learning with my hart. And thus benigne gentlemen, as I began, ſo in duety I end, euer preſt to do you all seruice.

                                       Thomas Edwards.

and Procris.

<small>A pariphrifis of the Night.</small>

Faire and bright *Cynthia*, Ioues great ornament,
Richly adorning nightes darke firmament,
Scoured amidſt the ſtarry Canapie
Of heauens celeſtiall gouernement, well nie
Downe to the euer ouer-ſwelling tide,
Where old *Oceanus* was wont t'abide,
At laſt began to crie, and call amaine,
Oh what is he, my loue ſo long detaines!
Or i'ſt *Ioues* pleaſure *Cynthia* ſhall alone,
Obſcure by night, ſtill walke as one forlorne:
Therewith away ſhe headlong poſtes along
Salt waſhing waues, rebellious cloudes among,
So as it ſeem'd minding the heauens to leaue,
And them of light, thus ſtrangely to bereaue.

<small>A defcription of the Morning.</small>

*With that *Aurora* ſtarting from her bed,
As one that ſtandes deuiſing, ſhakes his head,
Not minding either this or that to doe,
So are her thoughts, nor quicke, nor ouerflow;
  Phebus halfe wrothe to ſee the globe ſtand ſtill,
The world want light, a woman haue her will:

Cephalus and Procris.

To poſt foorth gan another *Phaeton*,
And ſwore once more, he ſhould the world vppon,
Or as tis thought to trie th' aduentrous boy.
Yet ſome ſuppoſe, he meant vpon this day,
A Sympathy of ſorrowes to aduaunce.
The boy thus proude-made, hotly gan to praunce,
And now heauens coape, *Ioues* pallace chryſtaline
Downe dingeth *Atlas*, and ſtraight doth decline
In ſuch aboundant meaſure, as tis ſaid,
Since that ſame day the light of heauens decaide;
A metamorphoſis on earth 'mongſt men,
As touching conſtancy hath bene ſince then,
And this is true maidens, ſince that ſame day,
Are ſaide for louers neuer more to pray.
  But to returne, *Phebe* in million teares,
Moanes to her ſelfe, and for a time forbeares,
Aurora ſhe her ſwift bright ſhining rayes,
On *Phebus* charyot toſſe, and oft aſſayes,
With her ſweete lookes, her fathers wroth t'appeaſe,
But all ſhe doth, he tels her, doth diſeaſe,
Like to the vncorrected headſtrong childe,
That neuer felt his parentes ſtrokes but milde,
Growne vp to ryper yeares, diſdaines a checke:
(For nature ouergon comes to defect:)
  So now *Aurora* hauing felt the pride
Of heauen and earth, turning her ſelfe a ſide,
Rapt with a ſuddaine extaſie of minde,
Vnto her ſelfe (thus ſaide) Goddeſſe diuine:
How hapt that *Phebus* mou'd amid his chaſe,
Should ſuch kinde frendſhip ſcorne for to imbrace,
I will no more (quoth ſhe) godd it along
Such vnaccuſtom'd wayes, ne yet among

Such

Cephalus and Procris.

Such as is *Titan*, better fittes it me,
With *Vesper* still to liue, then such as he,
Though well I wot, honor is set on high,
Yet gentle *Humilitie* is best, say I.
No more she spake, but like the swelling tide,
That hauing passage skymes, scorning a guide,
Vntill the vaste receipte of *Neptunes* bower,
Kils the hoat fume, euen so, away she skoures,
Lawlesse as twere sans thought or any dread,
Like to banditos mong'st the mountaine heard.

<small>Aurora filia Titanis & Terræ.</small>

And now vpon her gentle louely *mother,
Bright as the morning, comes the mornings honor,
All snowy white, saue purpled heere and there,
So beautifull as beauty might despaire,
And stand amaz'd, noting her wanton eie,
Which at a trice could all the world espie,
Vpon her head, a coronet did stand,
Of seuerall flowers gathered by *Titan*.

<small>*An imitation taken from the Thracians called Acroconiæ, that vsually weare long haire downe to their wasts.</small>

*A vale she wore downe trayling to her thighes,
The stuffe whereof, I gesse, of such emprize,
As Gods themselues are doubtfull of the arte,
Seeming as aire with otomie disperst,
Her handes, a meny Poets* dead and gone,
Haue heretofore (excelling) wrote vpon.
It shall suffize *Venus* doth grace to her,
In that she waites before, like to a Starre,

<small>*Dead as mê.</small>

Directing of her steps along'st the zone,
Neuer ouertaken by the *Horizon*,
Ne yet in daunger put of any Lake,
The frozen Pole she warnes her to forsake:

<small>Pleiades the seauen starres, supposed to be the daughters of Licurgus.</small>

And all *Licurgus* daughters *Dion* noates,
Base in respect of duetie, and out-coates,

8

Each

Cephalus and Procris.

Each God and Goddeſſe, ſuch is beauties pride,
That *Neptunes* honor hath no larger tide:
One laſtes but a time, till time is come againe,
The other euer ouer-rules too certaine.

   Thus at the laſt, *Aurora* vanquiſhing
Heauens glory, and earthes cauſe of mourning:
" For now the ſparckling vault of *Ioues* high ſeate,
" Was not ſo fild with ouer-ſwaying heate:
" Red-hoat diſdaine gaue beauty place, for why?
" *Venus* had conquered baſe neceſſitie.
Along'ſt ſhe paſſed by *Heſperides*,
Laden with honor of thoſe golden eies:
And ſtately bode them ſtoupe to honor vs,
And ſtoupe they did, thinking twas *Venus*.
Then from this golden Orchard to the Tower,
Where *Ioue* in likenes of a golden ſhower,
Rauiſht faire* *Danae*, ſhe in rauiſhment   Ouid lib. 2, de
Of ſtrange delightes, the day there almoſt ſpent.   Triſtibus.
Thence to th' *Idalian* mount, where *Venus* doues,
Plume on the feathers, ſent by their true loues:
As *Itis* Pheaſant feathers, *Progne*, and
Tereus, they the Lapwincke winges did ſend: Ouid Metam.
Faire *Philomela* from the Nightingale
Sent likewiſe feathers, plucked from her taile,
And many others that denying loue,
Dide with deſpight, and here their cauſe did moue,
Then on her ſwift-heeld *Pegaſus*, amaine
Of *Colchos* golden Fleece a ſight to gaine,
And with the ſwift windes Harrould *Mercury*,
The golden Sonne-beames of *Apolloes* tree:
Where valorous warlike Knightes, for feates ydone
Are regiſtred, yclept Knightes of the Sonne: Knightes

Cephalus and Procris.

Knightes of the Garter, auncient knightes of Rhodes,
She mainely poftes, and there a time abodes,
   I do not tell you all that fhe did fee,
In honor done of this fame golden tree.
Knightes did their due, and Poets had no leffe,
Then what for Triumphes euery one can geffe.
Hence twas that *Hermes* ftole from heauen the power,
To foueranize on fchollers idle howres,
And had not *Ioue* bene fauourable then,
They never fhould haue bene accounted men,
But liu'd as pefants, fhaddowes, imagies,
And nere haue had the princes *fimilies*.
   Hence poft we foorth vnto an *Ocean*
That beats againft the bankes of *Helycon*,
Whereon if fo the ruler of the Eaft,
But caft an eie, we are not meanely bleft,
No more but fo, for more were ouer much,
Gold is approu'd but by a flender touch.
   And now bright *Phebus* mounted, gan difplay
His Orient funne-beames, on the liuely day,
Aurora made vnto the Siluan fhore,
Where Satyres, Goat-heardes, Shepheards kept of yore,
A facred and moft hallowed criftall fpring,
Long'ft which oft *Cephalus* yode on hunting,
And much delighted in the murmyring water,
Whofe filent noates gaue Eccho of their author,
And as in Rondelaies of loue they fung,
It aunfweare made, yet bod them hold their toung:
No bafe groome durft his cafe here to bemoane,
But quench his thirft, and fo part, and be gone.
But *Cephalus*, a man of fome compare,
Bore hound, and horfe, through depth without defpaire,

Cephalus and Procris.

And when the heate of Sommer ſtung him thro,
His yuorie limbes heere bath'd, and waſht he to,
His Steede orecome with anger in the chaſe,
His dogs halfe tir'd, or put vnto diſgrace,
Heere, and but here, he ſought for remedie,
Nor durſt the *Siluans* ſhrincke, but aide him preſently.
What ſhall I ſay in pride of him and his?
Man, horſe, and dogs, pleaſd th'inamored *Procris:*
But how with him *Aurora* was in loue,
A richer braine the taske would highly moue.

   Vpon a milke white courſer ſwift as winde,
Betrapt with yſſyckles of gold, that chim'bde;
By ſweete *Zephirus*, and the gentle aire,
That breathed life (as twere) to kill deſpaire,
Rode he vpright as any heiſell wan,
His Steede was wrought, & now would needes be gon:
Whoſe ouer head-ſtrong prauncing checkt the earth,
In ſcornefull ſorte, and whoſe loude neighing breath
Rent throgh the clouds, like *Ioues* ſwift quickning thũder,
And paſſage bod, or it would paſh't in ſunder.
So war-like *Mars*-like fit for *Venus* Court,
Hotly the gallant gentleman did ſort,
Now here, now there, his Steede began to rage,
And ſent foorth fome to bid the cloudes a badge
Of his proud ſtomacke, who would not be proude,
That is well backt, and in his pride alloude?
" Heere could I tell you many a prettie ſtorie,
" Of ſome eterniz'd by an others glory,
" Of men transfourm'd to apes, of womens euils,
" Of fiendes made Angels, and of angels diuels,
" Of many braue knightes done to ſhame, and more,
" How ſchollers fauourites waxe ouer poore,
                                                      " But

Cephalus and Procris.

" But oh faire Mufe, let flip to treate of fuch,
" A taske thou haft, that tyres thee too too much,
" And none (Gods know) thy boldneffe will out backe,
" But naked trueth, that garded coates doth lacke.
" Heroicke Parramore of Fairie land,
" That ftately built, with thy immortall hand,
" A golden, Angellike, and modeft Aulter,
" For all to facrifice on, none to alter.
" Where is that vertuous Mufe of thine become?
" It will awake, for fleepe not prooues it dumme.
" And thou *Arcadian* knight, earthes fecond Sunne,
" Reapt ere halfe ripe, finifht ere halfe begunne,
" And you that tread the pathes, were thefe haue gone,
" Be your foules agentes in our tragicke fong,
" And when the daughter of difpaire is dead,
" And ougly nightes blacke *Æthiopian* head,
" Ycoucht, and woxen pale, for griefe and fhame,
" Then fhall our quill, lift honor to your name.
O high *Apollo*, giue thou skill to vs,
That we may queintly follow *Cephalus*,
That now is mounted, ready to furprize,
What game fo ere is feaz'd-on by his eies;
Aurora met him, in his furious chafe,
As winde doth reigne, fo did fhe him embrace,
And his fierce courage, on the harmefulle Boare,
Ere he did part, fhould be affwag'd fhe fwore.
His amber-couloured treffes, neuer yet cut,
Into her luke-warme buffome fhe did put.
She wringes his handes, and hugges him twixt her armes,
(Apes die by culling) yet he tooke no harme:
Anone with smiles, fhe threates his chaft conceites,
And (looking on his eies) him fhe entreates,

Cephalus and Procris.

With kiſſes, ſighes, and teares reuying them,
As though their ſexe of duetie ſhould woe men,
He ſtriuing to be gone, ſhe preſt him downe:
She ſtriuing to kiſſe him, he kiſt the growne,
And euermore on contrarieties,
He aunſweare made, vnto her Deitie,
Her garland deckt with many a prettie gemme,
And flowers ſweete as May, ſhe gaue to hem:
Her feete (immodeſt dame) ſhe bear'd to ſhow him,
And askt him, yea, or no, if he did know them,
And therewithall, ſhe whiſpers in his eare,
Oh, who ſo long, is able to forbeare!
A thouſand prettie tales ſhe tels him too,
Of *Pan* his *Sirinx*, of *Ioues Io*,
Of *Semele*, the *Arcadian* Nimphes diſport,
Their ſtealth in loue, and him in couert ſorte,
Like to th'vnhappie Spider, would intangle;
He flie-like ſtriues, and to be gone doth wrangle:
And tels, he can no more of loue or beautie,
Then ruffe-beard Satyres, that nere heard of duetie,
Therefore to cut of all diſquietneſſe,
Rudely he throwes her from his down-ſoft breſt:
And with his Steede cuts through the riotouſe tnornes,
That ſhipwracke make of what is not their owne:
His ſpeare halfe bleeding, with a ſharpe deſire,
To taint the hot-Boare ſeemed to aſpire:
The ruffe and hidious windes, twixt hope and feare,
Whiſle amaine into his greedie eares,
His Steede vpſtartes, and courage freſhly takes,
The Rider fiercely, after hotly makes.
Halfe droncke, with ſpitefull mallice gainſt the Boare,
He prickt him forward, neuer prickt before.

Cephalus and Procris.

The toyling dogs therewith do mainely runne,
And hauing found the game, their Lord to come
They yalpe couragioufly, as who would fay,
Come maifter come, the footing ferues this way.
Therewith more fierce then *Aoris* did hie,
In his swift chafe the game for to efpie,
He gets him gon, nor neede wa'st to say goe,
O cruell men, that can leaue wemen fo!
  By this the fport grew hot on either part,
Aurora fhe was bitten to the hart,
A dogged part it was, fhe telleth oft,
To bite so deadfully a hart fo foft,
Aie me, had *Cupid* bene a rightfull lad,
He neuer fhould haue fhot a dart fo bad.
But what preuailes? a meny fad laments,
And Madrigals with dolefull tunes fhe fent,
Vnto the heauens Lampe *Phebus* mournefully,
All balefull, treating pittie from his eies,
She does her orizons, and tels how many
Haue loued her, before nere fcorn'd by any:
Her handes fo white as yuorie ftreame,
That through the rockes makes paffage vnto him:
Halfe blacke with wrathfull wringing them together
She reares to heauen, and downe vnto her mother,
Anon fhe faintly lets them fall againe,
To heauen, earth, father, mother, all in vaine,
" For loue is pittileffe, rude, and impartiall,
" When he intendes to laugh at others fall.
  Afrefh the fport of *Cephalus* began,
Erewhile at fault, his dogges now liuely ran,
And he quicke-lifted, when he lift to heare,
Ore tooke them ftraight, and with his venum'd fpeare,

Cephalus and Procris.

Gaſhly did wound the Boare couragiouſly,
The dogs vpon him likewiſe liuely flie,
His entrals bleeding-ripe before for feare,
Now twixt their grim chaps, *pel mel* they do teare,
The maſter proude at ſuch a ſtately prize,
Fils his high thoughtes, and gluts his greedie eies,
He bathes himſelfe, (as twere) in Seas of bliſſe ;
But what is victorie, where no praiſe is ?
Pittileſſe he ſcornes the plaintes *Aurora* ſendeth,
For where her loue beginneth, his loue endeth,
And seeme ſhe neuer ſo ore-gone with griefe,
He treble ioyes ; o bare and baſe reliefe !
" Euen like two Commets at one inſtant ſpred,
" The one of good, the other ſhame and dread :
" Peſtering th' aire with vapours multiplying,
" So is our Theame now quicke, and then a dying.
  Once more ſhe met him, and thus gently ſpake,
(If wemen had no tounges, their hartes would breake,)
Oh *Cephalus* for pittie loue me ſweete !
Or if not loue, yet do me gently greete,
Tis Action ſhewes th' intent, but ſmile vpon me,
Or giue a kiſſe, a kiſſe hath not vndone thee :
(Quoth he) these deſertes haue I meny a time,
In winters rage, and in the Sommers prime,
Mounted as now with horſe, and houndes good ſtore,
Chaſte, and encountred with the gag tooth'd Boare,
Rouſd vp the fearefull Lion from his caue,
(That duld the heauens, when he began to raue)
Purſu'd the Lizard, Tyger and a crew
Of vntam'd beaſtes ; yet none tam'd me as yew.
Admit that woemen haue preheminence,
To make men loue ; yet for ſo foule offence,

Cephalus and Procris.

As for to violate the marriage bed,
Were ouer much to be inamored;
Her who I honor, and am tied to,
Would deeply fcorne, I fhould another woe:
Admit the contrary, is it no finne,
In loue to end, where I did not begin?
Oh tis a fault, a finne exceeding any!
Then pardon me, for I fcorne to loue many.
   Twixt fhame and feare fcorn'd, and denied fo,
Poore foule fhe blufht, not wotting what to do,
Her teares were iffueleffe, her fpeech was done,
" The fpring being ftopt, how can the riuer runne,
Her hart (poore hart) was ouercharg'd with griefe,
" Tis worfe then death to linger on reliefe.
   At laft fhe fpake, and thus fhe mildly faid,
Oh, who to choofe, would liue, and die a maide!
What heauenly ioy may be accounted better,
Then for a man to haue a woman debter?
Now thou art mine in loue: Loue me againe.
Then I am thine, is it not heartie gaine,
Vpon aduantage to take double fee?
Thou fhalt haue double, treble, pleafeth thee:
Thefe curled, and vntewed lockes of thine,
Let me but borrow vpon pawne of mine.
Thefe (oh immortall) eies, thefe facred handes,
Lend me I pray thee, on fufficient bandes:
Wilt thou not truft me? By the facred throne,
That *Phebus* in the mid day fits vpon,
I will not kepe them paft a day or twaine,
But Ile returne them fafely home againe,
   Thefe lockes (quoth he) that curled I do weare,
Within their folding billowes they do beare,

Cephalus and Procris.

The deere remembrance twixt my loue and mee,
Therefore I cannot lend them vnto thee,
Thefe eies delight, thofe eies did them mainetaine,
And therefore can not lend them foorth againe,
Thefe handes gaue faith of my true faithfulneffe,
And therefore will not lend them; pardons vs.
" All fad, and in her widdow-hood of forrow,
" Like to the Pilgrim longing for the morrow,
" Tires on the tedious day, and tels his cafe
" Vnto the rutheleffe Eccho what he was.
    So doth *Aurora* rioteoufly complaine
Of loue, that hath her hart vniuftly flaine,
And furioufly fhe throwes her armes about him,
As who would fay, fhe could not be without him;
Faft to his girted fide fhe neately clinges,
Her haire let loofe about his fhoulders flinges:
Nay twere immodeft to tell the affection
That fhe did fhow him, leaft it draw to action.
    " Faire *Cytherea*, miftris of delight,
" Heere was accompanied with foule defpight,
" The boy woxt proude to fee the morning pale,
" And hence it was *Ioue* plucked of his vale,
" That he might pittie her, and note his wrath,
" But fcornefully he fmiles, and helpeth nothe :
" Whereat reuengefully to loue he gaue,
" Perpetuall blindnes in his choice to haue,
" And too too true we finde it euery day;
" That loue fince then hath bene a blinded boy,
" And knowes not where (unhappy wegg) to dart,
" But defperately, vncounceld flayes the hart.
By this deepe chat on either part was one,
And *Cephalus* would now perforce be gone.

17   C   " What

Cephalus and Procris.

What can a woman more then to entreate?
Is it for men to practife on deceite?
Like to the toiling *Sifiphus* in vaine,
She roules the ftone, that tumbleth backe againe,
And ftriue fhe ne're fo much to conquer him,
It will not be for he hates fuch, fo finne:
Againe fhe pleades his conftancie to miffe,
Requitall in the loweft degree by *Procris*;
Inferring more to proue her argument,
That woemen cannot be with one content.
   Cephalus as now vnto her fpeech gaue heede,
Againe (quoth fhe) attir'd in marchants weede,
Home to thy faire fpoufe, moue her vnto ruth,
Pleade tedioufly on loue, boaft of thy youth,
And if not youth, nor loue, can her obtaine,
Promife rewardes for fome confent for gaine:
I fay no more, but if I were a man,
Thefe cheekes for loue fhould neuer look fo wan.
   Drown'd in a fea of ouerfwelling hate,
As one that lies before his enimie proftrate,
Willing to liue, yet fcorning to beg life,
So feares he now (as twere) with his falfe wife;
Sometimes he cals her faire, chaft, wife, and graue,
Anon with too too wrathfull tauntes he raues,
(Quoth he) fhall I, where erft I might commaunde,
Goe and intreate with knee, and cap in hand,
Or fhall I die, tormented thus in minde,
Iuft *Radamanth*, what torture canft thou finde,
For woemen that difloyall, counterfeite,
Loue to their peeres, and yet would flay their hartes?
Haft thou no more tubs bottomeleffe to fill?
Haft thou no more ftones to rowle vp the hill?

Cephalus and Procris.

Haft thou no more wheeles to teare of their flefh,
That fo difloyally in loue tranfgreffe?
Haft thou no torment, neuer yet inflicted
On woemens flefh, and all this while neglected?
If fo I pray thee graunt this boone to mee,
That *Procris* therewith may tormented be,
Oh! he is deafe, and damned let him liue,
He will not heare, his kingdome too well thriues.
Proferpina, great goddeffe of the Lake,
Some pittie fweete on the diftreffed take:
And when the *Chaos* of this worldes difdaine,
Hath fent this bodie to th' Elizium plaine,
And left this Center barren of repaft,
Ile honor thee eternall with my ghoft,
Which faid, "as one that banifht doth remaine,
" Would rather die then longing be detained,
Defperate he goes vnto his innocent wife,
What's fhe would wed t' abide fo bad a life?
And now the tombe that clofeth rotten bones,
(Deceitfull man) difguifed is come home,
He afketh for himfelfe, himfelfe being there,
Would it not make a thoufand woemen feare?
He tels her of his long indur'd laments,
By fea and land, that he for her hath fpent,
And would haue faid more, but fhe ftraight was gone,
Is not the fault efpeciall in the man?
Then after makes he by her flender vale,
He holdes her faft, and tels her meny a tale,
He threw her downe vpon the yeelding bed,
And fwore he there would loofe his maiden-head,
She (as fome fay, all woemen ftricktly do,)
Faintly deni'd what fhe was willing too:

Cephalus and Procris.

But when he faw her won to his defire,
(Difcourteous man) did heape flax on the fire,
What there did want in wordes moft fubtilly,
By liberall giftes he did the fame fupply,
Hauing purfued fo egerly his drift,
Procris vnarm'd fufpecting not his fhifte;
What for defire of ftealth in loue commended,
Or gold s' aboundant dealt, fhe him befrended,
At leaft gaue notice of her willing minde,
(*Æfopian* fnakes will alwaies proue vnkind,)
At firft content to parley hand in hand,
After fteale kiffes, talke of *Cupids* band,
And by degrees applide the tex fo well,
As (cunning counter-feite) he did excell,
And what but now gently he might obtaine,
O what but now, fhe wifht cald backe againe,
" The duskie vapours of the middle earth,
" Drawne from contagious dewes, & noifome breathes,
" Choakt the cleere day; and now from *Acheron*,
" Blacke difmall night was come the world vppon,
" Fitting true louers, and their fweete repaft,
" *Cinthia* arofe from *Neptunes* couch at laft.
Oh! then this fcape of *Cephalus* was fpide,
Treafon may fhadowed be but neuer hid;
Vnhappy woman, fhe the dull night fpent
In fad complaintes, and giddie merrymentes,
Sometimes intending to excufe her crime,
By vowes protefting, and an other time,
(Remotiue woman) would haue done worfe harme,
Hymen therewith fent forth a frefh alarme,
But *Chauntecleere* that did the morne bewray,
With his cleere noates gaue notice of the day,

Cephalus and Procris.

Whereat she starts, and in a desperate moode,
Skipt from the bed, all wrathfull where she stoode,
Vow'd to herselfe perpetuall banishment,
Mournefull complaintes, out-cries, and languishment;
Then to the craggie vaulted caues, whose sound
Small mourning doth a treble griefe resound,
Amid the thickest of the desertes, she
Distressed woman, forlorne, sollitarie,
With many a direfull song, fits the thicke groue,
And heere and there in vncouth pathes doth roue.
   Cephalus we leaue vnto his secrete muse,
     Lamie by chaunce some sacred herbe to vse,
On deere compassion of some louers plaintes,
Among the woods and moorie fennes she hauntes,
Such euill pleasing humours, fairie elues,
Obserue and keepe autenticke mong'st themselues;
And now was she of purpose trauailing,
Intending quietly to be a gathering
Some vnprophane, or holy thing, or other:
Good Faierie Lady, hadst thou bene loues mother,
Not halfe so meny gallants had bene slaine,
As now in common are with endlesse paine,
This Lady compassing her secret fauour;
Procris espi'd wondring at her behauiour,
Amaz'd she stoode at such a heauenly sight,
To see so debonary a saint at such a hight,
Her haire downe trailing, and her robes loose worne,
Rushing through thickets, and yet neuer torne,
Her brest so white as euer womans was,
And yet made subiect to the Sunnes large compasse:
Each so officious, and became her so,
As *Thames* doth Swannes, or Swans did euer *Po*,

Cephalus and Procris.

Procris in fteede of tearmes her to falute,
With teares and fighes, (fhewing her toung was mute)
She humbly downe vnto her louely feete,
Bow'd her ftraight bodie *Lamie* to greete:
Therewith the Lady of thofe pretie ones,
That in the twylight mocke the frozen zone,
And hand in hand daunce by fome filuer brooke,
One at an other pointing, and vp looke,
(Like rurall Faunes) vpon the full fa'ft Moone,
Intreating *Venus* fome heroicke boone,
Gently gan ftoupe, and with her facred haire,
Her louely eies, and face fo ouer faire,
She neatly couers, and her vngirt gowne,
Deafely commits vnto the lowly growne,
She dandleth *Procris* thereon prettily,
And chaunteth foueraigne fongs full merrily,
And gins to prancke her vp with many a flower,
And vow'd fhe fhould be *Oboron's* parramore.
" Euen like to one thats troubled in his fleepe,
" Amazed ftartes of nothe fcarce taking keepe,
" But in a furie tels what he hath done,
So fhe of *Cephalus* a tale begun,
Whereby the Lady quickely vnderftood,
The caufe fhe was fo grieued and fo wood,
Aie me, who can (quoth *Lamie*) be fo cruell,
As to conuert the building Oake to fuell?
Or rob the Ceder from his royall armes,
That fpread fo faire, or do a woman harme?
Waft not inough for *Læda's* Swanly fcape,
That *Iupiter* was author of the rape?
What can be more for *Cephalus* then this,
That *Cephalus* was author of thy miffe?

Cephalus and Procris.

The fault ydone muſt be to him alluded,
That in the complot hath thee ſo abuſed,
I pray thee tell me, who would not conſent,
Amorouſly boorded, and in merriment?
Say that thou hadſt not yeelded therevnto,
As one vnknowne, vnmaſkt thou would'ſt it do,
Methinkes the paſtime had bene ouer pleaſing,
So ſweetely ſtolne, and won by ſuch falſe leaſing,
A wonder ſure that *Cephalus* a man,
Giuen to hunting, with the game not ran;
But thou wilt ſay, he gaue thee too much law,
Whereby to courſe, his dogs the game not ſaw,
Tut twas in thee to bring the ſport to paſſe,
Knowing his dogs, and where the huntſman was,
In ſoothe, if he had hunted cunningly,
He ſhould haue prickt out where the game did lie,
But peraduenture I will not ſay ſo,
His dogs were tir'd: and if new ſport not kno,
For ſome a moneth, and meny men a weeke,
Cherriſh their curs before for game they ſeeke,
And then no maruaile though they backe did beate,
When they were ſtrengthleſſe, and orecome with heate,
If it be royall too, I heard ſome ſay,
Till warrant had, ther's none muſt coorſe or play,
But it is wonder, he on his owne land,
Would not ſtrik't dead, hauing't ſo faire at ſtand,
A was not halfe couragious on the ſport,
For who would yeeld when he hath won the fort?
An other time he vowes (perhaps) to kill,
But in meane while poore *Procris* wants her will,
It is but game (quoth ſhe) doth ſtand betweene you,
And what but ſporting doth he diſallow?

Cephalus and Procris.

To end which controuerſie (quoth ſhe) againe,
Shew him an other courſe vpon the plaine,
And if he then beate backe, or ſleeping follow,
Once more giue notice by a ſiluer hollow,
It may be he will haue ſome deep ſurmize,
That ther's new footing, note his greedie eies,
For thei' le be pliant, ſheuering in his head,
Like to a greedie *Priapus* in bed,
For pittie, ruthe, compaſſion, loue, or luſt,
He can not chooſe but yeeld perforce he muſt,
Perſwade thy ſelfe, a womans wordes can wound,
Her teares oh they are able to confound:
Then *Procris* ceaſe, and prey thee mourne no more,
There be that haue done ten times worſe before.
  Careleſſe of what the eluiſh wanton ſpake,
Procris begins a freſh her plaintes to make,
She kneeleth downe cloſe by the riuers ſide,
And with her teares did make a ſecond tide,
She vp to heauen heaues her immortall eies,
Caſting them downe againe ſhe ſeem'd to die,
No ſhew of pleaſance from her face did come,
Except the teares ioyd on her cheekes to runne,
Her handes full often would haue helpt each other,
But were ſo weake they could not meete together:
Some orizons I geſſe ſhe would haue done,
But they alack were finiſht ere begun.
Thus for a ſeaſon liueleſſe ſhe doth liue,
And prayes to death, but deafe he nothing giues;
Continuing for a ſpace thus deſolate,
The new ſprung flowers her ſences animate,
Her head and eies then ſhe ginnes to mainetaine,
As one halfe ſorrowing that ſhe liu'd againe,

Cephalus and Procris.

Their former strength her handes possesse at last,
Which serue to drie the teares that she doth wast.
   Thus in distressefull wise, as though she had
Bene rauisht, wounded, or at least halfe mad,
Like a *Thessalian Metra*, of our storie
To haue no part, nor rob vs of our glory,
She fiercely raues, and teares in carelesse sorte,
The louely flowers (God wot) that hurteth not.
At length the silent *Morpheus* with his lute,
About her tyring braine gan to salute
Her vnto rest, the *Driades* consent,
With downe of thissels they made her a tent,
Where softly slumbering shadowed from the Sunne,
To rest herselfe deuoutly she begun.
   But note the sequel, an vnciuill Swaine,
That had bene wandring from the scorched plaines,
Espi'd this *Amoretta* where she lay,
Conceited deedes base Clownes do oft bewray,
Rude as he was in action, roughe, and harsh,
Dull, sluggish, heauie, willfull, more then rash,
He paces long'st, and round about her tent,
And which way he had gone againe he went;
His rude borne basenesse holdes him thus excus'd,
In age we do the like in youth we vs'd,
Nor stood he long on tearmes, but rusheth in,
And boldly thus to boord her doth begin.
   O gentle Goddesse loues owne louely mother!
(For fairer then thy selfe, I know no other,)
What sacrilegious obsequies vndone,
Art thou perfourming to thy winged Sonne?
Or are these cloistred willow walles the show,
Of thy fell hate to him that thou doest owe,

Cephalus and Procris.

Tis mercenary toyling thus alone,
Tell me (I pray thee) wherefore doeſt thou moane?
Amid extreames who would not ſhow his griefe?
The riuer pent ſeldome yeeldes reliefe:
But being deuided flowes and nurſeth many,
Sorrow (I geſſe) did neuer good to any,
Thou art too peeuiſh, faith, be rul'd by me;
Who liues content, hath not ſecuritie,
And ſooner fades the flower then the weede,
Woemen are onely made on for their deedes,
Few reape the ſtubble, when the corne is gon,
A Hermitage compared to a region,
Hath no exceede, but takes diſgrace therein:
So woemen liuing ſollitarie, ſin,
More by the wrong they do commit thereby,
Then mong'ſt many acting the contrary:
This ſaid, he bow'd his body to embrace her,
Thinking thereby, that he ſhould greatly grace her,
And would haue told her ſomething in her eare,
But ſhe orecome with melancholy feare,
Diu'd downe amid the greene and roſey briers,
Thinking belike with teares to quench deſire,
Aie me (I wot) who euer the like tried,
Knowes tis a hell to loue, and be denied.
And who ſo is moſt politicke, true loue
Will ſend his wits, or headlong, or to *Ioue*.
The dowdy yongſter had by this ſo well
Perſwaded *Procris* from her ſolemne Cell,
That now as heeretofore through thicke and thin,
Like ſome pernitious hegg ſurpriz'd with ſin,
Cutting the aire with braine-ſick ſhreekes and cries,
Like a ſwift arrow with the winde ſhe highes,

Cephalus and Procris.

For that fame Swaine yfpoken of, did tell her,
Where and with what Nimphe *Cephalus* did err,
Still doth the morning add vnto our mufe,
And of *Auroraes* fweete fome fweete to vfe,
Lets mount couragioufly, ha done with hate,
Tis feruile ftill on forrow to dilate.
" The ftaring maffacres, blood-dronken plots,
" Hot riotous hell-quickeners, *Italian-nots*:
" That tup their wits with fnaky *Nemefis*,
" Teate-fucking on the poyfon of her mis,
" With ougly fiendes ytafked let them bee,
" A milder fury to enrich feeke wee,
" If *Homer* did fo well the feates ypaint
" Of an *Vlyffes*, then how much more quaint,
" Might his fweete verfe th' immortall *Hector* graced,
" And praife deferuing all, all haue imbraced?
" But what is more in vre, or getteth praife,
" Then fweete Affection tun'd in homely layes?
" Gladly would our *Cephalian* mufe haue fung
" All of white loue, enamored with a tounge,
" That ftill *Styll* muficke fighing teares together,
" Could one conceite haue made beget an other,
" And fo haue ranfackt this rich age of that,
" The mufes wanton fauourites haue got
" Heauens-gloryfier, with thy holy fire,
" O thrife immortall quickener of defire,
" That fcorn'ft this* vaft and bafe prodigious clime,   He mindes in
" Smyling at fuch as beg in ragged rime,   refpect of Po-
" Powre from aboue, or fauour of the prince,   ets and their
" Diftilling wordes to hight the quinteffence   fauourites.
" Of fame and honor: fuch I say doeft fcorne,
" Becaufe thy ftately verfe was Lordly borne,

" Through

Cephalus and Procris.

"Through all *Arcadia*, and the *Fayerie* land,
"And hauing fmale true grace in *Albion*,
"Thy natiue foyle, as thou of right deferued'ft,
"Rightly adornes one now, that's richly ferued :
"O to that quick fprite of thy fmooth-cut quill,
"Without furmife of thinking any ill.

<small>He thinkes it the duetie of euery one that failes, to ftrike maine-top, before that great & mighty Poet COLLYN.</small>

"*I offer vp in duetie and in zeale,
"This dull conceite of mine, and do appeale,
"With reuerence to thy
"On will I put that brefte-plate and there on,
"Riuet the ftandard boare in fpite of fuch :
"As thy bright name condigne or would but touch,
"*Affection* is the whole *Parenthefis*,
"That here I ftreake, which from our tafke doth miffe.

And now conclude we in a word or twaine,
Viragon-like, *Procris* the woods containe;
Where by direction from the Swaine fhe lay,
Shrowded with fmale bowes from the fcorching day,
Clofe by th' accuftom'd harbour of her loue,
Where he to follace did him felfe approue,
It was his guize through melancholy anger,
Heere to oppofe his body, as no ftraunger,
But well affected, and acquainted too,
With ftrange perfourmances, that oft did doo
Him honor, feruice, in refpect of her,
That in the skie fits honoured as a Starre,
Soft ftealing bare-foote Faieries now and then,
(That counted are as Iewels worne of men,)
Together with the fcornefull mocking *Eccho*,
Nymphes, *Driades*, and *Satyres* many mo
Then I can tell you, would full oft moft trim,
Like gliding ghoaftes about his cabine fwim,

Cephalus and Procris.

As what might feeme to imitate delight,
Sweete thoughts by day, and muficke in the night,
Caufing the one fo to confirme the other,
As Reuels, Mafkes, and all that *Cupids* mother,
Could fummon to the earth, heere was it done,
A fecond heauen, (aie me) there was begunne.
 She waues herfelfe, fuppofing that thereby,
Aurora to embrace he would come nie;
But he miftrufting fome deuouring beaft,
Till he could finde fome pray, himfelfe did reft,
Vnder that thicket, eft-foone with the dart,
He of *Aurora* had acted a part,
Fitter for fome rude martialift then one,
That should haue bene the accent of her moane.
Now in her bowels bathes the dart a good,
The liuely, frefh, and rofey couloured blood
Then did rebate, in fteade whereof pale death,
Lay with his furquedie to draw her breath,
Her fpeach paft fence, her fences paft all fpeaking,
Thus for prolonged life he fals entreating.
Thou faffron God (quoth he) that knits the knot
Of marriage, do'ft, heauës know, thou knoweft not what,
How art thou wrath, that mak'ft me of this wrong
Author and Actor, and in tragicke fong,
Doeft binde my temples, eke in fable cloudes,
Encampes the honor thereto is allowde,
O *Hymen* haft thou no remorfe in loue?
Then *Hyems* hencefoorth be till I approoue
Againe the fruites, and comfort iffueleffe,
Of Iealoufie in marriage had a mis.
 Heere was no want of hate, foule *Acheron*,
Styx, and *Cocytus*, dufkie *Phlegyton*,

L'Enuoy.

Eumenydes, and all the hell houndes then,
Spued foorth difgrace, oh what hath *Cupid* done!
Pherecydes, Puppius, and *Philocles* mourne,
Mourne with *Cephalus*, and your *Hymni* turne
To difmall nightes darke ougly ftratagems,
To tragicke out-cries, wonderment of men,
And thofe that take delight in amorous loue,
Be their *Heraclian* wits fubiect to moue
An other Sunne to grace our *Theater*,
That sadly mournes in blacke, with heauy cheere,
Duld with a ftill continuing heauineffe;
O! in extreames who comes to vifite vs?

FINIS.

Etwixt extreames
Are ready pathes and faire,
On ftraight and narrow went
Leades paffengers in dreames,
And euer as the aire,
Doth buzze them with content,
A cruelle ougly fenne;
Hated of Gods and men,

Cals out amaine,
O whether but this way:
Or now, or neuer bend,
Your fteps this goale to gaine,
The tother tels you ftray,
And neuer will finde ende,
Thus hath the Gods decreed,
To paine foules for their deedes.

L'Enuoy.

  Thefe monfters tway,
Ycleeped are of all,
Difpaire and eke debate,
  Which are (as Poets fay)
Of Enuies whelpes the fall,
And neuer come too late:
  By *Procris* it appeeres,
Whofe proofe is bought fo deere.

  Debate a foote,
And Iealoufie abroade,
For remedie difpaire,
  Comes in a yellow coate,
And actes where wyfardes troade,
To fhew the gazers faire,
  How fubtilly he can cloake,
The tale an other fpoake.

  O time of times,
When monfter-mongers fhew,
As men in painted cloathes,
  For foode euen like to pine,
And are in weale Gods know,
Vpheld with fpiced broathes,
  So as the weakeft feeme,
What often we not deeme.

  Abandon it,
That breedes fuch difcontent,
Foule Iealoufie the fore,
  That vile defpight would hit,
Debate his *Chorus* fpent,
Comes in a tragicke more,

L'Enuoy.

Then Actors on this Stage,
Can plaufiuely engage.

Oh *Cephalus,*
That nothe could pittie moue,
To tend *Auroraes* plaintes,
   Now fham'd to tell vnto vs,
How thou would'ft gladly loue,
So *Procris* might not faint,
   Full oft the like doth hap,
   To them that thinke to fcape.

   But aie me fhee,
Vnmercifully glad,
To fpie her wedded mate,
   Reft from all woemen free,
Yet amoroufly clad,
Thought on her bended knee,
   Of him to be receau'd
   But aie me was deceiu'd.

   Oft hits the fame,
For who the innocent,
To catch in fecret fnares,
   (And laughes at their falfe fhame,)
Doth couertly inuent,
Themfelues not throughly ware,
   Are oft beguil'd thereby,
   Woemen efpecially.

   Faire *Procris* fall,
The merriment of moe,
That tread in vncouth wents,
   Remaine for fample fhall,

L'Enuoy.

And learne them where to goe,
Their eares not so attent,
   To vile disloyaltie,
   Nurse vnto Iealousie.
   Aurora shee,
Too amorous and coye,
Toyde with the hunters game,
   Till louing not to see,
Spide loue cloth'd like a boy;
Whereat as one asham'd,
   She starts, and downe-ward creepes,
   Supposing all a sleepe.
   " The seruitor,
" That earst did brauely skoure,
" Against the frontier heate,
   " For fame and endlesse honor,
" Retir'd for want of power,
" Secure himselfe would seate,
   So she but all too soone,
   Her honor ere begun,
   Did famish cleane:
For where she sought to gaine,
The type of her content,
   By fatall powers diuine,
Was suddainely so stain'd,
As made them both repent,
   And thus enamoured,
   The morning since look't red.
   As blushing thro,
Some tinssell weau'd of lawne,
Like one whose tale halfe spent,
   His coulour comes and goes,
Desirous to be gone,
In briefe shewes his intent,

L'Enuoy.

Not halfe fo ftately done,
As what he erft begun,

Euen fo, and fo,
Aurora pittioufly,
For griefe and bitter fhame,
 Cries out, oh let me goe,
(For who but fluggards eie,
The morning feekes to blame?)
 Let fchollers only mourne,
 For this fame wretched tourne.

A iuft reward
To fuch as feeke the fpoyle,
Of any wedded ftate,
 But what do we regard?
So liue by others toyle,
And reape what they haue got,
 No other reckoning wee,
 Suppofe but all of glee.

 Aie me the Sonne,
Ere halfe our tale is quit,
His ftrength rebates amaine,
 A clymate cold and wan,
That cannot ftrength a wit,
By Arte to tell the fame,
 Faire *Cynthia* fhine thou bright,
 Hencefoorth Ile ferue the night.

FINIS.

Th. Edwards.

NARCISSVS

Aurora musæ amica.

LONDON
Imprinted by Iohn Wolfe.
1 5 9 5.

NARCISSVS

Y Ou that are faire, and fcorne th' effectes of loue,
You that are chafte, and ftand on nice conceites,
You *Delians* that the Mufes artes can moue,
You that for one poore thing make thoufands treate,
You that on beauties honor do curuate;
    Come fing with me, and if thefe noates be lowe,
    You fhall haue fome prickt higher ere ye goe.

I tune no difcord, neither on reproache,
With hideous tearmes in thwarting any dame,
But euen in plaine-fong, plodding foorth of each,
That Cynicke beauties vifor on doth frame,
Sing I, and fo fing all that beautie name:
    If there be any that account it harfh,
    Why let them know, it is *Narciffus* verfe.

Now geue me leaue, for now I minde to trie you,
Sweete Mufes but to harbour mong'ft fo many,
On rich *Parnaffus* mount, if not fo nie you,
O yet in fome low hollow Caue with any,
That but the name of *Poetry* do carry:
    Corycyus fome haue told you let lie vaft,
    There let me liue a while, though die difgra'ft.

Narcissus.

Euen word for word, fence, fentence, and conceite
I will vnfold, if you will giue me leaue,
Euen as *Narciffus* playning did entreate
Mee to fit downe, nor will I you deceive,
Of any glory that you can receive,
   By this fad tale, and if it do you pleafure,
   No doubt there will be better done at leifure.

With fixed eies, handes ioyntly vpwardes reard,
His bodie all to mournefull forrow bent,
Imbracing clowdie fighes, as one prepard,
To tell fome leaden-tale, not merryment,
With melancholy action onwardes went:
   And thus he fpake, and fmiling too, begun,
   And thus he wept, and ended to his fong.

Whileft I was young nurft in the bleffed heauen,
Of thofe fweete Ioyes, which men allude to loue,
Euen in the hight thereof was I bereauen,
Of thofe fweete pleafures, ere I could approue,
The effence of that organing from *Ioue:*
   For looke how Gnats foft finging fwarme together,
   So did faire Ladies round about me houer.

Aie me, I not refpected dalliance then,
Though many did incyte me to difport,
I knew not I what ioyes they gaue to men,
But as the banquet paft, they as the fhot,
Pleafing euils acting or acting not,
   Gods know I knew not, nor accounted euer
   Of faireft woemen but as fowleft weather.

Narcissus.

I thought no good compar'd vnto deceite,
Fancie was alwaies dull, and knew not mee,
When Ladies did with kisses me entreate,
As in a traunce I lay, and would not see,
Of dalliance so farre I stole in degree,
    What good did Nature giuing me such beautie,
    And would not shew me there to all the duetie?

I not regarded plaintes, or nice smiles speaking,
Eies modest wandering, toung alluring obiectes,
Sighes raysing teares, shame with the white rose streking,
But counted her, and her as natures abiectes,
He that nere paine did feele, all doubtes doth neglect;
    So carelesse were my thoughtes and all my actions,
    As I accounted nere to feele subiection.

I stood as nice as any she aliue,
On this curl'd locke the other wreathed haire,
And told how some had power to make men wiue,
And some againe to bring them to dispaire,
Had I but told them they could charme the aire;
    Such was beliefe, and such is still in louers,
    That one may cause them thinke, or ought discouer.

O had I bene lesse faire, or they more wittie,
Then had I not thus playn'd in tragicke song,
Then had I not bene pointed at by pittie,
Nor throwne my selfe Care-swallowing griefes among,
Nor these teares thus vnto the world haue throng'd:
    But what auailes, sigh, weepe, mourne, houle, lament?
    In vaine wordes, action, teares, and all are spent.

Narcissus.

Would some good man had massacred my face,
Blinde stroke my eies, as was my hart thereto,
Dasht in my throate, my teeth, done some disgrace,
For with my tounge some say they were vndoe,
Or me foredone to shame, ere they did woe.
   I am perswaded then, I had not beene,
   What now I am, nor halfe these griefes had seene.

" Looke how at suddaine thunder in the aire,
" Th' amazed starts, looking from whence it comes,
" So on report of any passing faire,
" The greedie people in the streetes do runne,
" Where first the Wonder-breeder it begunne:
   It was enough to say *Narcissus* came,
   The crie thereof gaue grace vnto my name.

How many times haue I been luld a sleepe,
In Ladies bowers, and carried to and fro,
Whilest but a stripling, Lord, how would they peepe
On this, and that, not knowing what to do?
Nature they blam'd, and yet they prais'd it to:
   Had *Priapus Narcissus* place enioy'd,
   He would a little more haue done then toy'd.

Some with *Still* musicke, some with pleasing songes,
Some with coy smiles, mixt now and then with frownes,
Some with rich giftes, all with alluring tounges,
And many with their eies to th' earth cast downe,
Sighing foorth sorrow that did so aboune,
   Sufficient to approue on thrice more coye,
   And yet (poore wenches) could not get a boy.

Anon

Narcissus.

Anone the fayrest gins thus to salute,
Narcissus, oh *Narcissus* looke vpon mee,
There are (quoth she) ten thousand that would greet
Her, who thou maist command, yet scornst I see.
Reak'st thou no more of loue, of life, of beautie?
  Ioues Iô was transform'd vnto a cow,
  So would I low, might I be lou'de of yow.

Another queintly thus disputes with me,
As now and then amongst my fellow peeres,
I wont to sport awaie the time, quoth she,
Well now (*Narcissus*) I perceiue a cheere,
You pricke a cast to touch the mistres neere.
  Ah short in faith, I wish you no more harme,
  Than that you had some *Marie* in your armes.

The cast is mine (quoth I) she it denide,
I wrangl'de, striu'de, and would not yeeld the thro,
Vnto a standing measure Ile be tride,
Whether (quoth she) that I haue won't or no,
Striue, wrangle, measure, doo what I could do:
  Somewhat she aild, and this I found at last,
  For want of rubs I ouerthrew the cast.

Then came the neatest one of all my louers,
The onely patterne of simplicitie,
Her sister-hood would not a thought discouer,
That should foretell whereon she did relie,
Not for a world, her loue was bent so holly,
  When she did sweare, her oath was by this booke,
  And then would kisse, and round about her looke.

Narciſſus.

I haue not tolde you in what neat attire,
She came to viſit me her onely brother,
Nor how ſhe cloakt her ſpirituall deſire,
That was ſo feruent towards me boue others,
Her chaſt not-foes, and toying lyke a mother:
   Nor will I tell you, leaſt ſome olde wife ſaie,
   Narciſſus was a cruell wanton boie.

" Oh what is beautie more than to the ſicke
" A potion adding ſpirit to the patient,
" Which for a time hath operation quicke,
" But when that nature workes her due euent,
" Is ruinous and quite without content:
   " Then youth and beautie hold not hands together,
   " For youth is beſt, where beautie hath another.

Yet youth and beautie hold you hands together,
For you are ſeemely ornaments of nature,
And will delight the ſonne of ſuch a mother,
And glad the Sire that put ſuch proofe in vre,
Beautie and youth are baites without a lure:
   That ſcorning pride, ſo farre exceed compare,
   As makes you ſeeme what yet you neuer were.

Faire *Adonis* in pride that ſhewes ſo hot,
Clad in rich purple haire, with amorous hew,
Cauſing to leaue her Doue-drawne chariot,
Loue ſole commander, and to follow yow,
Not for the palme of glorie but for *yew:*
   Come tune with me true deſolations noate,
   For none but we can beauties blindnes coate.

Narcissus.

For none but we, we, but none for vs mourne;
Thrice faire *Adonis* by this cooling water,
Come feate thy louely branches, and Ile turne
Thefe plains to meades, thefe meades to plaine teares after,
When with recording noates of their firft author;
   We'le take more ioy in counting ouer forrowes,
   Than *Venus* gazing on her ingling fparrowes.

Come, come *Adonis*, let vs meete each other,
Imbrace thou fighs, with teares I'le fil the aire,
And though we both were hapleffe boies together,
Yet let vs now contend againft the faire,
Beautie like winter bringeth on defpaire:
   Fruit ouer-ripe, Iems valued paft their worth,
   Redoune fmall honor to their bringer forth.

Nay if thou wilt not, choofe, feeft who comes here?
Tis one that hath the map of forrow drawen,
Welcome *Leander*, welcome, ftand thou neere,
Alacke poore youth, what haft thou for a pawne,
What, not a rag, where's *Heroes* vale of lawne?
   Her bufkins all of fhels yfiluered ore,
   What haft thou noth? then pack yonder's the doore.

Yet ftaie a while, for thou fhalt mourne with me,
Yet get thee gone, for I will mourne alone;
Yet ftaie awhile, extreames are bad we fee,
And yet it fkils not, for thou canft not mone,
Thou wilt not moane, thy teares were long fince done:
   And were thy griefes againe for to lament,
   Thou couldft not fhed fuch teares as I haue fpent.

Narcissus.

No, no *Leander*, thou lasciuiously
Didst plaie with loue, and with thy loue hadst sport,
Nere didst thou mourne, but as thou liuedst didst dy,
Telling *Musæus*, he the world of what
Thy dandling tresses of faire *Hero* got:
   I tearme her faire, for thou didst make her faire,
   For without men alacke they nothing are.

But tell me, tell me, whether art thou bent,
Hath *Tempe* now disgorg'd her loue-mates hether,
Or haue you licenfe for some merriment,
To visit faire *Elizium*, tell me whether,
What melancholy man, answerest to neither?
   It skils not much, for thought you will not saie,
   Abydos can your wantonnes display.

Oh ceafe *Narcissus*, be not so mis-lead,
Thou art in furie and deceiued quite,
Looke round about thee where are anie dead,
Or ghosts afrighting come to dim thy sight?
Thou doest mistake, and dreamst to serue the night:
   Night onely cheefe companion for thy care,
   Yet when he comes, canst not of him beware.

Thou sable winged messenger of *Ioue*,
True honor of content and sad complaints,
Comfort to them that liuing die in loue,
Hate to the scornfull and nice dames so quaint,
Deepe searcher of our secret teares and plaints:
   Wide ope thy wings, I'le houer twixt thy armes,
   And like the cock when morne comes found alarme.

Narcissus.

Was euer boy afflicted thus before?
Was euer man halfe partner of my griefe?
Was euer Nymph or Goddesse knowne of yore,
To languish thus and neuer haue reliefe?
Was euer goddesse, man, or boy the chiefe?
    The onely subiect for a wrathfull pen,
    Heauens iudge, earth deem, ges you the foules of men.

Is this the happie blisseful ioy of beautie?
Is this the summer sporting with delight?
Then cage vp me for winter's best, saie I,
And sing who list in such sunne-shining light,
Obscuritie and sweet thought wandering night
    Are fit companions for my troubled ghoast,
    Farewell, the Sunne's too hot to be my hoast.

I, I, *Narcissus*, in some pitchie caue,
Or vgly dungeon where the serpents lie,
There rest thy selfe, and when thou ginst to raue,
Their musicke shall consort melodiouslie,
Vnto thy sighs and deepe lamenting cries:
    For since the earth hath none that pittie moues,
    To tell thy tale, tell thou scornst such as loue.

I there's the sore, tell how thou scornst to loue,
Tell to thy shame, tell to thy ouerthrow,
Tell them beneath, or tell to them aboue,
Tell who thou wilt, long since ther's none but know,
And know *Narcissus*, more than thou canst show:
    For he that sorrow hath possest, at last
    In telling of his tale is quite disgra'st.

Narciſſus.

What ſhall I then but languiſh in complaining,
Since deepeſt teares haue ſmalleſt comfort ſhewen;
And if I had the richeſt wordes remaining,
That euer tragicke maſſacre made knowen,
Or poets imping them now perfect growen:
   Yet theſe and all, could not my thoughts diſcouer,
   And this I got ſcorning to be a louer.

Now comes the ſwelling ſoules ſhame to be told,
Now preſſeth on my long neglected care,
How ſhall I tell my griefe, or how vnfolde
The coie diſdaines I vſde, and what they were,
Or how with anie comfort ſhall appeare?
   The one halfe to the world of my diſtreſſe,
   You that did vrge this ſore make it ſeeme leſſe.

Now make it ſeeme leſſe, now or neuer do it,
You faire alluring Nymphs, you pretie ones,
Take from this broken ſong, or adde you to it,
Deſcant on which part beſt ſhall pleaſe, for none
Shall be accounted ſweet that ſing alone:
   Then faire dames ſing a treble to my baſe,
   With teares be yours, with ſighs Ile ſhew my caſe.

And if the world eſteeme of bare good will,
Then I am he, the onely ſubiect yet,
That ere inſerted to inrich a quill,
Or could command the ſterneſt muſe to write,
I craue not then for anie to indite,
   But to the world and ages yet to cum,
   Narciſſus poet ſhall not be found dum.

Narciſſus.

This ſaid, a million of deepe-ſearching ſighes,
(The meſſengers to tragike thoughts and cries)
Hee doth prepare as actors in his night,
And then addreſt to ſpeake he onward highes,
And thus gainſt loue begins to tyrannize:
  " If beautie bring vs ſo to be miſ-led,
  " Of ſuch a relique who's inamoured?

So witleſſe, fond, ſaue thou was neuer anie,
Forlorne *Narciſſus* to thy ſelfe complaining,
Oh cruell Loue that hath vndone ſo many,
Haſt thou yet power or anie hope remaining,
To chaſe from theſe faire ſprings hatefull diſdayning?
  Oh no, loues darts haue all but one euent,
  Once ſhooting, vertue of the reſt are ſpent.

See foulings Queene, ſee how thou trainſt me forth,
Thou gaueſt me beautie, which the world admir'd,
But when I came to talent out the worth,
What iſſue ioy'd it that my youth requir'd,
A brain-ſick hot conceit by loue inſpir'd,
  A flaming blaſt, no ſooner ſeene than gon,
  A ſinke to ſwallow vp the looker on.

" For as amid the troupe of warlike men,
" Their generall for ſafetie flies amaine,
" Who fatall death by fortunes aide doth ken,
" Sad meſſenger his hoped wiſh detaines,
" So was *Narciſſus* to his treble paine:
  " Loues generall, and mongſt his faire ones flew,
  " Whileſt in the troup was ſlaine ere ioyes he knew.

Narcissus.

And which I mourne for most, disastrous chance,
I tooke the Iewels which faire Ladies sent me,
And manie pretie toies, which to aduance
My future bane, vnwillingly they meant me,
Their whole attire and choice suites not content me;
   But like a louer glad of each new toy,
   So I a woman turned from a boy.

Which once perform'd, how farre did I exceed
Those stately dames, in gesture, modest action,
Coy lookes, deep smiles, faining heroique deeds,
To bring them all vnder my owne subiection,
For as a woman tired in affection,
   Some new disport neare thought on is requir'd,
   So now I long'd to walke to be admir'd.

The life obtaining fields, we liuely trace,
And like yong fawnes delight to sport each other,
Some framing odes, and others in their grace,
Chaunt soueraigne sweet Sonetto's to loues mother,
Thus euerie Nymph would gladly be a louer;
   And loue himselfe might have enamoured beene,
   If he had eies, and these choice dames had seene.

Yet I was carelesse, for selfe-loue orethrew me,
I scornd to heare how he could slaie or wound,
And yet full oft, so many nymphs as knew me,
Would saie that once blind loue would cast me downe,
Foule fall that poare blind boy whose power abownes;
   Well, well, I see tis shame to threat the Gods,
   Whose deepe authoritie gaines treble ods.

Narcissus.

As thus we like to wanton wenches were,
In seuerall sports best pleasing and delightfull,
Seuered at last I to a fount drew neere,
Oh that alone a boy should be so wilfull!
As children vse gainst pretie toies be spightfull:
   In playing till they spoiled be or harm'd,
   So playd I with this coole-spring till it warm'd.

For as I gaz'd into this shallow spring,
I rear'd my voice, mistrusting that nor this,
Oh what diuine Saint is it that doth sing!
Let me intreate to haue of thee a kisse,
See who *Narcissus* lou'd, see where's his misse:
   His owne conceit with that of his did fire him,
   When others actual colde it did desire him.

Lead by my attractiue Syren-singing selfe,
Vnto this Sun-shine-shadow for the substance,
Hard at the brinke, prying from forth the shelfe,
That grounded hath my ioyes and pleasing essence,
I claim'd th' authoritie of them were absence:
   And made this well my ill, this bowre my bane,
   This daily good become my hourly wane.

Yet dreading of no ill, close downe I lay,
By this same goodly fountaine deere and precious,
Beset with azured stones bonnie and gay,
Like a yong woer that should visite vs,
Oh that bright-seeming things should be so vicious,
   Base imperfection Nature doth abhorre,
   Then why should I deceiued be thus farre?

Narcissus.

Neuer was she more perfectly imbraced,
Than in her worke vnto *Narcissus* done,
If arte, proportion should haue thus disgraced,
Where should our artists then haue rai'sd theyr Sunne,
That in this cast vp *Chaos* is begunne?
   Loues minion did her deitie here show,
   That Nature should not claime what she did ow.

Immortall strife that heauens should be at iarre,
Why should the one seeke to disgrace the rest;
Were there no women, there would be no warre,
For pride in them claimes her due interest,
Presumptuous women thus to scorne the blest:
   But gainst their sex why doo I raue thus vile,
   That lou'd *Narciss;* in loue that was a child?

Now had my eyes betooke themselues to gaze,
On this cleere-spring where as a man distract,
The more I sought allusions forth to raze,
The more I found my senses in defact,
And could not choose but yeeld to this enact,
   That I beheld the fairest faire that euer
   Earth could desire, or heauens to earth deliuer.

Yet striue I did, and counted it deceit,
I chid the wanton fond toies that I vs'd,
And with sharpe taunts would faine haue found retreit,
And tolde my selfe how of my selfe refus'd,
Many faire Ladies were and how abus'd
   Through base disdaine, then calling vnto *Ioue*,
   He would not heare, thus I was for'st to loue.

Narcissus.

For'ſt vnto loue, I for'ſt perforce to yeld,
Not as the groueling coyne-imbracing fathers,
Doo now in common make their children yld,
By chopping them to church that like of neither,
But by ſtern fate vnweldie that was euer:
    Was I vnhappie that I was or any,
    Loues yong *Adultus* fauoured of ſo many?

" As when the Engliſh globe-incompaſſer,
" By fame purueying found another land,
" Or as the troupe at *Boſworth*, *Richards* err,
" Done to diſgrace, a taſke nere tooke in hand,
" By *Hercules* were readie for command:
    So hauing euer fortunatly ſped,
    Suppos'd that ſhaddowes would bee enamored.

For ſee how *Eſops* dog was quite forgone,
And loſt the ſubſtance weening further gaine,
So was I gazing on this Orient Sunne,
Stroke blinde, Gods knowe, vnto my treble paine,
Leaping at ſhaddowes, looſing of the maine:
    When I loues pleaſance thought to have imbraced,
    My ſun-ſhine light darke clouds ſent foul diſgraced.

Yet ſuch a humor tilted in my breſt,
As few could threat the none-age of my voice,
For though the heauens had here ſet vp their reſt,
I proudly boaſted that ſhe was my choice,
And for my ſake earth onely thus was bleſt:
    And tolde them ſince they faſhioned this golde,
    To coine the like, how they had loſt their mold.

Narcissus.

Sad and drier thoughts a foot, my wearied lims,
Clofe as I could to touch this Saint I couched,
My bodie on the earth fepulchrizing him,
That dying liu'd, my lips hers to haue touched,
I forc'd them forward, and my head downe crouched:
   And fo continued treating, till with teares
   The fpring run ore, yet fhe to kiffe forbare.

Looke on thofe faire eies, fmile to fhew affection,
Tell how my beautie would inrich her fauour,
Talke Sun-go-downe, no rules tending to action,
But fhe would fcorne, & fweare fo God fhould faue her,
Her loue burnt like perfume quite without fauour:
   Yet if (quoth fhe) or I but dreamt, fhe fpake it,
   Tis but a kiffe you craue, why ftoupe and take it.

Neuer the greedie *Tantalus* purfued,
To touch thofe feeming apples more than I,
Vow'd in conceit her fauour to haue vs'de,
I haftned forward, and her beckning fpie,
Like affection offering, and like curtefie:
   Now was the heauen, ah now was heauen a hell,
   I ioy'd, but what can anie louer tell?

A coole effect for my affections burning,
A fad receit to mittigate my paine,
What fhall I be like to the *Polyp* turning,
Or an *Orpheus* going to hel againe?
No, loue nere bled but at the mafter vaine:
   And there will I benum the liuely flefh,
   And ftrike by arte or nature fhall tranfgreffe.

Narcissus.

Then like a cunning pilate making out,
To gaine the *Oceans* currant ftem I forward,
Top gallant hoift amaine, fafely about
The loftie fer with fpread failes hal'd I onward,
To make fure paffage, but alacke too backward,
   The fea prefer'd our vintage, for the bloome
   Was blafted quite, ere fruit was feene to come.

For as I thought downe ftouping to haue kift her,
My loofe-borne treffes that were lawleffe euer,
Troubled the fpring, and caus'd me that I mift her,
Who fo before no fuch fond toies could feuer,
My hope to haue inioy'd her loue, but rather,
   Haire, hart and all would facrifiz'd and done,
   To fouleft fhame this faire one to haue wonne.

Who knowes not that in deepeft waters lies
The greateft danger, or who will not know it?
Monfters of time, whofe ruine each one fpies,
And to the world in teares lamenting fhow it,
That beautie hath fmall good for men to owe it:
   But as a relique for the fight alone,
   Is to be dandled, kift, and lookt vpon.

At laft, for what but time perfection giues?
Againe, O, O, againe my ladies fauour,
I haue obtain'd, at leaft againe fhe liues,
And now what doubt, but doubtleffe I fhal haue her,
It is the water, and not fhe that wauers:
   Slanderous men that count of them fo flightly,
   Who would exceed if you were what you might be?

Narcissus.

See when I spread my armes her to imbrace,
She casteth hers as willingly to meet me,
And when I blush, how it procures her grace,
If weepe or smile, she in same method greets me,
And how so ere I boord her, she salutes me,
　As willing to continue pleasance, yet,
　　Saue smiling kisses I can nothing get.

But how deceiu'd, what Saint doo I adore?
Her lips doo moue, and yet I cannot heare her,
She beckens when I stoope, yet euermore
Am farthest off, when I should be most neere her,
And if with gentle smiles I seeme to cheere her:
　Vnlike a louer weepes to see me sport,
　　And ist not strange? Ioyes when she sees me hurt.

Oh why doth Neptune closet vp my deere?
She is no Mermaid, nor accounted so,
Yet she is faire, and that doth touch him neere,
But she's a votarie, then let her go,
What beautie but with wordes men can vndo?
　Oh *Neptune* she's a *Syren*, therefore nay,
　　Syrens are fittest to adorne the sea.

Then tie me fast where still these eares may heare her,
Oh then I feare these eies will climbe too high!
Yet let me then these bankes be somewhat neerer,
Oh then this tongue will cause this heart to die,
And pining so for loue, talke ouer-lauishly:
　And yet they shal not, for with sighing praiers,
　　Ile busie them not thinking of the faire.

Narcissus.

Oh thrice immortall, let me come vnto thee,
Within whose limits linkt is natures pride,
Accept my vowes, except thou wilt vndoo me,
She is my loue, and so shall be my bride,
Then part vs not, least that I part this tide :
   In spite of *Ioue*, if thou doest her detaine,
   Ile fetch her forth, or quel th' ambitious maine.

Some saie the heauens haue derogated farre,
And gladly done on misconceited weeds,
To cloake their scapes, yet heauens scape you this starre
For know she is immortall for her deeds,
And wo to him that playes with Saints I reed :
   The earth a paradise where she is in,
   Equals the heauens, were it not toucht with sin.

"Now *Phœbus* gins in pride of maiestie,
" To streake the welkin with his darting beames,
" And now the lesser planets seeme to die,
" For he in throane with christall dashing streames,
" Richer than *Indiaes* golden vained gleames
   " In chariot mounted, throwes his sparkling lookes,
   " And vnawares pries midst this azured brooke.

At whose hot shining, rich-dew-summoning,
The gooddest Nymph that euer fountaine kept,
Her courage was euen then a womanning,
And sorrowful he sawe her there, she wept,
And wrung her hands, & downwards would haue crept,
   But that I staid her, ah I doo but dreame !
   It was a vapor that did dull the streame.

Narciſſus.

It was a vapor fuming, whoſe aſſent,
Looſing the vitall organ whence it ſprang,
Much like an vntrain'd faulkon loftly bent,
Wanting the meanes, tottering till tir'd doth hang
Beating the aire: ſo till the ſtrength was ſpent,
   This ſaffron pale congealed fuming miſt,
   Bearded my ſenſes when my loue I miſt.

And yet tis *Phœbus* or ſome richer one,
That ouerpries me thus, it cannot be,
But *Ioue* or ſome, that pittying my ſad mones,
Comes to redreſſe my plaints, and comming ſee,
My heauenly loue in her diuinitie:
   Ioue pittie not, nor hearken to my plaints,
   I treate to mortall ones, not heauenly ſaints.

Sufficeth you haue manie be as faire,
Beſides the queene of dalliance and her Nuns,
Chaſt votaries for Gods to chaſe th' aire,
And can Arcadian Nymphs neuer yet wun,
In naming godhood, them from hating turne:
   Alacke this is the daughter of a neat-heard,
   And I am treating but to be her ſhep-heard.

Some yet may fortune aſke me how my ſtate,
From lordly pompe, and fames eterniz'd throne,
Diu'd downe to yonger method and the mate,
Of each forſaken louer quite forlorne,
Am thus in baſtardie vnlawfull borne:
   Why are not princes ſubject to report,
   What cloiſtred ill but fame doth beare from court?

Narcissus.

Liui'as rich statues in his gallery,
Portraide by lyfe, as they in sundrie shapes,
Mask't through the cloudie stitched canapie,
Where *Venus* and her blind ones, acting rapes,
Incestuous, lawlesse, and contentious scapes ;
  Were they remembred, who would be a louer?
  Nor I, nor *Venus*, were she not loues mother.

Oh extreame anguish of the soules affliction!
Pining in sorrow, comfortlesse alone,
Hate to the heauens, admitting intercession,
But as a meanes to aggrauate our mones,
Prolonging dated times to leaue's forlorne :
  Raising new seeds to spring and shaddow vs,
  Whose ghosts we wrong'd, and thus do follow vs.

But how am I in passion for her sake?
That tyres as much, and equals teare with teare,
That beates the aire with shrikes, and praiers make,
In iust proportion, and with like sad feare,
As I haue done, a louing show doth beare ;
  Women doo yeeld, yet shame to tell vs so,
  Tis action more than speech doth grace a show.

And I not much vnlike the Romane actors,
That girt in *Pretextati* seamed robes,
Charged the hearts and eyes of the spectators,
With still continuing sorrow, flintie *Niobes*,
And of each circled eie fram'd thousand globes :
  And to become flat images, not men,
  So now must I with action grace the pen.

Narcissus.

For what with wordes the *Chorus* setteth forth,
Is but t' explaine th'ensuing tragicke scene,
And what is sayd, is yet of litle worth,
Tis I the siege must countenance, and then
Will leaue you all in murmuring sort like men.
  Hard at the point of some extremitie,
  Vnarm'd to fight, and know not where to flie.

Nor shall I want the meanes to grace my tale,
Abundant store of sweet perswasiue stories,
Though they haue past, and got the golden vale,
From artes bright eie, yet *Ascraes* gentle vallies,
Haue shrouded my sad tale, I in the glorie,
  Of well accepted fauour and of time,
  Thus poasted out, haue smiled on my rime.

Shame wer't to scape the telling of my shame,
How being faire and beautious past compare,
I scorn'd loue, yet lou'd one of my owne name,
My selfe complaining of my face too faire,
And telling how my griefes procured teares:
  Confused arguments, vaine, out of date,
  And yet it does me good to shew my state.

Long I continued as a doating matron,
Some new assault assailing her coole breast,
Delights to kisse yong children, plaie the wanton,
And would I know not what, thinking the rest,
Ioying in that I found vnhappiest:
  Carelesse of loue, respecting not her honor,
  Which now I feele in dotage looking on her.

Narcissus.

Nay on her shaddow, on her shaddow nay,
Vpon thy owne *Narcissus* loue thy selfe,
Fie wanton, fie, know'st not thou art a boy,
Or hath a womans weeds, thee sinful elfe,
Made wilfull like themselues, or how growen coy?
   Wer't thou a woman, this is but a shaddo,
   And seldome do their sex themselues vndo.

A forrest Nymph, whil'st thus I stood debating,
Gan oft and oft to tell me pleasing tales,
And sometimes talkt of loue, and then of hating,
Anone she trips it by the short nipt dales,
And then againe the tottering rockes she scales:
   But when I cald for her to come vnto me,
   A hollow siluer sound bad come and woo me.

Anon I chaunt on pleasing roundelaies,
That told of shepheards, and their soueraigne sportes,·
Then blith she pip'd to send the time awaie,
And clapt my cheekes, praising my nimble throate,
And kisse she will too twixt each sharpe prickt noate.
   But if I tell her all that's done is fruitles,
   She answeres I, I, to thy tother mistres.

Thus whil'st the Larke her mounted tale begun,
Vnto the downe-soft *Tythons* blushing Queene,
And rising with her noates sweet orizons,
At *Ioues* high-court gan *Phœbus* steads to weene,
How well appointed, and how brauely seene,
   That all in rage they tooke such high disgrace,
   The heauens dispatcht poast from *Auroraes* pallace.

Narciſſus.

Eccho complayning *Cythereas* ſonne,
To be a boy vniuſt, cruell, vnkinde,
The Gods before her tale was throughly done,
Thus for'ſt agreement twixt our wauering minde,
She to a voice, the *Syluans* plaints to finde :
    And for redreſſe of her increaſing ſorrow,
    To hold darke night in chaſe, to mocke the morrow.

This done, amaine vnto the ſpring I made,
Where finding beautie culling nakednes,
Sweet loue reuiuing all that heauens decaide,
And once more placing gentle maidenlikenes,
Thus ſought I fauour of my ſhaddowed miſtres ;
    Imbracing ſighs, and telling tales to ſtones,
    Amidſt the ſpring I leapt to eaſe my mones.

Where what I gain'd, iudge you that vainly ſue,
To ſhaddowes wanting appetite and ſence,
If there be anie comfort tell me true?
And then I hope you'le pardon my offence,
Pardon my tale, for I am going hence :
    Cephiſus now freez'd, whereat the ſea-nymphs ſhout,
    And thus my candle flam'd, and here burnt out.

Ovid. 3. Met. Narciſſus fuit Cephiſi fluuii, ex Liriope nympha, filius.

FINIS.

Narcissus.

 Carring beautie all bewitching,
Tell a tale to hurt it felfe,
Tels a tale how men are fleeting,
  All of Loue and his power,
Tels how womens fhewes are pelfe,
  And their conftancies as flowers.

Aie me pretie wanton boy,
What a fire did hatch thee forth,
To fhew thee of the worlds annoy,
  Ere thou kenn'ft anie pleafure:
Such a fauour's nothing worth,
  To touch not to tafte the treafure.

Poets that diuinely dreampt,
Telling wonders vifedly,
My flow Mufe haue quite benempt,
  And my rude fkonce haue aflackt,
So I cannot cunningly,
  Make an image to awake.

Ne the froftie lims of age,
Vncouth fhape (mickle wonder)
To tread with them in equipage,

L'Enuoy.

As quaint light blearing eies,
Come my pen broken vnder,
Magick-spels such deuize.

Collyn was a mighty swaine,
In his power all do flourish,
We are shepheards but in vaine,
    There is but one tooke the charge,
By his toile we do nourish,
    And by him are inlarg'd.

He vnlockt *Albions* glorie,
He twas tolde of *Sidneys* honor,
Onely he of our stories,
    Must be sung in greatest pride,
In an Eglogue he hath wonne her,
    Fame and honor on his side.

Deale we not with *Rosamond*,
For the world our sawe will coate,
Amintas and *Leander's* gone,
    Oh deere sonnes of stately kings,
Blessed be your nimble throats,
    That so amorously could sing.

Adon deafly masking thro,
Stately troupes rich conceited,
Shew'd he well deserued to,
    Loues delight on him to gaze,
And had not loue her selfe intreated,
    Other nymphs had sent him baies.

L'Enuoy.

Eke in purple roabes diftaind,
Amid'ft the Center of this clime,
I haue heard faie doth remaine,
   One whofe power floweth far,
That fhould haue bene of our rime,
   The onely obiect and the ftar.

Well could his bewitching pen,
Done the Mufes obiects to vs,
Although he differs much from men,
   Tilting under Frieries,
Yet his golden art might woo vs,
   To haue honored him with baies.

He that gan vp to tilt,
Babels frefh remembrance,
Of the worlds-wracke how twas fpilt,
   And a world of ftories made,
In a catalogues femblance
   Hath alike the Mufes ftaide.

What remaines peereleffe men,
That in *Albions* confines are,
But eterniz'd with the pen,
   In facred Poems and fweet laies,
Should be fent to Nations farre,
   The greatnes of faire *Albions* praife.

Let them be audacious proude,
Whofe deuifes are of currant,
Euerie ftampe is not allow'd,

Narcissus.

Yet the coine may proue as good,
Yourselues know your lines haue warrant,
   I will talke of *Robin Hood.*

And when all is done and past,
Narcissus in another sort,
And gaier clothes shall be pla'st,
   Eke perhaps in good plight,
In meane while I'le make report,
   Of your winnings that do write.

Hence a golden tale might grow,
Of due honor and the praise,
That longs to Poets, but the show
   were not worth the while to spend,
Sufficeth that they merit baies,
   Saie what I can it must haue end,
Then thus faire *Albion* flourish so,
As *Thames* may nourish as did *Pô.*

FINIS.

Tho: Edwards.

APPENDIX.

Epig. LIII.

Italiæ Vrbes potiſſimæ. Th. Edwards.

The 52 chief Cities of *Italy* concifely charactered in fo many Heroic Verfes.

[From

Enchiridium Epigrammatum
Latino-Anglicum
an Epitome of Eſſais Engliſhed out of Latin
&ᶜᵃ.
Doon by Rob: Vilvain of Excefter.
London. 1654.]

> **S**anƈta est Sanƈtorum celeberrima sanguine Roma:
> Cingitur Vrbs Venetum pelago, ditißima nummis.

Fertilis egre-
giis fulget Bo-
nonia clau-
ſtris.

> Inclita Parthenope gignit Comitesque Ducesque:
> Est Mediaolanum jucundum, nobile, magnum.
> 5 Excellit studiis fæcunda Bononia cunƈtis:
> Splendida solertes nutrit Florentia cives.
> Genoa habet portum, mercesque domosque superbas:
> Exhaurit loculos Ferraria ferrea plenos.

Omnes Vero-
næ tituli de-
bentur honor-
is.

> Verrona humanæ dat singula commoda vitæ:
> 10 Extollit Paduam Juris studium & Medicinæ.
> Illustrat patriæ Senas facundia linguæ:
> Maxima pars hominum clamat miseram esse Cremonam.
> Mantua gaudet aquis, ortu decorata Maronis:
> Vina Utini Varias generosa vehuntur ad Vrbes.
> 15 Brixia dives opum parce succurrit Egenis:
> Italicos Versus præfert Papia Latinis.
> Libera Luca tremit Ducibus vicina duobus:
> Flent Pisæ amissum dum contemplantur honorem.
> Commendant Parmam Lac, Caseus, atque Butyrum:

Per libras
vendit per-
pulchra Pla-
centia poma.

> 20 Non caret Hospiciis perpulchra Placentia claris.
> Taurinum exornant Virtus, pietasque, fidesque:
> Militibus validis generosa Placentia claret.
> Vercellæ lucro non deleƈtantur iniquo:
> Mordicus Vrbs Mutinæ Ranas tenet esse salubres.

hoc carmen
intelligēdum
eſt de ſolis vr-
bibus Piceni.
forum Liuii.

> 25 Contemnunt omnes Anconæ mænia Turcas:
> Litibus imponit finem Macerata supremum.
> Urbs Livii celebris nimis est proclivis ad arma:
> Emporiæ in portis consistit gloria clausis.

Rome Holy of Holies, renownd for Martyry:
Venice Sea-clofd moft rich in Treafury.
Moft noble *Naples* Dukes and Earls ingenders:
Millain is blith, and hir felf fplendid renders.
5   Fertil *Bonony* in al *A*rts doth excel:
Brav *Florence* maintains hir Inhabitants wel.
Genoa a Port, Wares and proud Houfes fhows:
Ferrary with hir Iron Mines poor grows.
Verona with al needful helps is crowned:
10 *Padua* for Law and Phyfick much renowned.
Siena famous is for Language purity:
Cremona (as moft think) brought to poverty.
Mantua wel watred, with *Virgils* birth adorned:
Utinas ftrong Wines to fundry States tranfported.
15 *Brefcia* is rich, yet helps Poor fparingly:
Papy prefers Italic to Latin Poetry.
Luca being neer two Dukes, trembles with pain:
Pifa having loft hir honor mourns amain.
Parma for Milk, Cheef, Butter, is extolled:
20 Fair *Placence* for ftatly Ins is inrolled.
Taurinum Virtu hath, Piety and Fidelity:
Gallant *Placentia* fhines with *A*rt military.
Vercellæ litle cares for wicked gain:
Mutinæ hold Frogs for wholfom food t' attain.
25 *Ancona* from hir wals did the Turcs fend:
Macerata puts to Law fuits a final end.
Great *Livies* City too prone is to debates:
Emporias glory ftands in fhutting their Gates,

Italiæ Vrbes potiſſimæ.

            Bergomum *ab inculta dictum eſt ignobile lingua:*
hoſpitalitas   30 *Omnibus exponit gladios* Aretium *acutos.*
Dominica-
norum com-   Viterbi *Conventus opem fert ſanctus Egenis:*
mendatur.   *Civibus humanis decorata eſt* Aſta *fidelis.*
            Fructibus, Anſeribus, Pomario Ariminum *abundat:*
            Fanum *formoſas Mulieres fertur habere.*
         35 *Odit mundanas ſincera* Novaria *fraudes:*
            Clara perantiquæ defecit fama Ravennæ.
Anglia plures   Anglia *habet paucos Comites,* Vincentia *multos:*
habet Comi-
tatus quam   *Omnes magnificant ficus groſſoſque* Piſauri.
comites, Vin-   *Caſtaneis, Oleo, Tritico* Paſtorium *abundat:*
centia plures
comites quam 40 *Ruſtica frugales nutrit* Dertona *colonos.*
comitatus.   *Poſtponit* Rhegium *cornuta animalia Porcis:*
            Dulcia fœlicem cingunt Vineta Ceſenam.
            Tarviſium *exhilarant nitido cum flumine Fontes:*
            Imola *diviſa eſt; nocet hæc diviſio multis.*
Ex ſola lucri 45 Urbinum *ſtatuit Ducibus clamare, valete:*
ſpe clamor
proucnit iſte.   *Nota eſt fictilibus figulina* Faventia *vaſis.*
            Spoletum *vocitat, Peregrini intrate, manete:*
            Urbs pingues Pompeia *boves producit, oveſque.*
            Narnia *promittens epulas, dabit ova vel uvas:*
         50 Aſſinum *ſancti* Franciſci *corpore gaudet.*
            Hoſpitibus Comum *piſces cum carnibus offert:*
            Quærit opes fragiles, ſtudiis Savena *relictis.*
              Sunt tot in Italia venerandi ponderis urbis:
              Quot vagus hebdomadas quilibet annus habet.

Italiæ Vrbes potiſſimæ.

  Bergamo is held baſe for their language rude:
30 *Aretium* their ſharp ſwords to al intrude.
  Viterbums holy Covent abounds with Charity:
  Aſta is famous for Citizens courteſy.
  Arimin with Fruits, Geeſ, Orchards doth abound:
  Fair Women in *Fanum* are ſaid to be found.
35 Honeſt *Novary* hates al worldly cheating:
  Ravenna's antient fame is quite defeating.
  Vincentia many Earls hath, *England* but few:
  Al *Piſaurs* Figs and Fruits as beſt doth ſhew.
  Paſtory hath ſtore of Cheſnuts, Oil, and Wheat:
40 *Derton* feeds Clowns, who frugal are to eat.
  Rhegium prefers Hogs to horned Cattle ſtore:
  Sweet vineyards compaſs *Ceſena* back and before.
  Tarviſium ſweet ſprings hath, with a River cleer:
  Imola' s divided, which is hurtful meer.
45 *Urbin* reſolvs to bid their Dukes farewel:
  Faventia in making Clay-pots bears the bel.
  Spoletum cries, Gueſts enter and make ſtay:
  Pompey fat Oxen and Sheep breeds alway.
  Narny bids Feaſts, but Egs or Grapes doth giv:
50 *Aſsinum* by Saint Francis Corps doth liv.
  Comum their Gueſts with Fiſh and Fleſh entertain:
  Saven their Studies leav and hunt for gain.
   So many Cities hath *Italy* of high price:
   *A*s every wandring yeer doth weeks compriſe.

[Bodleian Library; 306 Tanner MSS., fol. 175.]

f all the goddes would now agree
to graunt the thinge I would require
madame I pray you what judge ye
a bove all thinge I wold defire
in faithe no kingdome wold I crave
fuche Idle thoughte I never have

No Creffus woulde I wifhe to be
to have in ftore gret hord of gold
appollos gifte liketh not me
of riddells darke the trothe to unfold
nor yet to honor would I clyme
amideft the ftreames I love to fwyme

Nought I regarde that moft men crave
and yet a thinge I have in mynde
wh if by wifhinge I myght have
like lucke to me could not be affigned
but will you knowe what liketh me
madam I wifh yor ffoole to be

Whom you might bobe even as you lift
and loute and taunt in your fwete talke
aboute whofe head your litle fift
for your difport might often walke
who finelie might your chamber kepe
and when you lift whift you a fleape

And warme yor fhytes when you rife
and make the bede wherein you flept
but you to fee in any wife
eche thinge you do be clofelie kept
for all my fervice this graunt me
madame your chamber foolle to be

ffinis.

[Bodleian Library; 306, Tanner MSS. fol. 175.]

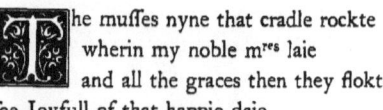he muſſes nyne that cradle rockte
wherin my noble m^{res} laie
and all the graces then they flokte
ſoe Joyfull of that happie daie
that thou ẃ ſilver ſoundinge voice
gan altogether to reioyce

Ther chīppinge charme did nature praiſe
whoſe fame alowde they all did ringe
of royall lynne that ſhe did raiſe
a princes by that noble kinge
whoſe memorie doth yet revive
all courtlie ſtates wrygtes that be alive

And when this folleme ſonge was done
in counſell grave they ſatt ſtreight waye
ẃ ſmylling chere then one begonne
faire oratour theis wordes to ſaie
behold q^d ſhe my ſiſter deare
how natures giftes doe here appere.

Let us therfore not feme unkinde
as nature hathe the bodie deckte
foe let our giftes adorne the mynde
of the godes left we be checkte
and you three graces in like forte
awaight uppon her princelie porte

To this w̔ handes cafte up an highe
theis ladies all gave ther confent
and kiffinge her moft lovinglie
from whence they came to heaven they went
ther giftes remayne yet here behinde
to bewtifie my m^{res} mynde

Wh̔ geven to her in tender yeres
by tracte of tyme of foe encrefte
a preles prince that fhe apperes
and of her kynde paffinge the reft
as farre in fkill as doth in fyght
the fonne exell the candle light

No wonder then thoughe noble hartes
of fondrie fortes her love dothe feke
her will to wynne they play ther partes
happie is he whom fhe fhall like
to God yet is this my requeft
hym to have her that loves her beft.

finis qd Edwardes.

[Bodleian Library, Ashmole MSS. 38, p. 176.]

On Mr. Edwards

A Dearly beloved Schoole Master.

Here lies the picture of pure honestye
   Here lies the fire of manye a learned sonn
   Here lies the zeale of Christianitye
Here lies the paterne of Religion
Here lies the Man whose Life was naught to none
Here lies that frind whom younge and old bemoane.

VARIOUS READINGS FROM

PARVVM THEATRVM VRBIVM

five

VRBIVM PRAECIPVARVM

TOTIVS ORBIS BREVIS ET MEthodica Defcriptio.

Authore Adriano Romano E.A.

Cum gratia & priuilegio Cæfareæ Maieſtatis ſpeciali ad decennium.

FRANCOFORTI
Ex officina Typographica Nicolai Baſſæi.
ANNO M.D. XCV.

Quarto, pp. 365 + 4 leaves preliminary, the fourth of which has the verſes in Latin Elegiac verſe, + 10 pages De Eminentia Theatri Vrbium, + 15 pages Index. [From a copy in the Bodleian Library, Oxford. 4to. R. 22, Art. Seld.]

NOVA, BREVIS, ET SYNCERA CELEBERRIMARUM VRBIVM ITAlicarum Defcriptio, Authore Thoma Eduardo Anglo.

	Vilvain's Text.	Adriani Romani Textus.
Line		
1	for *celeberrima*	read *pretiofo.*
4	Mediaolanum	r. MEDIOLANUM.
5	*Excellit ftudiis fœcunda* Bononia *cunctis.*	r. Omnibus excellit ftudiis BONONIA pinguis.
7	Genoa	r. GENVA.
9	Verrona	r. VERONA.
13	*Maronis*	r. MARONIS.
20	*Hofpiciis*	r. *hofpitiis.*
21	*Virtus*	r. *virtus*
22	*generofa* Placentia	r. *ftudiofa* PERVSIA.
24	*Ranas*	r. *ranas.*
27		r. 28 ⎫ [Thefe two lines are tranfpofed.]
28		27 ⎭
32	*civibus*	r. *Ciuibus.*
	eft	r. *est.*
33	*Anferibus*	r. *anferibus.*
	Pomario	r. *pomarium.*
38	*magnificant*	r. *commendat.*
39	Paftorium	r. PISTORIVM.
43	*exhilarant*	r. *exhilerant.*
47	*vocitat*	r. *clamat.*
48	*Urbs*	r. LAVS.
49	*epulas*	r. *epulum.*
50	Affinum	r. ASSISIVM.
52	Savena	r. SAVONA.

CEPHALVS AND PROCRIS.

[*From Golding's Tranflation of* Ovid's Metamorphofis, *London,
W. Seres*, 1567. *The Seventh Booke, fol.* 91, *verfo. The
original is printed in Black Letter with the names in Roman
Type.*]

With this and other fuch like talke they brought the day to ende,
The Euen in feafting, and the night in fleeping they did fpende.
The Sunne next Morrow in the heauen with golden beames did burne,
And ftill the Eafterne winde did blow and hold them from returne.
Sir *Pallas* fonnes to *Cephal* came (for he their elder was)
And he and they to *Aeacus* Court togither forth did paffe.
The King as yet was faft a fléepe. Duke *Phocus* at the gate
Did meete them, and receyued them according to their ftate.
For *Telamon* and *Peleus* alreadie forth were gone,
To mufter Souldiers for the warres. So *Phocus* all alone
Did leade them to an inner roume, where goodly Parlours were,
And caufed them to fit them downe. As he was alfo there
Now fitting with them, he beheld a Dart in *Cephals* hand
With golden head, the fteale whereof he well might underftand
Was of fome ftraũge and vnknowne tree. when certaine talke had paft
A while of other matters there, I am (quoth he) at laft
A man that hath delight in woods and loues to follow game
And yet I am not able sure by any meanes to ame

Cephalus and Procris.

What wood your Jaueling steale is of. Of Ash it can not bée.
For then the colour should be browne, and if of Cornell trée,
It would be full of knubbed knots. I know not what it is:
But sure mine eies did neuer sée a fairer Dart than this.
 The one of those same brethren twaine replying to him said:
 Nay then the speciall propertie will make you more dismaid,
Than doth the beautie of this Dart. It hitteth whatsoeuer
He throwes it at. The stroke thereof by Chaunce is ruled neuer.
For hauing done his feate, it flies all bloudie backe agen
Without the helpe of any hand. The Prince was earnest then
To know the truth of all: as whence so riche a present came,
Who gaue it him, and wherevpon the partie gaue the same.
Duke *Cephal* answerde his demaund in all points (one except)
The which (as knowne apparantly) for shame he ouerlept:
His beautie namely, for the which he did receiue the Dart.
And for the losse of his deare wife right pensiue at the hart,
He thus began with wéeping eies. This Dart O Goddesse sonne
(Ye ill would thinke it) makes me yirne, & long shall make me donne,
If long the Gods doe giue me life. This weapon hath vndonne
My deare beloued wife and me. O would to God this same
Had neuer vnto me bene giuen. There was a noble Dame
That *Procris* hight (but you perchaunce haue oftner heard the name
Of great *Orythia* whose renowne was bruted so by fame,
That blustring *Boreas* rauisht hir.) To this *Orythia* shee
Was sister. If a bodie should compare in ech degrée
The face and natures of them both, he could none other déeme
But *Procris* worthier of the twaine of rauishment should séeme.
Hir father and our mutuall loue did make vs man and wife.
Men said I had (and so I had in déede) a happie life.
Howbeit Gods will was otherwise, for had it pleased him
Of all this while, and euen still yet in pleasure should I swim.
The second Month that she and I by band of lawfull bed

Cephalus and Procris.

Had ioynde togither bene, as I my maſking Toyles did ſpred,
To ouerthrow the horned Stags, the early Morning gray
Then newly hauing chaſed night and gun to breake the day,
From Mount *Hymettus* higheſt tops that freſhly flouriſh ay,
Eſpide me, and againſt my will conueyde me quight away.
I truſt the Goddeſſe will not be offended that I ſay
The troth of hir.   Although it would delight one to beholde
Hir ruddie chéekes: although of day and night the bounds ſhe holde:
Although on iuice of Ambroſie continually ſhe feede:
Yet *Procris* was the only Wight that I did loue in déede.
On *Procris* only was my heart: none other word had I
But *Procris* only in my mouth: ſtill *Procris* did I crie.
I vpned what a holy thing was wedlocke: and how late
It was ago ſince ſhe and I were coupled in that ſtate.
Which band (and ſpecially ſo ſoone) it were a ſhame to breake.
The Goddeſſe being moued at the words that I did ſpeake,
Said: ceaſe thy plaint thou Carle, and kéepe thy *Procris* ſtill for me.
But (if my minde deceyue me not) the time will ſhortly be
That wiſh thou wilt thou had hir not.   And ſo in anger ſhe
To *Procris* ſent me backe againe, in going homeward as
Upon the Goddeſſe ſayings with my ſelfe I muſing was,
I gan to dreade bad meaſures leaſt my wife had made ſome ſcape.
Hir youthfull yeares begarniſhed with beautie, grace and ſhape,
In maner made me to beleue the déede already done.
Againe hir maners did forbid miſtruſting ouer ſoone.
But I had bene away: but euen the ſame from whom I came
A ſhrewde example gaue how lightly wiues doe run in blame:
But we poore Louers are afraide of all things.   Herevpon
I thought to practiſe feates: which thing repented me anon:
And ſhall repent me while I liue.   The purpoſe of my drifts
Was for taſſault hir honeſtie with great rewards and gifts.
The Morning fooding this my feare, to further my deuice,

Cephalus and Procris.

My fhape (which thing me thought I felt) had altered with a trice.
By meanes whereof anon vnknowne to *Pallas* towne I came,
And entred fo my houfe: the houfe was clearly void of blame:
And fhewed fignes of chaftitie in mourning euer fith
Their maifter had bene rapt away. A thoufand meanes wherewith
To come to *Procris* fpeach had I deuifde: and fcarce at laft
Obteinde I it. Affoone as I mine eie vpon hir caft,
My wits were rauifht in fuch wife that nigh I had forgot
The purpofde triall of hir troth, right much a doe God wot
I had to holde mine owne that I the truth bewrayed not.
To kéepe my felfe from kiffing hir full much a doe I had
As reafon was I fhould haue done. She looked verie fad.
And yet as fadly as fhe lookte, no Wight aliue can fhow
A better countenance than did fhe. Hir heart did inward glow
In longing for hir abfent fpoufe. How beautifull a face
Thinke you Sir *Phocus* was in hir whome forrow fo did grace:
What fhould I make report how oft hir chaft behauiour ftraue
And ouercame moft conftantly the great affaults I gaue:
Or tell how oft fhe fhet me vp with thefe fame words: To one
(Where ere he is) I kéepe my felfe, and none but he alone
Shall fure inioy the vfe of me. What creature hauing his
Wits perfect would not be content with fuch a proofe as this
Of hir moft ftedfaft chaftitie? I could not be content:
But ftill to purchafe to my felfe more wo I further went.
At laft by profering endleffe welth, and heaping gifts on gifts,
In ouerlading hir with wordes I draue hir to hir fhifts.
Then cride I out: Thine euill heart my felfe I tardie take.
Where of a ftraunge aduouterer the countenance I did make,
I am in déede thy hufband. O ynfaithfull woman thou,
Euen I my felfe can teftifie thy lewde behauior now.
She made none anfwere to my words, but being ftricken dum
And with the forrow of hir heart alonly ouercum,

Cephalus and Procris.

Forfaketh hir entangling houfe, and naughtie hufband quight:
And hating all the fort of men by reafon of the fpight
That I had wrought hir, ftraide abrode among the Mountaines hie,
And exercifde *Dianas* feates. Then kindled by aud by
A fiercer fire within my bones than euer was before,
When fhe had thus forfaken me by whome I fet fuch ftore.
I prayde hir fhe woulde pardon me, and did confeffe my fault.
Affirming that my felfe likewife with fuch a great affault
Of richeffe might right well haue bene enforft to yeelde to blame,
The rather if performance had enfewed of the fame.
When I had this fubmiffion made, and fhe fufficiently
Reuengde hir wronged chaftitie, fhe then immediatly
Was reconcilde: and afterward we liued many a yeare
In ioy and neuer any iarre betwéene vs did appeare.
Befides all this (as though hir loue had bene to fmall a gift)
She gaue me eke a goodly Grewnd which was of foote fo fwift,
That when *Diana* gaue him hir, fhe faid he fhould out go
All others, and with this fame Grewnd fhe gaue this Dart alfo
The which you fée I hold in hand. Perchaunce ye faine would know
What fortune to the Grewnd befell. I will vnto you fhow
A wondrous cafe. The ftraungeneffe of the matter will you moue.
The krinkes of certaine Prophefies furmounting farre aboue
The reach of auncient wits to read, the Brookenymphes did expoūd:
And mindleffe of hir owne darke doubts Dame *Themis* being found,
Was as a recheleffe Prophetiffe throwne flat againft the ground.
For which prefumptuous déede of theirs fhe tooke iuft punifhment.
 To *Thebes* in *Bæotia* ftreight a cruell beaft fhe fent,
Which wrought the bane of many a Wight. The coūtryfolk did féed
Him with their cattlell and themfelues, vntill (as was agréed)
That all we youthfull Gentlemen that dwelled there about
Affembling pitcht our corded toyles the champion fields throughout.
But Net ne toyle was none fo hie that could his wightneffe ftop,

Cephalus and Procris.

He mounted ouer at his eafe the higheft of the top.
Then euerie man let flip their Grewnds, but he them all outftript
And euen as nimbly as a birde in daliance from them whipt.
Then all the field defired me to let my *Lælaps* go:
(The Grewnd that *Procris* vnto me did giue was named fo)
Who ftrugling for to wreft his necke already from the band
Did ftretch his collar. Scarfly had we let him of of hand
But that where *Lælaps* was become we could not vnderftand.
The print remained of his féete vpon the parched fand,
But he was clearly out of fight. Was neuer Dart I trow,
Nor Pellet from enforced Sling, nor fhaft from Cretifh bow,
That flew more fwift than he did runne. There was not farre fro thence
About the middle of the Laund a rifing ground, from whence
A man might ouerlooke the fieldes. I gate me to the knap
Of this fame hill, and there beheld of this ftraunge courfe the hap
In which the beaft feemes one while caught, and ere a man would think,
Doth quickly giue the Grewnd the flip, and from his bighting fhrink:
And like a wilie Foxe he runnes not forth directly out,
Nor makes a windlaffe ouer all the champion fieldes about,
But doubling and indenting ftill auoydes his enmies lips,
And turning fhort, as fwift about as fpinning whéele he whips,
To difapoint the fnatch. The Grewnde purfuing at an inch
Doth cote him, neuer lofing ground: but likely ftill to pinch
Is at the fodaine fhifted of. continually he fnatches
In vaine: for nothing in his mouth faue only Aire he latches.
Then thought I for to trie what helpe my Dart at néede could fhow.
Which as I charged in my hand by leuell aime to throw,
And fet my fingars to the thongs, I lifting from bylow
Mine eies, did looke right forth againe, and ftraight amids the field
(A wondrous thing) two Images of Marble I beheld:
Of which ye would haue thought the tone had fled on ftill a pace
And that with open barking mouth the tother did him chafe.

Cephalus and Procris.

In faith it was the will of God (at leaft if any Goddes
Had care of them) that in their pace there fhould be found none oddes.
   Thus farre: and then he held his peace.   But tell vs ere we part
   (Quoth *Phocus*) what offence or fault committed hath your Dart?
His Darts offence he thus declarde.   My Lorde the ground of all
My griefe was ioy. thofe ioyes of mine remember firft I fhall.
It doth me good euen yet to thinke vpon that bliffull time
(I meane the frefh and luftie yeares of pleafant youthfull Prime)
When I a happie man inioyde fo faire and good a wife,
And fhe with fuch a louing Make did lead a happie life.
The care was like of both of vs, the mutuall loue all one.
She would not to haue line with *Ioue* my prefence haue forgone.
Ne was there any Wight that could of me haue wonne the loue,
No though Dame *Venus* had hir felfe defcended from aboue.
The glowing brands of loue did burne in both our brefts alike.
Such time as firft with crafed beames the Sunne is wont to ftrike
The tops of Towres and mountaines high, according to the wont
Of youthfull men, in woodie Parkes I went abrode to hunt.
But neither horfe nor Hounds to make purfuit vpon the fent.
Nor Seruingman, nor knottie toyle before or after went.
For I was fafe with this fame Dart. when wearie waxt mine arme
With ftriking Déere, and that the day did make me fomewhat warme,
Withdrawing for to coole my felfe I fought among the fhades
For Aire that from the valleyes colde came breathing in at glades.
The more exceffiue was my heate the more for Aire I fought.
I waited for the gentle Aire: the Aire was that that brought
Refrefhing to my wearie limmes.   And (well I beart in thought)
Come Aire I wonted was to fing, come eafe the paine of me
Within my bofom lodge thy felfe moft welcome vnto me,
And as thou heretofore art wont abate my burning heate.
By chaunce (fuch was my deftinie) proceeding to repeate
Mo words of daliance like to thefe, I vfed for to fay

Cephalus and Procris.

Great pleaſure doe I take in thée: for thou from day to day
Doſt both refreſh and nouriſh me. Thou makeſt me delight
In woods and ſolitarie grounds. Now would to God I might
Receiue continuall at my mouth this pleaſant breath of thine.
Some man (I wote not who) did heare theſe doubtfull words of mine,
And taking them amiſſe ſuppoſde that this ſame name of Aire
The which I callde ſo oft vpon, had bene ſome Ladie faire:
He thought that I had looude ſome Nymph. And therevpon ſtreight way
He runnes me like a Harebrainde blab to *Procris*, to bewray
This fault as he ſurmiſed it: and there with lauas tung.
Reported all the wanton words that he had heard me ſung.
A thing of light beliefe is loue. She (as I ſince haue harde)
For ſodeine ſorrow ſwounded downe: and when long afterwarde
She came againe vnto hir ſelfe, ſhe ſaid ſhe was accurſt
And borne to cruell deſtinie: and me ſhe blamed wurſt
For breaking faith: and freating at a vaine ſurmiſed ſhame
She dreaded that which nothing was: ſhe fearde a headleſſe name.
She wiſt not what to ſay or thinke. The wretch did greatly feare
Deceit: yet could ſhe not beleue the tales that talked were.
Onleſſe ſhe ſaw hir huſbands fault apparant to hir eie,
She thought ſhe would not him condemne of any villanie.
Next day as ſoone as Morning light had driuen the night away,
I went abrode to hunt againe: and ſpéeding, as I lay
Upon the graſſe, I ſaid come Aire and eaſe my painfull heate.
And on the ſodaine as I ſpake there ſéemed for to beate
A certaine ſighing in mine eares of what I could not geſſe.
But ceaſing not for that I ſtill procéeded natheleſſe:
And ſaid O come moſt pleaſant Aire. with that I heard a ſound
Of ruffling ſoftly in the leaues that lay vpon the ground.
And thinking it had bene ſome beaſt I threw my flying Dart.
It was my wife, who being now ſore wounded at the hart,
Cride out alas. Aſſoone as I perceyued by the ſhrieke

Cephalus and Procris.

It was my faithfull fpoufe, I ran me to the voiceward lieke
A madman that had loft his wits. There found I hir halfe dead
Hir fcattred garments ftaining in the bloud that fhe had bled,
And (wretched creature as I am) yet drawing from the wound
The gift that fhe hir felfe had giuen. Then foftly from the ground
I lifted vp that bodie of hirs of which I was more chare
Than of mine owne, and from hir breft hir clothes in haft I tare.
And binding vp hir cruell wound I ftriued for to ftay
The bloud, and prayd fhe would not thus by paffing fo away
Forfake me as a murtherer: fhe waxing weake at length
And drawing to hir death a pace, enforced all hir ftrength
To vtter thefe few wordes at laft. I pray thée humbly by
Our bond of wedlocke, by the Gods as well aboue the Skie
As thofe to whome I now muft paffe, as euer I haue ought
Deferued well by thée, and by Loue which hauing brought
Me to my death doth euen in death vnfaded ftill remaine
To neftle in thy bed and mine let neuer Aire obtaine.
This fed, fhe held hir peace, and I receyued the fame
And tolde her alfo how fhe was beguiled in the name.
But what auayled telling then? fhe quoathde: and with hir bloud
Hir little ftrength did fade. Howbeit as long as that fhe coud
Sée ought, fhe ftared in my face and gafping ftill on me
Euen in my mouth fhe breathed forth hir wretched ghoft. But fhe
Did féeme with better cheare to die for that hir confcience was
Difcharged quight and cleare of doubtes. Now in conclufion as
Duke *Cephal* wéeping told this tale to *Phocus* and the reft
Whofe eyes were alfo moyft with teares to heare the pitious geft,
Behold King *Aeacus* and with him his eldeft fonnes both twaine
Did enter in and after them there followed in a traine
Of well appointed men of warre new leuied: which the King
Deliuered vnto *Cephalus* to *Athens* towne to bring.

FINIS.

NARCISSUS.

[*From Golding's Tranſlation of* Ovid's Metamorphoſis,
Lond. 1567, *The Thirde Booke, fol.* 35, *verſo.*]

The firſt that of his ſoothfaſt wordes had proufe in all the Realme
Was freckled *Lyriop*, whom ſometime ſurpriſed in his ſtreame,
The floud *Cephiſus* did enforce. This Lady bare a ſonne
Whoſe beautie at his verie birth might iuſtly loue haue wonne.
Narciſſus did ſhe call his name. Of whome the Prophet ſage
Demaunded if the childe ſhould liue to many yeares of age.
Made aunſwere, yea full long, ſo that him ſelfe he doe not know.
The Soothſayers wordes ſeemde long but vaine, vntill the end did ſhow
His ſaying to be true indéede by ſtraungeneſſe of the rage,
And ſtraungeneſſe of the kinde of death that did abridge his age.
For when yeares thrée times fiue and one he fully lyued had,
So that he ſeemde to ſtande béetwene the ſtate of man and Lad,
The hearts of dyuers trim yong men his beautie gan to moue
And many a Ladie freſh and faire was taken in his loue.
But in that grace of Natures gift ſuch paſſing pride did raigne,
That to be toucht of man or Mayde he wholy did diſdaine.
A babling Nymph that *Echo* hight : who hearing others talke,
By no meanes can reſtraine hir tongue but that it néedes muſt walke,

Narcissus.

Nor of hir felfe hath powre to ginne to fpeake to any wight,
Efpyde him dryuing into toyles the fearefull ftagges of flight.
This *Echo* was a body then and not an onely voyce,
Yet of hir fpeach fhe had that time no more than now the choyce.
That is to fay of many wordes the latter to repeate.
The caufe thereof was *Iunos* wrath. For when that with the feate
She might haue often taken *Ioue* in daliance with his Dames,
And that by ftealth and vnbewares in middes of all his games.
This elfe would with hir tatling talke deteine hir by the way,
Untill that *Ioue* had wrought his will and they were fled away.
The which when *Iuno* did perceyue, fhe faid with wrathfull mood,
This tongue that hath deluded me fhall doe thée little good,
For of thy fpeach but fimple vfe hereafter fhalt thou haue.
The déede it felfe did ftraight confirme the threatnings that fhe gaue.
Yet *Echo* of the former talke doth double oft the ende
And backe againe with iuft report the wordes earft fpoken fende.
    Now when fhe fawe *Narcifts* ftray about the Forreft wyde,
    She waxed warme and ftep for ftep faft after him fhe hyde.
The more fhe followed after him and néerer that fhe came,
The whoter euer did fhe waxe as néerer to hir flame.
Lyke as the liuely Brimftone doth which dipt about a match,
And put but foftly to the fire, the flame doth lightly catch.
O Lord how often woulde fhe faine (if nature would haue let)
Entreated him with gentle wordes fome fauour for to get?
But nature would not fuffer hir nor giue hir leaue to ginne.
Yet (fo farre forth as fhe by graunt at natures hande could winne)
Ay readie with attentiue eare fhe harkens for fome founde,
Whereto fhe might replie hir wordes, from which fhe is not bounde.
By chaunce the ftripling being ftrayde from all his companie,
Sayde: is there any body nie? ftraight *Echo* anfwerde: I.
Amazde he caftes his eye afide, and looketh round about,
And come (that all the Forreft roong) aloud he calleth out.

Narcissus.

And come (sayth she:) he looketh backe, and seeing no man followe,
Why flifte, he cryeth once againe: and she the same doth hallowe,
He still perfiftes and wondring much what kinde of thing it was
From which that anfwering voyce by turne so duely seemde to paffe,
Said: let vs ioyne. She (by hir will defirous to haue said,
In fayth with none more willingly at any time or ftead)
Said: let vs ioyne. And ftanding fomewhat in hir owne conceit,
Upon thefe wordes she left the Wood, and forth she yeedeth ftreit,
To coll the louely necke for which she longed had so much,
He runnes his way and will not be imbraced of no fuch.
And fayth: I firft will die ere thou shalt take of me thy pleafure.
She aunfwerde nothing elfe thereto, but take of me thy pleafure.
Now when she faw hir felfe thus mockt, she gate hir to the Woods,
And hid hir head for verie shame among the leaues and buddes.
And euer fence she lyues alone in dennes and hollow Caues.
Yet ftacke hir loue ftill to hir heart, through which she dayly raues
The more for forrow of repulfe. Through reftleffe carke and care
Hir bodie pynes to fkinne and bone, and waxeth wonderous bare.
The bloud doth vanish into ayre from out of all hir veynes,
And nought is left but voyce and bones: the voyce yet ftill remaynes:
Hir bones they fay were turnde to ftones. From thence she lurking ftill
In Woods, will neuer shewe hir head in field nor yet on hill.
Yet is she heard of euery man: it is her onely found,
And nothing elfe that doth remayne aliue aboue the ground.
Thus had he mockt this wretched Nymph and many mo befide,
That in the waters, Woods and groues, or Mountaynes did abyde
Thus had he mocked many men. Of which one mifcontent
To fee himfelfe deluded fo, his handes to Heauen vp bent,
And fayd: I pray to God he may once feele fierce *Cupids* fire
As I doe now, and yet not ioy the things he doth defire.
The Goddeffe *Ramnufe* (who doth wreake on wicked people take)
Affented to his iuft requeft for ruth and pities fake.

Narciſſus.

There was a ſpring withouten mudde as ſiluer cleare and ſtill,
Which neyther ſhéepeheirds, nor the Goates that fed vpon the hill,
Nor other cattell troubled had, nor ſauage beaſt had ſtyrd,
Nor braunch nor ſticke, nor leafe of trée, nor any foule nor byrd.
The moyſture fed and kept aye freſh the graſſe that grew about,
And with their leaues the trées did kéepe the heate of *Phœbus* out.
The ſtripling wearie with the heate and hunting in the chace,
And much delighted with the ſpring and cooleneſſe of the place,
Did lay him downe vpon the brim: and as he ſtooped lowe
To ſtaunche his thurſt, another thurſt of worſe effect did growe.
For as he dranke, he chaunſt to ſpie the Image of his face,
The which he did immediately with feruent loue embrace.
He féedes a hope without cauſe why. For like a fooliſhe noddie
He thinkes the ſhadow that he ſées, to be a liuely boddie.
Aſtraughted like an ymage made of Marble ſtone he lyes,
There gazing on his ſhadowe ſtill with fixed ſtaring eyes.
Stretcht all along vpon the ground, it doth him good to ſée
His ardant eyes which like two ſtarres full bright and ſhining bée.
And eke his fingars, fingars ſuch as *Bacchus* might beſéeme,
And haire that one might worthely *Apollos* haire it déeme.
His beardleſſe chinne and yuorie necke, and eke the perfect grace
Of white and red indifferently bepainted in his face.
All theſe he woondreth to beholde, for which (as I doe gather)
Himſelfe was to be woondred at, or to be pitied rather.
He is enamored of himſelfe for want of taking héede.
And where he lykes another thing, he lykes himſelfe in déede.
He is the partie whome he wooes, and ſuter that doth wooe,
He is the flame that ſettes on fire, and thing that burneth tooe.
O Lord how often did he kiſſe that falſe deceitfull thing?
How often did he thruſt his armes midway into the ſpring?
To haue embraſte the necke he ſaw and could not catch himſelfe?
He knowes not what it was he ſawe. And yet the fooliſh elfe

Narcissus.

Doth burne in ardent loue thereof. The verie felfe fame thing
That doth bewitch and blinde his eyes, encreafeth all his fting.
Thou fondling thou, why doeft thou raught the fickle image fo?
The thing thou féekeft is not there. And if a fide thou go:
The thing thou loueft ftraight is gone. It is none other matter
That thou doeft fée, than of thy felfe the fhadow in the water.
The thing is nothing of it felfe: with thée it doth abide,
With thee it would departe if thou withdrew thy felfe afide.
    No care of meate could draw him thence, nor yet defire of reft.
    But lying flat againft the ground, and leaning on his breft,
With gréedie eyes he gazeth ftill vppon the falced face,
And through his fight is wrought his bane. Yet for a little fpace
He turnes and fettes himfelfe vpright, and holding vp his hands
With piteous voyce vnto the wood that round about him ftands,
Cryes out and fes: alas ye Woods, and was there euer any?
That looude fo cruelly as I? you know: for vnto many
A place of harbrough haue you béene, and fort of refuge ftrong.
Can you remember any one in all your time fo long?
That hath fo pinde away as I? I fée and am full faine,
Howbeit that I like and fée I can not yet attaine:
So great a blindneffe in my heart through doting loue doth raigne.
And for to fpight me more withall, it is no iourney farre,
No drenching Sea, no Mountaine hie, no wall, no locke, no barre,
It is but euen a little droppe that kéepes vs two a funder.
He would be had. For looke how oft I kiffe the water vnder,
So oft againe with vpwarde mouth he rifeth towarde mée.
A man would thinke to touch at leaft I fhould yet able bée.
It is a trifle in refpect that lettes vs of our loue.
What wight foever that thou art come hither vp aboue.
O pierleffe piece, why doft thou mée thy louer thus delude?
Or whither flifte thou of thy friende thus earneftly purfude?
I wis I neyther am fo fowle nor yet fo growne in yeares

Narciſſus.

That in this wiſe thou ſhouldſt me ſhoon. To haue me to their Féeres,
The Nymphes themſelues haue ſude ere this. And yet (as ſhould appéere)
Thou doſt pretende ſome kinde of hope of friendſhip by thy chéere.
For when I ſtretch mine armes to thée, thou ſtretcheſt thine likewiſe.
And if I ſmile thou ſmileſt too: And when that from mine eyes
The teares doe drop, I well perceyue the water ſtands in thine.
Like geſture alſo doſt thou make to euerie becke of mine.
And as by mouing of thy ſwéete and louely lippes I wéene,
Thou ſpeakeſt words although mine eares conceiue not what they béene
It is my ſelfe I well perceyue, it is mine Image ſure,
That in this ſort deluding me, this furie doth procure.
I am inamored of my ſelfe, I doe both ſet on fire,
And am the ſame that ſwelteth too, through impotent deſire.
What ſhall I doe? be woode or wo? whome ſhall I wo therefore?
The thing I ſéeke is in my ſelfe, my plentie makes me poore.
O would to God I for a while might from my bodie part. ⎫
This wiſh is ſtraunge to heare a Louer wrapped all in ſmart, ⎬
To wiſh away the thing the which he loueth as his heart. ⎭
My ſorrowe takes away my ſtrength. I haue not long to liue,
But in the floure of youth muſt die. To die it doth not grieue.
For that by death ſhall come the ende of all my griefe and paine ⎫
I would this yongling whome I loue might lenger life obtaine: ⎬
For in one ſoule ſhall now decay we ſtedfaſt Louers twaine. ⎭
   This ſaide in rage he turnes againe vnto the forſaide ſhade, ⎫
   And rores the water with the teares and ſloubring that he made, ⎬
   That through his troubling of the Well his ymage gan to fade. ⎭
Which when he ſawe to vaniſh ſo, Oh whither doſt thou flie?
Abide I pray thée heartely, aloud he gan to crie.
Forſake me not ſo cruelly that loueth thée ſo déere,
But giue me leaue a little while my dazled eyes to chéere
With ſight of that which for to touch is vtterly denide,
Thereby to féede my wretched rage and furie for a tide.

Narcissus.

As in this wife he made his mone, he ftripped off his cote
And with his fift outragioufly his naked ftomacke fmote.
A ruddie colour where he fmote rofe on his ftomacke fhéere,
Lyke Apples which doe partly white and ftriped red appéere.
Or as the clufters ere the grapes to ripeneffe fully come :
An Orient purple here and there beginnes to grow on fome.
Which things affoone as in the fpring he did beholde againe,
He could no longer beare it out.   But fainting ftraight for paine,
As lith and fupple waxe doth melt againft the burning flame,
Or morning dewe againft the Sunne that glareth on the fame :
Euen fo by piecemale being fpent and wafted through defire,
Did he confume and melt away with *Cupids* fecret fire,
His liuely hue of white and red, his chéerefulneffe and ftrength
And all the things that lyked him did wanze away at length.
So that in fine remayned not the bodie which of late
The wretched *Echo* loued fo.   Who when fhe fawe his ftate,
Although in heart fhe angrie were, and mindefull of his pride,
Yet ruing his vnhappie cafe, as often as he cride
Alas, fhe cride alas like wife with fhirle redoubled found.
And when he beate his breaft, or ftrake his féete againft the ground,
She made like noyfe of clapping too.   Thefe are the woordes that laft
Out of his lippes beholding ftill his wonted ymage paft.
Alas fwéete boy beloude in vaine, farewell.   And by and by
With fighing found the felfe fame wordes the *Echo* did reply.
With that he layde his wearie head againft the graffie place }
And death did clofe his gazing eyes that woondred at the grace }
And beautie which did late adorne their Mafters heauenly face. }
And afterward when into Hell receyued was his fpright
He goes me to the Well of *Styx*, and there both day and night
Standes tooting on his fhadow ftill as fondely as before }
The water Nymphes his fifters wept and wayled for him fore }
And on his bodie ftrowde their haire clipt off and fhorne therefore. }

Narciſſus.

The Woodnymphes alſo did lament.   And *Echo* did rebound
To euery ſorrowfull noyſe of theirs with like lamenting ſound.
The fire was made to burne the corſe, and waxen Tapers light.
A Herce to lay the bodie on with ſolemne pompe was dight.
But as for bodie none remaind: In ſtead thereof they found
A yellow floure with milke white leaues new ſprong vpon the ground.

FINIS.

CEPHALUS AND PROCRIS

FROM

> A petite Pallace
> *of* Pettie *his*
> *Pleafure.*
>
> Containing many pretie Hiftories, by him fet forth in comely colours, and moft delightly difcourfed.
>
> *Omne tulit punctum,*
> *qui mifcuit utile dulci.*
>
> Imprinted at London, by
> G. *Eld*, 1608.

Small quarto. Black letter : not paged :
Signatnres A to Z + * = 192 leaves, the laft blank.
Bodleian Library, Oxford, Wood, C. 33.

The previous edition, London, by R. W. [1567], and the third, 1613, are alfo in the Bodleian. In the Title of the firft Edition "delightly" is "delightfully," and there are many diverfities in the fpelling, but probably no variations of confequence.

"CEPHALUS AND PROCRIS."

"*Cephalus*, a luftie young gallant, and *Procris*, a beautifull girle, both of the *Duke* of *Venice* Court, become each amorous of other, and notwithftanding delayes procured, at length are matched in marriage. *Cephalus*, pretending a farre iourney and long abfence, returneth before appointed time to trie his wives truftineffe. *Procris*, falling into the folly of extreme ieloufie over her hufband, purfueth him priuilie into the woodes a hunting, to fee his behauiour: whom *Cephalus* hearing to rufhe in a bufhe wherein fhe was fhrowded, and thinking it had beene fome game, flayeth her unwares, and perceiuing the deede, confumeth himfelfe to death for forrow."

IT is the prouident pollicy of diuine power, to the intent we fhould not be too proudly puft up with profperity, moft commonly to mixe it with fome fowre fops of adverfity, and to appoint the riuer of our happines to run in a ftreame of heauines, as, by all his benefits bountifully beftowed on vs we may plainly perceiue, whereof there is not any one fo abfolutely good and perfect, but that there be inconueniences as wel as commodities incurred therby. The golden glifering Sonne, which gladdeth all earthly wights, parcheth the Summers gréene, and blafteth their beauty which blaze their face there in. The fire, which is a moft neceffary Element vnto vs, confumeth moft ftately towres and fumptuous cities: The Water, which we vfe in euery thing we

Cephalus and Procris.

do, deuoureth infinite numbers of men, and huge heapes of treasure and riches: the ayre, whereby we liue, is death to ye diseased or wounded man, and being infected, it is the cause of all our plagues and pestilences: the earth, which yéeldeth foode to sustaine our bodies, yéeldeth poysen also to bane our bodies: the goods which doe vs good, oftentimes worke our decay and ruine: children which are our comfort, are also our care: mariage, which is a meane to make vs immortal, & by our renuing offspring to reduce our name from death, is accompanied $\tilde{w}$ cares, in number so endlesse, and in cumber so curelesse, that if the preservation of mankind, and the propagation of our selues in our kinde, did not prouoke vs therto, we should hardly be allured to enter into it. And amongst all the miseries, that march vnder the ensigne of mariage, in my fancy there is none that more tormenteth vs, then that hatefull helhound Jelousie, as the history which you shall heare, shall shew.

You shall vnderstand in the Dukes Court of *Venice*, spent his time one *Cephalus* a Gentleman of great calling, and good qualities, who at the first time he insinuated himselfe into the society of the Ladys & Gentlewomen, made no speciall or curious court to any one, but generally vsed a dutiful regard towards them all, and shewed himselfe in sporte so pleasant, in talke so witty, in manners so modest, and in all his conuersation so comely, that though he were not specially loued of any, yet was he generally liked of all, and though he himselfe were not specially vowed to any, yet was he specially viewed of one, whose name was *Procris*, a proper Gentlewoman, descended of noble parentage. And though at the first her fancy towards him were not great, yet she seemed to receive more contentation in his company, then in any other Gentleman of ye troupe. But as material fire in short time groweth from glowing coales to flashing flames: so the fire of loue in her, in short time grew from flitting fancy to firme affection, & she began to settle so surely in good will towards him, that she resolued with her selfe, he was the onely man she would be matched too, if shée were euer marryed. And being alone in her lodging, shée entred with her selfe into this reasoning.

Cephalus and Procris.

How vnequally is it prouided, that thofe which worft may are driuen to holde the Candle? that we which are in body tender, in wit weake, by reafon of our youth vnfkilfull, and in al things without experience, fhould be conftrained to beare y⁰ loathfome burden of loue, whereas riper yéeres, who hath wifdome to wield it, and reafon to repreffe it, are feldome or neuer oppreffed with it? Good God, what fiery flames, of fancy doe fry within? What defire? What luft? What hope? What truft? What care? What difpaire? What feare? What fury? that for me, which haue always liued frée and in pleafure, to be tormented therewith, féemeth litle better then the pangues of death. For as the Colt, the firft time he is ridden, fnuffeth at the fnaffle, and thinketh the byt moft bitter vnto him fo y⁰ yoake of loue féemeth heauy vnto me, becaufe my necke neuer felt the force thereof before, and now am I firft taught to draw my dayes in dolour and gréefe. And fo much the leffe I like this lotte, by how much the leffe I looked not for it, and fo much the more fower it is, by how much the more fodaine it is. For as the Birde that hops from bough to bough, and vttereth many a pleafant note, not knowing how néere her deftruction draweth on, is caught in fnare, before fhe be ware: fo, while I fpent my time in pleafure, affoone playing, affoone purling, now dauncing, now dallying, fometime laughing, but alwayes loytering, and walking, in the wide fields of fréedome, and large leas of liberty, I was fodainly, inclofed in the ftraite bondes of bondage. But I fée, and figh and forrow to fée, that there is no cloth fo fine, but Mothes will eate it, no yron fo hard but ruft will fret it, no Wood fo found, but Wormes will putrifie it, no Metall fo courfe, but fire will purifie it, nor no Maide fo frée, but Loue will bring her into thraldome and bondage. But féeing the Gods haue fo appointed it, why fhould I refift them? féeing the deftinies haue decréed it, why would I withftand them? féeing my fortune hath framed it, why fhould I frowne at it? féeing my fancy is faft fixed, why fhould I alter it? féeing my bargaine is good, why fhould I repent it? féeing I loofe nothing by it, why fhould I complaine of it: féeing my choice is right worthy, why fhould I miflike it: féeing *Cephalus* is my Saint, why fhould I not

Cephalus and Procris.

honour him: féeing he is my ioy, why fhould I not enioy him? féeing I am his, why fhould he not be mine: yes *Cephalus* is mine, and *Cephalus* fhall be mine, or elfe I proteft by the Heauens that neuer any man fhall be mine.

Euer after this fhe obferued all opportunities to give him intelligence, as modeftly as fhe might, of her good will towards him. And as it happened a company of Gentlewomen to fit talking together, they entred into commendation of the Hiftories which before had beene tolde them, fome commending this Gentlemans ftories, fome that, according as their fancie forced them: but *Procris* féemed to preferre the hiftories of *Cephalus*, both for that (faith fhe) his difcourfes differ from the reft, and befides that, me thinkes the man amendeth the matter much. *Cephalus* though out of fight, yet not out of hearing, replied in this fort. And furely, (Gentlewoman) that man thinketh himfelfe much mended by your commendation, and affure yourfelfe, you fhall readily commaund, as you courteoufly commend him.

The Gentlewoman blufhing hereat, faid fhe thought he had not beene fo neere, but touching your anfwere (faith fhe) I haue not fo good caufe to commaund you as to commend you : for as I thinke you well worthy of the one, fo I thinke my felfe far vnworthy of the other : but be bolde of this, if at any time I commaund you, it fhall be to your commoditie. I cannot (faith he) but count yout commaundement a commoditie, onely in that you fhall thinke me worthy to do you feruice : neither will I wifh any longer to liue, then I may be able, or at leaft willing, to doe you due and dutifull feruice. If fir (faith fhe foftly vnto him) it were in my power to put you to fuch feruice as I thought you worthy of, you fhould not continue in the condition of a feruant long, but your eftate fhould be altred, and you fhould commaund another while, and I would obey. It fhall be (good Miftreffe faith he) in your power to difpofe of mee at your pleafure, for I wholly commit my felfe to your courtefie, thinking my ftate more frée to ferue under you, then to reigne ouer any other whatfoeuer : and I fhould count myfelfe moft happy, if I might eyther by feruice, dutie,

Cephalus and Procris.

or loue, counteruaile your continuall goodneſſe towards me. Vpon this the company brake off, and therwith their talke. But *Cephalus*, ſéeing her good will ſo great towards him began as faſt to frame his fancy towards her, ſo that loue remained mutuall betwéene them. Which her father perceiuing, and not liking very well of the match, for that he thought his daughter not old enough for a huſband, *Cephalus* rich enough for ſuch a wife, to breake the bond of this amity went this way to worke. He wrought ſo with the Duke of *Venice*, that this *Cephalus* was ſent poſt in ambaſſage to the Turke, hoping in his abſence to alter his daughters affection. Which iourney, as it was nothing ioyfull to *Cephalus*, ſo was it ſo paynefull to *Procris*, that it had almoſt procured her death. For being ſo warily watcht by her waſpiſh parents that ſhe could neither ſée him, nor ſpeake with him before his departure, ſhe got to her chamber window, and there heauily beheld the Ship wherein he was ſorowfully ſailing away: yea ſhe bent her eyes with ſuch force to behold it that ſhe ſaw the ſhip farther by a mile, then any elſe could poſſibly ken it. But when it was cleane out of her ſight ſhe ſayd: Now farewell my ſwéet *Cephalus*, farewell my ioy, farewell my life? ah if I might haue but giuen thée a carefull kiſſe, and a fainting farewel before thy departure, I ſhould haue béen the beter able to abide thy aboode from me, and perchance thou wouldeſt the better haue minded me in thy abſence, but now I know thy will will wauer with the winds, thy faith will fléete with the floodes, and thy poore *Procris* ſhall be put cleane out of thy remembrance. Ah, why accuſe I thée of inconſtancy? No, I know the Seas will firſt be dry, before thy faith from me ſhall flie. But alas, what ſhall conſtancy preuaile: if thy life doe faile? me thinkes I ſée the hoyſing waues like a huge army to aſſayle the ſides of thy Ship, me thinkes I ſée the prouling Pirates which purſue thée, me thinkes I heare the roaring cannons in mine eare which are ſhot to ſinck thee, me thinkes I ſée the ragged rocks which ſtand ready to reaue thy Ship in ſunder, me thinkes I ſée the wilde Beaſts which rauenouſly runne ẃ open mouthes to deuour thée, methinkes I ſée the théeues which rudely ruſh out of the woods to rob thée, me thinkes I

Cephalus and Procris.

heare the trothleſſe *Turkes* enter into conſpiracy to kill thée, me thinkes I féele the furious force of their wicked weapons pitiouſly to ſpoyle thee. Theſe ſighes and thoughtes, depriued her both of ſéeing and thinking, for ſhe fell herewith downe dead to the ground: and when her wayting-woman could not by any meanes reuiue her, ſhe cried out for her mother to come helpe; who being come, and hauing aſſayed all the meanes ſhe could for her daughters recouery, and ſéeing no ſigne of life in her, ſhe fell to outragious outcries, ſaying, O uniuſt Gods, why are you the authors of ſuch vnnaturall and vntimely death? O furious féend, not God of loue, why doeſt thou thus diueliſhly deale with my daughter? O ten times curſed be the time that euer *Cephalus* ſet foote in this Court. At the name of *Cephalus* the maide began to open her eyes, which before death had dazeled, which her mother perceiuing, ſayd; Behold, daughter, thy *Cephalus* is ſafely returned, and come to ſée thée. Wherewith ſhe ſtart from the bed whereon they had layde her, and ſtaring wildly about the Chamber, when ſhe could not ſée him, ſhée ſunke downe againe. Now her parents perceiuing what poſſeſſion loue had taken in her, thought it labour loſt to endeuour to alter her determination, but made her faithfull promiſe ſhe ſhould haue their furtherance, and conſent to haue her *Cephalus* to huſband at his returne, wherewith ſhe was at length made ſtrong to endure the annoy of his abſence. It were tedious to tell the praiers, the proceſſions, the pilgrimages, the Sacrifices, the vowes ſhe made for his ſafe returne: let this ſuffice to declare her rare good will towards him, that hearing of his happie comming towards the Court, ſhe feared leaſt his ſodaine ſight would bring her ſuch exceſſive delight, that her ſenſes ſhould not be able to ſuppreſſe it, and therefore got her into the higheſt place of the houſe, and beheld him comming a farre of, and ſo by little and little was partaker of his preſence, and yet at the meeting, ſhe was more frée of her teares, then of her tongue, for her gréeting was onely wéeping, word ſhe could ſay none.

 Cephalus inflamed with this her vnfaigned loue, made all the friends he could to haſten the mariage betwéene them. But the old ſaying is,

Cephalus and Procris.

haſt maketh waſt, and bargaines made in ſpeed, are commonly repented at leaſure. For maried they were, to both their inexplicable ioy, which ſhortly after turned to both their vnſpeakable annoy. For the increaſe is ſmall of ſeed too timely ſowne, the whelps are euer blind that dogs in haſt do get, the fruits full ſoone do rot, which gathered are too ſoone, the Mault is neuer ſwéete, vnleſſe the fire be ſoft, and he that leapeth before he looke, may hap to leape into the brooke. My meaning is this, that *Cephalus* his ſhare muſt néedes be ſorrow, who would ſo raſhly and vnaduiſedly enter into ſo intricate an eſtate as wedlock is. The Philoſophers willeth vs to eate a buſhell of Salt with a man, before we enter into ſtrict familiarity with him: but I thinke a whole quarter little enough to eate with her, with whom we enter into ſuch a bond that only death muſt diſſolue. Which rule if *Cephalus* had obſerued, he had preſerued himſelfe from moſt irkeſome inconueniences. But he at al aduentures ventred vpon one, of whom he had no triall, but of a little trifling loue. I like but little of thoſe marriages, which are made in reſpect of riches, leſſe of thoſe in reſpect of honours, but leaſt of all, of thoſe in reſpect of haſty, fooliſh, and fond affection. For ſoone hot, ſoone cold, nothing violent, is permanent, the cauſe taken away, the effect vaniſheth, and when beauty once fadeth (whereof this light loue for the moſt part ariſeth) good will ſtraight fayleth. Well, this hot loue ſhe bare him, was onely cauſe of his haſty and heauy bargaine, for womanlineſſe ſhe had none, (her years were too young) vertue ſhe had little (it was not vſed in the Court) modeſty ſhe had not much (it belongeth not to louers) good gouernment and ſtayed wit ſhe wanted (it is incident to few women) to be ſhort, his choiſe was rather grounded vpon her goodlines, then her godlineſſe, rather vpon her beauty, then vertue, rather vpon her affection then diſcretion. But ſuch as he ſowed, he reapt, ſuch as he ſought he found, ſuch as he bought he had, to wit, a witleſſe Wench to his Wife. Therefore I would wiſh my friends, euer to ſow that which is ſound, to ſéeke y^t which is ſure, to buy that which is pure. I meane, I would haue them in the choiſe of ſuch choice ware, chiefly to reſpect good conditions and vertue, that is the onely ſeed which will yéeld

Cephalus and Procris.

good increaſe, that is the onely thing worthy to be ſought, that is the onely thing which cannot be too dearely bought. And whoſoeuer he be, that in any other reſpect whatſoeuer, entereth into the holy eſtate of matrimony, let him looke for no better a peniworth then *Cephalus* had, which was a loathſome life, and a deſolate death. For within a yeare or two after they had been married, his fancie was in a manner fully fed, and his diſordinate deſire of her began to decay, ſo that he began plainly to ſee, and rightly to iudge of her nature aud diſpoſition, which at the firſt the partiality of his loue, or rather outrage of his luſt, would not permit him to perceiue. And ſeeing her retchleſſe regards and light lookes, which ſhe now vſed towards all men, remembring therewithall how lightly he himſelfe won her, he began greatly to doubt of her honeſt dealing towards him : and hauing occaſion of a far iourney, and long abſence from her, he wrought this practiſe to trie her trueth. He told her, his abode from her muſt of neceſſity be forty wéekes: but at the halfe years end, by that time his hayre was wildly growne, he apparrelled himſelfe altogether contrary to wonted guiſe, and by reaſon of his hayre ſo diſguiſed himſelfe, that he was not knowne of any: which done, his neceſſary affaires diſpatched, he returned into his own Country, and came to his own houſe in maner of a ſtranger which trauailed the Country where he found his wife in more ſober ſort then he looked for, and receiued ſuch courteous entertainement, as was conuenient for a Gueſt. Hauing ſoiourned there a day or two, at conuenient time, he attempted her chaſtity in this ſort.

  If (faire Gentlewoman) no acquaintance might iuſtly craue any credit, or little merits great méed, I would report vnto you ye cauſe of my repaire, & craue at your hands the cure of my care: but ſéeing there is no likelyhood that either my words ſhall be beléeued, or my wo reléeued, I thinke better with paine to conceale my ſorrow, then in vaine to reueale my ſuite. The gentlewoman ſomewhat tickled with theſe trifling words, was rather deſirous to haue him manifeſt the miſtery of his meaning, then willing he ſhould deſiſt from his purpoſe, and therefore gaue him this anſwer.

  I am (Sir) of opinion, that credit may come diuers waies beſides

Cephalus and Procris.

acquaintance, and my felfe haue knowne much good done to many without defart: and therefore if your words be true, and your defire due, doubt not, but you fhall be both credited, and cured.

For the trueneffe of my words (faith he) I appeale to the heauens for witneffe, for the dueneffe of my defire I appeale to your courtefie for iudgement, the words I haue to vtter are thefe.

There chaunced not long fince to trauell through the Country, wherein lyeth my liuing, a knight, named *Cephalus*: and though the report of the porte and houfe which I maintaine be not greate, yet it is fuch, that it fendeth me many guefts in the yeare: it pleafed this *Cephalus* to foiourne the fpace of thrée or four dayes with me, and in way of talke, to paffe away ye time, he made relation at large vnto me of his country, of his condition and ftate, of his fpeciall place of abode and dwelling, of his lands and liuing, and fuch like. I demaunded of him whether he were married, faying: All those things before rehearfed, were not fufficient to the attaining of a happy life without a beautifull, faire, and louing wife. With that he fetcht a déepe figh, faying: I haue (Sir) I would you knew, a wife, whofe beauty refembleth the brightnes of the Sun, whofe face doth difgrace all Ladies in *Venice*, yea *Venus* her felfe, whofe loue was fo excéeding great towards me, that before I was maried vnto her, hauing occafion to go in Ambaffage to the *Turke*, fhe almoft died at my departure, and neuer was rightly reuiued til my returne, Good God, faid I, how can you be fo long abfent from fo louing a wife? How can any meate doe you good, which fhe giueth you not? How can you fléepe out of her armes? It is not lawfull (faith he) for euery man to do as he would, I muft do as my bufines bindeth me to do. Befides that, euery man is not of like mind in like maters. Laftly, it is one thing to haue bin happy, it is another thing to be happy. For your bufineffe (said I) it feemeth not to be great, by the good company, which I thanke you, you have kept me thefe foure dayes: For your mind, I know no man that would willingly be out of the company of fuch a wife: For your prefent happineffe, indeed it may be your wife is dead, or y^t

Cephalus and Procris.

her loue is tranflated from you to fome other. No (faith he) fhe liueth, and I thinke loueth me; but what good doth gold to him that careth not for it? And can you (faid I) not care for fuch a golden Girle? Then may I fay, you have a wife more faire than fortunate, and fhe a hufband more fortunate then faithfull. Alas (faith he) with teares in his eyes, it is my great care that I do fo little care, but no more hereof I befeech you. But my blood being inflamed with the commendation which he gaue to your beauty, and pittying your cafe to have fo careleffe a hufband ouer you, I lay very importunately vpon him to impart the whole matter vnto me, and with much a doe I wrong thefe words from him. Sir (faith he) I fhall defire you to impute my doings not to my fault, but to my fates, and to thinke that what fo euer is done ill, is done againft my will. It is fo, that I remained marryed with my wife the terme of two whole years, what time I did not onely make of her, but I made a goddeffe of her, and rather doltifhly doted on her, then duely loued her : Now whether it were the punifhment of the gods for my fond Idolatry committed vpon her, or whether they thought her too good for me, or whether the deftinies had otherwife decreed it, or whether loue be loft when fancy is once fully fed, or whether my nature be to like nothing long, I know not, but at the two yéers end I began fodainly in my heart to hate her as deadly, as before I loued her déepely : yea her very fight was lothfome vnto me, that I could not by any meane indure it. And becaufe her friends are of great countenance, and I had no crime to charge her withall, I durft not féeke deuorcemēt, but priuily parted from her, pretending vrgent affaires which conftrained me thereto. Hereafter I meane to beftow my felfe in the warres vnder the Emperour, not minding to returne while fhe liueth. And for my maintenance there, I haue taken order fecretly with my friends, to conueigh vnto mée yearely the reuenues of my land. Thus crauing your fecrefie herein, I haue reuealed vnto you my carefull cafe. The ftrangeneffe of this tale made me ftand a while in a maze, at length I greatly began to blame his difloyalty, to conceaue without caufe fo great difliking, where there was fo great caufe of good liking. But Gentlewoman, to

Cephalus and Procris.

confeſſe the trueth vnto you, my loue this time was ſo great towards you, that I neuer perſwaded him to returne vnto you, meaning my ſelfe to take that payne, and knowing him better loſt then found, being no better vnto you. Shortly after this he departed from me towards the Emperours Court, and I tooke my iourney hither as you ſee. And this is the tale I had to tell you.

Procris hauing heard this forged tale, with diuers alterations and ſundry imaginations with her ſelfe, ſomtime fearing it was true, for that he rightly hit diuers points which had paſſed betwéen her huſband and her, ſometime thinking it falſe, for that ſhe had firme confidence in her huſbands faith and loyalty towards her, aſſoone caſting one likelyhood one way, aſſoone another, another way: at length fully reſoluing with her ſelfe that his words were vtterly vntrue, ſhe replyed vnto them in this ſort.

Good God, I ſée there is no wooll ſo courſe, but it will take ſome colour, no matter ſo vnlikely, which with words may not be made probable, nor nothing ſo falſe which diſembling men will not faigne and forge. Shall it ſinke into my head that *Cephalus* will forſake me, who did forſake all my friends, to take him? Is it likely he will leave countrey, kinſſolk, friends, lands, liuing, and (which is moſt of all) a moſt louing wife, no cauſe conſtraining him thereto? But what vſe I reaſons to refell that which one without eyes may ſee is but ſome coyned deuice to cozen me? No ſir knight, you muſt vſe ſome other practiſe to effect your purpoſe, this is too broad to be beléeued, this colour is ſo courſe, that euery man may ſée it, and it is ſo black, that it will take no other colour to cloud it, the thred of your hay is ſo byg, that the Cunnies ſee it before they come at it, your hooke is ſo long, that the bayte cannot hide it; and your deuice is too far fetcht, to bring your purpoſe néere to an end.

Gentlewoman (ſaith *Cephalus*) I ſée it is ſome mens fortune not to be beléeued when they ſpeake truely, and others to be well thought of when they deale falſely, which you haue verified in your huſband and me, who doubt of my words which are true, and not of his deeds

Cephalus and Procris.

which are falſe. And this I thought at yᵉ firſt, which made me doubt to discloſe this matter vnto you: for I know it commonly to be ſo, that trauellers words are not much truſted, neither great matters ſoone beléeued. But when the time of your huſbands returne is expired, and he not come, then will you ſay, that Sir *Sulahpec* (for ſo turning his name he termed himſelfe) told you true. For my part, notwithſtanding the great good will I beare you, would not ſuffer me to conceale this matter from you, that you might prouide for your ſelfe: yet I am very well content you ſhould giue no credit to my words, for I would not you ſhould beléeue anything which might gréeue you any way, and I would wiſh you to thinke well, till you ſée otherwiſe: for euery euil bringeth greefe enough with it when it commeth, though the feare before procure none. Therefore I craue no credite for my words: my deſire is, that you will beléeue that which you ſée, which is, yᵗ for your ſake I haue trauelled with great perill and paine out of mine owne country hither to your houſe, that vpon the report of your beauty I was ſo ſurpriſed therewith, that I thought euery houre a yeare till I had ſéene you, that hauing ſéene you, I haue reſolued with myſelfe to liue and die in your ſeruice and ſight. Now if in conſideration hereof it ſhall pleaſe you to graunt me ſuch grace, as my good will deſerueth, you ſhall find me ſo thankfull and gratefull for the ſame, that no future fortune ſhall force me to forget the preſent benefit which you ſhall beſtow vpon me: and if it chaunce that your huſband returne, you ſhal be ſure alway to enioy me as your faithfull friend, and if he neuer come againe, you ſhall haue me, if you pleaſe, for your louing Spouſe for euer. Yea marry (faith *Procris*) from hence came theſe teares, hereof procéeded your former fetch, this is it which hath ſeparated my huſband from me, which hath ſent him to the Warres, which will cauſe him neuer to returne: a fine fetch forſooth, and cunningly contriued. Did that report which blazed my beauty (which God knoweth is none) blemiſh my name (which I would you knew is good) in ſuch ſort, that you conceiued hope to win me to your wicked will? Were you ſo vaine to aſſure your ſelfe ſo

Cephalus and Procris.

furely of my vanity, that onely thereupon you would vndertake fo great a iourny? No, you are conuerfant with no *Creffed*, you haue no *Helen* in hand, we women will now learne to beware of fuch guileful guefts. No, if you were as cunning as *Ioue*, that you could conuert your felfe into the likeneffe of mine owne hufband (as *Ioue* came to *Alcmena* in the likeneffe of her hufband *Amphetrion*) I doubt how I fhould receiue you, till the prefixed time of my hufbands comming were come: much leffe fhall your forged tales or importunities conftraine me to receiue you into that credite, and admit you into that place, which is, and fhall be onely proper to my hufband. And this anfwere I pray you let fuffice you, otherwife you may leaue my houfe when yée lift. *Cephalus* liked this geare reafonable well, and perfwaded himfelfe, that though he had a wanton Wife, yet he had no wicked Wife. But knowing it the fafhion of Women at firft to refufe, & that what angry face foeuer they fet on the matter, yet it doth them good to be courted with offers of curtifie, he meant to prooue her once againe, and went more effectually to work, to wit, from craft to coyne, from guiles to gifts, from prayers to prefents. For hauing receiued great ftore of gold and Jewels for certaine Land, which he fold there whither he trauelled (the onely caufe in déed of his trauaile) he prefented it all vnto her, faying he had fold al that he had in his own Country, minding to make his continual aboad with her, and if fhe meant fo rigoroufly to reiect his good will, he wylled her to take that in token thereof, and for himfelfe, he would procure himfelfe fome defperate death, or other, to auoyd that death which her beauty and cruelty a thoufand times a day draue him to.

The Gentlewoman hearing thofe defperate words, and feeyng that rich fight, moued fomewhat with pitty, but more with pention, began to yeeld to his defire, and with *Danae* to hold vp her lap to receiue the golden fhewre. O god gold, what canft thou not do? But O diuill woman, that will do more for gold then for good will. O Gentlewomen what fhame is it to fel vilely, that which God hath giuen fréely, and to make a gaine of that, which is more grateful to women then men, as

Cephalus and Procris.

Tiresias gaue iudgement. Hereof came that odious name whore, which in Latine is *Meritrix a merendo* of deseruing or getting: a thing so vnnaturall, that very beasts abhor it: so vnreasonable, as if one should be hired to do ones selfe good: so vnhonest, that the common stewes thereof first tooke their beginning. But to returne to our story. *Cephalus* seeing the lewdnesse of his wife, bewraied himselfe vnto her who he was: whereupon she was surprised with such shame, and he with such sorrow, that they could not long time speake each to other: at length she fell downe vpon her knées, humbly crauing his pardon. *Cephalus* knowing women to be too weake to withstand the might of money, and thinking that her very nature violently drew her to him, whom being her husband though to her vnknown she loued intierly, he thought best for his own quiet, and to auoyd infamy, to put vp this presumption of euil in his wife patiently, and to pardon her offence: and so they liued quietly together a while. But within short time, shée partly from want of gouernement, and partly thinking her husband would reuenge the wrong which she would haue done to him, fell into such a furious iealousie ouer him, that it wrought her own destruction, and his desolation. For this monstrous mischeife was so merueilously crept into her heart, that she began to haue a very carefull and curious eye to the conuersation of her husband, and with her selfe sinisterly to examine all his words and works towards her. For if he vsed her very familiarly, she supposed that he flattered her, and did it but to collour his falshood towards her: if he looked solenmely on her she feared the alteration of his affections, and the alienation of his good will from her, and that he rowed in some other streame: if he vsed any company and frequented any mans house, she thought by and by that there dwelt the Saint whom he serued: if he liued solitarily, and auoyded company, she iudged forthwith y^t he was in loue some where: if he bidde any of his neighboures to his house, why, they were his goddesses: if he inuited none, she thought he durst not, least she should spie some priuy trickes betwéene them: if he came home merrily, he had sped of his purpose: if sadly, he had receiued some repulse: if he talked pleasantly,

Cephalus and Procris.

his Miftreffe had fet him on his merry pins: if he faid nothing, fhe remembred it was one of the properties of loue to be filent: If he laughed it was to thinke of his loue: if he fighed, it was becaufe he was not with her: if he kift her, it was to procure appetite againft he came to his miftres: if hée kift her not, he cared not for her: if he atchiueth any valiant enterprife at armes, it was done for his miftreffe fake: if not, he was become a carpet knight: if he fell out with any, it was fome open enemy to his priuy friend: if he were friends with all men he durft difpleafe none, leaft they fhould detect his doings to her: if he went curioufly in apparrell, it was to pleafe his miftreffe: if negligently he liued in abfence: if he ware his haire long, he mourned becaufe he could not be admitted: if fhort, he was receiued into fauour: if he bought her any apparrell, or any other prity trifling trickes, it was to pleafe her, and a bable for the foole to play with: if he bought her nothing, he had inough to doe to maintaine other in brauery: if he entertained any feruant, he was of his miftreffe preferment: if he put any away, he had fome way offended her: if he commended any man, he was out of queftion his baude: if he praifed any woman, fhe was no doubt his whore: and fo of other his thoughts, wordes, and deedes, fhe made this fufpitious fuppofe and iealous interpretation. And as the Spider out of moft fwéet flowers fucketh poyson: fo fhe out of moft louing and friendly déedes towards her, picked occafions to quarrell, and conceyued caufes of hate. And fo long fhe continued in thefe carefull coniectures, that not onely her body was brought low, by reafon that her appetite to meat failed her, but alfo fhe was difquieted in minde, that fhe was in a manner befides her felfe: whereupon in great penfiueneffe of heart, fhe fell to preaching to her felfe in this fort.

Ah fond foole, wilt thou thus wilfully worke thine owne wracke and ruine: if thy hufband commit treafon againft thee, wilt thou commit murder vpon thy felfe: if he confume himfelfe away with Whores, wilt thou then confume away thy felfe with cares: wilt thou increafe his mifchiefe with thine owne miferie: if he be fo wickedly bent, it is not my

Cephalus and Procris.

care can cure him: for that which is bred in the bone, will not out of the flesh. If he be difpofed to deale falfly with me, it is not my wary watching which will ward him from it: for loue deceiued *Argus* with his two hundred eyes. If he fhould be forbidden to leaue it, he wil vfe it the more: for our nature is to run vpon that which is forbidden vs: vices the more prohibited, the more prouoked, and a wild Colte, the harder he is rained, the hotter he is. If I fhould take him tardie in it, it would but increafe his incontinent impudency: for being once knowne to haue tranfgreffed the lawfull limittes of loue and honefty, he would euer after be careleffe of his good name, which he knew he could neuer recouer againe. And why fhould I féeke to take him in it? fhould I féeke to know that, which I ought to féeke not fo much as to thinke on? was euer wight fo bewitched to run headlong vpon her owne ruine? So long as I know it not, it hurteth me not, but if I once certainely knew it, God knoweth how fodainely it would abridge my daies. And yet why fhould I take it fo grieuoufly? am I the firft that haue béen fo ferued? Hath not *Juno* her felfe fuftained the like iniury? But I reafon with my felfe as if my hufband were manifeftly conuicted of this crime, who perchance, good Gentleman, be as innocent in thought, as I wrongfully thinke him to be nocent in déed: for to confider aduifedly of the matter, there is not fo much as any likelyhood to leade me to any fuch opinion of him, he vfeth me honeftly, he maintaineth me honorably, he loueth me better then my lewde dealing toward him hath deferued. No, it is mine owne vnworthineffe that maketh me thinke I am not worthy the proper poffeffion of fo proper a Gentleman: it is mine own luftful defire that maketh me afraide to loofe any thing: it is mine owne weakneffe, that maketh me fo fufpitious of wrong: it is mine own incontinency, which maketh me iudge him by my felfe. Well, the price of my preiudiciall doings towards him is almoft paide, and if paine be a punifhment, then haue I endured a moft painfull punifhment: but let this deare bought wit do me fome good, let me now at légth learne to be wife, and not to thinke of euils before they come, not to feare them before I haue caufe, not to doubt of them in whom is no

Cephalus and Procris.

doubling, nor to miftruft them in whom is no treafon, and faithfully to loue him, that unfainedly loueth me. After this fhe indeuoured to do fuch fond toyes forth of her head, and for a while fhe liued louingly and quietly with her hufband, but fodainly, by reafon of one looke which he caft vpon one of his neighbours, fhe fell into her old vaine of vanity againe. And as fecond falling into ficknefle is euer moft dangerous, fo now her folly was growne to fuch fury, and her difeafe for incurable, that fhe could not conceale it any longer, but flatly told her hufband to his teeth, y^t fhe thought he did mifufe her.

Cephalus knowing his owne innocency, and feeing her imbecility, gently prayed her not to conceiue any fuch euill opinion of him, faying: If neither regard of God, neither refpect of men, neither reuerence of the reuerent ftate of mariage, could feare me frō fuch filthineffe, yet affure your felf, the loyall loue I beare you, would let me from fuch lafciuiouf- neffe. For beléeue me, your perfon pleafeth me fo well, that I thinke my felfe fwéetely fatiffied therewith. Yea if *Venus* her felfe fhould chance vnto my choice, I am perfwaded I fhold not prefer her before you. For as her beauty would intifingly draw me to her, fo my dutie would neceffarily driue me to you. Therefore (good Wife) trouble not your felfe with fuch toyes, which will but bréed your owne vnreft, and my difquiet, your torment and my trouble, yea and in time perchance both our vntimely deaths. Let *Deianyra* be a prefident for you, who fufpecting her hufband *Hercules* of fpoufe-breach, fent him a fhirt dyed with the bloud of the *Centaure Neffus*, who told her that fhirt had vertue to reuiue loue almoft mortified: but *Hercules* had no fooner put it on, but it ftuck faft to his flefh, and fryed him to death, as if it had béene a fury of hell: which when fhée knew, with her owne hands fhée wrought her owne deftruction. See the vnworthy end which that monfter iealoufie brought this worthy couple to, and forefée (fwéete wife) that it bring not vs to the like bane. Thefe words could worke no effect w̃ her, but rather increafed her fufpition, perfwading her felfe, that as in faire painted pots poyfon is oft put, and in goodly fumptuous Sepulchres rotten bones are rife, euen fo faireft words

Cephalus and Procris.

are euer fulleſt of falſhood. Yea the more courteously he ſhowed himſelfe, the more culpable ſhe thought him to be. Which *Cephalus* ſéeing, becauſe he would take away all cauſes of ſuſpicion, abandoned all good company, and ſpent his time ſolitarily, hunting in the woods, and ſéeking the ſpoile of ſpoiling ſauage beaſts. But this helhound Jelouſie did ſo haunt and hunt her, that ſhe could in no place be in reſt, but made her plod from her pallace to the woods, to watch whether he there hunted a chaſte chaſe, or not. And one day as ſhe dogged him wher he was layd downe to reſt amongſt ye gréen leaues, ſhe heard him utter theſe words, Come gentle *Ayre*, and refreſh my wearied ſpirits: ẃ ſuch like words of dalliance, which he (being hot) ſpake to the gale of wind which pleaſantly blew vpon him. But ſhée thought he had ſpoken to ſome woman with him, whereupon ſhe furiouſly fell to the ground, tearing her hayre, and ſcratching her face: and though her griefe would not giue her leaue to ſpeake, yet to her ſelfe ſhe thought this: and can the Traitor thus treacherouſly deale with me? Had the ſorow which I ſuſtained only for his abſence before I was married to him, or any way owed him any thing, almoſt coſt me my life? and now ſhall his preſence procure my death? Did I powre out penſiue praiers for his ſafe return from the *Turkes*? and doth his returne, returne my good will with ſuch diſpight? O would to God the *Turkes* had torne him in péeces, that he had neuer come home to martir me in this manner. But Woolues neur pray vpon Woolues: his fraud was nothing inferiour to their falſhood, and therefore it had béen in vaine for him to haue halted before a Créeple: but me, being but a ſimple ſhéepe, ſée how ſoone this ſubtile foxe could deceiue. Is this the fruite of my feruent loue? Is this the felicity I expected in marriage? had I knowne this, I would neuer haue knowne what the ſubtill ſexe of men had meant. I would rather, as they ſay, haue led Apes in hell after my death, then haue felt al ye torments of Hel in my life. But had I wiſt, is euer had at the worſt: they that caſt not of cares before they come, cannot caſt them off when they do come. It is too late to caſt Anchor, when the ſhip is ſhaken to péeces againſt the Rockes: it booteth not to ſend for a Phiſition, when the ſick

Cephalus and Procris.

party is already departed. Well, I will yet go feé the curfed caufe of my careful calamity, that I may mittigate fome part of my martirdome, by fcratching her incontinent eyes out of her whorifh head: and thereupon rowfed her felf out of the fhrub wherein fhe was fhrowded. *Cephalus* hearing fomewhat rufh in the bufh, thought it had bin fome wild beaft, and tooke his dart and ftrocke the tame foole to the heart. But comming to the place, and feéing what he had done, he fell downe in a fwoune vpon her: but with her ftriuing vnder him with ye panges of death, he was reduced to life, and faid: Alas my *Procris* by my felfe is flaine. Which fhe (not yet dead) hearing, faid, Alas your *Ayre* hath brought me to this end. With that he vnderftood how the matter went, and faid, Alas (fweét Wife) I vfed thofe words to the winde. Why then (faith fhe) not you but that winde gaue me this wound. And fo ioyning her lips to his, fhe yéelded vp her breath into his mouth, and dyed. And he, with care confumed, tarried not long behind her, to bewaile eyther his owne déed, or her death.

Now Gentlewomen, let this cafuall end of this Gentlewoman be a *Cauøat* to kéepe you from fuch wary watchings of your Hufbands, it is but a meane to make them fall to folly the rather, as the thoughtful care of the rich man caufeth the théefe the fooner to féeke fpoyle of him. But if you will know the chiefe way to keepe your Hufbands continent, is to keepe your felues continent: for when they fhall fee you, which are the weaker veffels, ftrong in vertue & chaftity, they wil be afhamed to be found faint in faith & loyaltie: when they fhall fee you conftant in good wil towards them, they wil feare to be found fickle in faith towards you: when they fhall fee you loue thē faithfully, you fhal be fure to haue them loue you feruētly. But if you fhal once fhake off the fhéete of fhame, & giue your felues over to choife of change: then affuredly make account, your hufbands will efchew your companies, loath your lips, abandon your beds, and frequent the familiarity of they care not who, if not of you.

FINIS.

THE STORY OF

NARCISSVS

FROM

CHAUCER ROMAUNT OF THE ROSE.

1455-1548.   Aldine Edition, 1852.

---

nd ſo befell, I reſted mee
　　Beſides a well under a tree,
　　Which tree in Fraunce men call a pine,
But ſith the time of King Pepine
Ne grew there tree in mannes ſight
So faire, ne ſo well woxe in hight,
In all that yard ſo high was none.
And ſpringing in a marble ſtone
Had nature ſet, the ſooth to tell,
Under that pine tree a well,
And on the border all without
Was written on the ſtone about
Letters ſmall, that ſaiden thus,
Here ſtarſe the faire Narciſſus.
　　Narciſſus was a bachelere,
That Love had caught in his daungere,
And in his nette gan him ſo ſtraine,
And did him ſo to weepe and plaine,

Narcissus.

That need him muft his life forgo:
For a faire lady, that hight Echo,
Him loved over any creature,
And gan for him fuch paine endure,
That on a time fhe him tolde,
That if he her loven holde,
That her behoved needes die,
There lay none other remedie.
  But natheleffe, for his beaute
So fierce and daungerous was he,
That he nolde graunten her afking,
For weeping, ne for faire praying.
  And when fhe heard him werne her fo,
She had in herte fo grete wo,
And tooke it in fo grete defpite,
That fhe without more refpite
Was dead anon: but ere fhe deide,
Ful pitoufly to God fhe preide,
That proude hearted Narciffus,
That was in love fo daungerous,
Might on a day ben hampered fo
For love, and ben fo hote for wo,
That never he might to joy attaine;
Then fhould he fele in very vaine
What forrow true lovers maken,
That ben fo villainoufly forfaken.
  This prayer was but reafonable,
Therefore God held it firme and ftable:
For Narciffus fhortly to tell,
By aventure came to that well
To reft him in the fhaddowing
A day, when he came from hunting.

Narcissus.

This Narciſſus had ſuffred paines
For renning all day in the plaines,
And was for thurſt in great diſtreſſe
Of herte, and of his wearineſſe,
That had his breath almoſt benomen.
Whan he was to that well ycomen,
That ſhaddowed was with braunches grene,
He thought of thilke water ſhene
To drinke and freſh him wele withall,
And downe on knees he gan to fall,
And forth his necke and head outſtraught
To drinke of that well a draught:
And in the water anon was ſene
His noſe, his mouth, his eyen ſhene,
And he thereof was all abaſhed,
His owne ſhaddow had him betraſhed,
For well wend he the forme ſee
Of a childe of great beautee,
Well couth Love him wreke tho
Of daungere and of pride alſo
That Narciſſus ſometime him bere,
He quite him well his guerdon there,
For he muſed ſo in the well,
That ſhortely the ſooth to tell,
He loved his owne ſhaddow ſo,
That at the laſt he ſtarfe for wo:
For when he ſaw that he his will
Might in no manner way fulfill,
And that he was ſo faſte caught
That he him couthe comfort naught,
He loſt his wit right in that place,
And died within a little ſpace,

Narcissus.

And thus his warison he tooke
For the lady that he forsoke.
  Ladies I praye ensample taketh,
Ye that ayenst your love mistaketh :
For if of hir death be you to wite,
God can full well your wile quite.
  When that this letter of which I tell,
Had taught me that it was the well
Of Narcissus in his beaute,
I gan anon withdrawe me,
When it fell in my remembraunce,
That him betide such mischaunce.

FINIS.

THE STORY OF

NARCISSVS

FROM

GOWER CONFESSIO AMANTIS,

Book i. p. 118, ed. Pauli, London, 1857.

CONFESSOR . . . . orthy, my fone, if thou wolt live
                      In vertue, thou muft vice efcheue
                      And with lowe herte humbleffe fue,
So that thou be nought furquedous.
AMANS. . . . . . . My fader, I am amorous,
Wherof I wolde you befeche
That ye me fome enfample teche,
Which might in loves caufe ftonde.
CONFESSOR . . . . My fone, thou fhalt underftonde
In love and other thinges alle,
If that furquedrie falle,
It may to him nought well betide,
Which ufeth thilke vice of pride
Which torneth wifdom to wening
And fothfaftneffe into lefing
Through foll imagination.
And for thin enformation
That thou this vice as I the rede
Efcheue fhalte, a tale I rede,
Which fell whilom by daies olde,
So as the clerke Ovide tolde.

Narcissus.

Hic in speciali tractat confessor cum amante contra illos, qui de propria formositate presumentes amorem mulieris dedignantur. Et narrat exemplum, qualiter cuiusdam principis filius nomine Narcizus estivo tempore, cum ipse venacionis causa quendam cervum solus cum suis canibus exagitaret, in gravem sitim incurrens necessitate compulsus ad bibendum de quodam fonte pronus inclinavit, ubi ipse faciem suam pulcherrimam in aqua percipiens putabat se per hoc illam nimpham, quam poete Ekko vocant, in flumine coram suis oculis pocius conspexisse, de cuius amore confestim laqueatus, ut ipsam ad se de fonte extraheret, pluribus blandiciis adulabatur, sed cum illud perficere nullatenus potuit, pre nimio languore deficiens contra lapides ibidem adjacentes caput exverberans cerebrum effudit. Et sic de propria pulchritudine qui fuerat presumptuosus de propria pulchritudine fatuatus interiit.

There was whilom a lordes sone,
Which of his pride a nice wone
Hath caught, that worthy to his liche
To sechen all the worldes riche
There was no woman for to love.
So high he set him selfe above
Of stature and of beaute bothe,
That him thought alle women lothe.
So was there no comparison
As towarde his condition.
This yonge lord Narcizus hight.
No strength of love bowe might
His herte, whiche is unaffiled.
But ate laste he was beguiled.
For of the goddes purveiaunce
It felle him on a day perchaunce,
That he in all his proud fare
Unto the forest gan to fare
Amonge other, that there were,
To hunten and disporte him there.
And whan he cam into the place,
Where that he wolde make his chace,
The houndes weren in a throwe
Uncoupled and the hornes blowe,
The great herte anone was founde
With swifte feet set on the grounde.
And he with spore in horse side
Him hasteth faste for to ride,
Till alle men be left behinde.
And as he rode under a linde
Beside a roche, as I the telle,
He sigh where spronge a lusty welle.

Narciſsus.

The day was wonder hote withalle,
And ſuch a thurſt was on him falle,
That he muſt outher deie or drinke.
And downe he light and by the brinke
He tide his hors unto a braunche
And laid him lowe for to ſtaunche
His thurſt. And as he caſt his loke
Into the welle and hede toke,
He ſigh the like of his viſage
And wende there were an ymage
Of ſuche a nimphe, as tho was ſay,
Whereof that love his herte aſſay
Began, as it was after ſene
Of his ſotie and made him wene
It were a woman, that he ſigh.
The more he cam the welle nigh,
The nere cam ſhe to him ayein.
So wiſt he never what to ſain,
For whan he wepte he ſigh her wepe,
And whan he cried he toke good kepe,
The ſame worde ſhe cried alſo,
And thus began the newe wo,
That whilom was to him ſo ſtraunge.
Tho made him love an harde eſchaunge
To ſet his herte and to beginne
Thing, whiche he might never winne.
And ever amonge he gan to loute
And praith, that ſhe to him come oute.
And other while he goth a fer
And other while he draweth ner
And ever he founde her in one place.
He wepeth, he crieth, he axeth grace,

Narciſſus.

                    There as he mighte gete none.
                    So that ayein a roche of ſtone,
                    As he that knewe none other rede,
                    He ſmote him ſelf til he was dede,
                    Wherof the nimphes of the welles
                    And other that there weren elles
                    Unto the wodes belongende
                    The body, which was dede ligende,
                    For pure pite that they have
                    Under grave they begrave.
                    And than out of his ſepulture
                    There ſpronge anone peraventure
                    Of floures ſuche a wonder ſight,
                    That men enſample take might
                    Upon the dedes whiche he dede.
                    And tho was ſene in thilke ſtede,
                    For in the winter freſh and faire
                    The floures ben, which is contraire
                    To kinde, and ſo was the folie
                    Which felle of his ſurquedrie.
CONFESSOR . . . Thus he, which love had in diſdeigne,
                    Worſt of all other was beſeine,
                    And as he ſet his priſe moſt hie,
                    He was leſt worthy in loves eye
                    And moſt bejaped in his wit,
                    Wherof the remembraunce is yit,
                    So that thou might enſample take
                    And eke all other for his ſake.

The fable of Ouid treting of Narcissus, trāſlated out of Latin into Englyſh Mytre, with a moral ther vnto, very pleaſante to rede.

M.D.LX.

God reſpſteth the proud in euery place
But vnto the humble he geueth his grace.
Therfore truſt not to riches beuti nor strēgth
All theſe be bayne, & ſhall conſume at length.

Imprynted at London by Thomas
Hackette, and are to be ſold at hys
shop in Cannynge ſtrete, ouer
agaynſte the thre
Cranes.

In the original the borders are filled in with rude woodcuts, which do not appear to have any reference to the ſtory, and therefore have not been reproduced.

⁋ THE PRENTER TO THE BOOKE.

⓮ 𝕷yttell Booke do thy Indeuoure
to all eſtates, that vyce doeth refuſe,
In the maye be learned how to perceuer
ſynne to abhorre vertue to vſe.
The wyſe the aucthour wyll excuſe
by cauſe he inuayeth, agaynſt ſynne and pryde,
Who cauſeth many a one, pariloufly to ſlyde.

In the may the wyſe learne vertue in dede
In the maye the ſtronge manne, of hym ſelfe knowe
In the maye the ryche manne, of hym ſelfe reed
how to gather hys ryches, or them to beſtowe
wyth moſt worthy matter in the doeth flowe
who ſeketh in the for profyt and gayne,
Of excellent matter ſone ſhall attayne.

THE ARGUMENT OF THE FABLE.

Lireope had a Sonne by Cephicious named Narciſſius, whose contynuaunce of lyfe Tyricias a prophete, affyrmyd to be longe, yf the knowledge of hym felfe, procuryd not the contrary, whofe fentence here howe Ecco the callynge Impe, from whome Iuno had berefte the ryght vfe of fpeche, fo loued this Narcyſſus, that throughe the thought and care that fhe fuftayned, for the gettynge hys good wyl that euer defpyfed her, fhe confumed the relykes, of whiche confumed Carcas were torned into ftones. The greate dyfdayne of Narcyſſus, herein Ramufia Straungely reuenged, for he heated through hūtinge by the drynkynge of a well, fuppofynge to quenche hys thurfte efpyed therein the fhadowe, of hys face, wherewyth he was
 fo rauyfhed that hauynge no power to leue hys
  blynde defyre for the attaynyng of an impofe-
   belytye, there he ftarued. For the pre-
    peration, whofe buryall the Nim-
     phes, had ordyned fouch fur-
      nituer as ther vnto apper-
       teyned & had. Retornyd
        to the folemne,
         Erthynge
    and buryall of fuche a carcafe, they
    founde in fted of the ded Corpis
     a yelow floure which with
      vs beareth the name
       of a daffa-
        dylly.

THE ENDE OF THE ARGUMENT.

Ireope whome once Ciphicious, dyd embrace,
    and raufhe ī his crokid floudes wher fhe was fhut frō grace.
    Dyd trauell and brynge forth when tyme of berth befel
a chyld euen then whō loue had lyked well,
    And hym Narciffus named of whome the lot to learne,
yf he fhoulde number manye yeares, and perfecte age difcerne
    The reder of hys fate Tiricious yea dyd faye
If that the knowledge of hym felfe, his life dyd not decaye,
    Ful longe a vayne pronounce, this femed tyll hys death,
By furye quaynte dyd make it good, and vnfene lofe of brethe
    For twentye yeares and one, Narciffus death efcaped
What tyme no chylde was feene fo fayre, nor yong man better fhapyd,
    A nomber bothe of men and maydes, did hym defyre,
But bewtye bente wyth proude dyfdayne, had fet hym fo on fyre
    That nether thofe whome youthe in yeares, had made his make
Nor pleafaunte damfels frefhe of heue, coulde wyth him pleafure take
    This man the fearfull hartes, inforcynge to hys nettes
The caulyng nimphe one daye, behelde that nether euer lettes
    To talke to thofe that fpake, nor yet hathe power of fpeche
Before by Ecco this I mene, the dobbeler of fkreeche
    A body and no voyce, was Ecco yet but howe
The blabbe had then none other vfe of fpeach, then fhe hath now
    The later ende to geue of euery fence or claufe,
wherof the wyfe of Jupiter, was fyrft and chyfe the caufe
    For that when fhe dyd feke, the fyllye Imphes to take
that oft fhe knewe wythin the hylles, had lodged wyth her make
    This Ecco wyth a tale, the goddes kepte fo longe
that well the Imphes myght her efcape, but whē fhe fawe this wrong
    This tonge quod fhe where wyth, fo ofte thou dydefte dyfceaue
the goddes Juno lyttyll vfe of fpeche, fhall erfte receaue
    And fo her thretininges proue, yet Ecco endyth fpeche
wyth dobling found the wordes fhe heareth, & fendeth againe w^t fcrech

The Moralization of the Fable

Thus when Cyphicious Sonne, the defartes walkinge fafte
wyth wandrynge pace fhe had efpyed, her loue and on hym cafte
 Wyth ftealyng fteppes, fhe foloweth faft her hote defyre
and ftyl the nerer that fhe comes, the hotter is her fyre
 None other wyfe then as the nerer fyre dothe lye
to brimftone matters mete to borne to flayme doth more applye,
 Howe ofte oh wolde fhe fayne, wyth plefaunte wordes him glad
and faune on hym wyth prayers fwete, but nature it forbad,
 And letteth her to begynne, but that fhe doth permytte
full prefte is Ecco to perfourme accordyng to her wytte,
 In lyftynge for to heare, fome founde hys mouth efcape
whereto her wordes fhe myghte applye, and him an aunfwere fhape,
 By chaunce Narciffus, led from companye alone
dyd faye is anye here to whome, fhe anfwereth her a none,
 He mufyth and amafyd, doth loke on euerye fyde
and cauling loude come nere he fayth, whom fhe byds yeke abyde,
 Agayne he looketh aboute, and feynge none that came,
Whyftlyft thou me quod he, who harde her anfwere euen the fame
 He ftayeth and not knowyng, whofe this founde fhould be
come hether let vs mete he fayde, and let vs mete quod fhe
 Then with fo good a wyll, as thoughe fhe neuer harde
a found that lyked her halfe fo well, to anfwere afterwarde
 And to perfourme her wordes, the woodes fhe foone forfooke
and to imbrace that fhe defyred, aboute the necke hym tooke
 He flyeth fafte awaye, her foulded armes that fprede
aboute hys necke he cafte awaye, and euer as he flede
 Death would I chufe, ere thou haft power of me quod he
whom fhe none other anfwere made, but thou haft power of me
 and after that wyth leues, fhe hid her fhamefaft face
wythin the woodes in hollow caues, maketh her dwellynge place,
 Yet loue dothe no whyt more decrefe, but wyth her fmarte
agmentith ftyll and watchynge cares, confumyth her wretched harte,

in Ouid of Narciſſus.

By lenenes eke her ſkyne is dryed, and to eare
her bloude confumeth, ſo hath ſhe nought, but voyce & bones to ſpare,
Whereof is nothinge lefte, but voyce for all her bones
they ſaye as to her lykeſte ſhape, were tourned into ſtones,
And ſence the woodes hath bene, her home her ſelfe to hyde
from euerye hyll and nought, but founde in her dothe none abyde
Thus here they other nymphes, of wooddes and waters borne
had he dyſceaued, and youngmen yeke, a nomber had in ſkorne,
At laſt wyth handes lyft vp, ſoone to the goddes dyd playne
that ſo hys hap myght be, to loue and not be loued agayne,
Wherto it ſemed wel, Ramuſya gaue eare
and ſought to graunte this iuſte requeſt, it after dyd appeare
A ſprynge there was ſo fayre, that ſtremes like ſyluer had
whiche nether ſhepardes happe to fynde, nor gotes that vpwarde gad
Uppon the rocky hyls, nor other kynde of beſte,
wyth flaſhing feete to foule the ſame, or troble at the leſte,
Wherein them ſelues to bathe, no byrdes had made repare,
nor leffe had fallen from any tree, the water to appeare,
About the which the grounde had made ſome herbes to growe
and eke the trees had kept the ſunne, from cōmynge doune ſo lowe
Narcyſſus theare through heate, and wery hunters game
glad to take reſt dyd lye hym downe, and faſt beheld the ſame,
And as he thought to drynke, hys feruent thurſte to ſlake
A dryer far deſyre hym toke, by lokyng in the lake
For ſeynge as he dranke, the image of hys grace
therewyth he rapt, fell ſtreyght in loue, wyth ſhadowe of his face
And muſeth at hym ſelfe, wyth whych aſtonyed cheare,
as image made of marble whyte, his countenance dyd apeare,
Lyke ſtarres he ſeyth hys eyes, and bacchus fyngeres ſwete
he thought he had on goulden heares, for Phebus not vnmete
A necke lyke yuery whyte, a mouth wyth fauoure good
a face wyth ſkynne as whyte as ſnowe, well coleryd wyth bloud

The Moralization of the Fable

All whych he wonders at, and that he lyketh well
is euen him felfe that wonder makes, with fmall aduice to dwell
 He fees that he doeth afke, agayne doth hym defyre
together he doeth burne him felfe, and kyndel eke the fyre
 The well that him dyfceaued, how ofte kyft he in vayne
howe ofte there in his armes he dround, in hope for to attayne
 The necke, that he defyred fo muche to imbrace
and yet himfelfe he could not catche, in that vnhappye place
 Not knowyng what he feeth, therewith he is in loue
and thofe fame eyes that, erroure blindes, to errour doth him moue
 Ah foole, why doeft thou feke, the fhape that wyll not byde
nor beyng hathe, for turne thy face, away and it wyll flyde
 The fhadowe of thy felfe, it is that thou doeft fee
and hath no fubftaunce of it felfe, but comes and bydes with thee
 Yf thou canfte go awaye, with thee it wyll departe
yet nether care for meate or flepe, could make him thus aftarte
 But in that fhadowe place, befyde the well he lyes
where he behelde his fayned fhape, with vncontented eyes
 And lyfting vp thofe eyes, that his, deftruction made
vnto the trees that ftode aboute, he raught his armes and faide
 Hath euer loue, oh woodes delte crueller with man
you knowe that hyding place, hath bene to louers now and than
 Now can you call to mynde, you that fuche worldes haue lafte
that euer anye pyned fo, by loue in ages pafte.
 I fee and lyke it well, but that I lyke and fee
yet fynde I not fuche errour loe, this loue doth bring to mee
 And to increafe my grefe, no fay nor yrkefome waye
no hylles nor valeys, with clofyd, gates, dothe faye our meting nay
 A lytle water here, dothe feuer vs in twayne,
he feketh I fee, that I defyre, to be imbraced as fayne,
 For looke how ofte my lippes, I moue to kyffe the lake
fo oft he fheweth his mouthe, content, full well the fame to take

in Ouid of Narciſſus.

To touche thee, might full well, a man wolde thinke be dime
it is the lefte of other thinges, that louers oughte to ſhine
What ſo thou be come forthe, why dofte thou me diſſeyue
why flyeſt thou hym, that the ſomuche, defyreth to receyue
My bewtie and mine age, truely me thynkes I ſe
it is not that thou dofte miſlyke, for nimphes haue loued me
Thou promyſte to me a hope, I wotnot howe
with friendly cheare, and to mine armes the ſame thou doſt vnbowe
Thou ſmyleſt when I laughe, and eke thy trekeling teares
when I doe weepe I ofte eſpy, with fines thy countenaunce ſteares
By mouing of thy lyppes, and as I ges I lerne
thou ſpeakeſt words, the ſence whereof, myne eares can not deferne
Euen this I am I ſe, my proper ſhape I knowe
wyth louing of my ſelfe, I borne I mone, & beare the glowe
What ſhall I doe, and if I aſke what ſhall I craue
aboundaunce brings me want, with me, it is that I would craue
Oh wolde to God I myght, departe my body fro
in hym loues this that wyſhe is ſtrang, hys lyking to for go
But nowe my ſtrength, throughe payne is fled, and my yeares
full ſone or lyke to ende, thus dethe away my youth it beares
Yet dethe that endeth my wooes, to me it is not ſo ſure
He whom I loue ryght fayne, I wold myght lyue alenger houre
Nowe to one quod he, together let vs dye
In euell eſtate and to his ſhape, returneth by and by
And wyth his guſſhynge tearys, ſo vp the water ſtarte
hys ſhape that therby darkened was, whiche when he ſawe departe
Nowe whether doſte thou go, abyde he cryed faſte
forſake not hym ſo cruelly, hys loue that on the caſt
Thoughe thee I may not touche, my ſorowes to aſſwage
yet maye I looke, relefe to geue vnto my wretched rage
And whyleſt he thus tormentes, he barred all his cheſte
before the well with ſtonye fyſtes, and beates his naked breſte

The Moralization of the Fable

With a carnacion hue, by ſtrockes thereon dyd leaue
none other wyſe then apples whyte, wyth ruddy ſydes receaue,
   Or as the growyng grapes, on ſundry cluſters ſtrepe
a purpyll coler as we ſe, or euer they be rype,
   Whyche as he dyd eſpye, wythin the water clere
no lenger coulde he duere the payne, he ſawe he ſuffred there.
   But as by fyre, to waxe ameltyng doth inſue
and as by hete the ryſing ſunne, conſumeth the mornynge due,
   So feblyd by loue, to waſte he doth begynne
at lenght and quyte conſumeth, by heate of hydyng fyre wythin,
   And nether hath he nowe, heare of red and whyte
no lyuelynes nor luſty ſtrength, that earſt dyd eyes delyte
   Nor yet the corpys remaynes, that Ecco once had loued
whiche tho wyth angry mynd ſhe vewed, to ſorow ſhe was moued,
   And loke howe ofte alas, out of hys mouth dyd paſſe
ſo ofte agayne wyth boundyng wordes, ſhe cryed alas alas,
   And when that he hys ſydes, wyth rechles handes dyd ſtryke
ſhe alſo then was hard to make, a ſounde lamentynge lyke
   Thus lokyng in the well, the laſt he ſpake was thys
alas thou ladde to much in vayne, beloued of me a mys,
   Whych ſelfe ſame wordes a gayne, this Ecco ſtreight dyd yell
and as Narciſſus toke hys leue, ſhe bad hym eke fayre well
   Hys hed that hym abuſed, vnder the graſſe he thraſte
and deth ſhut vp thoſe eyes, that on there maſter muſed faſte
   And when he was receyued, into that hyllye place
be yeke wythin the ogly ſtype, behelde hys wretched face
   The wood and wattrye nimphes, that all hys ſuſterne were
bewayles hys lot as is ther wonte, wyth cuttynge of theyr heare
   Whoſe waylinge Eccoes ſounde dyd mournyng lyke declare
for graue pompe, a bayre wyth lyghtes and fyre they dyd prepare
   Then body was ther none, but growing on the ground
a yelowe flower wyth lylly leaues, in ſted therof they founde.

                FINIS. *FABVLE.*

❡ THE MORALIZATION OF THE FABLE IN OUID OF NARCISSUS.

 Tale wherein some wyſdome may be founde
May be alowed, of ſuch as lyes refuſe,
Hereon I meane not, that my wytte can grounde
A matter fytte for all menne to vſe,
The prayſe hereof I vtterly refuſe,
And humbly them beſeche to reade the ſame,
Me to excuſe or by theyr Judgement blame.

  For neither I preſume, by youthfull yeares,   The vm-
To clayme the ſkyl that elder folkes, doe wante,   belnes of
Nor vndertake that wyſer often feares,   yᵉ author.
To venter on my ſpites, then would pante
Right well I knowe, my wyttes be all to ſkante
But I by your correction, meane to trye,
If that my head to reaſon can applye.

  I meane to ſhewe, according to my wytte   To ſuche
That Ouyd by this tale no follye mente   as inbra-
But ſoughte to ſhewe, the doynges far vnfytte   ſe not kno-
Of soundrye folke, whome natuer gyftes hath lente,   lege.
In dyuers wyſe to vſe, wyth good in tente
And howe the bownty torneth to theyr payne
That lacke the knowledge, of ſo good a gayne.

The Moralization of the Fable

Profitable coūfel.

Whiche Ouid now this Poete fure deuine
Doth collour in fo wonderfull a forte
That fuche as twyfe, refufe to reade a lyne
Wyth good aduice, to make their wytte reforte
To reafons schole, their Leffons to reporte
Shall neuer gather Ouids meanyng ftraunge
That wyfdome hydeth, with fome pleafaunt chaunge.

Hys tales doe Joyne, in fuche a godly wyfe,
That one doth hange vpon a nothers ende,
As who fhould faye, a man fhould not defpyfe,
To loke before whiche waye hys worke wyll bende
And after howe he maye the fame amende
Thus Ouid bydes hys readers for to knowe
The thynges aboue as well as thofe belowe.

The fable that he tretyd of before
Is howe that Juno fell in argumente
Wyth Jupiter, which after leafuer more
To wryte at lardge, then tyme conueniente
For fouche acaufe haue in defferente
But to be fhorte, Tericious was theyr iudge
Whofe fentence Juno femed for to grudge

For fhe becaufe he fayde not as fhe wolde
Bereft him of his eyes and made him blinde
As one vnfitt to vew the worlde that coulde
No better Judge vnto a womans mynde
Redres where of none Jupiter colde find
But with fome honour to releue his wooe
Eche thinge to come he made him surely knowe.

in Ouid of Narciſſus.

The formeſte profe, where of in this same tale
Lireope, the nymphe receued now
That dyd demaunde an anſwere not to fayle
If that her Childe, to home her lykinge vowe
Euen at the fyrſte was geuen him to allowe
Shoulde not parfite years, and manie growe
Yea yea quod, he him ſelfe yf he not knowe.

Here as I ſayd, appearith that the ende
Of euery tale another doth begynne
Here lykewiſe may we ſe the poette, bende
To byd vs loke his meaninge here with in
Suppoſinge that, ther wittes be verye thin
That will be bolde the ſkabard of the blade
And not the knife wherfore the ſhethe was made.

Deſſerne the truth of euery thynge.

For if that Ovids meaninge was to wryghte
But how Narciſſus, drinkinge of a wel
With ſhade of him ſelfe dyd ſo delyghte
That there til deth he thoughte to ſtarue and dwell
Bothe him a foole, a ly in verſe to tell
The wiſe mighte think, and thoſe that rede the ſame
To be vnwyſe and merite greatier blame.

The torninge of Lycaon to a, beaſt
Doth well declare that to the wicked sorte
Full heneous plagis preparid be at leaſte
Of god that to ther doinges will reſorte
With Juſtice hande at home they cannot ſporte
But yf they seke for to withſtande his wyll
They finde to worke them ſelues a waye to ſpill.

God puniſheth for ſinne.

The Moralization of the Fable

God preserueth the Juste.

By sayinge eke, of Pirha, and her make
Dengalyon from the confuming floude
What elfe is mente but god a boue dothe take
An order euer to prefarue the good
From perill ftill, in timis that they be woode
That few or none but fouche as god doth chufe
Can happie lyue, or them from harme excufe.

A prayfe of verginite.

And Daphus chaunginge to the laurer grene
Whofe leues in winter neuer lofte there hue
Doth well to vs betoken as I wene
That fouche as to virgynitie be true
Mortall glorye euer fhall enfue
And as the laurer lyues in winters rage
So fhall ther prayfe though death deuour there age.

A good warning to yonge people.

Of Pheton eke Appolles wretched fonne
That wolde prefume his fathers carte to gyde
Of corage more, then counsell wel begonne
What may be thoughte, but fouche as will a byde
With small aduice not from there will to flyde
And do refufe ther fathers councel fuer
There helpeles harmis, vnto them felues procuer.

The hede wyfdome of the poetes.

What nedyth me examples to reherfe
Sith I do take an other thinge in hande
Thefe fhewe that poetties colour vnder verfe
Souch wyfdome as they can not vnderstande
That lyghtelye lyft to loke on lernynges lande
But fuche as wyth aduyce, wyll vewe the fame
Shall leffons fynde therby, ther lyues to frame.

in Ouid of Narciſſus.

And now to tourne vnto the tale I meane
To treate vppon when that the dome was rede,
Of this Cephicious ſonne, by one that cleane
Had loſt the ſyght of all that nature brede
A vayne pronounce, it ſemed that he ſprede
Whoſe ſentence hym ſelfe, dyd not know
To perfyght age hys lyfe he ſhall beſtowe.

Tericias heare whome maye we lyke vnto
Euen ſuche a man, as hath no mynde to gayne
Wyth ryghteus lyppes, that ſeke no wronge to do
That yelde to ryches, for no maner of payne
Ne yet the truthe in anye thinge wyll layne
Which ſhall as he was blynde for Juſtice ſake
Be quyte berefte of all that he can make.

Happy ar they that do soo.

For he that wylnot Junoſe ſeruaunte be
I meane not now the pleaſyng of the ſtoute
And myghty dames that wolde haue all agre
Unto theyr fancees that they go aboute
But he I ſaye, and profe doth put no doute
That wyl not ſeke the ryche foulke to pleaſe
Through hate and wronge, hath often lyttle eaſe.

Truth is often ſhente.

Yet when they lacke this vſe of worldely ſyghte
That lyttel haue they lefte on erthe to ſee
And that by wronge another hath theyr ryghte
Bycauſe to wyll, ther wyttes wolde not agre
By loſſe herof they got a greater fee
For god of good doth gyue the knowledge more
Then all the gayne of erthe coulde the reſtore.

The Moralization of the Fable

<table>
<tr><td>The cars of the worlde letteth vertue.</td><td>

For wher theyr eyes be cafte from worldely welth
And haue refpecte to thynges that be aboue
In moche more perfecte wyfe the certayne helthe
Shall they dyfcerne, then fouche as haue a loue
To vayne defyers that ryfe for to remoue
And forther be they a byll to a vowe
Of hydden thinges then worldlye folke alowe.
</td></tr>
<tr><td>The folifh people regard no vertu nor good coūfell.</td><td>

But as Teryffus Judgemente femed vayne
In the foreredyng of Narcyffus fate
So folyfhe folke, from credyt wyll refrayne
Of wyfdomes voice, that feldome comes to late
They only marke, the prefente erthely ftate
Without regarde of anye thynge at all
What in this lyfe or after may befaule.
</td></tr>
<tr><td>Profecies be doughtful to medell with all.</td><td>

And yeke agayne regarde how Ouid heare
Of prophecies doth fhow the doughtefulnes
Whofe meanynge neuer playnely doth appeare
In doughtefull wordes that hath a hid pretence
Wheron we geffe, but greate experience
Full ofte we fynde and prouynge of the fame
Doth well declare our iudgementes be by ame.
</td></tr>
<tr><td>We mufte refer thofe thynges yt paffeth our knowledge.</td><td>

Wherfore we nether oughte to make to lyghte
By the depining of a fkylfull voyce
Nor yet prefume to fare aboue oure myght
As of the certayne fkanning to reioyce
Of hedden thinges that reche beyonde our choyfe
For who can furely fay it will be fo
Or dyffaloue the thinge they do not knowe.
</td></tr>
</table>

in Ouid of Narciſſus.

Tericyas voice dyd Pentheus deſpyſe
In countynge faulſe the thynges that he foreſawe
Yet of his deth they geſſe dyd ſeme to wyſe
Which he for tould by hys deuininge law
And Pirechus iugemente yeke appeared vayne
That wolde preſume of dowtfull ſpeche to make
A certayne ſence the meaning to myſtake.

   So that herby righte well we may regarde   People to
What happe they haue that worke by doughteful geſſe   take on them yt
To ſkorninge folke, & yeke the euile rewarde   yt paſſeth
That often faulyth the poete doth expreſſe   there know-
Thus two extremes he teachis to redreſſe   ledge.
And by Narciſſus warnith vs to be ware
Of the miſhap, that pride doth ſtill repare.

   For wel Narciſſus may betoken here
Souche one as hath that other members wante
As ſtrengthe and power a cauſe of weakers feare   Pride mar-
A paſſing witte aboue the ingnoraunte   reth al.
Of beughtie ffayer in riches nothinge ſkante
And to conclude frome chefe of natuers packe
That hath the choyſe that other thouſandes lacke.

   Who beinge decked with ſo goodlye giftes
Shall haue a nomber that will moche requier
Of the acquayntaunce, for the diuers dreſtes
Which fancie craueth to content deſyre
But yf he haue the ſame a buſyd fyer
That this Cephicious ſonne did her receaue
Exampile take him ſelfe he ſhall deſceaue.

The Moralization of the Fable

<small>A proude harte cōmeth to confuciō.</small>

  The man that thinkes him felfe to haue no make
Eche offred frendefhip, ftreighte, will quite refufe
For fo narciffus carid not to take
The felowefhip of fouch as fought to chufe
His companie a boue the refte to vfe
But as by pride he grwe in great difdayne
So for rewarde his ende was full of payne.

<small>That rich is and bewty be vayne.</small>

  Whofe ftrengthe is fouche that it can moch preuayle
Yet cannot faye, I am the moofte of ryghte
Whofe heapis of golde, be of foul hyghe a vayle
Yet nede not brage, to be the ritcheft wight
Whofe bewghtie yeke full pleafaunte is in fyghte
Yet hath no caufe to faye aboue the refte
I all dyfpice for natuer made me befte.

<small>A notabill exiāpell for proude people.</small>

  No Cretuer hath euer yet bene foche
That can iuftely faye, I mofte excell
God thought here of the pride was verye moche
When Lucyfer he cafte from heauen to hell
In fhowynge wher prefuminge folkys fhould dwell
None oughte to trufte to ryches or to ftrengthe
To power or bewtye, all confumith at lengthe.

<small>To the ryche or dyfdainfull man.</small>

  The Ryche, and proude, dyfdaynefull welthye man
That Lazarus forbad, the crommes to eate
Whiche from his borde fhoulde fall mighte after ban
His mouche a boundaunce and his dentye meate
Which was the caufe of all his torment greate
Yet yf he coulde haue vfed well his gayne
He lyttel fhoulde haue had of all his payne.

in Ouid of Narciſſus.

Now Creſſus yeke, the welthy kinge of Lide   Marke thys.
Whoſe ſoms of goulde wer paſſinge to be toulde
Dyd ſe at laſte his ritches wolde not byde
As Solon ſayde his ende that did be houlde
Wherfor we proue, who potteth ther truſte in golde
Or ſlypper welthe ar ſene in care to dwell
And loſe at laſte, the good they like ſo well.

Of ſtrengthe agayne, who will him ſelfe auaunce   No man oughte to truſte in his owne ſtrength.
ſhall ſe that conqueſte goes not all by myghte
This Dauid made the Phelyſtians, to graunte
That ſlue there giaunte Golyas ther kinghte
Agaynſte the which noman the thought to wyghte
For al his pride yet ſawe they at the laſte
Him ouer throwe and ded by Dauydes caſte.

Nowe Sampſons ſtrengthe that cauſed all this wooe   A notabell exſampell for the hy mynded.
I euer pas & Miloes mighte ſo ſtraunge
That coulde induer a forlonge wel to go
And on his backe an oxe to beare the raung
For all his mighte to weke eſtate did chaunge
When that his ſtrengthe did bringe his latter oure
To ſhow the ende of myght and mortall power.

Senacharyb the ſtronge aſſyryan kynge
Dyd put his whole affyaunce in his power
Yet Ezechias, prayers good dyd brynge   God is ye geuer of vyctorye.
His ſore deſtruction in a ſoden ower
By myghte the Angell, dyd hys hoſte deuower
Wyth death where by Senacharib, myght knowe
That God full ſoone, his might could make full lowe.

The Moralization of the Fable

<small>many pro-
fytable ex-
famples.</small>

    Darius flighte, which Ferres ouer throwe
And Terus flaughter, by the Siciɗthian Quene
Be fytt examples, for to let vs knowe,
That who to power, wyll put their truft and wene
By onely might to vanquyfhe, all befene
Of this their purpofe oftentymes to fele
When fortune lyft to turne her happie whele.

<small>Pryde is
the deftro-
yer of ma-
ny good
gyftes.</small>

    That bewties babes, mufte bide the hard prepare
That ofte is fente, to bate their Iolye chere
Emonge the refte, doth Abfalon declare
When not wythftanding, all his bewtie clere
And eke his fayre and yelowe golden heare
Betwene the bowes dyd hange, tyl that hys foes
Wyth deathes defpatche, dyd ryd hym of his wooes.

<small>The tran-
fitory thi-
ges of this
world are
not to be
truftyd.</small>

    The forowes greate, of Menelawes wyfe
Whofe bewtie fayre, fo farre to fe was fought
The wretched ende, of Cleopatres lyfe
Whofe ryche araye, was all to derely bought
Dothe plainly fhewe, that all was vaine and nought
Thus riches ftrengthe and power, confeffe we mufte
Wyth bewtie eke, to flypper be to trufte.

    Agayne we fe, eche mortall thynge decaye
A damage by dyfpleafure, hath the ryche
And bewties blomis, full fone are blowne awaye
The ftronge by fyckenes, feles a feble ftitche
From wele to woe, thus by promyfe pytche
Our tyme is tofte, with fuche vnfuerties change
As to beholde, aduice maye thinke full ftrange.

in Ouid of Narcissus.

Yet some ther be so pouffed vp with pride   *Disdayn-*
And as Narcissus, drouned in dysdayne   *fullnes*
That lyghte regarde they haue what will abide   *and ora-*
So farre vn ware of ther in suing paine   *bell vice.*
Of other folke vnreakinge they remayne
As tho they thoughte, who wothie wer to be
A mate sulmete, & felowe fite for me.

To whome it happes as to Cephicious sonne
It chaunced her which Ecco did dyspise
The caulinge nimphe which ernist loue begonne
In hastie sorte dyd ende in wofull wise
Not muche vnlyke the vayne desyers that rise
By fruteles thoughts to get some solyshe thinge
Which harme, or else repentance farre will bring.

But by thys fable some there be suppose   *A flaterar*
That Ouyd mente to showe the fauinge sorte   *is not to*
Of flattringe folke whose vsage is to glose   *be trus-*
With prayers swete, the men of gretiest, porte   *ted.*
And moste of welthe to whome the still resorte
In hope of gete, refusing nought to lye
The ende of speche as Ecco they applye.

For yf the men by whome they wane to gayne   *No man*
shall saye me thinketh that this is verye well   *shal learn*
Euen verye well they aunswer strayght agayne   *the truth*
As tho aduice had byd them so to tell   *of a flate-*
When verye nought they same mighte, reason spell   *rar.*
The ende of euerye fortunes darlinges voice
Thus they repete without a forther choyse.

The Moralization of the Fable

The con-
dycyons
of a flate-
rar.

Nowe yf a tiraunte faye it fhall be fo
None other thinge but fo they haue to fpeake
Although it tourne a thoufande vnto wooe
The ftrong maye floupe to wracke maye goo the weke
So they the Riche, maye pleafe they nothinge racke
The fame, they faye, they aunfwer after warde
As though it twife were worthye to be harde.

Bocas a
wryter of
this fame.

And lefte I feme to ouerfkippe the fence
Of anye wryghter worthye to be knowne
Wherby the poettes wife and hid pretence
With other wittes by trauell greate, great hath fowne
To fhowe what good of Ouides feede, is growen
Through my defaute may fkanned be a myffe,
Uppon this fable, Bocafe wryghtethe this.

By Ecco whiche dothe, fpoken wordes repleate
And els is dome, I faine doo vnderftande
That mortaule folke dothe loue with feruente heate
And foloweth fafte, in euery plafe and lande
As thinges wheron, her beinge all dothe ftande
And yet the fame a nomber will forfake
And lyghte efteme for folyfhe pleafures fake.

Within whofe well of fhininge, gaye delyghtes
That we maye lyke vnto a water coulde
That flydynge is fome time as Bocafe, wryghtes
Them felues that is, ther glorye, they be holde
And are fo fure in lufte and pleafure coulde
That rapte therewith not abyll to aftarte
From thenfe they be or from ther madnes parte.

in Ouid of Narcissus.

 And there at Laste, they dye which shame forsoke   Fame o-
That them somoche desyred to embrace   ther good
Whose lyfe so loste, for lyttell prayse dyd loke   or euell.
Of vertuse voyce, that bydes in euerye place
And byddeth fame to euery Coste to chafe
There prayses greate that cause well deserue
Not with there Corpis to let, there name to starue.

 But suche as, will make lyght the loue, of fame
For Lycorous luste, that lyketh them so well
By good desarties, and rekes for no good name
Howe muche in wytte, or beughtie they excell
Howe stronge or ryche so euer they shall dwell
Ther deinty ioyes, there body name and all
They lose at ones, which dethe ther lyfe, dothe call.

 And yf pare happes, that natuer dyd bestowe
More good of them in lyfe then of the reste
And that ther by there some remembraunce growe
Of natuers bountye, gyuen them for the beste
Euen lyke a fadinge flower, this flytinge geste
I maye recimbell, which is freshe to daye
And yet or night is wetherid clene awaye.

 What Bocas mente thus somwhat haue I toulde   Of youth
The skanninge to of others ges herein   full tyme
I haue and will at laste at large vnfoulde   yll spent.
But where I left, nowe fyrste I will begynne
To showe howe moche the hastye sorte shall winne
By there dysdayne, the which Narcissus here
Dothe represente to me as dothe appeare.

The Moralization of the Fable

For fyrſte who was his bewtye and his ſhape
There with and notes of others his dysdayne
And then ſhall marke of his ende and his myſhape
Who blinded was with his to good a gayne
As in a glaſſe ſhall ſe the picture playne
Of a full proude and ouer weninge wyghte
That natures gyftes dyſdayne to vſe arighte.

And ſythe I haue declared here before
What lyttell truſte, of ryghte we ought to haue
To that, whiche we receue, for to reſtore
To hym that firſte our pleaſynge treaſures gaue
To ſuer to Ioye but when he lyſte to craue
The good he ſente the ſame he takyth a waye
Or we be ware, our hap ſo ſoone decaye.

Nowe wyll I ſhowe that erſte I ſayd I wolde
Of this ſame talke in ſome Comparing ſorte
What I conceue, the whiche not as I ſholde
Yf I declare, and that my wittes reſorte
Without the reche of wiſdomes ſober porte
Nowe of the learned I doo craue
And of my Iudgmente here the ſence you haue.

I fayne a man, to haue a godly wytte
The ſelfe ſame yeares that this Narciſſus hade
With lyke dyſdayne of others farre vnfytt
And then immagin one that wolde be glade
With counſayle good to cauſe him for to knowe
To make his witte bothe ſober wiſe and ſade
That prides rewarde is to be made ful lowe.

in Ouid of Narciſſus.

And thiſſame one I, Ecco preſuppoſe
By whome I geſſe that good aduice is mente
Whiche is ful lothe a godly witte to loſe
And forye moche to ſe the ſame yl spente
She foloweth him therfore for this intente
To make him marke and well regarde the ende
Of euerye thinge that he dothe once intende.

    Her nature is not to be full of talke   To ſuche
Not to deuice, but to aduice full well   as ſpeke
                                                                                                                                                       with out
wordyes yᵗ ſpringe frō youthefull thoughtes at walke   ad viſe
Not greinge ſtill to reaſons ſober ſpelle   mente.
The endinge ſence whereof ſhe aye doth yel
As who ſhoulde ſaye we ought to regarde the cauſe
And ende of ſpeche ofte ſpoke with lyttel, pauſe.

    For ſythe eche wordys and doinge oughte of righte
To be refarred vnto ſome reaſons ende
With out reſpecte, whereof lyttel mighte
Our doinges reſte which to no purpoſe bende
To ſharpiſte wittes, aduice, her loue douth ſende
As fyttiſte foulkes, to gayne her greate good will
If they receyue the good, ſhe profers ſtil.

    Nowe howe ſhe waues this man, that hath this witte
I nede not tell, ſyth Ouyd doth declare
But hym ſhe foloweth as ſhe thinkes it fitte
Tell that ſhe ſe him, voyde, of wanton care
To ſhape an aunſwere then ſhe dothe prepare
To euerye cencethat he ſhall ſpeake or ſounde
To cauſe him marke therof the certayne grounde.

The Moralization of the Fable

To fuche
as geue
them fel-
ues ouer
to pleafur
of vanites.

The ende of euerye fence fhe repetis
Where by for what he fpake he maye deferne
But he that on the vaynes of plefuer beatis
His wanton fhippe without aftedye ftarne
Of good aduice fhall nothynge racke to learne
But her refufe when fhe wolde him imbrace
Affection fo a waye doth reafon chafe.

Wytte
well vfed
mofte ne-
des be pro-
fitabell.

So this fame man whome nature witte hath lente
A vertue greate to them that vfe it well
Aduice, perhappes canne be contente
To heare and lyften what her wordes can fpell
But when he once efpies fhe thinketh to dwell
Contenually with him to be his make
Here offrid frendefhippe ftrayght he doth forfake.

To lyue by loffe his good he doth refufe
Unbrydelyd will oh whether wilte thou trayne
This wandring witte that hath no power to chufe
The reddye waye to fouche a perfite gayne
But as the blynde to paffage right, dothe paine
Him felfe no more then when he goith amis
To winne thy woys afmouche thy trauayle is.

Pryde is
a vayne
thinge.

But whye accaufe I will that maye be charmed
By good aduice yf thou haddefte not dyfdayne
Thy pride, thy pryde, hath worfte of all the harmed
That poufes the vp vppon prefumcions vayne
Whiche maketh thofe, continue, that wold be fayne
Of thy good will to make thy wittes full wife
Whofe loue thou hafte, the proffet to defpife.

in Ouid of Narcissus.

    This witte refusing good aduice loue
And wandringe faste to willes vncertayne reach
Dothe let her starne, that sought a waye to moue
Then happye ende that profe doth planelye teache
Is full prepared, dysdaynefull folke to appeache
Whose pride is souche as puttes a waye the sighte
Of counsayle good and euerye iugement righte.

To suche as dysdaynes good counsayl.

    And so aduice I leue forsaken quite
As Ecco was for all her greate good will
And will declare, wittes rashe and madd dyspite
Of suche a frende neglect for lacke of skyll
Wherby he faste procures him selfe to spill
As one vnware, of all his wooes to come
Whose reckles lyfe receueth a wretched dome.

    A careles lyfe thus led in youthfull yeares
A wilfull waye be semeth well to take
So this same witte as wilde desyer him steres
Unconstantely, for luste and pleasures sake
From this to that his vayne inuenciones wake
A resteles time in nedeles worke doth spende
Till that hereof he findes the folyshe, ende.

    Then werye quite of all this wanton sporte
And trustinge moche to tast a more stabyll drynke
To prayse well bycause he dothe resorte
Whereby mishappe, he rather comes I thynke
Whose pleasaunte fare, and swete delyghtinge drinke
Who shall approche will thinke a thousand yeare
Tyll they haue sene there, in the water cleare.

The Moralization of the Fable

Which hath in it no foule nor oglye fyghte
Nor lothfome lokiynge ther a bate to ftande
The filuer ftreames fo fhininge be and brighte
As can delyghte the greateft lorde in lande
The Ladys yeke full fayer wyth hande in hande
Will fafte repare vnto this pleafaunte well
Wherewith aduice, I wyfhe them all to dwell.

Whiche for bycaufe that witte dyd quite dyfpyfe
Nowe marke his harme, and harde predeftenid woo
This well he fafte behouldes in mufynge wife
And lyes to drinke where more his thurfte dothe growe
A laffe for that him felfe he doth not knowe
For ther he feethe the image of his grace
Hys fhape and yeke proporcion of his face.

His wittes his ftrengthe and euerye other gyfte
That maye be thoughte a vertue anye waye
Appeareth therwith euerye fondrye fhifte
That nature fendeth to make the carkes gaye
And yeke that Fortune lendes for eche affaye
There nought is hid that is worthye prayfe to pyke
Nor ought is fene, that men might well miflike.

Where on they fafter that his eyes be cafte
There at the more his maruell doth increace
And yeke the more his maruel thus doth lafte
The leffe he fekes his blinde defyer to ceafe
Which for fyth loue to putte him felfe in prefe
To lyke the thyng that better ware to lacke
Then by fouche loue to bringe him felfe to wracke.

in Ouid of Narciſſus.

For who ſo Couettes that he cannot catche
And moſte aloweth that nedyth mooſte amendes
With ſo good will, and ſtill defyres to watche
Suche wretched Joyes a corſid, lyfe that ſpendeth
As profe doth teache vnto dyſtruccion bendes
Delyted ſo with that he ſhoulde refuſe
And quite for ſakinge that he oughte to chuſe.

But of his loue ſuche is the blynde, reſpecte
And ſuche the ſwete, delightinge wretched plighte
That his a vaile he blyndelye doth neglecte
To helpe him ſelfe as one that hath no mighte
So rauiſhed is he with the pleaſinge ſighte
Of that to him whiche lyttell pleaſure gaynes
Unleſſe we counte the wynning good of paynes.

For in this well to well he vewes the forme
Of euerye gyfte, and grace that nature gaue
To hym for that he chefelye ſhoulde perfourme
With good, moche good, his good therby to ſaué
Yet be his good, as ſure is euel to haue
He gaynis the loſſe that other neuer fele
Which haue not wone ſuche welthe by fortunes whele.

And whye bycauſe he demes not as he oughte   There
Eche vertue lyketh value of the ſame   be to ma-
His face, the beſte that euer was wrought   ny ſuche.
And ſhape he thinkes deſerueth no maner blame
By wytte he wennes ful wyunderus thinges to frame
And what he hathe he thinkes all the beſte
Beſyds him ſelfe difpicinge all the reſte.

The Moralization of the Fable

All though in dede, he nether be fo fayer
So well proporſinid, nor fo fuerlye wife
Ne yet in ſtrengthe, be abyll to compayre
With halfe the nomber that he dyd dyſpiſe
Aboue them al he thinkes him felfe to priſe,
Whiche ouer weninge, wins him all his wooe
A ſimpyll gayne I count, that hurtes me fo.

To fuche
as flatter
thē ſelues.

For rapte fo faſte, through his abuſed eyes
Euen on him felfe, whereof he doth delighte
With in this well no fautes he euer ſpies
Whereby him felfe he anye waye might ſpite
But as eche face appearithe, fayre & quyte
Thoughe it be foule with in the flatringe glas
This lyinge lake, ſhewes euerye gyfte to paſſe.

Wherto he ſtrayght confentes by Judgemente blind
And grauntes to haue asmuch as femeth, and more
So eaſye lo, felfe loue is nowe to kinde
So fome is had, fo fwete agreuous fore
So glade he is to kepe his harmis in ſtore
So moche defyrous for to abyde his woo
And yeke fo lothe his mifchefe to for goo.

Which cauſith this, bycauſe of natuere all
Be pleaſed well, well of them felues to here
And yet the wyfe, with good aduice will calle
Unto them felues yf they, deferue to beare
The prayſys greate which feme fo true & cleare
By others mouthes whiche euer taulke the beſte
Of them they fe, in good eſtate to reſte.

in Ouid of Narciſſus.

Now witte that wantes all that wiſdome willes
The wiſe to haue is voyd of this reſpecte
For what he hath he thinkes it greatlye ſkylles
But what he is, the whylſt he dothe neglecte
Thus Joye to haue, ſo mouche doth him infecte
That care to be, ſo good as he appeares
He quite forſaketh, ſo blyndely loue him bleres.

Through which he loſythe euerye verteous ſtrengthe
And lackes the ſkyl, ſo godlye gyftes to vſe
So euery good doth tourne to bade at lengthe
And he conſumeth, him ſelfe that doth abuſe
This lot is ſente to him that will refuſe
Aduices loue, to lyghte on prayſeth well
Wher tyll he ſtarue he ſtill delytes to dwell.

To ſtarue I meane, the good he hath to loſe
To whiche I thinke him ſelfe he ſuer doth binde
That of him ſelfe more good doth preſuppoſe
By lokinge in this preſent well ſo blinde
Them in him ſelfe a wiſer man can finde
For who dothe couet him ſelfe of wiſer ſkole
Then dedes him ſhowe, doth proue him ſelfe a fole.

Who thinkes he hath more then he doth poſſes
In this not only is dyſſeued quite
But hath ſo moche of that he hath the leſſe
Of wit I meane, wherin who ſhall delyghte
More then he oughte him ſelfe doth this dyſpite
Un wittinge clene, the more he thinkes he hathe
Euen by ſomoche, hath leſſe as Plato ſayth.

The Moralization of the Fable

Suche as thinkes them felues wife and yet ar folyſh.

    So he that demes, his witte aboue the reſte
So moche the leſſe, then others, hath here by
And he that thinkes, his one of all the beſte
The worſte of all it reaſon will replye
Al though the ſame he neuer can eſpie
Bycauſe he truſteth the lyinge well of prayſe
Whereby his wit and all he hath decayes.

    For ſyth, the well of prayſe, as well conſteſſe
Uppon the ſpringes of vnaduiſed talke
As of the voyce of wiſdome, that reſiſtes
The ſpeches of foolys, whoſe tonges a wrye will walke
Beſydes the pathe, of reaſons, gidinge balke
It maye welbe that ſuche them ſelues dyſſeaue
As of vntrouth, a certayne truthes conſeue.

We muſt not truſte our owne wittes heſte.

    Thus what hath made, this witte to ſtarue we ſe
Selfe loue the very hid conſuming ſore
Of godly wittes, that elſe could well agre
To euery ſence of wiſdoms preſent lore
And now to ſhowe the very cauſe wherfore
They loſe the ſtrength of this ſo good a gayne
And leue aduice, forſothe it is dyſdayne.

    This enuius heare, dyſdayne, this dayntie, thynge
When it begins to harbour, in thy breſte
Of anie man this harme it fyrſte doth bringe
Contempte of thoſe in better ſtate, that reſte
Then he is in, that counteth to be beſte
So that his faultes, who fayne wolde haue him knowe
And by his frende he countes him as his foe.

in Ouid of Narciſſus.

    Then of contemptes procedyth, hautye pride   *The con-*
The which who gettes ſhall neuer lyghtely leue   *temptes*
So grete an euel ſo faſte as ſene to byde   *of vertue*
Euen to the beſte when it beginneth to cleue   *commeth*
That honour, wit, or anie gyfte receue   *by pryde.*
This of dyſdayne, contempte, wherof procedes
The poyſon pride, this ſame ſelfe loue that bredes.

    Wherfore hereby I may conclude, a right   *All dyſ-*
That as contempte, dyd cauſe Narciſſus quayle   *dayne ful*
So by dyſdayne eche wyghte, doth loſe his myghte *folkes are*
And euery vertue through thiſſame, doth faile   *compared*
As well Narciſſus proueth in this ſame tale   *vnto Nar-*
Who loſte through loue eche thinge he mooſte dyd lyke *cyſſus.*
For his dyſdayn who worſe reuenge could pike.

    Can greter woo to anie man betide
Then that to loſe wherin he moſte delites
No ſuer and yet to ſyrcuyte and pride
This is the Juſte reuenge, that ſtill requites
Ther grete dyſdayne, and al ther oulde diſpites
To lacke of that, at laſte they lyke ſo well
Which wante aboundaunce, makes with them to dwel.

    This ſence is ſtraunge, & yet as true as quainte   *This is*
That plentie ſhoulde be cauſe of greter, lacke   *worthy*
A man in helthe can neuer, lyghtlye faynte   *to be*
The happye man no miſſery dothe ſmacke   *marked.*
The Riche, by ritches, feles no nedye, wracke
Agayne who ſittes in honours ſhyning chare
Is farre inough from wretched peoples ſhare.

The Moralization of the Fable

<small>A true saynge.</small>

 And what can happe, thus harme the happie man
Or can fuche welth, ther maifter bringe to woo
Can honors, forfe ther honors them to ban
Can all this good fo greue vs thus what no
Yes yes alas it proueth often fo
Of agis pafte exaumpils neuer grounde
Of thefe our dayes to manie may be founde.

<small>Honor & Ryches by godes good gyftes.</small>

 Be therfore al thefe godly gyftes to blame
Bycaufe they come to wracke that them poffeffe
Na to be ryche it is no maner fhame
Ne honour hurtis that helps to redres
The wronged foulke whome rigour doth oppres
Nor oughte is euel wherof the rightefull vfe
Who fhall obferue maye haue a Jufte excufe.

<small>Be ware of a buiynge honor and ryches.</small>

 But this aboundaunce who fhall euell abufe
And quite forget from whence thefe vertues flowe
The good they haue therby they quite refufe
And euery gyfte vnto agrefe fhall growe
Myfufe of good thus them fhall ouer throwe
Euen as Minaruais pipis that Marcias founde
Mifufed him harmed with fwetenes of the found.

 This Marcias, was a boyfterous country man
The pleafaunte pipes of pallafe once he founde
The which to blowe affone as he began
Euen of them felues dyd gyue fo fwete a founde
That better thoughte he not aboue the grounde
Wher in he ftrayghte dyd take fo grete a pride
As though his mouthe dyd al, this mufyke gyde.

162

in Ouid of Narciſſus.

Through whiche the muſys with ther armonye
He thoughte could not ſo ſwete a ſounde prepare
And eke Appollo god of melodye
He maye dyſſende doune from his ſhininge chare
Alſo with him preſuminge to compare
Full well contente to loſe his lyfe if he
Made not his pypes more ſwetely to agre.

Then muſikes god who ſeinge all his pride
Him fyrſte dyd farr excel in conning playe
And then to make him by his couenaunte, byde
He made the ſkyn, of all his bodye flaye
An euell rewarde for this his vayne aſſaye
Unhappye gyfte that gyues no better gayne
Naye folyſhe man, that gydes it to thye payne.

So that heareby I gather euerye gyfte   *Good gyf-*
Miſuſyde maye harme the honours of the ſame   *tes myſſe*
And though to ſome, that natures bountye lyfte   *vſed.*
A grace where of a nother ſhall be lame
This godly gefte, is not a whyte to blame
Although their honours through the ſame ſhall quayle
The rightefull vſe, that lacke, of ſouche a vayle.

For yf ſo be, that Marcias had knowen
That of him ſelfe, not all his conning came
He nether wolde haue ſtriuen to haue blowne
Ne yet preſumed to venter for the game
With him that was the auƈther of the ſame
If he had knowen howe, well to vſe this gaine
He it mighte well haue kepte & not bene flayne.

The Moralization of the Fable

<small>That deɪ dain is the deſtroyer of the wiſdome.</small>

    But who can knowe, that wil dyſdayne to learne
And who can lerne that reckes not to be taughte
So well to vſe his welthe who can deſerne
That this dyſdayne, this vename, greate, hath caughte
This ſame made Marcias, that he neuer raught
To knowe of whome his melodye dyd riſe
This made Narciſſus, Ecco yeke dyſpiſe.

    And to conclude this cauſyde, witte forſake
Aduice whoſe lacke, dyd loſe him all his gayne
For loke euen as Narciſſus by the lake
His beughtie loſte by bewtyes ſore dyſdayne
And that his profet purcheſte, all his payne
So witte, that hath dyſdayne, ſhall ſo preſume
That throughe his witte, his wit ſhall clene conſume.

<small>A good vſe of the Auꞓther.</small>

    Wherfore, this vice, that euerye vartue marres
That priuate weale, conuerts to preuate woo
That eche degre, ther rightefull dewtye bares
Who redyth, this tale, I wiſhe, ſo well mighte knowe
That in ther hartes, no ſede therof mighte growe
Where of eche, wighte deuoïde, by good aduiſe
Maye ryghtely vſe there gyftes of greatiſte priſe.

    Thus haue you harde the ſimpill ſence
That I haue gatherid by my ſymple witte
Of Ouides tale, whoſe wiſe & hid pretence
Though as I ſhoulde parhappes I haue not hitte
Yet as I could and as I thoughte it fitte
I haue declared, what I can conſeue
Full glade to learne, what wiſer folke parceaue.

in Ouid of Narciffus.

 And now to kepe my couenaunte & procede   Fyfius a
Of others Jugementes, to declare the fecte   writer of
Of thiffame tale, Ficius wrytes in dede   the fame.
A wife oppinion not to be neglecte
Of fouche affeme, to be of reafons fecte
The which I wolde not fkip emonge the refte
Leafte his Inuencion, fome maye thinke the befte.

 A rafhe mans minde, that hath no fkyl fayth he
By this Narciffus verye well is mente
His proper fhape, that hath no power to fe
That is the proper, office which is fente
Unto the minde, by no meane can conuente
To fe and marke, as eche man oughte of righte
And to performe accordinge to ther mighte.

 But as Narciffus, onlye dyd defyer
Hys fhadowe in the water to imbrace
So this fame minde dothe nothinge els requier
Of brittil bewtye, but to marke the cafe
That in the bodie hath the bydinge place
Which onlye is the fhadowe of the minde
As it mighte knowe in cafe it were not blinde.

 Thus minde, thus noughte defyringe, but his fhade
That is the beutie in the carcafe frayle
Not beinge abyl to deferne the trade
The which it oughte of righte for to affayle
Hereby forfaketh, quite the one a vayle
And lofyth bothe his proper fhape herein
And yeke his fhadowe hath no power to win.

The Moralization of the Fable

  For euery minde, becoms the bodys man
In fo louinge it, it felfe, dothe quite defpife
The boddys vfe, and yet it no waye can
Enioy and haue accordinge to the guife
And order due that natuer doth deuice
But thus doth both the bodys vfe myftake
And of it felfe the office true forfake.

<small>Better it is to haue the mynd garnifhed w^t vertu then a folyfhe bodi bewty ful.</small>

  The office of the minde is to haue power
Uppon the bodye, and to order well
The bodys office yeke in euery hower
It is of the minde to lerne the perfite fkyll
The vayne defyers that rife, him by to kill
Wherby the mynde dothe kepe his perfite ftrength
And yeke the bodye vanquifhe lofte at length.

  Now where the minde is drowned with defyre
Of fuche delyghtis as to the bodye longe
The boddye then mofte nedes confume with fyer
Of raginge luftes aboute the fame that thronge
So that the minde, is caufe of bothe ther wronge
To put it felfe, out of the proper place
And bringe the bodye, to fo euel a cafe.

<small>The mīd beynge replenyfhed with euyl bryn grth body & foule to confufion.</small>

  For thus the minde, that oughte of righte, to be
The teacher of the bodye to do well
Doth make the fame to euery euill agre
Procuringe that it fhoulde of right expell
Wherby in bothe, a mouinge blinde doth dwell
Euen as within Narcyffus dyd remayne
That through his fhadowe to be foche agayne.

in Ouid of Narciffus.

And as Narciffus, neuer coulde attayne
His fhadowe which he wiffhed for fo fafte
And that his loue dyd lede him to his payne
Euen fo thys minde that reafons bondes hath pafte
It felfe and from, the proper place hath cafte
Shall neuer gayne that it dothe mofte defyer
Suche is to folye ftyll the folowinge hire.

The rewarde of fuche as geue thē felues to vayne pleafurs.

    For thoughe it Couet moche, a fafe eftate
And feke it felfe to plante in perfite plighte
Yet this defyer, profedyth all to late
When will is bente, to loue vayne delight
Whofe rafhe regarde defcerns not blacke from whyte
Who wolde be well, worketh other wife
Of beinge well, the fuertie dothe defpife.

    And when this minde, hath wroughte fomoche amiffe
Thus blindely from his perfecte, place to fall
We mofte nedys graunte a kinde of dethe it is
A thinge deuine, and perfecte, to be thrall
Unto the carcas mofte corrupt of all
When this immortall minde, fhall feke to ferue
Eche mortall thinge, his vertue nedes mufte fterue.

    This is the meaninge of Ficius fence
That in this wife one Plato doth wryghte
And nowe to fhow, the learned mennes pretence
With Ouides tale the reders to delyghte
Two there were that fomewhat dyd indite
Of this fame fable, whiche I will declare
Leafte anye wryter I maye feme to fpare.

The Moralization of the Fable

The one hereof, afence deuine, doth make
No foole he femethe, that walles hath to name
And englyfhe man, whych thus doth vndertake
For fowles behoufe, to defkant on this fame
There by sayth he a nomber moche to blame
That as Narciffus, lettes there bewty quale
Becaufe they quite mifufe there good auayle.

For dyuers whych in bewty, much excell
Eyther infhape that in the bodys gyft
In knowledge elf whych in the mind, doth dwell
Or to conclude in ryches, which is lyft
To fundry men by fortunes hydynge fhyft
Before the fame fo puffed vp wyth pryde
That all, to bafe, they thynke with them to byde.

What then, to thys what is the due reward
Forfoth thefe derlynges wyth theyr great dyfdayne
Wythin the well of worldly wealth, regarde
Thyf fame apperaunce of their blyffull gayne
Whych laftith not, but as the fhadowe, vayne
Doth paffe a waye, euen fo doth come to goe
Eche thynge we haue the vfe affyrmeth fo.

Now in thys welle the apperaunce of theyr ftate
Doth them fo pleafe and eke fo well contente
That feynge it they nothynge elfe awaite
The nought can lowe they nothyng can confent
To prayfe or lyke but all to thys intente
Them felues, full farr aboue the reft aduaunce
And ftyll to glorye of there happye chaunce.

in Ouid of Narciſſus.

Thus through this glorye of ther lyfe to moche
The chefeſte lyfe, the lyfe of ſoules the loſe
There blinde deſyer and fonde regarde is ſoche
Them ſelues in all this daunger, for to cloſe
This Englyſhe wryter heare of doth thus ſuppoſe
The other nowe whome Italye dyd brede
As foloweth wrytes, to them that ſhall yet rede.

In Grece there was a paſſinge fayer yonge man
Whoſe beutye broughte him vnto ſuche a pride
That through theſſame vnto ſuch dyſdayne he ran
As but him ſelfe he none could well a bide
But counted other all as vile beſyde
Through which his ende was wretchedly to dye
With in the woodes to ſtarue and ther to lye.

A Learnyd man of Italye a writer of y^e ſame.

And wheras Oued, doth hereof affirme
That this Narciſſus, was tranſformed at laſte
Into a flower, he only doth confirme
That youth and bewghte, come and ſoone be paſte
Euen as the flower, that wetherithe full faſt
And for by cauſe, in wodes the nimphes do dwell
His deathe bewaylyd of them dothe Ouid tell.

Mannes lyfe is lyke a flowere.

Agayne where the poete dothe a vowe
That this Narciſſus dyed by a lake
It maye well be, by cauſe he dyd a lowe
None fette or worthye to become his make
But euery man deſpyſing, dyd for ſake
That ſome of hatrid and of malyce fell
For his dyſdayne dyd drowne him in a well.

The Moralization of the Fable

   Thus moche this fame Italyan wryter here
Doth finde as true, his wryghtinges do proffes
So it maye well be all that wrote appeare
Of this fame fable other more or leſſe
That ſtil dyſdayne doth cauſe the greter diſtres
Of euery good that natuers bountie gyues
To eche eſtate, vppon the yearthe that lyues.

   Wherfore who hath, no ſparckel of this vice
Are lyke to kendel in them ſelues no flame
Of anie euel but ſtyll by good aduice
Shall ſo them ſelues and all there doinges frame
As ſhall at all deſerue no maner blame
Whoe wantes this vice therby ſhall chefely ſtaye
To euerye euell the very reddy waye.

   Thus haue you harde what hath ben thought
By ſoundry folke, of thiſſame Ouides tale
Whereby I proue that al herin haue ſoughte
To ſhowe that Ouid wryt for good a vale
Declaringe howe they lykeſt ar to quayle
That greatyſt ſtore of anie good receyue
The ryghtful vſe therof and leaſte perceue.

   To moche poſſes ſo that it is no prayſe
But thynges poſſeſſed, ryghtfully to vſe
For each poſſeſcion, by and by decayes
And ſuche as by poſſeſcinge ſhall abuſe
All they poſſes, with ſhame, ſhall ſone refuſe
Wherfore the moſte, ar worthy to poſſes
Whoſe ſpotleſſe dedes, the rycheſt vſe expreſſe

in Ouid of Narciſſus.

And thus my ſimpel trauayle I commende
Unto euery one, prayinge you to take
The fame in worthe and when more yeares ſhall ſende
More wyt and yeke more knowledge ſhall awake
Suche labours lyke I mene not to forſake
As knoweth god who kepe vs alwaye
Saue and defend vs from all decaye.

F I N I S. Quod. T. H.

METAMORPHOSIS OUIDIANA

Moraliter a Magiſtro Thoma VValeys Anglico de profeſſione predicatorum ſub ſanctiſſimo patre dominico: explanata.

Uenundantur in edibus Franciſci Regnault : in vico ſancti Jacobi ſub interſignio ſancti Claudii commorantis.

Alia Editio.

METAMORPHOSIS OUIDIANA

Moraliter a Magiſtro Thoma Walleys Anglico de Profeſſione predicatorum ſub ſanctiſſimo patre Dominico : explanata.

Venundantur in Ædibus Aſcenſianis Johannis Parvi, et ſub Pellicano in vico Sancti Jacobi Parrhiſiis. 4to. 1511 ad Nonas Apriles.

METAMORPHOSEOS MORALISATE.

Liber tertius.   Fo. xxxvii.

FABULA XI.

Cum tyrefias daret refponfa veriffima petitum fuit fi filius Lyriopes nymphe, nomine narciffus qui erat puer pulcherrimus diu effet victurus: qui refpondit fic. Si fe non noverit inquit. Ac fi diceret quod diu erat victurus : dum tamen fuam formam et pulchritudinem non effet vifurus. Cum igitur narciffus a nymphis et puellis pluries effet requifitus, et omnes contemneret et de pulchritudine fuperbiret, ita quod echo nympham vociferam ipfum infequentem et eum alloqui cupientem, fed non valentem, eo cum loqui quod non poterat fed folum ad verba ultima refpondere, fugeret et ejus amorem penitus exhorreret: propter quod ipfa echo ex toto evanuiffet; et in vocem deceffiffet: factum eft quod idem narciffus quadam vice cum fatigatus effet; ad quendam clariffimum fontem veniffet, et bibere vellet, incepit vmbram fuam pulcherrimam refpicere : et fuam imaginem cepit tam ferventer amare: quod cum ipfam non poffet tangere; et pre amore vmbre recedere nollet, neceffe habuit ibi fame et inedia perire. Anima igitur ejus apud inferos fe in aquis ftigiis adhuc refpiciens mirabatur. Corpus autem ejus in florem purpureum eft converfum. Ovidius; nufquam corpus erat: croceum pro corpore florem Inveniunt foliis medium cingentibus albis. ¶ Revera talis fententia tyrefie quotidie verificatur in multis, quia multi funt qui fpiritualiter viverent fi fe et fuam pulchritudinem non viderent nec attenderent. Sed quia plerumque accidit quod quidam fumma pulchritudine vigent ita quod pulchritudinem corporis quantum ad formam, pulchritudinem anime quantum ad fcïentiam, pulchritudinem fortune quantum ad opulentiam magnam habent, ideo ipfi in fuperbiam elati omnes alios defpiciunt, nulliufque volunt focietatem aut copulam: immo alios indignos focietate et familiaritate fua credentes ipfos fatue vilipendunt. Quid igitur? Pro certo ifti in fonte mundane profperitatis videntes vmbram et eminentiam ftatus fui quæ omnia tranfeunt ficut vmbra.

Metamorphoseos Moralisate.

Sapientie V. Ita ferventer ipsam diligunt: et se in ea ita glorificant, quod anime vitam perdunt. Bonum igitur est quod homo se non videat: et quod ad suas naturales temporales et morales pulchritudines per complacentiam non respiciat ne ex hoc alios vilipendat. Et ideo bene commendatur ignorantia canticorum, i, vbi anime dicitur. Si ignoras te o pulchra inter mulieres egredere et abi: et sequitur. Pulchre sunt gene tue.

FABULA XII.

Echo fuit quedam nympha loquacissima, quæ Jovi in adulteriis favens quum nymphas in montibus opprimebat, Junonem Jovis uxorem, ne maritum in adulterio deprehenderet, in verbis Echo tenebat. Cum igitur fraudem Echûs Juno quadam die percepisset et se illusam ab ea cognovisset indignata est, ab ea garrulitatem abstulit et potestatem loquendi vel respondendi ipsi interdixit et quod solum ad ultima verba possit respondere licentiam ipsi dedit. Ex tunc igitur echo in silvis montibus et fluminibus habitavit, et quotiens ipsi aliquid dicitur quæ dicta sunt replicat. Corpore fuit privata, et in vocem tota mutata et ad resonandum in montibus ordinata. Ista igitur est vox quæ in montibus et silvis auditur quando aliquid dicitur aut clamatur.

¶ Dic quod echo significat adulatores qui et montes i. prælatos; silvas, i. religiosos: flumina, i. seculares et delicatos frequentant, et circa ipsos resonant, et clamant: si enim contingat aliquid ab aliquo dici statim solent ad verba ipsius respondere: et verbum ejus tanquam benedictum replicare. Vnde textus, Hec in fine loquendi Ingeminat voces; auditaque verba reportat. Eccle. xiii. Dives locutus est, et omnes tacuerunt; et verbum illius usque ad nubes produxerunt. ¶ Vel dic quod tales echo sunt quædam litigiose et brigose mulieres, vel etiam quidam servitores queruli qui ultimum verbum semper volunt habere: et ad omnia quæ dicuntur a maritis atque Dominis respondere. Et si ab eis reprehenduntur semper murmurant. Contra illud Leviti. xix. Non eris criminator aut susurro in populis. ¶ Vel dic contra derisores: qui verba aliorum deridendo referunt et resumunt ipsique si quæ sibi placentia vel placida non audiunt sepe multiplicant atque dicunt.

Metamorphoseos Moralisate.

In "La Bible des Poetes. metamorphoze. nouellemēt imprime a paris, Ant. Verard" (no date) on Fol. xxxii., verso, begins the story of Narcissus: on Fol. xxxiv., verso, col. 2, is the "Sens historial."

"Narcissus fut beau iouuenceau et fut dit de lui que assez viuroit sil se gardoit de lui mesmes veoir. Il se vit, car il senorgueillit pour sa grande beaulte qᵘ tantost lui faillit. Telle gloire est vaine & deceuable, car tost passe beaute mondaine. Si est fol cellui qui pour elle senorgueillit. Maladie, fieure, vieillesse et puis mort lont tantost gastee & perie. Narcisus pour sa beaulte senorgueillit tellement q'l lui sembloit q̃ au monde nauoit son pareil. Il en hait honnies & fennies et lui mesmes trop ayma & se trahit par le miroir de la fontaine de ce monde ou tant mira sa vaine beaulte que la mort lui vint et deuint fleur telle de quoy parle le psalmiste, que au matin fleurist et au vespre est cheuste & fletrie, tost est aneatie la vaine beaulte des gens. Si est trop fol celluy qui pour telle beaulte tost passee pert la ioye pardurable et se mue en tenebreuses peines denfer.

"Qui bien veult apprendre ceste fable on peut par Narcisus entendre les folz orgueilleux des biēs temporelz habondans qui se mirent dedans les faulses vanitez de ce monde qui les enyure et plonge en forsennerie de douloureux bruuage duquel qui plus en boit et plus a soif angoisseux et soliciteux et qui plus y muse moins y exploicte. Cest la deceuable fōtaine qui fait cuyder vraye lombre muable et cuydent tousiours prendre ce qui ne fine deschapper."

The same moralisation by Thomas Waleys will be found in the edition by Colard Mansion, Bruges, folio, 1484, p. lxiii.

A burlesque version of the story is contained in L'Ovide Bouffon, ov les Metamorphoses travesties en vers Bvrlesqves [par L. Richer] 4ᵐᵉ. ed., Paris, MDCLXV., pp. 278-306.

Metamorphoſeos Moraliſate.

In the following work "Metamorphoſeos del excelente poeta Ovidio Naſſon. Traduzidos en verſo ſuelto y octava rima: con ſus allegorias al fin de cada libro. Por el Doctor Antonio Perez Sigler natural de Salamanca. En Burgos, 1609, 12mo," p. 82., is another verſion of the moralization:

"Por Echo deſpreciada de Narciſſo, ſe entiende la fama y inmortalidad del nombre, amada de los eſpiritus altos y nobles, mas tenida en poco y deſpreciada de aquellos que dandoſe a los deleytes ſe enamoran miſeramente de ſi miſmos, y al fin ſon transformados en flor, que a la mañana eſta freſca, y en la tarde marchita: aſſi eſtos llegando a la muerte, que dan ſepultados con ſus nombres eternamente, ſin aprovecharles los plazeres y deleytes, en que han gaſtado la vita."

METAMORPHOSEOS MORALISATE.

Liber Septimus. Fol. lxv, verſo: lxvi.

FABULA XXXII.

Cephalus Eolides uxorem habuit Procrin nomine filiam Eriĉtei regis Athenarum quæ fuit pulcherrima et a Cephalo tam dileĉta quod dea Aurora ab ipſo fuit contempta quæ tamen ipſum rapuerat et diligere propoſuerat. ſed Procrin quam de novo duxerat plus amavit. et præ amore faĉtus zelotypus temptare voluit ſi eſſet pudica. Favente igitur Aurora quam contempſerat ipſe faciem et formam mutavit et ſe alienum ſimulans domum propriam introivit, qui cum Procrin arĉtiſſime ſollicitaſſet et illa diutiſſime et fortiſſime denegaſſet tandem tanta cepit promittere quod eam dubitare coegit. Quod videns Cephalus fiĉtam figuram depoſuit, et ſe maritum oſtendit. Pro quo Procris occulte fugiens omne genus hominum horrere cepit, et per montes diu vagata et Dianæ in venando aſſociata tandem a Cephalo excuſante dolente et veniam deprecante recuperata eſt. et canem et telum quæ ſibi Diana dederat in pignus amoris perpetui ipſi dedit.

Iſtud applica contra ſuſpitioſos maritos qui ſunt zelotypi et incipiunt de uxore quærere: et ſic quandoque multa inveniunt quæ non ſunt vtilia ſcire. Ideo dicitur Eccl. iii. Non eſt tibi neceſſarium ea quæ abſcondita ſunt videre oculis tuis, et in ſupervacuis rebus noli ſcrutari. ¶ Vel dic non eſt aliqua mulier ita caſta quin precibus et muneribus vacillare cogatur.

FABULA XXXIII.

Cum Procris fugitiva fuiſſet et cum Diana ſtetiſſet in ſilvis, et tandem ad Cephalum conjugem rediiſſet marito ſuo dedit quoddam telum quod illi Diana dederat cujus mirabilis erat virtus. Ad quodcunque enim animal emittebatur inevitabiliter evolabat ipſumque ſine defeĉtu occidebat:

Metamorphoseos Moralisate.

et tandem ad manum mittentis redibat. Ipsa tamen proprio telo fuit occisa. Accidit enim quod cum Cephalus omni die ad sylvas pro venatione iret, et calefactus pro refrigerio auram vocaret "Aura veni" dicens, nostroque medere labori, et hoc multotiens replicaret: audivit quidam rusticus hoc, et credens quod aliquam vocaret juvenculam illud uxori Procri detulit: quæ facta zelotypa illud probare voluit: ita mane virum ad venationem sequens sub foliis se abscondit. Vir igitur de venatione veniens calefactus auram pro refrigerio vocans procrim inter ramos et folia susurrantem audivit: qui eam feram esse credens telum emisit, et sic dominam propriam interfecit, et ad manum Cephali revolavit. Ipsa igitur moriens maritum suum excusatum habuit; et ipse tristabilem casum videns telum semper secum portabat, et quotiens casum meminerat ipse flebat.

Potes istud applicare contra mulieres suspiciosas quæ nituntur suos explorare maritos: quod cum faciunt ineuitabili telo. i. inenarrabili zelo leduntur. ¶ Vel dic contra relatores verborum qui odia et suspitiones suscitant et tandem pericla et mortem parant vel pariunt. ¶ Vel dic quod tale telum est amor qui a diana, id est luna, quæ soli sæpissime conjungitur, dicitur dari pro eo quod ex conjunctione et frequentia nimia solet amor in hominibus generari. Igitur amor est telum ineuitabile: quod pro certo nullus est qui posset euitare quin ab aliquo diligatur. Amor in morem istius teli reciproce est nature: quia postquam ad aliquem vulnerandum et diligendum emissus fuerit ad illum qui eum emisit statim redit. Naturale enim est quod si aliquis aliquem dilexerit ipse illum diligat a quo diligitur. Ideo dicit Seneca, Docebo te inquit breue amatorium sine carmine. Ama si vis amari. ¶ Vel dic quod tale telum est bonus obediens qui infallibiliter vadit ad exequendum opera injuncta a superiore, et statim redit ad manum mittentis, ut iterum exhibeat se paratum: ut de bonis mittentibus et obedientibus dicatur illud Job xxxviii. Numquid mittes fulgura et ibunt, et reuerentia dicent tibi assumus. ¶ Vel dic quod tale telum est verbum detractorium. Istud enim irreuocabiliter interficit in quantum fama quam aufert vix aut nunquam poterit restitui vel reuocari.

Metamorphoſeos Moraliſate.

"La Bible des Poetes. metamorphoze. nouellemēt imprime a paris. Ant. Verard." Fol. lxxxvii. p. iii. verſo.

Sens alegoricq̄ a la fable deſſuſdicte.

A ceſte fable de Cephalus et de procris ſe peuēt amener pluſiers entendemens. Premierement ſe doit garder ſur toutes choſes le ſage mary deſtre ialoux de ſa femme et ne doit delle enquerir la choſe quil ne vouldroit trouuer: car ſelle eſt bonne & elle ſappercoit quil doubte de ſa chaſtete ce luy eſt vng aguillan de mal faire & ſi len aimera moins Selle eſt pute et il la trouue elle doublera ſa honte & ſi ſe mettra en ſes deuoirs de lui priuer de la vie por doñer lieu a ſon amy. Sēblablement la bonne fēme ſe doit ſur tout garder que nenquiere trop les fais et les voies de ſon ſeigneur, car grans inconueniens en ſont aduenus. Ou diſons quil neſt ſi chaſte femme que par prieres et dons on ne feiſt de ſon honneur varier. Nous pouons auſſi entendre le dart cephalus eſtre la langue des detracteurs et rapporteurs de mauuaiſes nouuelles Leſquelz par icelles engendrent ſouuent la mort.

This Moraliſation is alſo contained in the edition by Colard Manſion, Bruges, 1484, p. cli.

In the "Metamorphoſeos del excelente poeta Ovidio Naſſon Traduzidos por Sigler, Burgos 1609.," p. 184, is the following:

La hiſtoria de Cephalo y Procris ſignifica (como nos aduierten las ſacras letras) que el hombre no deue procurar ſaber mas de lo que le conuiene ſaber, porque incurrira ſiempre en el error de Cephalo que paſſo de una vida feliz a vna miſera y llena de infelicidad, por auer querido hazer mayor prueua que era licito hazer, en ſu amada Procris. Por el perro que dio Diana a Procris, ſe entiende la fidelidad, que deue ſiempre la caſta muger el marido, no auiendo otro animal mas fiel al hōbre que el perro. Por el dardo, que jamas ſe tiraua en vano, ſe entiende el penſamiēto caſto que ahuyenta y deſecha la deſhoneſta laſciuia, figurada por el monſtruo de Beocia, que era vna zorra, porque el amor deſhoneſto va ſiēpre fundado en engaños como la zorra.

From "Boccacius de Mulieribus Claris. Ulmæ, Czeiner, 1473."

De Procri Cephali Conjuge. Capitulum xxvi.

Procris pandionis athenarum regis nata et Cephalo Eoli regis filio nupta, uti avaricia fua pudicis matronis exofa eft fic et viris accepta, qm̃ per eam ceterarum mulierum vicium adapertum fit. Nam cum leto pioque amore vir et uxor viventes gauderent, eorum infortunio factum eft, ut defiderio Cephali caperetur aura, feu potius aurora quædam ut placet aliquibus fpectandæ pulchritudinis mulier, quem cupidine procris fuæ detentum, aliquamdiu fruftra in fuam fententiam trahere cōnata eft. Ex quo inquit indignans penitebit te Cephale adeo fervidè dilexiffe procrim! Comperies faxo fi fit qui temptet eam aurum amori præpofuiffe tuo. Quod audiens juvenis experiri avidus peregrinationem longinquam fingens abiit, flexoque in patriam gradu per intermedium muneribus conftanciam temptavit uxoris, quæ quantumcunque grandia fponderentur impetu primo moviffe nequivere. Eo tandem perfeverante et jocalia augente ad ultimum hefitantem flexit animum, illique nox optatique amplexus, fi detur fponfum aurum, promiffi funt. Tunc Cephalus mærore contriftatus (al. ed. confternatus) apparuit quoniam dolo frivolum Procris amorem intercepiffet, quæ rubore confperfa et confcientia impulfa facinoris confeftim in filvas abiit, et fe folitudini dedit. Juvenis autem amoris impatiens ultro venia data precibus afpernantem revocavit in gratiam. Sed quid refert? nullæ funt indulgentiæ vires adverfus confcientiæ morfus, agebatur Procris in varios animi motus, et zelo partita, ne forte id in fe blandiciis auroræ vir ageret, quod ipfa in illum auro mercata fuerat, clam per fcopulos et abrupta montium juga valliumque fecreta venatorem confequi cæpit. Quod peragens contigit, dum inter vallium herbida calamofque paluftres latitans moveretur Procris, credita a viro bellua, fagitta confoffa periit. Ignoro quid dixerim potius an nil effet potentius auro in terris, aut ftolidius quærere quod comperiffe non velis. Quorum dum utrumque infipiens mulier approbat, fibi indelibilem notam et mortem invenit, quam minime inquirebat, sed (ut auri immoderatum defiderium finam quo ftolidi fere trahuntur omnes) quefo tam obftinato zelo correpti dicant, quid inde fibi emolimenti fentiant? quid decoris? quid laudis? aut gloriæ confequantur? Meo quippe judicio hæc ridicula mentis eft egritudo a pufillanimitate patientis originem ducens, cum non alibi viderimus quam hos penes, qui fe adeo dejectæ virtutis exiftimant, ut facile fibi quofcunque preponendos fore concedant. _{al. ed. trahimur.}

A full account of this edition, with feveral facfimiles of the curious woodcuts with which it is illuftrated, is given by Dr. Dibdin in the Bibliotheca Spenceriana, vol. iv. pp. 580-586. (The reference to it in the Index, p. x., under Boccacio, is erroneoufly printed 578.) At p. 584 there is a copy of part of the woodcut of Cephalus and Procris; on which Dibdin notes "A man is however interpofed between Cephalus and Procris, in the act as if of wooing the latter. Fol. xxviii. *rev.*" It is merely one fcene in the ftory, the whole being included in the fame plate, as is frequently feen in early works of art.

JOHAN BOCACIO DE LAS MUJERES ILLUSTRES EN ROMĀCE.

La preſente obra fue acabada en la inſigne, 't muy noble ciudad de Caragoça de Aragon: por induſtria 't expenſas de Paulo hurus Aleman de Cōſtancia a xxiiij. dias del mes de Octubre: en el año de la humana ſaluacion, Mil quatrocientos nouenta 't quatro.

The Colophon, on p. cvi. ſign. p. iiij. There are ff. cix.

Capitulo xxvi. de Prochris: mujer de Cephalo.

¶ Yo mas culparia, ſi juez de tal cauſa me fizierā: al indiſcreto cephalo, q̄ ala tēptada 't con tanto afinco procris ſu mujer: porq̄ no ſolamēte el dio comēço al mal: y endemas por creer de ligero ala competidora 't verdadera enemiga de ſu mujer: 't mucho peor, por ſe pcurar el miſmo ſu infamia, 't porfiar tan ſobrado: q̄ no fue grā marauilla, mujer tan moça, e tan ahinçada: 't a poder de dinero ſalir a barrera: q̄ ya el refrā diʒe, q̄ el dar quebrāta las peñias: pues q̄nto mas vna flaca mujer, y en abſencia del marido: 't cō ſperāça q̄ ſe terna ſecreto ſu mal. No le abaſtara 't le ſaliera mucho mejor, q̄ pues tāto ſe le defendia, publicara ſu mujer por cōſtante: 't a el por marido de mujer tā honeſta: q̄ ni aḥñ por dadivas grandes hauia ofendido a ſu virtud, q̄ no porfiar faſta llegar tan alcabo: q̄ mas por importunidad q̄ por amor la vincieſſe: aſſi q̄ ſi cayo: derribola, no ſola ſu flaqueza 't mollez: q̄ mujer era 't muelle como las otras lo ſon: mas aq̄lla comū ſentencia q̄ diʒe: porfia mata venado: 't bien parecio en la ſegūda, q̄ mas por engaño q̄ por voluntad falleſcio: ca luego tomo vengāça de ſi miſma: 't ſe condēpno al rigor delos yermos 't penitēcia lloroſa, que por eſſo agrado tāto alla caſta Diana que le dio muchas joyas:

Metamorphoseos Moralisate.

y en especial vna flecha, que ningun tiro erraua: ꝗ ala postre de que hauia fecho caça, ella misma boluia al que la hauia tirado, que significa ppriamente los celos, que no solo matan al triste que fieren: mas a la postre se bueluen a aql que los causa: ca son tan incurables ꝗ dañosos al vno ꝗ al otro, q̃ matã al uno, ꝗ al otro no dexan: q̃ al vno dan muerte de temor ꝗ cuydado, al otro dan guerra de quexos injustos: assi q̃ nunca en la casa do entran los celos hay paz, sossiego, folgança: ni bien: ni fallecẽ boȝes, riñas, enojos, ꝗ mal: pues monta q̃ si entrada les days, les fallares para nuca remedio ꝗ salida. Preguntad lo a los tocados dessa dolencia, que nunca saben della sanar.

This characteristic defence of Procris against the temptations of her husband Cephalus is peculiar to the Spanish version, neither the original Latin of Boccacio, nor the French Translation, having any corresponding comment.

The above extract from the Spanish version of Boccacio is printed from a copy in the Library collected by the late Michael Wodhull, Esq., of Thenford, Northamptonshire, now the property of John Edmund Severne, Esq., M.P. To the courtesy of his mother, Mrs. Severne, who still resides at Thenford House, I am indebted for the privilege of consulting this most rare volume—perhaps the only copy in the kingdom. It is not mentioned in the Bibliotheca Spenceriana, nor does Brunet in his Manuel du Libraire, i. 991, refer to any copy, merely saying "Edit. fort rare decrite par La Serna Santander."

JOHN BOCACIO ON ILLUSTRIOUS WOMEN OF ROMANCE.

The prefent work was finifhed in the celebrated and very illuftrious City of Saragoffa of Aragon by the induftry and at the expenfe of Paul Hurus Aleman de Conftancia, on the 24th day of the month of October in the year of Our Lord one thoufand four hundred and ninety four.

Colophon—p. cvi. Sign p. iiij. There are ff. cix.

⁋ I fhould rather blame—were I to make myfelf a judge in fuch a caufe—the indifcreet Cephalus than his much tempted wife Procris, fince not only was he the firft that began the evil, and further, by too readily believing the rival and real enemy of his wife, but worfe ftill by himfelf procuring her difgrace or fall and fo obftinately perfifting in it, that, it was no great marvel that a woman fo young, fo eager and influenced by the power of money, fhould expofe herfelf to public reproach, for the proverb fays, "*gifts foften Rocks*"* much more, then, a weak woman in the abfence of her hufband, and in the hope that her wrong would be kept fecret. Would it not have fufficed and have been better, fince there was fo much in her defence, for him to have proclaimed his wife conftant and himfelf the hufband of a woman fo virtuous that even the greateft gifts would not make her offend againft her virtue, than to perfift in going to fuch extremes, in as much as fhe was conquered, more by dint of importunity, than by love? So that if fhe fell, it was not only her

* Que el dar quebranta las peñas.

weaknefs and pliability which caufed her to fall, for fhe was but woman after all, and weak like other women, but as the common faying is, "*it's perfeverance that kills the deer*"* and this is well borne out by the fequel as it was more out of error than by defire fhe perifhed, for immediately fhe took revenge upon herfelf, and condemned herfelf to the privations of the defert and tearful penitence, by which fhe pleafed the virtuous Diana fo much that fhe gave her many gifts, and efpecially an arrow that would never mifs and which after hitting its mark would return to the hand that fent it off, thus properly fignifying jealoufy, which not only kills the unfortunate object whom it wounds, but in the end comes back to him who caufed it, and it is as incurable and hurtful to the one as to the other; it kills the one and does not fpare the other: to one, it gives the death of fear and anxiety, to the other the war of unjuft complaints; fo that in no houfe where it enters is there ever peace, tranquillity, happinefs or welfare of any kind: angry words never ceafe; quarrels, bickerings and wickednefs, give them but once entrance and no remedy or efcape can be found.

Afk thofe that have fuffered from this affliction and you will learn that for them there is no cure.

* Porfia, mata Venado.

THE TALE OF

CEPHALUS AND PROCRIS,

FROM

"*POEMS*

Written by

Mr. WILLIAM SHAKESPEARE,

reprinted for

THOMAS EVANS, *No.* 50 *Strand, near York Buildings.*"

pp. 189-192.

" An edition of Shakefpeare's Sonnets was publifhed in 1640, in fmall octavo, which, though of no authority or value, was followed by Dr. Sewell and other modern editors. The order of the original copy was not adhered to, and, according to the fafhion of that time, fantaftick titles were prefixed to different portions of thefe poems: *The glory of beauty; The force of love; True admiration,* &c. Heywood's tranflations from Ovid, which had been originally blended with Shakfpeare's poems in 1612, were likewife reprinted in the fame volume." MALONE.

"In the 1640 edition, on L 2, commences a Head Title 'An Addition of fome excellent Poems to thofe precedent of Renowned Shakfpeare by other Gentlemen.' Some of thefe poems are copied from Thomas Heywood's 'General Hiftory of Women'." LOWNDES by BOHN.

THE TALE OF
CEPHALUS AND PROCRIS.

Beneath *Hymettus'* hill, well cloth'd with flowers,
A holy well her soft springs gently pours:
Where stands a cops, in which the wood-nymphs shrove,
(No wood) it rather seems a slender grove.
The humble shrubs and bushes hide the grass,
Here laurel, rosemary, here myrtle was:
Here grew thick box, and tam'risk, that excels,
And made a mere confusion of sweet smells:
The triffoly, the pine; and on this heath
Stands many a plant that feels cold Zephyrs breath.
Here the young *Cephalus*, tir'd in the chace,
Us'd his repose and rest alone t 'embrace;
And where he sat, these words he would repeat,
' Come air, sweet air, come cool my mighty heat!
' Come, gentle air, I never will forsake thee,
' I'll hug thee thus, and in my bosom take thee."
Some double duteous tell-tale hapt to hear this,
And to his jealous wife doth straitway bear this;
Which *Procris* hearing, and withal the name
Of air, sweet air, which he did oft proclaim,
She stands confounded, and amaz'd with grief,
By giving this fond tale too sound belief.

Cephalus and Procris.

And looks, as do the trees by winter nipt,
Whom froft and cold of fruit and leaves half ftript.
She bends like corveil, when too rank it grows,
Or when the ripe fruits clog the quince-tree boughs.
But when fhe comes t' herfelf, fhe tears
Her garments, eyes, her cheeks, and hairs;
And then fhe ftarts, and to her feet applies her,
Then to the wood (ftark wood) in rage fhe hies her.
Approaching fomewhat near, her fervants they
By her appointment in a valley ftay;
While fhe alone, with creeping paces, fteals
To take the ftrumpet, whom her lord conceals.
What mean'ft thou, *Procris*, in thefe groves to hide thee?
What rage of love doth to this madnefs guide thee?
Thou hop'ft the air he calls, in all her bravery,
Will ftrait approach, and thou fhalt see their knavery.
And now again it irks her to be there,
For fuch a killing fight her heart will tear.
No truce can with her troubled thoughts difpenfe,
She would not now be there, nor yet be thence.
Behold the place her jealous mind foretels,
Here do they ufe to meet, and no where elfe;
The grafs is laid, and fee their true impreffion,
Even here they lay! aye, here was their tranfgreffion.
A body's print fhe faw, it was his feat,
Which makes her faint heart 'gainft her ribs to beat.
Phœbus the lofty eaftern hill had fcal'd,
And all moift vapours from the earth exhal'd.
Now in his noon-tide point he fhineth bright,
It was the middle hour, 'twixt noon and night.
Behold young *Cephalus* draws to the place,
And with the fountain-water fprinks his face.

Cephalus and Procris.

Procris is hid, upon the grafs he lies,
And come fweet *Zephyr*, come fweet air he cries.
She fees her error now from where he ftood,
Her mind returns to her, and her frefh blood;
Among the fhrubs and briars fhe moves and ruftles,
And the injurious boughs away fhe juftles,
Intending, as he lay there to repofe him,
Nimbly to run, and in her arms inclofe him.
He quickly cafts his eye upon the bufh,
Thinking therein fome favage beaft did rufh;
His bow he bends, and a keen fhaft he draws;
Unhappy man, what doft thou? Stay, and paufe,
It is no brute beaft thou would'ft 'reave of life;
O! man unhappy! thou haft flain thy wife!
O heaven! fhe cries, O help me! I am flain;
Still doth thy arrow in my wound remain.
Yet tho' by timelefs fate my bones here lie,
It glads me moft, that I no cuck-quean die.
Her breath (thus in the arms fhe moft affected)
She breathes into the air (before fufpected)
The whilft he lifts her body from the ground,
And with his tears doth wafh her bleeding wound.

INTRODUCTION
TO
CEPHALUS AND PROCRIS.

"Amores *Cephali et Procridis* notissimi sed diversis modis narrati: suavissimè ab Ovid. Met. vii.; antiquior ratio Pherecydis est in Schol. Od. λ. (xi.) 321. (Heyne, Observationes ad Apollodorum iii. 15, 1. Gottinge 1803. 8ᵛᵒ.)

Φαίδρην τε, Πρόκριν τε ἴδον." Odyss. xi. 321.

To this brief mention of Procris, as one of the heroines whose shades appeared to Ulysses, the Scholiast has appended a narrative from the seventh book of Pherecydes of Athens, a logographer who flourished in the earlier half of the fifth century B.C., which gives the history of these lovers in the simplest form, without any of the strange details which are found in some subsequent writers.

Κέφαλος ὁ Δηϊονέως γήμας Πρόκριν τὴν Ἐρεχθέως ἐν τῇ Θορικῷ κατῴκει. Θέλων δὲ τῆς γυναικὸς ἀποπειρᾶσθαι λέγεται εἰς ἀποδημίαν ἐπὶ ἔτη ὀκτὼ καταλιπὼν αὐτὴν ἔτι νύμφην οὖσαν. ἔπειτα κατακοσμήσας καὶ ἀλλοειδῆ ἑαυτὸν ποιήσας ἔρχεται εἰς τὴν οἰκίαν ἔχων κόσμον, καὶ πείθει τὴν Πρόκριν, δέξασθαι τοῦτο καὶ συμμιγῆναι αὐτῷ. ἡ δὲ Πρόκρις ἐποφθαλμίσασα τῷ κόσμῳ καὶ τὸν Κέφαλον ὁρῶσα κάρτα καλὸν συγκοιμᾶται αὐτῷ. ἐκφήνας δὲ ἑαυτὸν ὁ Κέφαλος αἰτίαται τὴν Πρόκριν. οὐ μὴν ἀλλὰ καταλλαγεὶς ἐξέρχεται ἐπὶ θήραν πυκνῶς δὲ αὐτοῦ τοῦτο δρῶντος ὑπώπτευσεν ἡ Πρόκρις ὅτι μίσγεται γυναικὶ ἑτέρᾳ. προσκαλεσαμένη οὖν τὸν οἰκέτην ἔλεγεν εἰ σύνοιδεν. ὁ δὲ θεράπων ἔφη τὸν Κέφαλον ἰδεῖν ἐπί τινος ὄρους κορυφῶν, καὶ λέγειν συχνῶς, Ὦ νεφέλη παραγενοῦ, καὶ τοῦτο μόνον συνειδέναι. ἡ δὲ Πρόκρις ἀκούσασα ἔρχεται εἰς ταύτην τὴν κορυφὴν καὶ κατακρύπτεται. καὶ τὸ αὐτὸ λέγοντος αὐτοῦ πυθομένη προστρέχει πρὸς αὐτόν. ὁ δὲ Κέφαλος ἰδὼν αὐτὴν αἰφνιδίως ἔξω ἑαυτοῦ γίνεται, καὶ ὥσπερ εἶχε βάλλει τῷ μετὰ χεῖρα ἀκοντίῳ τὴν Πρόκριν καὶ κτείνει. μεταπεμψάμενος δὲ τὸν Ἐρεχθέα θάπτει πολυτελῶς αὐτήν. ἡ δὲ ἱστορία παρὰ Φερεκύδῃ ἐν τῇ ἑβδόμῃ.

Cephalus and Procris.

Πρόκρις Ερεχθέως θυγάτηρ Κέφαλον τὸν ἑαυτῆς ἄνδρα συνεχῶς ἐπὶ θήραν ἐπιόντα ἐτήρει λαθραίως διὰ ζηλοτυπίαν· ὁ δὲ Κέφαλος, νομίσας εἶναι θήριον ἀπὸ τοῦ τῆς ὕλης κτύπου ἔλαθεν αὐτὴν Πρόκριν κατακοντίσας. Schol. Vulg.

The next version of the story is that of Apollodorus, who flourished c. 140 B.C., in which the flight of Procris to Crete is added, in consequence of her amour with Pteleon having been detected by Cephalus. He informs us that "Erechtheus King of Athens had four daughters, Procris, Creusa, Chthonia, and Oreithuia, whom Boreas carried off. Boutes married Chthonia, and Xuthus Creusa.

Πρόκριν δὲ Κέφαλος ὁ Δηϊόνος. ἡ δὲ λαβοῦσα χρυσοῦν στέφανον, Πτελέοντι συνευνάζεται· καὶ φωραθεῖσα ὑπὸ Κεφάλου, πρὸς Μίνωα φεύγει. ὁ δὲ αὐτῆς ἐρᾷ, καὶ πείθει συνελθεῖν. εἰ δέ γε συνέλθοι γυνὴ Μίνωι, ἀδύνατον ἦν αὐτὴν σωθῆναι· Πασιφάη γὰρ, ἐπειδὴ πολλαῖς Μίνως συνηυνάζετο γύναιξιν, ἐφαρμάκευσεν αὐτόν, καὶ ὁπότε ἄλλῃ συνηυνάζετο, εἰς τὰ ἄρθρα ἐφίει θηρία, καὶ οὕτως ἀπώλλυντο. ἔχοντος οὖν αὐτοῦ κύνα ταχὺν, ἀκόντιόν τε ἰθυβόλον, ἐπὶ τούτοις Πρόκρις, δοῦσα τὴν Κιρκαίαν πιεῖν ῥίζαν, πρὸς τὸ μηδὲν βλάψαι, συνευνάζεται. δείσασα δὲ αὖθις τὴν Μίνωος γυναῖκα, ἧκεν εἰς Ἀθήνας· καὶ διαλλαγεῖσα Κεφάλῳ, μετὰ τούτου παραγίνεται ἐπὶ θήραν· ἦν γὰρ θηρευτική. διώκουσαν γὰρ αὐτὴν ἐν τῇ λόχμῃ ἀγνοήσας Κέφαλος ἀκοντίζει, καὶ τυχὼν ἀποκτείνει Πρόκριν. καὶ κριθεὶς ἐν Ἀρείῳ πάγῳ φυγὴν ἀΐδιον καταδικάζεται. Apollodori Bibliotheca, iii. 15, 1.

εἶτα Κέφαλος ὁ Δηιονέως, ὅστις Πρόκριν τὴν Ἐρεχθέως ἔχων γυναῖκα, καὶ ἀποκτείνας, ἐξ Ἀρείου πάγου δίκην ὡς δικασθεὶς ἔφυγεν ἐξ γενεαῖς ὕστερον.

Scholiast. on Euripides, Orestes, 1648.

The story receives further variations in the Metamorphoses of Antoninus Liberalis (he flourished c. 140 A.D.), who probably dovetailed several versions together.

Κέφαλος ὁ Δηϊόνος ἔγημεν ἐν Θορίκῳ τῆς Ἀττικῆς Πρόκριν τὴν θυγατέρα τὴν Ἐρεχθέως· ἦν δὲ ὁ Κέφαλος νέος καὶ καλὸς καὶ ἀνδρεῖος. ἐρασθεῖσα δὲ διὰ τὸ κάλλος ἥρπασεν αὐτὸν Ἠὼς, καὶ ἐποιήσατο σύνοικον· τότε δ' οὖν ὁ Κέφαλος ἐπειρᾶτο τῆς Πρόκριδος, εἰ συμμένειν ἀδιάφθορος αὐτῷ ἐθελήσαι· καὶ αὐτὸς μὲν καθ' ἥντινα πρόφασιν ἐσκέψατο εἰς θήρας ἰέναι. Πρόκριδι δὲ εἰσαπέστελλεν ἄνδρα οἰκέτην ἀγνῶτα φέροντα χρυσὸν πολὺν, καὶ αὐτὸν ἐδίδασκε λέγειν πρὸς τὴν Πρόκριν, ὅτι ἀνὴρ ξένος ἐρασθεὶς διδοῖ τοῦτο τὸ χρυσίον, εἰ αὐτῷ συγγένοιτο· ἡ δὲ Πρόκρις τὸ μὲν πρῶτον ἀπολέγεται τὸν χρυσὸν, ἐπεὶ δὲ διπλάσιον εἰσέπεμψε,

Introduction.

ὁμολογεῖ καὶ προσδέχεται τὸν λογον· ὁ δὲ Κέφαλος ὅτε αὐτὴν ἔγνω παρελθοῦσαν εἰς τὸν οἶκον, καὶ κατακλινεῖσαν ὡς παρὰ τὸν ξένον, δᾷδα καιομένην παρήνεγκε, καὶ κατεφώρασεν αὐτήν. Πρόκρις δὲ καταλιποῦσα τὸν Κέφαλον ὑπ' αἰσχύνης, ᾤχετο φεύγουσα παρὰ Μίνωα τὸν βασιλέα τῶν Κρητῶν· καταλαβοῦσα δ' αὐτὸν ἐχόμενον ὑπ' ἀτεκνίας, ὑπισχνεῖτο διδάσκειν τὸν τρόπον ᾧ γένοιντο παῖδες αὐτῷ· ὄφεις γαρ καὶ σκορπίους καὶ σκολοπένδρας ὁ Μίνως οὔρεσκε, καὶ ἀπέθνησκον αἱ γυναῖκες ὅσαις ἐμίγνυντο· Πασιφάη δ' ἦν Ἡλίου θυγάτηρ ἀθάνατος· ἥγ' οὖν Πρόκρις ἐπὶ τῇ γονῇ τοῦ Μίνωος μηχανᾶται τοιόνδε· κύστιν αἰγὸς ἐνέβαλεν εἰς γυναικὸς φύσιν, καὶ ὁ Μίνως τοὺς ὄφεις πρότερον ἐξέκρινεν εἰς τὴν κύστιν, ἔπειτα δὲ παρὰ τὴν Πασιφάην εἰσιὼν, ἐμίγνυντο· καὶ ἐπεὶ αὐτοῖς ἐγένοντο παῖδες, ὁ Μίνως διδοῖ τῇ Πρόκριδι τὸν ἄκοντα καὶ τὸν κύνα· τούτους δὲ οὐδὲν ἐξέφυγε θηρίον, ἀλλὰ πάντα ἐχειροῦντο· καὶ ἡ Πρόκρις δεξαμένη, ἀφίκετο εἰς Θορικὸν τῆς Ἀττικῆς, ὅπου ᾤκει ὁ Κέφαλος, καὶ σὺν αὐτῷ ἐκυνηγέτει, ἐξαλλάξασα τὴν ἐσθῆτα, καὶ τὴν κουρὰν τῆς κεφαλῆς εἰς ἄνδρα, καὶ οὐδεὶς αὐτὴν ἰδὼν ἐγνώρισε. Κέφαλος δε ἰδὼν, ὅτι αὐτῷ μὲν οὐδὲν ἐπετύγχανε τῶν πρὸς τὴν θήραν, ἅπαντα δὲ συνέφερε πρὸς τὴν Πρόκριν, ἐπεθύμησεν αὐτὸς τὸν ἄκοντα τοῦτον λαβεῖν· καὶ προσυπέσχετο δώσειν, εἰ αὐτῇ τῆς ὥρας ἐθελήσαι τῆς ἑαυτοῦ χαρίσασθαι· ὁ δὲ Κέφαλος παραδέχεται τὸν λόγον, καὶ ὅτε κατεκλίνησαν, ἐξέφηνεν ἑαυτὴν ἡ Πρόκρις, καὶ ὠνείδισε τὸν Κέφαλον, ἧς αὐτὸς πολὺ αἴσχιον ἐξάμαρτοι. Καὶ τὸν μὲν κύνα καὶ τὸν ἄκοντα λαμβανει Κέφαλος. Antoninus Liberalis, cap. 41.

Servius, the commentator on Virgil, who lived about the beginning of the fifth century A.D., and Hyginus, whose date ranges from the time of Augustus to the latest days of the Roman Empire, have left us their respective versions, in both of which the love of Aurora for Cephalus is a leading incident.

"His Phædram Procrinque locis . . . cernit."—Virgil, Æn. vi. 445. On which Servius: "Procrinque." Filia Iphicli, uxor Cephali fuit, qui cum venandi studio teneretur, labore fessus, ad locum quendam ire consueverat, et illic ad se recreandum *auram* vocare. Quod cum sæpe faceret, amorem in se movit Auroræ, quæ ei canem velocissimum, Lælapa nomine, donavit: et duo hastilia inevitabilia, eumque in amplexus rogavit. Ille respondit jusjurandum se habere cum conjuge mutuæ castitatis. Quo audito Aurora respondit; ut probes igitur conjugis castitatem muta te in mercatorem; quo facto ille it ad Procrin, et oblatis muneribus, impetratoque coitu, confessus est maritum se esse: quod illa dolens, cum audisset a rustico quodam amare eum Auram, quam invocare consueverat, ad sylvas profecta est, et in frutetis latuit ad deprehendendum maritum cum pellice. Qui cum more solito *auram* vocaret, Procris egredi

Cephalus and Procris.

cupiens fruteta commovit; sperans Cephalus feram hastam inevitabilem jecit, et ignarus interemit uxorem.

Procris Paudionis filia. Hanc Cephalus Deionis filius habuit in conjugio: qui cum mutuo amore tenerentur alter alteri fidem dederunt, ne quis cum alio concumberet. Cephalus autem cum studio venandi teneretur, et matutino tempore in montem exisset, Aurora Tithoni conjux cum adamavit, petitque ab eo concubitum. Cui Cephalus negavit, quod Procri fidem dederat. Tunc Aurora ait: Nolo ut fallas fidem, nisi illa prior fefellerit. Itaque commutat eum in hospitis figuram, atque dat munera speciosa, quæ Procri deferret. Quo cum Cephalus venisset, immutata specie, munera Procri dedit, et cum ea concubuit: tunc ei Aurora speciem hospitis abstulit. Quæ cum Cephalum vidisset, sensit se ab Aurora deceptam, et inde profugit in Cretam insulam, ubi Diana venabatur. Quam cum Diana conspexisset, ait ei: Mecum Virgines venantur, tu virgo non es, recede de hoc cœtu. Cui Procris indicat casus suos, et se ab Aurora deceptam. Diana misericordia tacta, dat ei jaculum, quod nemo evitare posset; et jubet eam ire, et cum Cephalo contendere. Ea capillis demptis, juvenili habitu Dianæ voluntate ad Cephalum venit, eumque provocavit: quem in venatione superavit. Cephalus ut vidit tantam potentiam canis atque jaculi esse, petit ab hospite, non æstimans conjugem suam esse, ut sibi jaculum et canem venderet. Illa negare cœpit: regni quoque partem pollicetur: illa negat. Sed si utique, ait, perstes id possidere da mihi id quod pueri solent dare. Ille amore jaculi et canis incensus, promisit se daturum: qui cum in thalamos venissent, Procris tunicam levavit et ostendit se fœminam esse, et conjugem illius: cum qua Cephalus muneribus acceptis, redit in gratiam. Nihilominus illa timens Auroram, matutino tempore secuta eum, ut observaret, atque inter virgulta delituit, quæ virgulta cum Cephalus moveri vidit, jaculum inevitabile misit, et Procrin conjugem suam interfecit. Ex qua Cephalus habuit filium Archiam, ex quo nascitur Laertes Ulyssis pater.—Hygini Fabulæ, 189.

Ed. Muncker. Amst. 1681.

The story has a place in the Ἰωνιὰ or Violarium of the Empress Eudocia, compiled in the latter part of the eleventh century A.D. (see p. 346 of the edition published by Villoison at Venice in 1781), and is briefly summed up by another Byzantine author, John Tzetzes, a century later, in the following *versus politici*.

Περὶ κύνος τοῦ Κεφάλου.

Πρόκρις ἡ Ἐρεχθέως τε καὶ Πραξιθέας κόρη
Κέφαλον σχοῦσα σύνευνον τὸν τοῦ Δηϊονέως,

Introduction.

Λαθροκοιτεῖ Πτελέοντι χρυσοῦν λαβοῦσα στέφος·
Φεύγει δὲ πρὸς τὸν Μίνωα, Κεφάλῳ φωραθεῖσα.
Μίνως δὲ ταύτῃ μίγνυται λαθραίᾳ συνουσίᾳ
Δοὺς εὔστοχον ἀκόντιον καὶ κύνα ταχύδρομον,
Ὅστις θηρίον τάχιστον ἅπαν ἀνῄρει τρέχων.
Ταῦτα λαβοῦσα τοιγαροῦν παλινδρομεῖ Κεφάλῳ.
Διαλλαγεῖσα τούτῳ δὲ πρὸς θήραν συνεξῆλθεν·
Ὃς πρὸς θηρίον βέλεμνον ἀφεὶς αὐτὴν ἀνεῖλε.
Ἀρείῳ πάγῳ δὲ κριθεὶς ἀειφυγίαν φεύγει.

Joannes Tzetzes Historiarum Variarum Chiliades, i. 542-552.

Apollodorus (Bibliotheca iii. 14, 3, 1.) mentions another Cephalus, of earlier date ; "Ερσης δὲ καὶ Ἑρμοῦ Κέφαλος, οὗ ἐρασθεῖσα Ἠὼς ἥρπασε. This may be only an euphemism for an early death according to Eustathius, and the author of the longer Scholia (printed in the Oxford edition of 1827) on the Odyssey, v. 121. Heraclides, in his Allegoriæ Homericæ, cap. 68, explains it in the same sense :

δεῖ δὲ ἡμᾶς οὐδὲ τὰ μικρὰ παροδεύειν, ἀλλὰ καὶ δι' ἐκείνων τὴν λεπτὴν ἐξετάζειν Ὁμήρου φροντίδα. τὸν γὰρ Ἡμέρας καὶ Ὠρίωνος ἔρωτα, πάθος οὐδ' ἀνθρώποις εὔσχημον, ἠλληγόρησεν.

"Ὡς μὲν ὅτ' Ὠρίων' ἕλετο ῥοδοδάκτυλος Ἠώς. (Od. v. 121.)

παρεισάγει γὰρ αὐτόν, ἔτι νεανίαν, ἐν ἀκμῇ τοῦ σώματος, ὑπὸ τοῦ χρεὼν πρὸ μοίρας συνηρπασμένον. ἦν δὲ παλαιὸν ἔθος τὰ σώματα τῶν καμνόντων, ἐπειδὰν ἀναπαύσηται τοῦ βίου, μήτε νύκτωρ ἐκκομίζειν μήθ' ὅταν ὑπὲρ γῆς τὸ μεσημβρινὸν ἐπιτείνηται θάλπος, ἀλλὰ πρὸς βαθὺν ὄρθρον, ἀπύροις ἡλίου ἀκτῖσιν ἀνιόντος. ἐπειδὰν οὖν εὐγενὴς νεανίας, ἅμα καὶ κάλλει προέχων, τελευτήσῃ, τὴν ὄρθριον ἐκκομιδὴν ἐπευφήμουν Ἡμέρας ἁρπαγήν, ὡς οὐκ ἀποθανόντος, ἀλλὰ δι' ἐρωτικὴν ἐπιθυμίαν ἀνηρπασμένου.

However this may be, the legends of the two have been united, as is well stated in the following passage from the Biographie Universelle, under " Cephale," in the Partie Mythologique, vol. 53, p. 563. Paris, 1832.

L'histoire de Céphale se compose de deux légendes, l'une Cypriote, l'autre Athénienne. A Cypre appartient le fils de Mercure et d'Hersé, l'amant enlevé par l'Aurore, le père de Phaéthon, le bel et brillant adolescent en rapport avec la famille des Cinyrades : le reste est grec: quant à la fusion des deux récits elle n'eut rien d'absurde. L'Aurore aime la beauté, l'éclat, l'extrême jeunesse.

vi *Cephalus and Procris.*

L'époux de Procris offre ces caractères. En Egypte l'Aurore chérit la ville de Tpé : Tpé comme Képhalê signifie tête. L'Aura qui inspire de la jalousie à Procris n'est peut-être pas sans rapport avec l'Aurore ; le dernier de ces deux noms a pu donner lieu à l'autre.

By all these writers, as well as by Ovid, the persons introduced are spoken of as really existent, and we may almost say historical, and in a similar spirit Thomas Edwards has constructed his poem, with that mixture of the mythological which his classical authorities had grafted upon the original narrative. There seemed no incongruity in thus intermingling gods and men, and it was only exercising their undoubted right according to the Horatian rule, "pictoribus atque poetis Quidlibet audendi semper fuit æqua potestas." What Homer began had just received a fresh stamp from Shakspeare in his Venus and Adonis.

Modern scholarship, however, has now thrown a new light on these early traditions, and it seems to be admitted that the Story of Cephalus and Procris, like many others, is only a solar myth representing the several phenomena of the dawn of day. This view was put forward by Professor Max Müller in his famous Essay on Comparative Mythology, printed in the Oxford Essays for 1856, and has been adopted in the work on the Mythology of the Aryan Nations by Sir G. W. Cox—as will be seen by the following extracts from the above publications.

"As we have mentioned, Kephalos was the beloved of Eos, and the father of Tithonos ; we may add, that Kephalos also, like Tithonos and Endymion, was one of the many names of the Sun."

Kephalos, however, was the rising sun—the head of light—an expression frequently used of the sun in different mythologies. In the *Veda*, where the sun is addressed as a horse, the head of the horse is an expression meaning the rising sun. Thus, the poet says, *Rv.* i. 163, 6, "I have known through my mind thyself when it was still far—thee, the bird flying up from below the sky; I saw a head with wings, proceeding on smooth and dustless paths." The Teutonic nations speak of the sun as the eye of Wuotan, as Hesiod speaks of

Πάντα ἰδὼν Διὸς ὀφθαλμὸς καὶ πάντα νοήσας ;

And they also call the sun the face of their god. In the *Veda* again the sun is called (i. 115, 1) "the face of the gods," or the face of Aditi (i. 113, 9) and it is said that the winds obscure the eye of the sun by showers of rain. (v. 59, 5.)

A similar idea led the Greeks to form the name of Kephalos; and if Kephalos is called the son of Herse—the Dew—this meant the same in mythological language, that we should express by the sun rising over dewy fields. What is told of Kephalos is, that he was the husband of Prokris, that he loved her, and that they vowed to be faithful to one another. But Eos also loves Kephalos; she tells her love, and Kephalos, true to Prokris, does not accept it. Eos, who knows her rival, replies, that he might remain faithful to Prokris, till Prokris had broken her vow. Kephalos accepts the challenge, approaches his wife disguised as a stranger, and gains her love. Prokris, discovering her shame, flies to Kreta. Here Diana gives her a dog and a spear, that never miss their aim, and Prokris returns to Kephalos disguised as a huntsman. While hunting with Kephalos, she is asked by him to give him the dog and the spear. She promises to do so only in return for his love, and when he has assented, she discloses herself, and is again accepted by Kephalos. Yet Prokris fears the charms of Eos, and while jealously watching her husband, she is killed by him unintentionally, by the spear that never misses its aim.

Before we can explain this mythe, which, however, is told with many variations by Greek and Latin Poets, we must dissect it, and reduce it to its constituent elements.

The first is, "Kephalos loves Prokris." Prokris we must explain by a reference to Sanskrit, where prush and prish mean "to sprinkle," and are used chiefly with reference to raindrops. For instance, $Rv.$ i, 168, 8. "The lightnings laugh down upon the earth, when the winds shower forth the rain."

The same root in the Teutonic languages has taken the sense of "frost"— and Bopp identifies prush with O. H. G. frus, frigere. In Greek, we must refer to the same root, πρώξ, πρωκός, a dewdrop, and also Prŏkris, the dew. Thus the wife of Kephalos is only a repetition of Herse, her mother—Herse, dew, being derived from Sanskrit vrish—to sprinkle. The first part of our mythe, therefore, means simply—the sun kisses the morning dew.

The second saying is, "Eos loves Kephalos." This requires no explanation: it is the old story, repeated a hundred times in Aryan mythology—"the dawn loves the sun."

The third saying was, "Prokris is faithless; yet her new lover, though in a different guise, is still the same Kephalos." This we may interpret as a poetical expression for the rays of the sun being reflected in various colours from the dew drops—so that Prokris may be said to be kissed by many lovers : yet they are all the same Kephalos, disguised, but at last recognised.

The last saying was, "Prokris is killed by Kephalos," *i.e.*, the dew is absorbed by the sun. Prokris dies for her love to Kephalos, and he must kill her because he loves her. It is the gradual and inevitable absorption of the dew by the glowing rays of the sun, which is expressed with so much truth by the unerring shaft of Kephalos thrown unintentionally at Prokris hidden in the thicket of the forest. " La rugiada Pugna col sole." Dante, Purgatorio, i. 121.

We have only to put these four sayings together, and every poet will at once tell us the story of the love and jealousy of Kephalos, Prokris, and Eos. If anything was wanted to confirm the solar nature of Kephalos, we might point out how the first meeting of Kephalos and Prokris takes place on Mount Hymettos, and how Kephalos throws himself afterwards, in despair, into the sea, from the Leukadian Mountains. Now, the whole myth belongs to Attika, and here the sun would rise, during the greater part of the year, over Mount Hymettos like a brilliant head. A straight line from this, the most eastern point, to the most western headland of Greece, carries us to the Leukadian promontory—and here Kephalos might well be said to have drowned his sorrows in the waves of the ocean." Oxford Essays, 1856. Comparative Mythology, by Max Müller, M.A., pp. 53—55.

"The involuntary departure of the sun from the dawn, or his capricious desertion of her, is exhibited in the myths of a long series of maidens wooed and forsaken, whether by Phoibos himself, or by heroes on whose head rests his might and majesty. With the story of Korônis, the mother of Asklêpios, the myth of Prokris is in close accordance. Her birthplace is Athens, the City of the Dawn, and her mother is Hersê, the Dew, while her own name denotes also simply the sparkling drops. We are thus prepared for the myth which tells us that Kephalos, a Phokian chief, coming to Athens, won her love, and plighted his faith to her. But Kephalos was loved also by Eôs, who sought to weaken his love for Prokris with a purpose so persistent that at last she induced him to make trial of her affection. He therefore deserts Prokris, to whom after a time he returns in disguise. When in this shape he has won her love, he reveals himself, and Prokris in an agony of grief and shame flies to Crete, where she obtains from Artemis the gift of a spear which shall never miss its mark, and of a hound which can never fail to seize its prey. With these gifts she returns to Kephalos, who after seeing her success in the chase longs to possess them. But they can be yielded only in return for his love, and thus Prokris brings home to him the wrong he has done to herself, and Eôs is for the time discomfited. But Prokris still fears the jealousy of Eôs, and watches Kephalos as he goes forth to hunt, until, as one day she lurked among the thick bushes, the unerring dart of Artemis, hurled by Kephalos, brings the life of the gentle Prokris to an end. This myth explains itself.

Kephalos is the head of the sun, and Kephalos loves Prokris, in other words, the sun loves the dew. But Eôs also loves Kephalos, *i.e.*, the dawn loves the sun, and thus at once we have the groundwork for her envy of Prokris. So, again, when we are told that though Prokris breaks her faith, yet her love is still given to the same Kephalos, different though he may appear, we have here only a myth formed from phrases, which told how the dew seems to reflect many suns which are yet the same sun. The gifts of Artemis are the rays which flash from each dewdrop, and which Prokris is described as being obliged to yield up to Kephalos, who slays her unwittingly, as Phoibos causes the death of Daphnê, or Alpheios that of Arethousa. The spot where she dies is a thicket, in which the last dewdrops would linger before the approach of the mid-day heats. Cox, Mythology of the Aryan Nations, i. pp. 430, 431.

NOTES TO CEPHALUS AND PROCRIS.

Dedication, p. 3, l. 1, *Resyant.*] Inherent in, belonging to; of which meaning I have met with no other instance. Resyant is resident. Kelham, Norman-French Dictionary, London, 1779, " Resseant, resiant deinez le manoir: *one that continually abides within the manor.*" Hence applied more generally to residents, whether permanent, as in Sir Th. More's Workes, p. 900; "as for in Myddlesex, I remember none, or in the cytye selfe, eyther of resiauntes therein, or of resorters thereto, Englyshe men or straungers." Or to mere sojourners, as B. Jonson, Catiline, iv. 3, vol. iv. p. 310, ed. Gifford, 1816 :—

"Now, friends, 'tis left with us. I have already
Dealt, by Umbrenus, with the Allobroges,
Here resiant in Rome."

On which Gifford notes, "*Resiant* was common with our ancestors for resident. It is now a mere law term. The last person in whose writings it occurs as a current expression, is, I believe, Sir John Hawkins, who has it, more than once, in his Life of Dr. Johnson."

Spencer, F. Q. c. iv. b. xi. 28, uses *resiant* of things inanimate. "The famous Troynovant, In which her kingdom's throne is chiefly resiant." On which Upton says, "Resident: lodged, placed. Lat. Barb. *resiantia*, residence." Examples of this will be found in Ducange.

George Daniel, Idyll iii. 97 (Works, vol. iv. p. 222, ed. 1878) has the derivative form "*irresiant*"—a word not in Dictionaries: —

"Th' old charter lost, new letters-pattent give
Vs libertie to wander with a briefe ;
Irresiant, now content."

L. 2. *Meritorious.*] Merited, deserved: so Thomas Middleton, the Wisdom of Solomon Paraphrased, chap. i. v. 9, vol. v. p. 340, ed. Dyce, 1840 :—

"Many there be, that, after trespass done,
Will seek a covert for to hide their shame,
And range about the earth, thinking to shun
God's heavy wrath and meritorious blame."

In this sense I do not find the word in Dictionaries.

Cephalus and Procris.

Previously Skelton had used *meritory* in the same way in his "Garlande of Laurell," l. 429 :—

"So am I prenentid of my brethern tweyne
In rendrynge to you thankkis meritory."

On which Dyce says, " deserved, due."

In Shakspere "meritorious" occurs three times, but always in the usual meaning, of "deserving," "meriting."

Line 2. *Statelesse.*] Not dignified. A word not in Richardson, or Johnson by Todd or Latham. In Ogilvie, Webster, and Worcester, but without a reference.

Line 3. *Straine it foorth.*] Compare p. 27 :—

"Distilling words to hight the quintessenc
Of fame and honour."

Line 4. *To tilt against the Sunne.*] Either to be over ambitious, to attempt the impracticable (like Don Quixote with the windmills) as in the "Passionate Morrice," re-printed by the New Shakspere Society, p. 54, "He building castles in the aire, and setting trappes in the sunne to catch the shadowe of a coy queane." And Shakspere, 2 H. VI. iii. l. 158, "and dogged York that reaches at the moon." Pericles ii. 2, 20, "And his device Is a black Æthiope reaching at the sun." Or more probably to tilt with the sun in his eyes—like the Latin, *adverso sole*, and thus at a disadvantage, as Barnabe Barnes, in his "Foure Bookes of Offices, Lond. 1606," folio iv. verso, in the Dedication to the King, writes, "Against the sunne (vpon which no reasonable creature can stedfastly fix his mortall eyes, least they be dazeled, infeebled, or blinded with the pretious cleeretie thereof, (being another type of Sacred Majestie) that imperiall bird soueraigning over the swift fethered creatures of the ayre by nature opposeth his sight." So Shakspere, 3 Hen. VI. ii. 1. 92 :—

"Now, if thou be that princely eagle's bird,
Show thy descent by gazing 'gainst the sun."

And Butler, Remains, i. 71 :—

"As eagles try their young against his rays,
To prove if they're of generous breed or base."

The phrase "against the sun" is in Chaucer's Legend of Good Women, where speaking of the Daisy, l. 46-48, he says :—

——" There dawnth me no day
That I nam up and walking in the mede,
To seen this floure ayenst the sunne sprede."

Notes.

Again, l. 110-112 :—

> "For to been at the resurrection
> Of this floure, whan that it should unclos
> Again the sunne, that rose as redde as rose."

And in Shakspere, Othello, ii. 3, 382 :—

> "Tho' other things grow fair against the sun."

P. 3, .l. 6 *With their hartes-soule.*] Hamlet, iii. 2, 78 :—

> ———"Give me that man
> That is not passion's slave, and I will wear him
> In my heart's core, ay, in my heart of hearts."

P. 3, l. 6. *Artes persuasive Mistress.*] T. Randolph Amyntas, i. 2 :—

> *Laurinda.*   How now *Thestylis?*
> Grown orator of late? Has learned *Mopsus*
> Read Rhetorique unto you, that you come
> To see me with Exordiums?
> *Thestylis.*   No, *Laurinda,*
> But if there be a charm call'd Rhetorique
> An art that woods and forests cannot skill;
> That with perswasive magick could command
> A pity in your soul, I would my tongue
> Had learn'd that powerful art!

P. 3, l. 9. *To praise the light.*] See Cowley's Hymn to Light, "one of the most exquisite pieces in the whole body of English Poetry."—Sir E. Brydges' Introduction to Davison's Poetical Rhapsody, i. p. 53. Lee Priory ed., 1814.

P. 3, l. 12. *To staine obscuritie.*] Gascoigne Flowers, Praise of his Mistres, ed. Hazlitt :—

> "Since she doth pas you al as much as Titan staines a starre."—p. 55
> "She Helene staines for hewe. —p. 55.

Matthew Grove, Poems (1587) ed. Grosart, p. 35 :—

> "Who staynes each courtly dame that shines
> For beauties gift so brave."

Barnabe Barnes, Parthenophil and Parthenophe (1593) Sonnet i. 4 :—

> "And staine in glorious loveliness the fayrest.
> Oh! matchlesse bewtie bewties bewtie stayning."—Sonnet xlvi
> "Nymphes which in bewtie mortal creatures staine."—Sonnet lv. 1.

Cephalus and Procris.

He also uses "*distaine*" in a similar sense :—

> "Returne, and Florae's pride distaine,
> Her lillyes, roses, and daffadilles:
> Thy cheekes and forehad disaray
> The rose and lillyes of their grayne."—Ode i. p. 10A.

J. Dickenson, The Shepheard's Complaint, ed. Grosart, p. 20 :—

> "Wood-Nymphes came, whose golden lockes, staining the beautye
> of Titans beames hoong loose about their shoulders."—p. 20.

Fletcher, Piscatorie Eclogues, vii. 3 :—

> "Nymphs,
> "Whose faces snow their snowy garments stain."

Stain: Old Fr. *desteindre*, Fr. *teindre*, from L. tingo to tinge, dye. "*Stain* is formed from *distain*, as *sdain* from disdain.—Richardson." This and its synonyms all imply the act of diminishing brightness, or injuring the appearance of an object; but to stain is stronger than the other terms, and is variously applied.—Worcester.

P. 3, l. 12. *Inur'd supposes.*] Long established, inveterate falsities, or pretences. Tarquin and Lucrece, 321 :—

> "This glove to wanton tricks is not *inur'd*."

Twelfth Night, ii. 5, 160 :—

> "And to *inure* thyself to what thou art like to be,
> Cast thy humble slough, and appear fresh."

Bacon, Essay xxxvi. 47. "At the least, a prince may animate and inure some meaner persons to be scourges to ambitious men." On which Dr. Edwin Abbott observes: "To habituate, put 'in *ure*,' i.e., in *use*. ' *Ure* ' is derived through the French from Latin ' *usura*.' The word ' *ure* ' occurs in Essay vi. 87, ' lest his hand should be out of *ure*.' Here, however, he gives another derivation, ' Ure, a use, from the French *heur* (not *heure*, hour) which is derived from Latin *augurium*. Hence *destiny, experience*. Hence *enure*, or *inure* is ' to put in experience,' ' to practice.' (Bacon's Essays, Lond. 1876.) This latter derivation is more fully set forth in Wedgwood's Dictionary of English Etymology under 'enure.'

Line 12 *Supposes*] Taming of the Shrew, v. i. 121 :—

> "While counterfeit *supposes* bleared their eyne."

Drayton, John to Matilda, 31 :—

> ' And tells me those are shadows and *supposes*."

P. 3, l. 13. *To blindfold Envie.*] J. Dickenson, Arisbas, p. 75, ed. Grosart, first printed 1594, in The Worth of Poesie devotes two stanzas to a description of Envy.

P. 3, l. 13. *Barbarisme.*] Marlowe, Hero and Leander, "To beat back *Barbarism* and Avarice," p. 38. Spenser's Tears of the Muses, Thalia, st. 3, l. 187 :—

"Ugly barbarisme."

Guilpin's Skialetheia Epigr., 1, 10 :—

"So England's wits,
Having confounded monstrous barharismes."

Return from Parnassus, p. 267 :—vol. iii. ed. Hawkins. Oxford 1773.

"Vile barbarisme was used to dandle thee."

Ben Jonson, Poetaster, i. i. p. 409 :—

"Your only harbarism is to have wit and want."

Shakspere, Love's Labour Lost, i. 1, 112 :—

"And though I have for barbarism spoke more."

Winter's Tale, ii. 1, 84 :—

"Lest barbarism, making me the precedent,
Should a like language use to all degrees,
And mannerly distinguishment leave out
Between the prince and beggar."

P. 3, l. 16. *Margining Reproach.*] The Return from Parnassus, p. 214 :—

"Yet subject to a critic's marginal."

Decker, London Triumphing (iii. 251) :—

"Nor the margent quoate
With any act of thine which may disgrace
This citie's choice, thyself or this thy place."

Hall, Prologue to Satires, 7, "Envy the margent holds."

P. 3, l. 16. *Gloses.*] "Gloses," more commonly glosses—comments, remarks, as in Spenser, Shepherd's Calendar at end of each month.

P. 3, l. 19. *Where never path was seen.*] The customary phrase with poets :—

"Avia Pieridum peragro loca nullius ante
Trita solo."—Lucretius, i. 925.

But do these words imply that T. Edwards was not acquainted with the Poem on the subject of Cephalus and Procris, attributed by T. Nash to Anthonie Chute, and entered in the Stationer's Register, Oct. 22, 1593?

Cephalus and Procris.

P. 3, l. 20. *In shadie groves, twisting the myrtle green.*] Perhaps there is a reference to Virgil, Æneid. vi. 440-445 :—

> "Nec procul hinc partem fusi monstrantur in omnem
> Lugentes campi: sic illos nomine dicunt.
> Hic quos durus amor crudeli tabe peredit,
> Secreti celant calles ; et *myrtea* circum
> *Silva* tegit; curæ non ipsa in morte relinquunt.
> His Phædram Procrinque locis — cernit."

Ovid appropriates the myrtle to Elegy :—

> "Elegian muse that warblest amorous lays,
> Girt my shine brow with sea-bank myrtle sprays."—
> Marlowe, Ovid. Eleg. i. (vol. iii. p. 108. ed. Dyce 2.)

Hence, Milton in Lycidas unites the myrtle with the laurel :—

> "Yet once more, O ye Laurels, and once more
> Ye myrtles brown, with ivy never sere."

Where T. Warton observes, "that these plants are not appropriated exclusively to elegy—they are symbolical of general poetry. Theocritus Epigr., i. 3, dedicates myrtles to Apollo." Still, as Virgil represents Procris among the unfortunate lovers amid the myrtle grove, this tree too being generally sacred to Venus, there is a peculiar propriety in the adoption of the myrtle here instead of the laurel or ivy, for a love story with so melancholy an issue.

For the origin of the myrtle, see R. Chester, Poems, p. 104, ed. Grosart. *Green.*] Horace, Od. i. iv. 9 :—

> "Viridi nitidum caput impedire myrto."

P. 4, l. 1. " Parthenophil and Parthenophe," published by Barnabe Barnes in May 1593, has on the Title a dedication " To the right noble and Vertuous Gentleman, Mr. William Percy, Esquier, his deerest friend," followed by an address " To the Learned Gentlemen Readers The Printer," in which he requesteth their favourable censures, and submits his Poems to their friendly patronages. " Arisbas, Euphues amidst his slumbers: Or Cupid's Journey to Hell, by J. Dickenson," 1594, is dedicated " To the right Worshipfull Maister Edward Dyer, Esquire, Mæcenas of Worth, and mirror of all admired perfections," followed by " an Epistle to the Gentlemen Readers " beginning, " Learned and curteous Gentlemen" and ending " Thus Gentlemen, committing my Pamphlet to your friendly view, and submitting myself to your curteous censures, I end, wishing to you al, several good fortunes &c."

Notes. 195

In the same way T. Edwards dedicates his volume "To the Right Worshipfull Master *Thomas Argall Esquire*," and then submits it " To the Honorable Gentlemen and true favourites of Poetry," in an address beginning, " Judiciall and Courteous," and ending, " And thus benigne Gentlemen, as I began, so in douty I end, ever prest to do you all service." Here, and in the marginal note on p. 27, he seems to use "favourites " for " favourers," and, so patrons of Poetry ; and from his frequent mention of Sidney and Spenser may possibly have intended some reference to them and their immediate friends, Dyer, Gabriel Harvey, and others, who as we learn from a letter of Spenser to G. Harvey, had some years before set themselves up as a court of Areopagus in poetry, and who, though mistaken in their attempt at introducing " the Hexameter, and certain laws of quantity of English syllables for English Verse," yet exercised a strong critical influence over their contemporaries.

P. 4.1.3. *Judiciall.*] Having the power to judge, judicious. So Daniel in his Defence of Rhime (Works, i. 29, ed. 1718) speaks of " The most judicial and worthy spirits of this land," (p. 15) that " It is not Books, but only the great Book of the World, and the all over-spreading Grace of Heaven, that makes men truly judicial," and in a more limited sense (p. 27,) " Nature and a judicial ear," a phrase used also by Hall, Satires, Postscript to the Reader. On the other hand Shakspere used *judicious* for *judicial* in Coriolanus, V. 6, 128. " His last offences to us Shall have judicious hearing."

P. 4. l. 4. *Irus.*] The name given by the suitors to the Ithacan beggar Arnæus, Odyssey xviii. 5—7 ; and hence the appellative for a beggar ; as " Irus et est subito qui modo Crœsus erat." Ovid. Trist. iii. 7—42. " No Crœsus-rich, nor yet an Irus-poore." John Vicars, Life of Sylvester, in his Du Bartas, ed. 1648. fol. A. 6.

P. 4 l. 9. *Slak't,*] and p. 61 *aslakt,* quieted : so Marlowe, Hero and Leander, second Sestiad, p. 27, l. 3, ed. Dyce 1850. " To slake his anger if he were displeas'd." Wedgwood gives the primary meaning as, " loose ; whence to slake is to diminish the active force, to still pain or thirst, to quench the fire, to put out."

P. 4. l. 15. *Live in bastardy.*] Not able to acknowledge their own issue, but obliged to publish under another's greater name, as we learn from T. Nash, Pierce Penilesse, p. 44 (Shakspere Soc. ed. 1841.) " He fathered one of the bastards (a booke I meane) which being of thy begetting was set forth under his name." "Parthenophil and Parthenophe," by Barnabe Barnes 1593, is an instance of this practice, and as there is only one copy of the original edition, and only thirty of the reprint by Dr. Grosart in 1875, the author's lines, appended to the Epistle to the Reader, in which he avails himself of it, may claim insertion here.

> " Go barstard Orphan packe thee hence,
> And seeke some straunger for defence:
> Now ginnes thy basenesse to be knowne,
> Nor dare I take thee for mine owne:
> Thy leuity shall be discried.
> But if that any haue espied,
> And question with thee of thy Sire,
> Or Mistrisse of his vaine desire,
> Or aske the place from whence thou came,
> Deny thy Sire, Loue, Place, and Name:
> And if I chance vnwares to meet thee,
> Neither acknowledge mee, nor greet mee,
> Admit I blush, perchance I shall,
> Passe by, regard me not at all,
> Be secrete, wise, and circumspect,
> And modesty sometimes affect :
> Some goodman that shall thinke thee witty,
> Will be thy patrone, and take pitty :
> And when some men shall call thee base,
> He for thy sake, shall him disgrace:
> Then with his countenance backt, thou shalt
> Excuse the nature of thy fault :
> Then if some laddes, when they goe by,
> Thee bastard call, give them the ly,
> So get thee packing and take heede,
> And though thou goe in beggars weede,
> Hereafter when I better may,
> I'le send relief some other day."

P. 4. l. 17. *Cynthia.*] Q. Elizabeth.
P. 4. l. 17. *Tralucent.*] Marlowe, Hero and Leander, first Sestiad, p. 17.

> " And, as she spake,
> Forth from those two tralucent cisterns brake
> A stream of liquid pearl."

on which Dyce observes, " *Tralucent* a form of *translucent* common in our early writers."

P. 4. l. 20. *Honor.*] Rank, dignity of birth or station.

Notes. 197

P. 4, l. 21. *Sowzed.*] Richardson in his Dictionary places all the meanings under the one head " souse ;" Wedgwood more correctly, it seems, refers some to " soss, souse," to plunge in water ; " They *soused* me over head and ears in water when a boy." Addison ; and others to " souce, souse," (from French saulce, Lat. salsus) to season with pickle, as N. Breton in Wits Trenchmoor, p. 10, col. 1, ed. Grosart, " The cunger must be sowst." Perhaps Edwards implies both meanings. " Honor and the living sparkes " (or as in the Sonnet to Henrie Earl of Southampton, prefixed to Florio's World of Words, " Honors ingendred sparkles ") are but of little account without the additional glories they receive (as it were a condiment in which they are immersed) from art, either Sculpture, Painting or Poetry, to which he successively alludes.

P. 4, l. 21, 22. *Adamantine goat-bleeding impression.*] This seems to refer to the cutting of gems, and so to the art of sculpture generally. The belief that adamant or diamond was infrangible unless steeped in goat's blood is traceable to Pliny—from whom it was repeated by Solinus, Isidorus, and Marbodæus de Gemmis, who writes

" Cujus durities solidissima cedere nescit,
Ferrum contemnens, nulloque domabilis igne,
Hæc tamen hircino calefacta cruore fatiscit. i. 5-7.

Pliny's account is in his Naturall Historie, Translated by Philemon Holland, London, Adam Islip, 1634. The seven and Thirtieth Booke, chap. iv. p. 610 K.] " Moreover as touching the concord and discord that is between things naturall, which the Greekes call Sympathia and Antipathia (whereof I have so much written in all my bookes, and endeavoured to acquaint the readers therewith) in nothing throughout the world may we observe both the one & the other more evidently than in the Diamant: For this invincible minerall (against which neither fire nor steele, the two most violent and puissant creatures of natures making, have any power, but that it checketh & despiseth both the one and the other) is forced to yeeld the gantelet and give place unto the bloud of a Goat, this only thing is the means to break it in sunder, howbeit care must be had, that the Diamant be steeped therein whiles it is fresh drawn from the beest before it be cold : & yet when you have made all the steeping you can, you must have many a blow at the Diamant with hammer upon the anvill: for even then also, unlesse they be of excellent proofe & goode indeed, it wil put them to it, and break both the one & the other: But I would gladly know whose invention this might be to soake the Diamant in Goats bloud, whose head devised it first, or rather by what chance was it found out and known? What conjecture should lead a man to make an experiment of such a singular and admirable secret, especially in a goat, the filthiest beast one of them in the whole world? Certes I must ascribe both this invention & all such like to the might and benificence together of the divine powers: neither are we to argue & reason how and why nature hath done this or that? Sufficient it is that her will was so, and thus she would have it. But to come againe to the Diamant, when this proofe taketh effect to our mind, so that the Diamant once crackt, you shall see it break and crumble into so small pieces, that hardly the eie can discerne the one from the other. Wel, lapidaries are very desirous of Diamants, and seek much after them: they set them into handles of yron, and thereby they with facility cut into anything, be it never so hard."

The same notion is to be found in two writers subsequent to Edwards; see J. Dickenson, "Greene in Conceipt," (1598) p. 103, ed. Grosart, 1878.

"If then the strongest marble bee in time worn by weake droppes of raine, the hardest Adamant (though otherwise impenetrable) pearc'd by Goates warme blood."

Poems of Robert Chester (who distinguishes the Adamant from the Diamond) a Dialogue (1611) pp. 109, 110, ed. Grosart, 1878.

"The *Adamant* a hard obdurate stone,
Invincible, and not for to be broken—
 *   *   *   *   *
Yet with a Goates warme, fresh and liuely blood,
This *Adamant* doth break and riue in sunder,
That manie mightie, huge strokes hath withstood."

For a full account of the Diamond, see the Natural History of Precious Stones and Gems, by C. W. King, London, 1865, pp. 19—48.

P. 4, l. 23. *Well could Homer paint, &c.*] If Edwards were alluding to the Art of Painting, he may have used the phrase "*paint on the shield of Ulysses*" with a tacit reference to the Shield of Achilles described in Iliad. xviii., and to the shields of the Seven Chiefs in the "Seven against Thebes" of Æschylus. Otherwise the phrase would simply mean Word-painting as afterwards on p. 27, lines 13—16.

P. 4, l. 25. *Amintas.*] There is here some difficulty in ascertaining who was intended by this name. If a Poet be meant, it is probably Thomas Watson, who wrote *Amyntas* in 1585, *Amintæ Gaudia* in 1592. Spenser in his Colin Clout 434—443 praises an Amyntas, who is supposed by Malone (Shakspere by Boswell, ii. 265—273) and Todd on Spenser, to be Ferdinando

Earl of Derby. The praises of an Amintas are also set forth by T. Nash in Pierce Penilesse (p. 91, ed. 1841), as to whom Collier observes in his note, " Possibly the Earl of Southampton, to whom Nash dedicates several tracts, was the Nobleman intended." In this note Collier erroneously states that Watson celebrated Sir Francis Walsingham under the name *Amyntas*; it should be *Melibæus*. Watson's poem *Melibæus*, was reprinted by Mr. Arber in 1870, wherein p. 147, the author advertises the reader that " He figures Sir Francis Walsingham in *Melibæus*." Edwards's words might be interpreted either of a poet, or a patron of poets, but as in *L'Envoy* to Narcissus, p. 62, *Amintas* is mentioned with other poets, the more natural inference seems to be that a poet, and if so Watson, is here designated under that name.

P. 4, l. 28. *The teares of the Muses.* Spenser's Poem under this Title, printed in 1591, is probably referred to; it begins

" Rehearse to me, ye sacred Sisters nine,
Those piteous plaints and sorowfull sad tine,
Which late ye powred forth as ye did sit
Beside the silver springs of Helicone, &c."

P. 4, l. 28. *Teared.* Wept: I have found no other instance of this verb. A similar play on words on p. 5, " Why temporize I thus on the intemperature of our clymate," and "trip it of in buskin till I feare me they will have nothe but skin," referring apparently to those who wrote for the stage, and found it a poor livelihood.

P. 5, l. 19. *Warme themselves.* Nicholson in his Acolastus (1600) l. 37, 38, has

" Our neighbour countries burne in civill fire
And *Nero*-like we warme us by the flame."

P.5, l. 26. *Prest.* Ready. Lat. præsto, at hand. See Teshes Verses on the Knights of the Garter, in Ballads from Manuscripts, vol. ii. part ii. 119. Ballad Society, 1873; on the motto of the Talbot family " Prest d'accomplir."

" The redie mynde respecteth never toyle,
But still is prest t'accomplish hartes intent:
Abroad, at home, in enerie Coste or soyle,
The deed performs what inwardly is ment;
Which makes me saye, in euerie virtuous deed,
I still am prest t'accomplish what's decreed.
    *   *   *   *   *
Prest to accomplish, what you will commaunde,
Prest to accomplish, what you shall desire:
Prest to accomplish, your desir's demaunde;
Prest to accomplish, Heaven for happie hire:
Thus do I ende, and at your will I rest,
As you shall please in every Action prest."

Cephalus and Procris.

P. 6, margin. *A pariphrisis of the Night.*] The same marginal note occurs in Marlowe's Hero and Leander, first Sestiad (iii., 13, ed. Dyce, 1850. Though not printed till 1598, this poem was entered in the Stationers' Book, 28th Sept. 1593, four months after the author's death, and was no doubt circulated in manuscript after the custom of that period. T. Edwards was evidently a great admirer of it.

P. 6, l. 3. *Scoured.*] Moved quickly. So p. 8 "away she skoures;" p. 33 "that erst did bravely skoure." Shakspere uses this verb once in this sense. "Never saw I men scour so on their way." Winter's Tale ii 1., 35. It occurs in the Romance of Kyng Alisaunder 3722, ed. Weber 1810, "Hit is beter that we to heom schoure." H. Coleridge, Glossarial Index of 13th Cent. explains "scour, v.n. to rush quickly" and connects it with It. scorrere, as do others, from Lat. excurrere. But this notion seems to spring from the ordinary meaning of the word to cleanse by rapid movement, in which sense the verb exists in all the Teutonic languages. To skir, scur, scurry, are variations. See Nares' Glossary in Skir.

P. 6, l. 3. *Canapie.*] Originally a bed with mosquito curtains (κωνωπεῖον), hence a covering of state; metaphorically the sky. Shakspere, Coriolanus iv. 5, 40, and Hamlet ii. 2, 310 "this most excellent canopy, the air look you, this brave o'erhanging firmament, this majesticall roof fretted with golden fire." R. Barnfield. The Affectionate Shepheard, 1594, 1, 2:—

"Scarce had the morning starre hid from the light
Heavens crimson canopie with stars bespangled."

Talbot in his English Etymologies, 1847, pp. 5, 6, derives it from the Latin *cannabis*.

P. 6, l. 4. *Gouernement.*] This seems here to mean that which is governed, the realm, an unusual sense of the word.

P. 6, l. 10. *One forlorne.*] Shelley in his Posthumous Poems (iv. 61, ed. F. Buxton) speaks of the moon

"Wandering companionless
Among the stars."

P. 6, l 11. *Headlong.*] Marlowe, Hero and Leander, p. 28 :—

"The Morn—All headlong throws herself the clouds among."

Postes.] Hastens. Very commonly used in this sense by writers of the Elizabethan age, and afterwards. Wordsworth has it in the Idiot Boy:—

"Away she posts up hill and down."

The various meanings of the word were first collected together by Horne Tooke, Diversions of Purley, Part ii. chap. ii., p. 319; and their connection is well traced by Archbishop Trench in his " Study of Words," Sect. vi.

" Post is the Latin positus, that which is placed; the piece of timber is placed in the ground and so a post; a military station is a post, for a man is placed in it, and must not quit it without orders; to travel post, is to have certain relays of horses placed at intervals, that so no delay on the road may occur; the post-office is that which avails itself of this mode of communication; to post a ledger is to place or register its several items."

So Eastwood and Wright in the Bible Wordbook

" —— a station where horses are kept for travelling; thence transferred to the person who travelled in this way using relays of horses; and finally to any quick traveller."

Milton, Samson Agonistes, 1538

" For evil news rides post, while good news baits."

Tacitus so describes the death of Agricola, c. 43 :—

" Supremo quidem die momenta ipsa deficientis per dispositos cursores nuntiata constabat, nullo credente sic accelari quæ tristis andiret."

From the account in Herodotus viii., 98 it appears that the system of posts was first instituted by the Persians, and by them was called ἀγγαρήϊον. And Xenophon Cyr. Pæd. viii., 6, 9, p. 232, attributes its institution to Cyrus. In the book of Jeremiah, li., 31 :—

" One post shall run to meet another, and one messenger to meet another, to shew the king of Babylon that his city is taken at one end."

Modern inventions have rendered such methods of communication, and travelling obsolete, but the verb to post will remain as a memento of former notions of speed.

P. 6, l. 15. *Aurora.*] As Cynthia sets in Ocean, Edwards probably implies that Aurora rises therefrom, as Virgil states in Æneid iv. 129, ' Oceanum interea surgens Aurora relinquit" and Homer in the Hymn to Hermes 185, 'Ηὼς δ'—ὤρνυτ' 'απ' 'Ωκεανοῖο— So Thomas Watson in his " Amintas for his Phillis," in England's Helicon, p. 139 :—

" Aurora now began to rise againe
From watry couch and from old Tithon's side:
In hopes to kisse upon Acteian plaine,
Young Cephalus, and through the golden glide
On easterne coaste he [forte, she] cast so great a light
That Phœbus thought it time to make retire
From Thetis bower, wherein he spent the night,
To light the world againe with heavenly fire."

Cephalus and Procris.

As "in the Homeric poems Eos not only announces the coming Helios but accompanies him throughout the day" (Smith Dict. of Biogr. and Mythol. in Eos) Edwards gives her journey through the sky in the following pages. Modern philologers tell us that Eos and Aurora are the same.

"The simpler form of ἠώς is preserved in the Æolic αὔως. The morning in Sanskrit is *ushas*, in Latin *Aurora*. Do these words which have the same meaning agree in form also; not of course judged by mere identity of sound, which is no guide at all, but according to the phonetic laws of their respective languages? They do; and all point to the root US to burn. This appears as USH in Sanskrit, from which *Ushas* is regularly formed, with no vowel-modification. The Græco-Italian people raised the vowel by regular process to *au*, and formed *ausos*: which received no further increase in Greek, but in Latin a secondary noun was formed from the primary one, that is, *ausos- a*. Now both Greeks and Italians, as is well known, disliked the sound *s* between two vowels; the Greeks generally dropped it, and so got here αὐ(σ)ως, αὔως, ἠώς; the Latins changed it into *r*, and made *Aurora*: the verb appears as *uro*."

Peile, Introduction to Greek and Latin Etymology, 1869. Pref. p. xii.

P. 6, l. 19. *The world stand still.*] See Transactions of New Shakspere Society, 1877-9, Part iii. Paper xvii. by Mr. Furnival, for the notions of astromony prevalent in Shakspeare's time.

P. 7, l. 1. *Another Phaeton.*] Hero and Leander, p. 9:—

"As if another Phaeton had got
The guidance of the sun's rich chariot."

Gower introduces the story of Phaeton in the fourth book of his Confessio Amantis as an illustration of the evil arising "through the slouth of negligence." § 4, vol ii. p. 34, ed. Pauli, 1857.

P. 7, l. 6. *The boy thus proude-made.*] Gower, Confessio Amantis, vol. ii., 35:—

"But he such veine gloire hadde."

P. 7, l. 7. *Heavens Coape.*] In Gower, Confessio Amantis, vol. iii., 138:—

"Under the cope of heaven."

Milton, P. L. iv. 992 :—

"The starry cope of heaven."

Shelley, Hellas, last chorus.

"Beneath heaven's cope."

Cope is used alone by Shakspere in the same sense, Pericles iv., 6, 131 :—

"The cheapest country under the cope."

Wedgwood quotes similar phrases from Italian, French, and Dutch, see his Dictionary in Cope, cap, cabin.

"All apparently from a root *cap*, signifying cover, which is found in languages of very distinct stocks."

P. 7, l. 8. *Downe dingeth.*] Hero and Leander, p. 38:—
"Danged down to hell."

Skelton, ed. Dyce ii. 47:—
"And the devyll downe dynge."

Drayton, Battle of Agincourt,
"This while our noble king,
His broad sword brandishing,
Down the French host did ding."

Willobies Avisa, 1594, p. 50:—
"And dinges them downe to fiery lake."

P. 7, l. 27. *Extasie.*] Any violent perturbation of mind. Marlowe, i., 254, Jew of Malta, Act i.
"Our words will but increase his ecstasy."

Venus and Adonis, 895:—
"Thus stands she in a trembling exstasy."

Hamlet iii. 4, 74; 138, 139, as madness.
"This bodiless creation ecstasy is very cunning in.
Hamlet. Ecstasy! My pulse as yours doth temperately keep time."

Milton, Il Penseroso, 165:—
"Dissolve me into extasies."

P. 7, l. 31. *Godd it.*] Spenser, Colin Clout, 810, speaking of Cupid, says
"That Jove himselfe his powre began to dread
And taking up to heaven, him godded new."

that is deified. So Shakspere, Coriolanus, v. 3, 11:—
"Loved me above the measure of a father; nay godded me indeed."

But Edwards uses the word in a different sense, to play the God; more like "Goddize" in Warner's Albion's England, ix. c. 44:—
"And faire, lov'd, fear'd Elizabeth, here goddized ever since."

I have met with no other instance of this use of the word.

P. 8, l. 6. *Skymes.*] To skim is to take off the scum, froth, foam; to move lightly over the surface of a liquid: to glide along:—
"The swallow *skims* the rivers watery face."—Dryden.
"Where the false tide *skims* o'er the cover'd land."—Dryden, Annus Mirabilis.
"Flies o'er th' unbending corn and *skims* along the main."—Pope.

See Talbot. English Etymologies p. 84. for its connection with the Latin Spuma. But "skyme" here may be to rise like scum, to foam. Stratmann has,

'scûmin, O. H. Germ. scûmen, to scum, spumare. Promptorium. 450.'

In this sense it is used in Berners' Froissarts Cronycle vol. ii. p. 49 :—

" Golde and sylver was no more spared then thoughe it had rayned out of the clowdes, or *scomed* out of the sea."

P. 8. l. 7. *Receipte.*] The place where any thing is received, or contained. St. Matthew ix. 9 "at the receipt of custom, τὸ τελώνιον." Shakspere, Macbeth, i. 7, 76, " and the receipt of reason A limbeck only." Earlier instances are given by Stratmann, p. 397 under recet. " O. Fr. recet, receipt, receptus. Robert of Gloucester 98, 19. Manning, History of England 4464." The whole line is a periphrasis for the Ocean.

P. 8. l. 8. *Kils the hoat fume.*] This is not very intelligible. Fume is connected with foam by Skinner, " Spuma enim rarescens instar fumi vel nebulæ est; certe proximum ei raritatis gradum obtinet," and foam seems more appropriate here as the effect of "the swelling tide." Is the simile to this purport? The first streaks of dawn spread till they are lost in the universal extension of light over the sky, as the swelling tide of some river with its hot foam (*i.e.* the foam produced by its violent rapid course) is lost in the ocean. "The swelling tide scorning a guide," *i.e.* unrestrained "skymes," foams along on its flood, and Aurora "lawlesse skoures," hastens swiftly, and unrestrained as "banditos 'mongst the mountaine heard."

P. 8. l. 10. *Banditos.*] Marston, Scourge of Villanie. 1599, Sat. iii. 117 :—

" When swarmes of mountebanks and bandeti."

Coryat, vol. iii. O, 4 verso :—

" Continually to stand in feare of the Alpine cut-throats called the Bandits."

Shakspeare 2 Hen. VI. iv. 1. 135 :—

" A Roman sworder and banditto slave Murder'd sweet Tully."

Milton, Comus, 426 :—

" No savage fierce bandite, or mountaneer."

We now use the plural banditti. " From the Mid. Latin bannire, bandire, to proclaim, the Italian participle *bandito* signifies one denounced, proclaimed, put under the ban of the law, and hence in the same way that English *outlaw* came to signify a robber *It. banditti* acquired the like signification." Wedgwood.

P. 8. l. 12. *The mornings honor.*] "That which confers distinction: boast: ornament." "A late eminent person the *honor* of his profession for integrity and learning." Burnet quoted in Worcester's Dict. Here Aurora herself is the mornings honor.

P. 8. l. 13. *All snowy white.*] Compare Milton P. L. xi. 133-5:—

" Meanwhile,
To resalute the world with sacred light
Leucothea waked."

On this passage Bishop Newton remarks; "Leucothea is the *White Goddess* as the name in Greek imports, the same with Matuta in Latin, as Cicero says, Leucothea nominata a Græcis Matuta habetur a nostris. Tusc. i. 12. Quæ Leucothea a Græcis a nobis Matuta dicitur. De Nat. Deor. iii. 19. And *Matuta* is the early morning that ushers in the Aurora rosy with the Sunbeams, according to Lucretius, v. 655:—

" Tempore item certo roseam Matuta per oras
Ætheris Auroram defert, et lumina pandit."

Elsewhere Milton describes this first stage of the morn by the epithet gray, as in P. L. vii, 373,

" The gray dawn,"

And more fully in Lycidas 187,

"While the still morn went out with sandals gray."

P. 8. l. 13. *Save purpled.*] Milton P. L. xi. 173-5:—

" The—morn begins her rosy progress."

So P. L. v. 1, 2,

" Now morn her rosy steps in th' eastern clime
Advancing, sow'd the earth with orient pearl."

She was pale and white before, now she is rosy red, which is the second stage in the progress, the third being when the sun has risen. On this subject see Richardson,s note to P. L. Book v. 1.

Shakspere, Hamlet i. 1, 166, has the epithet russet, (which is russeus, red, ruddy):—

" But look, the morn in russet mantle clad
Walks o'er the dew of yon high eastern hill."

2 E

Cephalus and Procris.

Purple is a very dark red color, and is applied to the Morn by Spenser, F. Q. i. 2, 7 :—

> " Now when the rosy-fingred Morning faire
> Weary of aged Tithones saffron bed,
> Had spread her purple robe through deawy aire."

Milton also uses the verb to purple, P. L. vii. 30. " Or when morn Purples the East." And describes the color, P. L. xi. 241 :—

> " A military vest of purple flow'd
> Livelier than Meliboean, or the grain
> Of Sarra."

in both following Virgil, quam plurima circum Purpura Mæandro duplici Melibœa cucurrit, Æn. v. 251, and Sarrano indormiat ostro, Georg. ii. 506.

P. 8. l. 15, *Wanton eie.*] Shakspere, Richard III. Act iii., 7, 187, "made prize and purchase of his wanton eye" in the first and second Folios, but printed in the Globe edition "lustful eye" in which sense it occurs in Isaiah iii. 16, " walk with wanton eyes." But this is probably a secondary meaning of the word though from its uncertain etymology it is hard to assign the primary signification. Edwards from his words " which at a trice could all the world espie" implies that the eye of Aurora was quick glancing, rapid in movement, unrestrained, more like Shakspere's application of the word wanton to the "air," or "wind," as sportive, roving. Trench, Synonyms of New Test. §. xvi., notes the two senses of "wantonness" as making it the best rendering for ἀσέλγεια.

P. 8. l. 16, *At a trice.*] Shakspere says "in" or "on" a trice. Horne Took, Diversions of Purley, p. 292, derives " trice" from the French "trois;" and says, "in a manner similar to Anon it means the time in which one can count three, one, two, three and away. " Gower, Conf. Amant. vol. i. p. 142, ed. Pauli, " all sodeinlich as who saith treis." But on this compare Grimm, Deutsche Grammatik, iii. 232, 3. Wedgwood says " Sp. *tris*, crack, noise made in breaking, thence in a trice, an instant. So in Sc. *in a crack*, immediately. Jamieson."

P. 8. margin, *Acroconiæ.*] A more correct reading would be Acrocomæ. But see the Dictionarium Historicum et Poeticum contained in Cooper's Thesaurus 1573, a work which our Poet seems to have used. " Acroconiæ, Certaine Thracians having their heare over their foreheads womanlike."

Notes. 207

They are mentioned in the Iliad, iv. 533, Θρήικες ἀκροκομοι: on which Heyne notes "Potest epitheton plures habere significatus. Suspicor Thraces erectos in vertice habuisse cincinnos ut multi barbari Germani quoque prisci, et nunc Americæ populi habere solent." Edwards translates "long-haired" and this is one of the meanings admitted by Eustathius λίαν κομῶντες, though he elsewhere disapproves of it.

P. 8, l. 20. *Emprize.*] An old word for enterprise, attempt. It is in Coleridge's Glossarial Index of 13th Century Words—in Spenser's Shepheards Calendar, September, 83, "Wronge emprise." In Milton, Comus, 610, and P. L. xi., 642 "bold emprise." It does not occur in Shakspeare. Edwards uses it in the sense of workmanship, texture.

P. 8, l. 22. *Otomie.*] This word seems to be used for "gossamer," the floating cobwebs seen in fine weather in the air, as described by Nares, who quotes Shakspere, Romeo and Juliet, ii., 6, 18:

"A lover may bestride the gossomers
That idle in the wanton summer air,
And yet not fall."

Nabbes, Hannibal and Scipio, B. 2, 1637:—

"By the bright tresses of my mistresse hair
Fine as Arachne's web, or gosshemere,
Whose curls when garnished by their dressing shew
Like that thinne vapour when 'tis pearled with dew."

In one place I find it corrupted to *gothsemay*, in Lady Alimony 1659, D. 2:—

"I shall unravel
The clew of my misfortunes in small threads
Thin spun, as is the subtil *gothsemay.*"

A little further corruption might make "otomie." Or it may be meant for "atomy," a word used by Shakspere in Romeo and Juliet, i. 4, 57; As You Like It, iii. 5, 13; for which Nares says "*Otamy*" was also used by old writers without any design to burlesque their language." But he gives no reference, nor have I succeeded in finding an instance of it. Dyce in his Glossary to Shakspere in atomy says, "So Ottamy. *Craven Dialect.*" For a wonderful abundance of gossamer on September 21st, 1741, see White's Selborne, Letter xxiii. He says that "these cobweblike appearances, called gossamer, are the real production of small spiders

Cephalus and Procris.

which swarm in the fields in fine weather in the autumn, and have a power of shooting out webs from their tails, so as to render themselves lighter than air." The French say that it is caused by the Virgin "qui file."

Garments of this fine texture were called ἀραχνώδεις. Eustathius de Ismeniæ et Ismenes Amor. 42, "'Αραχνώδης ὁ χιτὼν τῇ παρθένῳ," like those mentioned by Horace, Sat. i. 2, 101. " *Cois* tibi pene videre est Ut nudam," by Propertius, iv. 2, 23, " Indue me *Cois*," by Petronius, Cap. 55. Æquum est induere nuptam *ventum textilem*, Palam prostare nudam *nebula linea*;" and by Fulgentius, Mythologicon, i. p. 13, ed. 1681. " Astiterant itaque *syrmate nebuloso lucidæ* ternæ virgines," one of whom is described as "talo tenus discinctam recolligens vestem," as Edwards represents " Aurora's vale downe trayling to her thighes."

P 8, l. 23. *Her hands.*] The reference is to ῥοδοδάκτυλος so frequent in Homer and Hesiod, and always as epithet of 'Ηὼς, which Spenser F. Q. i. 2, 7, renders "the rosy-fingered Morning faire;" while strange to say neither Shakspere nor Milton have an equivalent epithet though the latter has something like it in P. L. vi. 3, 5 :—

> " Till morn,
> Waked by the circling hours, with *rosy hand*
> Unbarred the gates of light."

Of it Aristotle, Rhetoric, iii. 2, 23, observes, Τὰς δὲ μεταφορὰς ἐντεῦθεν οἰστέον ἀπὸ καλῶν, ἢ τῇ φωνῇ, ἢ τῇ δυνάμει, ἢ τῇ ὄψει, ἢ ἄλλῃ τινὶ αἰσθήσει· διαφέρει δ' εἰπεῖν οἷον " ῥοδοδάκτυλος ἠώς," μᾶλλον ἢ " φοινικοδάκτυλος," ἢ ἔτι φαυλότερον " ἐρυθροδάκτυλος."

The latter reminds one of the burlesque description in Hudibras, Part ii. Canto. ii. 31, 32 :—

> " And like a *Lobster* boyl'd, the *Morn*
> From *black* to *red* began to turn."

The Latin poets, owing to the genius of their language and the necessities of their metres, were unable to introduce a similar compound, and were limited to the use of " rosea " in divers combinations.

Compare in the 31st of the Homeric Hymns, l. 6, 'Ηῶ τε ῥοδόπηχυν, a very inferior epithet, though applied by Sappho to the χάριτες, and missing the peculiar force of ῥοδοδάκτυλος, on which the Scholiast well observes, ἀπὸ τοῦ σχήματος τῶν τῆς χειρὸς δακτύλων παρίστησι τὸ τῶν ἀκτίνων σχῆμα.

P. 8, l. 25. *Venus.*] Or, "The morning star that guides the starry flock," P. L. v. 708. Cicero de Nat. Deor. ii. xx, 53. " Infima est quinque errantium, terræque proxima stella Veneris, quæ Φωσφόρος Græcè, Lucifer Latinè dicitur cum antegreditur Solem ; cum subsequitur autem Hesperos." So Pliny Nat. Hist. ii. 8—" præveniens quippe, et ante matutinum exoriens, Luciferi nomen accipit, ut Sol alter, diem maturans." P. L. vi. 166-169. Shakspere, Mid. N. Dr. iii. 2, 380.

"And yonder shines Aurora's harbinger."

A close resemblance to Edwards' line.

"In that she waites before like to a starre."

Milton's May Morning begins

"Now the bright morning star, day's harbinger,
Comes dancing from the east."

All traceable to the Homeric ἑωσφόρος, Il. xxiii. 226.

Ἦμος δ' Ἑωσφόρος εἶσι φόως ἐρέων ἐπὶ γαῖαν,
ὅντε μέτα κροκόπεπλος ὑπεὶρ ἅλα κίδναται Ἠώς.

Upon these astronomical expressions see Transactions of the New Shakspere Society, 1877-9, Part iii. Paper xvii. by Mr. Furnival. Wordsworth addresses a sonnet to "Venus as an Evening Star," but in his Ode on May Morning calls her "the star that led the morn."

P. 8, l. 31. *Dion.*] For Dione, the mother of Venus, but here used for Venus herself. So in Britain's Ida, printed in Spenser's Works, Argument to Canto ii.

"*Diones* Garden of Delight
With wonder holds Anchises' sight."

While in the third line it is called "Faire *Venus* grove"

P. 8. Margin. *Pleiades.*] In the Dict. Histor. in Cooper's Thesaurus—

"Pleiades, the seven starres, which mariners use in triyng of coastes : Poetes feign them to be the seven daughters of Lycurgus, or Atlas."

From this it would seem Edwards took his note. They are all but universally called the daughters of Atlas. In fact, I can find only one passage wherein Lycurgus is said to be their father, viz., in the Scholia

Cephalus and Procris.

Vetera Latina on Germanici Arateu Phœnomena, 255 (Aratus ed. Buhle, 1801, vol. ii. p. 65.

"Pleiades a pluralitate Græci vocant, Latini eo quod vere exoriantur Vergilias dicunt. Dicit autem Pherecydes Athenæus septem sorores fuisse Lycurgi filias, ex Naxo insula, et pro eo quod Liberum educaverunt a Jove inter sidera sunt relatæ."

For the modern view of them, see Cox's Mythology of the Aryan Nations, ii. 286.

P. 8, Margin. *Seaven Starres.*] See the Transactions of the New Shakspere Society, 1877-9, Part iii. Article xvii. p. 448, for a note by Mr. W. Aldis Wright, from which it appears that the Pleiades are generally meant by the Seven Stars, though a second note by Mr. P. A. Daniel adduces several passages in which the seven planets seem to be intended.

P. 8, l. 32. *Base in respect of duetie.*] Base is here lowly, ordinary; as the rising of the Pleiades indicated the time for adventuring to sea, and their setting the time for planting wheat, both ordinary, common, matters. See Virgil, Georg. i. 138, 221. The phrase occurs in Hero and Leander, p. 14 "Base in respect of thee."

P. 8, l. 32. *Outcoates.*] This word seems one coined by Edwards. I can find no other instance of it. The Pleiades, as daughters of Lycurgus, are supposed to be clothed with garments of light, but these "outcoates" are "base," that is the outward surface emits or reflects but a dim light, they are not "bright luminaries," "bright officious lamps" like most stars, whose duetie is "merely to officiate light round this opacous earth" (P. L. viii. 22). So they are described by Aratus Phænom, 264, "αἱ μὲν ὅμως ὀλίγαι καὶ ἀφεγγέες," rendered by Cicero "Hæ tenues parvo labentes lumine lucent." Their appearance at sunrise has attracted the notice also of Milton in P. L. vii. 374, "The gray Dawn, and the Pleiades before him danc'd."

P. 9, l. 1. *Each God, and Goddess.*] Each star, named after God or Goddess, "Dion noates;" "beauties pride," "the mornings honor" spreading over all the heavens, like "Neptune's honor" the tide, over the Ocean, "as the waters cover the sea" (Is. xi. 9). But one tide lasts only till another comes, beauty "ever over-rules." Such may be the meaning of these obscure lines. The power of beauty is well described by Spenser in Colin Clout, 873 :—

Notes.

> " Beautie, the burning lamp of heavens light,
> Darting her beames into each feeble mynd :
> Against whose powre, nor God, nor man can fynd
> Defence, ne ward the daunger of the wound."

P. 9, l. 6. *Heavens glory.*] The starry heavens.
Earth's cause of mourning.] The darkness of night.
Both " vanquished by Aurora," before whom they disappear. This is confirmed by what Wordsworth says of the Sun " Hail, orient conqueror of gloomy night." Ode for General Thanksgiving, 1816. Compare Narcissus, p. 55 :—

> " Now Phœbus gins in pride of majestie,
> To streake the welkin with his darting beames,
> And now the lesser planets seem to die,
> For he in throne with Cristall dashing streames,
> Richer than Indiaes golden vained gleames
> In chariot mounted, throwes his sparkling lookes."

P. 9, l. 9, *Red-hoat.*] "The vowel in *hot* was formerly long" (Skeat in v.), as the spelling adopted by Edwards and others indicates; see p. 8, " Kils the *hoat* fume." R. Carew's Tasso p. 118 ; Gabriel Harvey's Pierce's Supererogation pp. 55, 78, 145. So Edwards pp. 9, 10, 59, has " noates " for notes ; p. 59 " poast " for post; and Gascoigne i. 379 " boane " for bone ; i. 175 " hoapte " for hoped.

The Poet's meaning seems to be that so long as " Venus " (the morning star) is shining the " beauty " of the morning continues, though " when the sparckling vault is fild with over-swaying heate," it must give place of necessite, and that is " base ; " " What ! upon compulsion ? No," as Falstaff says, (1 Hen. IV. ii. 4, 261.)

P. 9, l. 11, *Along'st.*] This form is here applied with great propriety, " as it means much more than 'along.' Precisely as 'along' is formed from ' a ' and ' long,' so along'st is formed from the superlative of 'lángr, löng, lángt.' This is 'löngst' or 'lengst,' and out of this an adverb 'álengst' or 'álöngst' has been formed, which means not 'along' but ' alongest,' it being, as is common enough in old Norse, a superlative adverb, meaning not *longe* but *longissime* in Latin." Dasent, Jest and Earnest, ii. 59, 60. It does not appear in Stratmann's Dictionary of Early English from the 12th to the 15th centuries, nor in Skelton, Spenser, Shakspere or Milton. The earliest quotation in Richardson's

Cephalus and Procris.

Dictionary is from Niccol's Thucydides, 1550. Halliwell quotes it from Holinshed; Boucher in his Glossary from Carew's Cornwall and The Beehive of the Romish Church, and says that "this annexation of the termination of the superlative degree to prepositions, though very ancient, and practised by the Saxons, is now, I believe entirely confined to the people of Scotland." Nares's Glossary, ed. 2, has two quotations from poets, viz., John Taylor, and Du Bartas by Sylvester—both subsequent to Edwards, who seems therefore to have been the first to introduce this form into poetical language.

P. 9, l. 11. *Hesperides.*] Properly the daughters of Hesperus, the guardians of the islands in which were "those Hesperian gardens famed of old;" P. L. iii. 568, but sometimes applied to the islands also, as by Shakspere L. L. L., iv. 3, 341, 2.

"For Valour is not Love a Hercules
Still climbing trees in the Hesperides."

and by Milton in Paradise Regained, ii. 357,

Ladies of th' Hesperides.

a passage in Pliny, N. H. vi. 36, "Hesperides insulæ," which would have justified this usage, is now read "Hesperidum insulæ." Edwards appears to include both meanings—for Aurora " passes by Hesperides laden with honor of those golden eies," as if he meant the place—while "stoupe they did, thinking 'twas Venus," implies the act of the "Ladies" themselves.

P. 9, l. 12. *Golden Eies.*] The golden apples, $\mu\hat{\eta}\lambda a$ τε χρυσέα καλὰ παρ' Ἑσπερίδων λιγυφώνων. Orpheus ap. Clem. Alex. Protrepticon, p. 15, ed. Potter, παγχρύσεα μῆλα in Ap. Rhod. iv. 398, "fulgentia poma," Lucan, ix. 366, "mala" simply in Virgil, "Tum canit Hesperidum miratam mala puellam."—Ecl. vi. 61.

"The fair Hesperian tree laden with blooming gold." Comus, 393,4.
"Fruit burnished with golden rind." P. L. iv. 249.

Ovid more fully:—

"Arboreæ frondes auro radiante nitentes
Ex auro ramos, ex auro poma tegebant." Met. iv. 636, 7.

On which T. Warton remarks (Comus, 981) "that he is the only ancient author who says the trees were of gold," an idea adopted by Milton (Comus, 981):—

> "All amidst the gardens fair
> Of Hesperus, and his daughters three
> That sing about the golden tree."

and previously by Marlowe, who in Hero and Leander, p. 36, speaks of "the fruit of the golden tree." The Dict. Hist. in Cooper's Thesaurus (a work which Edwards was familiar with) under Hesperidum Horti has "The gardens wherein were the golden apples, now called Orenges." Others from the two senses of μῆλον, take them for sheep. Vossius more poetically interprets this fable of the Hesperides φυσικώς: "Per hortum Hesperidum intelligitur cœlum stellatum—mala aurea sunt stellæ—Draco qui custodit vel Zodiacus est, vel Horizon. Quod Hercules rapuisse fertur mala Hesperidum, eo signatur Solem exortum luce suâ præstringere lumen stellarum.

The latest, and, probably, the correct interpretation is given by Cox in his Comparative Mythology—

> "Far away in the west is the dwelling of the Hesperides—but near the hounds of everlasting darkness—hence the dragon Ladon guards with them the golden apples which Gaia gave to Hebe when she became the bride of Zeus, these apples being the golden-tinted clouds or herds of Helios, the same word (μῆλα) being used to denote both." ii. 32.

The metaphorical expression "golden eies" is nowhere else applied to fruit, so far as I am aware, but is used by Shakespeare of flowers in the Song in Cymbeline, ii. 3, 25 (written in 1609).

> "And winking Mary-buds begin
> To ope their *golden eyes*."

Milton in Lycidas has

> "Ye valleys low,—
> Throw hither all your quaint *enamell'd* eyes,
> That on the green turf suck the honied showers,
> And purple all the ground with vernal flowers."

On which T. Warton observes that the term *eyes* is technical in the botany of flowers. Shakespeare has, in the Tempest, ii. 1, 54—

> "The ground indeed is tawny, with an *eye* of green in it."

On which Malone says that

> "Eye is used for a small portion of any thing."

This might apply to the fruit amid the foliage—but its brilliant look seems more likely to have suggested the metaphor to a poet.

2 F

P. 9, l. 15. *Golden Orchard.*] Marlowe, Hero, and Leander, p. 36 :—

"Leander now like Theban Hercules
Enter'd the orchard of th' Hesperides."

So Lucan, ix. 360 :—

"Fuit aurea silva,
Divitiisque graves, et fulvo germine rami,
Virginensque chorus, nitidi custodia luci,
Et nunquam somno damnatus lumina serpens
Robora complexus rutilo curvata metallo."

P. 9, l. 15. *Tower.*] Marlowe, Hero, and Leander, p. :—

"For know that underneath this radiant flour
Was Danaes Statue in a brasen tower."

P. 9, l. 15. Margin. *Ovid lib.* 2, *de Tristibus.*] In this book Ovid merely refers to Danae in line 401.

"Quid Danaen, Dannesque nurum, matremque Lyæi?"

But in his Amores, ii. 19, 27, 28, he writes :—

"Si nunquam Danaen habuisset aënea turris
Non esset Danae de Jove facta parens."

And again in the De Arte Amandi, iii. 415, 416 :—

"Quis Danaen nosset si semper clansa fuisset,
Inque sua turri perlatuisset anus."

P. 9, l. 20. *Plume on.*] To plume in falconry is to pluck off the feathers from a bird :—

"It is when a hawke caseth a fowle, and pulleth the feathers from the body."—Latham.

Nares in v. *To Plume on*, as used here of "Venus' Doves" is therefore a very correct phrase for inserting or putting on feathers as described by our Poet, whose notion of the metamorphosed lovers sending their feathers to the Idalian mount as a sort of tribute to Venus is also, so far as I am aware, due to his own invention.

P. 9, l. 21. *Itis—Progne.*] Their story is told by Gower, Confessio Amantis Book v. pp. 313—330, ed. Pauli.

P. 9, l. 27. *Her Swift-heel'd Pegasus.*] Not a mere figure of speech to indicate the rapid spread of the morning light, but in accordance with the Antient Mythologists. Tzetzes in his Scholia on Lycophron, 16, 17, after recording that Homer (Od. xxiii. 246) calls the horses of the Day Lampos and Phaethon (the bright, and the shining), adds, οἱ δὲ νέοι τῷ

Πηγάσῳ ἐποχουμένην αὐτὴν (sc. Ἡμέραν) εἰσάγουσι μυθικῶς, ὥσπερ ὁ Λυκόφρων. And after Pegasus had been received into the skies by Jupiter, "Ἡ γοῦν Ἡμέρα παρὰ Διὸς τοῦτον αἰτεῖται, ὡς ἂν ἐποχουμένη αὐτῷ τὸν ἡμερήσιον κύκλον βαδίζῃ. So in the Scholia on Iliad vi. 155, τὸν δὲ ἵππον λαβεῖν τὴν Ἠῶ, δεηθεῖσαν τοῦ Διὸς, δῶρον πρὸς τὸ ἀκόπως περιιέναι τὰς τοῦ κόσμου περιόδους. The passage of Lycophron 16, 17, is, Ἠὼς μὲν αἰπὺν ἄρτι Φηγίου πάγον
Κραιπνοῖς ὑπερποτᾶτο Πηγάσου πτεροῖς.

Instead of the characteristic epithet for Pegasus, πτερόεις (the wingy) as in Pindar Ol. xiii. 122, Isth. vii. 63, Euripides Ion 202, or πτερωτὸς (the winged), Schol. in Iliad vi. 155—in Latin, "ales," Hor. Od. iv. 11, 27—the English poet has preferred the "swift-heeled," ὠκυποὺς, in Homer always epithet of horses. Hofman in his Lexicon, after Vossius, says "Nec absurdè tamen per Pegasum etiam intelligantur nubes, quæ in altum subvolant, et per mediam aeris regionem avis instar deferuntur: uti nec incommodè Neptuni proles censentur, cùm vapores attollantur è mari." This is now the received interpretation: "Not less significant is the myth of Pegasus, the magnificent piles of sunlit cloud, which seem to rise as if on eagles' wings to the highest heaven, and in whose bosom may lurk the lightnings and thunders of Zeus. Like Athênê and Aphroditê, like Daphnê and Arethousa, this *horse of the morning* (Eôs) must be born from the waters: hence he is Pegasos sprung from the fountains (πηγάι) of Poseidôn, the Sea."—Cox, Aryan Mythology, ii. 288.

P. 9, l. 28. *Colchos.*] The name of the land is *Colchis*, of the people *Colchi*, but our Poets have adopted the form *Colchos; e.g.*, Gower, Confessio Amantis, Bk. v.; Shakespeare, Merchant of Venice, ii. 171. "Colchos' Strand." Even a scholar like Sandys in the notes to his translation of Ovid's Metamorphoses speaks of "the expedition to Colchos." Sylvester's Du Bartas Fifth Day, "The pride of Greece That sail'd to Colchos for the Golden Fleece."

P. 9, l. 28. *Golden Fleece.*] The story of the Golden Fleece is told by Gower, Conf. Am. Bk. v. vol. ii. ed. Pauli, 1857, pp. 236—273.

> "The fame of thilke shepes felle,
> Whiche in Colchos, as it befelle,
> Was all of gold, shal never die."—p. 269.

Cephalus and Procris.

There is something prophetic here, for, in addition to the three Epics which have come down to us from classic times by Orpheus, Apollonius Rhodius, and Valerius Flaccus, the memory of the Argonautic Expedition has been revived in our day by the poem on "the Life and Death of Jason," by William Morris.

P. 9, l. 29. *Swift Windes Harrould Mercury.*] In the Hymn εἰς Ἑρμῆν 3, he is styled ἄγγελος ἀθανάτων. In the Iliad and Odyssey διάκτορος, the guide—and in later writers the messenger. Hesiod calls him κήρυξ— strictly the herald. Op. 80, Th. 939. In Horace he is the " magni Jovis et deorum Nuntius." Od. i. x. 5.

If we may transpose the two words " swift windes," and read " wind-swift," the compound would equal ποδήνεμος, ἀελλόπος, epithets of Iris in the Iliad, of which Phurnutus in his Treatise de Natura Deorum, cap. xvi., καὶ γὰρ τὴν Ἶριν ποδήνεμον διά τοῦτο, καὶ ἀελλόποδα καλοῦσιν ἄγγελον, ἀπὸ τοῦ ὀνόματος παρεισάγοντες. Hinc nominant etiam Irim ποδήνεμον, id est velocem, et ἀελλόποδα, id est pernicem ipso nomine nuncium significantes. Gale, Opuscula Mythologica Amst., 1688, p. 166. Nonnus also in his Dionysiaca, ix. 93, describes Ἑρμῆς, as Ἠέρι δινέων ἀνεμώδεα ταρσὰ πεδίλων, with which we may parallel Milton's " throws his steep flight in many an aery wheel." P. L. iii. 741. His association with Aurora by Edwards is quite in harmony with the views of modern comparative mythology, as may be seen in the following extract. " But even in the Hermes of Homer and other poets, we can frequently discover the original traits of a *Sáraméya,* (the Dawn-son) if we take that word in the sense of twilight, and look on *Hermes* as a male representative of the light of the morning. He loves *Herse,* the dew, and Aglauros her sister, among his sons is *Kephalos,* the head of the day. He is the herald of the Gods, so is the twilight, so was *Sáramá,* the messenger of Indra." Max Muller Lectures on Language, 2nd series 476. Marlowe, Hero and Leander, p. 20, calls him " Heavens *winged* herald Jove-born Mercury." Edwards may have written" swift-winged."

P. 9, l. 30. *Golden sonne-beames.*] It will be observed that our poet takes Aurora to visit three ancient localities with golden traditions: the Hesperides famed for the golden apples; the tower of Danae for the shower of gold; and Colchos for the golden fleece. Venus is apparently left at the Idalian Mount, and Mercury takes her place, with whom " she (Aurora) mainely posts to Colchos, and there a time abodes."

Under "Colchos and the golden fleece" there is probably some covert allusion to England and the trade in wool, one of the chief sources of the national wealth. " In 1297 it was estimated at half the rent of the Kingdom."—Pearson's England, ii. 284. In the reign of James I. " nine-tenths of the commerce of the kingdom consisted in woollen goods."—Hume, app. to ch. xlix. That individuals became wealthy in consequence is implied in the sneer of the Earl of Arundel in 1621 at Lord Spencer, " My Lord, when these thing were doing, your ancestors were keeping sheep," alluding to the numerous flocks kept by his grandfather, Sir John Spencer, who died in 1586. Collins' Peerage by Brydges, i. 391.

The poet's argument is, that if they registered at "Apolloes tree the feates ydone by valorous warlike knights," and received crowns of baies, *i.e.*, praise and fame, they ought also to receive from their patron Apollo, with the help of their friend Mercury, the "golden sonnebeames," that is, the substantial rewards for their verses.

P. 9, l. 30. *Apolloes tree.*] Apolloes tree is the Laurus or Bay. Ovid in his legend of Apollo and Daphne accounts for it thus:—

" Cui Deus, At conjux quoniam mea non potes esse,
Arbor eris certe, dixit, mea. Semper habebunt
Te coma, te citharæ, te nostræ, Laure, pharetræ.
Tu ducibus Latiis aderis, quum læta triumphum
Vox canet ; et longas visent Capitolia pompas."—Met. i. 557-561.

Hence not only conquerors but poets were crowned with it. Horace speaks of Pindar as

" Laureâ donandus Apollinari."—Od. iv. 2, 9

And Ovid,

" Te precor incipiens, adsit tua laurea nobis,
Carminis et medicæ Phœbe, repertor opis."—Rem. Am. 75, 6.

See Chaucer's Poem of "The Floure and the Leafe" for the typical meaning of such crowns of leaves.

Professor Daubeney in his Essay on the Trees and Shrubs of the Ancients, Oxford, 1865, says that

" The term *Laurus* was employed by the ancients with great laxity. The *Royal Laurel*, sacred to Apollo, and known as the Augustan, being used in triumphs to encircle the brow of the conqueror, is the Bay, or *Laurus Nobilis* of Linnæus, belonging to the family of *Laurineæ*, and possessing something of the aroma so remarkable in certain tropical species of the same family, namely, in the cinnamon and cassia. Sibthorp identifies it with the Δάφνη of Dioscorides."—pp. 119-121.

"That which is the commonest of any at the present day, using the term Laurel in its popular sense, namely, the *Cerasus Laurocerasus* or Laurel Cherry, appears to have been unknown to the Ancients, having been introduced into Europe from Trebizond in 1576, by Clusius under great difficulties, for which see London's Arboretum, vol. ii. p. 717."—Ibid. p. 123.

Now T. Edwards always speaks of the bay, *e.g.*, p. 4, "Deckt gloriously with bayes." P. 62., "Other nymphes had sent him baies." P. 63, "To have honoured him with baies." And p. 64, "Sufficeth that they merit baies," but he apparently here refers to the common Laurel, then a novelty, as he sends Aurora under the special guidance of Mercury to Colchos, close to Trebizond, the region in which it grows wild, " to gaine a sight of it." Loudon says that the Laurel is not mentioned in the first edition of Gerard's Herbal, published in 1597, two years after this poem; notwithstanding this, some specimens may have been introduced into this country by 1595. By 1633 it was in many of our choice gardens—and in 1629 Parkinson in his *Paradisus* says he had a plant of it, calling it the Bay Cherry, as he does in his Theatrum Botanicum, 1640, p. 1516. There is a notice of it in Evelyn's Silva, Book ii., chap. vi.

P. 9, l. 31. *Where.*] This refers to "Apolloes Tree," as implying the works of poets, whose crowns ("doctarum præmia frontium") are of its leaves, and who register in their verses the praises of their heroes. Compare Horace:—

"Vixere fortes ante Agamemnona
Multi, sed omnes illacrimabiles
Urgentur, ignotique longa
Nocte, carent quia vate sacro."—Od. iv. ix. 25.

P. 9, l. 32. *Knightes of the Sonne.*] There is no Order of Knights bearing this title, but among the heroes of Romance few are more celebrated than the Knight of the Sun, whose claim to pre-eminence was stoutly maintained by Master Nicholas, the barber-surgeon, in the disputes with Don Quixote and the Parish Priest, at La Mancha. His life was published by Ortunez da Calahorra in 1562, and in 1578 translated into English, under the title of "The Mirror of Princely Deedes and Knighthood, wherein is shewed the worthinesse of the Knight of the Sunne and his brother Rosicleer, &c." This book was popular, and there is a tacit reference to it here as a model for Knights, whose qualifications are summed up in the following acrostic of the word Miles, by the Cardinal Petrus Capucius, (Ashmole's Order of the Garter, p. 40.)

"Each Knight should be M agnanimus in adversitate :
        I ngenuus in consanguinitate :
        L argifluus in honestate :
        E gregius in Curalitate
        S trenuus in virili probitate."

Be such, says our poet, and we followers of Apollo will eternize your names in our verses, and you also shall be enrolled under our own patron, under his other name of Phœbus, the Sun, as a new order, and be yclept "Knights of the Sonne." We will pluck the leaves of the bay in singing your "featès ydone," while you will shed on us in return "golden sonne beames." There is something to the purpose in Chaucer:—

"Now fair madame, quoth I,
If I durst ask what is the cause, and why,
That Knightis have the ensigne of honoure
Rathir by the lefè, than by the flour ?
Sothly, daughtir quoth she, this is the trouth,
For Knightes ever shoud be persevering.
To seke honour, without faintise, or slouth:
Fro wele to bettir in all manir thing,
In signe of which, with levis ay lasting,
Thay be rewardid after ther degre,
Whose lusty grene may not appairid be."
        The Floure and the Leafe, 543—553

The editions of "The Knight of the Sun" will be found in Brunet's Manuel under "Ortunez," "Rosset," and a different work under "Villalumbrales." The Italian editions also in Ferrarios Bibliografia dei Romanzi, 1829; the English in Lowndes, p. 1573, under "Mirror;" in Hazlitt's Hand-book and Collections under "Knight of the Sun;" and in the Huth Catalogue under "Mirror of Princely Deedes."

P. 10, l. 1. *Knightes of the Garter.*] This mention of an English Order confirms the conjecture that under Colchos he has England in view—and refers perhaps to the verses on the Order of the Garter by William Teshe, written in 1582, printed by Sir Harris Nicolas in his Orders of Knighthood, vol. ii., 1842 ; and again by the Ballad Society "Ballads from Manuscripts," vol. ii., part ii., pp. 115-129, from the Harl. MS. 3437, in the British Museum. These, like other poems, were no doubt circulated in MS. But we have a distinct celebration of the Knights of the Garter by one contemporary with the formation of the Order, viz., Chaucer in the Floure and the Leafe :

> "Eke there be Knightis old of the Gartir,
> That in ther timis did right worthily,
> And the honour they did to the laurir,
> Is for by it they have ther laud wholly,
> Ther triumph eke, and martial glory,
> Which unto them is more perfite riches
> Than any wight imagin can or gesse."—519-525.

Spenser also is supposed to intend the Knights of the Garter, though mentioned under another title in compliment to the Virgin Queen, in his Fairy Queen, Book i., Canto vii. 46.

> "At last, yled with far reported praise,
> Which flying fame throughont the world had spred,
> Of doughty Knights, whom Faery land did raise,
> That noble order hight of Maidenhed,
> Forthwith to Court of Gloriane I sped."

The history of the Order may be read in the works of Ashmole, Anstis, Nicolas, and Beltz.

P. 10, l. 1. *Auncient Knights of Rhodes.*] Called auncient because they were now Knights of Malta. Founded as an Order in 1092 or 1099, and instituted as Knights by King Baldwin the First in 1104, they bore the name at first of "The Hospitalars of St. John Baptist in Jerusalem." When Saladin had taken Jerusalem they retired first to Acre, and then seized the Island of Rhodes in 1308. Here they remained 214 years, till 1522, when Solyman the Great took the island by force. The Emperor Charles V. granted them the island of Malta in 1530, and they have ever since been called Knights of Malta. Vertot has written the history of the Order : Caoursin an account of the siege of Rhodes. Brunet, in the Table Methodique, 21977-22008, enumerates the chief works on these "Ordres de Chevalerie." "The Knights of St. John" was the subject for the English Verse Prize at Oxford in 1836, when the successful competitor for it was F. W. Faber, of University College.

P. 10, l. 6. *Triumphes.*] Triumphal songs, or odes such as those of Pindar and Simonides, the latter of whom is said to have been the first to take money for his poems. Aristotle Rhet. iii. ii. 14 has an anecdote of him that when Anaxilaus of Rhegium offered him a small fee to write an Epinician Ode on his victory at Olympia in the mule race he declined, ὡς δυσχεραίνων εἰς ἡμιόνους ποιεῖν, ἐπεὶ δ' ἱκανὸν ἔδωκεν, ἐποίησε, " Χαίρετ' ἀελλοπόδων θύγατρες ἵππων" καίτοι καὶ τῶν ὄνων θύγατρες ἦσαν. Perhaps Edwards had in mind the liberal payments made to Chœrilus by Alexander the Great:

"Gratus Alexandro regi Magno fuit ille
Chœrilus, incultis qui versibus et male natis
Rettulit acceptos, regale nomisma, Philippos."—Epist. ii. i. 232—234.

P. 10, l. 7. *Hermes, &c.*] In the Homeric Hymn to Hermes when Apollo had received from Hermes the lyre which he had invented, he promises in return

ὄλβον, καὶ πλόυτου δώσω περικαλλέα ῥάβδον,
χρυσείην· (529, 530.)

To this Zeus appears to have been a consenting party as in 505 he rejoices at the reconciliation between the two Gods, and thus " Jove may have bene favourable then " to Hermes, the patron of poets, possessing also the golden rod which would enable him to procure them their reward.

P. 10, l. 11. *Pesants.*] In the Prologue to his Satires Persius says—

"—— ipse semipaganus," 6.

P. 10, l. 12. *Similies.*] N. Breton, " The Courtier and the Countryman," p. 5, col. 2, l. 29, ed. Grosart, "if there may be a *similie* of heaven upon earth." " The prince's similies " would be the image or likeness of the prince on his coins, and hence the coins themselves, as above, " regale nomisma, Philippos.'

P. 10, l. 15. *The ruler of the East.*] Is this Apollo whose " golden sonne-beames " were spoken of on p. 9, and who is invoked on p. 12, l. 19?

P. 10, l. 18. *Gold is approv'd.*] Whitney's Emblems, p. 139—

" The tocche doth trye the fine and purest goulde."

See Nares' Glossary in v. The Poet alludes to himself under the figure of the touch-stone, and implies that a " slender " reward would be " approved" by him as true metal. So in Bodenham's Belvedere, p. 55—

" Poets scant sweetly write, except they meet
With sound rewards, for sermoning so sweet."

Cephalus and Procris.

P. 10, l 29. *Groome.*] Here used in its wider sense, as in Lucrece, 1013,

"Poor grooms are sightless night, kings glorious day."

Though this word generally carries the sense of a menial, Spenser seems sometimes to have allowed it a higher meaning. In the Fairy Q. vi. viii. 27.

"It was his owne true groome, the gentle squire;"

and in Colin Clout, 12 —

"One of those groomes, a jolly groome was he
As ever piped on an oaten reed."

The letter *r* has probably been inserted so that it is from the A. S. guma, a man; or as Horne Tooke, Pt. ii. ch. iv. thinks from gyman curare, so that "it applies to the person by whom something is attended."

P. 10, l. 29. *Of some compare.*] Worthy of comparison with others, and so of some mark and dignity. Shakspere, V. and A. 8, "Sweet above compare"; Lucrece, 40, "Braving compare"; and in Troilus, iii. ii. 182,

"When their rhymes
Full of protest, or oath, and big compare,
Want similes, truth tired of iteration—
Yet after all comparisons of truth,
As 'True as Troilus' shall crown up the verse."

The word is found in other writers of the period, and is used by Milton, P. L. i. 588, and four other passages, by Waller, and by Suckling.

P. 11, l. 3. *Anger.*] Is here eagerness, excitement. For the history of the word see "Jest and Earnest," by Sir G. W. Dasent, ii. pp. 90-92.

P. 11, l. 7. *In pride.*] That is, in praise or exaltation of.

P. 11, l. 15. *Heisell wan.*] Is hazel wand. Wan is for wand, as on p. 13, growne for ground; and p. 20, tex for text. The simile was possibly suggested by Marlowe's line, H. and L. p. 8, "His body was as straight as Circe's wand." See Baring-Gould's Curious Myths of Middle Ages, 1st ser. p. 78, where there is an engraving of a *straight* divining rod; and Brand's Pop. Ant. iii. 176, ed. Knight, 1841, where a passage from Ammianus Marcellinus is quoted about the Alani, "Futura miro præsagiunt modo: nam *rectiores* virgas vimineas colligentes," &c.

P. 11, l. 17. *Checkt.*] So Marlowe, H. and L. p. 30, "and with his hoves checks the submissive ground."

P. 11, l. 22. *Sort.*] Go forth. Fr. sortir; Lat. sortiri, separate, divide by lot, go

Notes. 223

out, cf. *partiri*, to depart and to part. Brachet, Fr. Etym. Dict. Littré dissents from this, and traces it to Lat. *surgere*, to rise through the form *surrectire*. The verb occurs in Bacon's Essays, vii. 35, xxvii. 48, "sorteth to discord"—"to inconvenience." On the former Dr. Abbott notes, "It turns out, from Lat. *sors*, a lot that is drawn or shaken out of a helmet." But in a note to Essay xxii. 120, he seems to approve Littré's derivation.

P. 11, l. 27. *Many a prettie story.*] A few names, instead of general allusions, would have removed the obscurity of the following lines.

P. 11, l. 29. *Men transformed to Apes.*] See Ovid. Met. xiv. 90—100, where he narrates how Jupiter transformed the Cercopes for their perjury into Apes.

P. 11, l. 30. *Fiends made Angels, &c.*] If the Poet intended any reference to Scripture, he may have had in view these passages, 2 Cor. xi. 14, "For Satan himself is transformed into an angel of light." And St. Jude, 6, "And the angels which kept not their first estate, but left their own habitation, he hath reserved in everlasting chains under darkness unto the judgment of the great day."

P. 11, l. 32. *How Schollers fauorites waxe ouer poore.*] That is Poets, or Patrons. If the former it may refer to Marlowe, H. and L. p. 20 - 24, who has a myth that Mercury in order to gratify his mistress having stolen some nectar from Hebe, was thrust from heaven, but by help of Cupid and the Destinies, dethroned Jove for a time, till becoming faithless to the Destinies they restored Jove, and with regard to himself as a punishment, they added this—

> "That he and poverty should always kiss,
> And to this day is every scholar poor,
> Gross gold from them runs headlong to the boor."

He may, however, have used "favourites" in the sense of "favourers" "patrons" as on p. 4 he possibly does, and thus be lamenting their inability or unwillingness to reward adequately.

P. 12, l. 2. *Too too.*] This reduplicated form, common to the writers of that day, occurs several times. See pp. 17, 18.

P. 12, l. 4. *Garded coats.*] In The Arte of Logique by Thomas Wilson, ed. 1552, p. 92. "Suche a man weareth a livery coote garded with velvet, and all the yeoman sarvantes have but plain coates, ergo he is one of the gentlemen." Rider in his English-Latin Dictionary, Oxon. 1589, has "A garde, homme, or welt of a garment, fimbria, lacinia, limbus, instita." Marston, Scourge of Villanie, Sat. vii. 60—65.

> "Would not some head,
> That is with seeming shadowes only fed,
> Sweare yon same damaske coat, yon garded man,
> Were some grave, sober Cato Utican?
> When, let him but in judgements sight nncase,
> He's naught but budge, old gards, browne fox-fur face."

P. 12, l. 5. *Parramore.*] Originally written *par amour*, as in Chaucer, C. T. 1157, "par amour I loved hire;" on which Tyrwhitt notes, "From hence paramour or paramours in one word was used vulgarly to signify love, or a mistress." Afterwards it meant a lover of either sex (Rider in his Eng. Lat. Dict. renders it by *amasius* and *amasia*), while it has now acquired a bad sense. But Edwards here applies it in its most exalted signification to Spenser, whose friend Gabriel Harvey had previously in 1593 included him under the same appellation, as it seems, in his Pierce's Supererogation, p. 65, "Meanwhile it hath pleased soome sweete wittes of my acquaintaunce (whome Heaven hath baptized the Spirites of Harmony, and the Muses have enterteyned for their *Paramours*) to reacquite Sonnets with Sonnets, and to snibb the Thrasonicall rimester with Angelicall meeter," &c. Spenser also himself uses it with a similar meaning in his F. Q. ii. ix. 34.

P. 12, l. 9, 10.] This silence of Spenser is perhaps referred to by himself in Colin Clout, 180-184:

> "He gan to cast great lyking to my lore,
> And great dislyking to my lucklesse lot,
> That banisht had my selfe, like wight forlore,
> Into that waste, where I was quite forgot."

Todd, in his Life of Spenser, mentions no publication after Daphnaida, in 1592, till Colin Clout, which he assigns to Dec. 1594 or 1595. See pp. lxxxvii and xcvii. This reference to Spenser's temporary silence is valuable, and confirms Todd's opinion of the later date of Colin Clout.

P. 12, l. 11. *Arcadian knight.*] Sir Philip Sidney.

P. 12, l. 13. *And you that tread the pathes.*] Many of these poets are enumerated by Spenser in his Colin Clout, 380-454.

P. 12, l. 27. *Never yet cut.*] So Marlowe says of Leander, p. 7:
"His dangling tresses that were never shorn."

P. 12, l. 30. *Apes die by culling.*] See Whitney's Emblems, 1586, p. 188.
" With kindenes, lo, the Ape doth kill her whelpe,
Through clasping harde, and lulling in her armes."

T. Bancroft, Heroical Lover, 1658, canto ii. p. 18, speaking of Aselgeia,
" Some of them, as Apes their young,
She by embracing kills."

J. Lyly, Euphues and his England, 1579, p. 215 (ed. Arber), in the Epistle Dedicatory,—" Lest I should resemble the Ape, and kill it by cullyng it." The ultimate authority is Pliny, Nat. Hist. viii. 54 (80). "Simiarum generi præcipua erga fetum affectio. Gestant catulos, quæ mansuefactæ intra domos peperere, omnibus demonstrant, tractarique gaudent, gratulationem intelligentibus similes. Itaque magnâ ex parte complectendo necant." As Philemon Holland translates it, " The she apes are wondrous fond of their little ones, and such as are made tame within house will carry them in their armes all about so soon as they have brought them into the world, keep a shewing of them to every bodie, and they take pleasure to have them dandled by others, as if thereby they tooke knowledge that folke joyed for their safe deliverance; but such a culling and hugging of them they keep that in the end with very clasping and clipping they kill them many times." Oppian, however, in his Cynegetica, ii. 605—611, asserts that the apes bring forth only two, one of which they love, and the other they dislike, which is therefore squeezed to death. " αὐτὸς δ' ἀγκαλίδεσσιν ἑῶν τέθνηκε τοκήων." This seems also in some degree to have been the notion of Æsop in the Fable of The Ape and her two young Ones, of one of which she was doatingly fond, while she disregarded and slighted the other.

P. 13, l. 1. *Revying.*] Outwagering, outbidding, exceeding. Ben Jonson has " Slight here's a trick vied and revied!" Every Man in his Humour, iv. 1, on which Gifford notes (vol. i. 106), " To *vie* was to hazard, to put down, a certain sum upon a hand of cards; to *revie* was to cover it with a larger sum, by which the challenged became the challenger, and was to be *revied* in his turn with a proportionate increase of stake. This vying and revying continued till one of the party lost courage, and gave up the whole, or obtained for a stipulated sum a discovery of his antagonist's cards; when the best hand swept the table. The term was in use at many games." To vie is derived by Wedgwood from It. *invitare.* Prov. en-*vidar, enviar.* Fr. *envier,* to invite or propose to throw for certain stakes; and *renvier* to revie from *reinvitare* is in Brachet's Etymol. Dict. H. Coleridge (Gloss. XIIIth Cent.) adopts the view of Burguy (Grammaire de la Langue D'Oil, 1856), who connects it with avoier, voie, via, to urge on the way; which is the explanation in Richardson's Dict. A very different origin is suggested by Cockayne in his work " Spoon and Sparrow," No. 438, p. 110, where Vie is said to be identical with Fight. Both words vie and revie occur in Drayton's Muses Elysium Nymphal, ii. near the end. "LIROPE. Vie and revie like chapmen proffered."

P. 13, l. 4. *Growne.*] For ground, as wan for wand.

P. 13, l. 7. *Gemme.*] This being derived from gemma (i.e. gen-ima shortened into gemma, from geno, gigno, to produce) a bud, is applied to pearls and such precious stones as are distinguished by roundness of form, and like buds—though Wedgwood, less probably, connects it with "ON. gimlir, splendour; gim-stein or shining stone, from gima, for glima, to shine." Aurora's gems, the dew-drops, combine both notions for round as pearls they are also "gems of purest ray serene." In the juxtaposition here of "many a prettie gemme, And flowers sweete as May," Edwards has anticipated Shakspere, in whose xxi. sonnet, 6, 7, they are introduced

"With sun and moon, with earth and sea's rich gems,
With April's first-born flowers."

P. 13, l. 14. *Pan his Syrinx.*] See Ovid Met. i. 689—712.

P. 13, l. 14. *Joves Io.*] Ovid Met. i. 587, *sqq.*

P. 13, l. 15. *Semele.*] Ovid Met. iii. 256, *sqq.*

P. 13, l. 15. *Arcadian Nimphes disport.*] Calisto. See Ovid Met. ii. 401, *sqq.* Who calls her Virgo Nonacrina, 409, and Parrhasis, 460.

P. 13, l. 20. *Ruffe-beard.*] Barnfield, R., Affectionate Shepheard, 2nd day, vii. p. 19, Roxb. Club ed. has, "Ile give thee fine *ruffe-footed* Doves to keepe."

P. 13, l. 23. *Riotouse.*] Wild, unchecked. Generally of persons. Chaucer, C. T. 4406, "so fareth it by a riotous servant." Riot is either from Fr. rioter, a dim. from rire, ridere, excess of laughter; or, as Diez, ii. 402, thinks, from ahd. riban, reiben, to rub; Kilian has "Ravotten" tumultuari, Angl. riot'.

Notes. 227

P. 13, l. 26. *Taint.*] " Our old writers seem to use this word as equivalent to touch, or touch lightly," Richardson. Berner's Froissart, ii. c. 168, " The ii course they *tainted* eche other on ye helmes and passed by." Gascoigne's Works, i. 333:—

> " Bothe concht their launces full agaynst the face,
> But heaven it noldo that there they should them *teinte*."

It seems to be a recognised term in tilting, as in Ben Jonson, ii. 55, " He will taint a staff well at tilt;" and in Massinger, ii. 293, on each of which passages Gifford has a note.

P. 13, l. 32. *Prickt.*] Gower, Conf. Amant. i. 110:—

> " And some gone, and some ride,
> And some prick her horse aside,
> And bridle hem now in now oute."

So Milton, P. L. ii. 535-6:—

> " Before each van Prick forth the aery knights, and couch their spears."

P. 14, l. 5. *Aoris.*] This is apparently an instance of Edwards' having made use of Cooper's Thesaurus, as in the Dict. Hist. appended to it occurs, " Aoris the sonne of Aras a great hunter and warrior." This hero is mentioned by Pausanias, ii. 12, 5: "Ἄραντος δὲ υἱὸς "Αορις, καὶ θυγάτηρ ἐγένετο 'Αραιθυραία· τούτους φασὶ Φλιάσιοι θηράσαι τε ἐμπείρους γενέσθαι, καὶ τὰ ἐς πόλεμον ἀνδρείους. Eustathius also, on Il. ii. 571, in which line 'Αραιθυραία is reckoned among the territories of Agamemnon, having been so named by Aoris in memory of his sister, who died before him, says τούτους Φλιάσιοι θηρατάς φασι καὶ πολεμικούς.

P. 14, l. 12. *Deadfully.*] I find no mention of this word in the Dictionaries. Deathful (Pope), Deathfulness (Jeremy Taylor) are given.

P. 14, l. 13. *Aie me.*] This common interjection is satirically alluded to by Drayton in Sonnet I. To the Reader of his Poems (vol. iv. p. xviii. in Chalmers' ed. of Poets ; p. 441, Drayton's Poems, Roxb. Club, ed. 1856):

> " Love from mine eye a tear shall never wring,
> Nor in *ah-mees* my whining sonnets drest,
> (A libertine) fantastickely I sing.

P. 14, l. 14. *Shot a dart.*] Marlowe, H. and L. p. 14, " shot a shaft."

Cephalus and Procris.

P. 14, l. 16. *Madrigals.*] From mandra, a sheepfold, and originally a shepherd's song, so used with propriety by Milton, Comus, 495.

> "*2nd Brother.* O brother, 'tis my father's shepherd, sure.
> *Elder Brother.* Thyrsis? whose artful strains have oft delay'd
> The meddling brook to hear his madrigal.

and in Marlowe's immortal Passionate Shepherd's Song:

> "By shallow rivers to whose falls
> Melodious birds sing madrigals."

Edwards therefore uses the term appropriately here for Aurora's passionate songs, though "dolefull in tune," as Dryden, Art of Poetry, c. 2, would allow:

> "The madrigal may softer passions move,
> And breathe the tender ecstacie of love."

P. 14, l. 17. *Heaven's Lampe, Phœbus.*] Shakspere, V. and A. 860-2:

> "O thou clear god, and patron of all light,
> From whom each lamp and shining star doth borrow
> The beauteous influence that makes him bright."

"So when heavens lamp that rules the genial day."—S. Duck, The Shunamite.

The ancient poets, however, had already led the way:

> "Forsitan et roseâ sol alte lampade lucens."—Lucretius, v. 608.

and before him, Sophocles makes Antigone lament,

> οὐκ ἔτι μοι τόδε λαμπάδος ἱερὸν ὄμμα
> θέμις ὁρᾶν ταλαίνᾳ.—879, 880.

P. 14, l. 21. *Yvorie streame.*] White as the foam—that is like ivory—where a stream makes passage for itself through the rocks.

P. 14, l. 27. *For love is pitilesse.*] Compare Marlowe, H. and L. p. 36 :—

> "Love is not full of pity, as men say,
> But deaf and cruel where he means to prey."

P. 14, l. 32. *Venom'd spear.*] Deadly as if poison'd. Shakspere uses the phrase metaphorically, K. Richard II. i. 1, 171:—

> "Pierced to the soul with slander's venom'd spear."

P. 15, l. 1. *Gashly.*] A word peculiar to Edwards. Quarles has the adjective, gashful; whence might come gashfully, and perhaps gashly has that sense. Or may it be a misreading for ghastly? Shakspere, 2 Henry IV. ii. 4,

212, has "ghastly, gaping wounds"; and Milton P. L. vi. 368, "ghastly wounds." Shakspere also uses ghastly adverbially, 2 Hen. VI. iii. 2, 170, "staring full *ghastly* like a strangled man."

P. 15, l. 3. *Bleeding-ripe.*] Nares in v. ripe, "In a state ready for any particular act; as *reeling-ripe* in a state of intoxication fit for reeling," as in the Tempest, v. 1, 279, "And Trinculo is reeling-ripe." He instances "crying-ripe," "smarting-ripe"; to which add from N. Breton, "Fortunes of Two Princes," p. 25, col. 2, 14 (ed. Grosart), "her eyes weeping-ripe."

P. 15, l. 4. *Pel mel.*] Promiscuously, confusedly. It is found several times in Shaksp., in Hudibras, i. 3, 506; and in Milton's Prose Works, North's Plutarch, and Bishop Hall. It is from the French "*Pêle-mêle,* formerly *pesle-mesle,* properly to move (*mêler*) with a shovel (*pelle*)." Brachet and Skeat Etymol. Dict. This may be; but the explanation in Wedgwood is simpler, "Formed by a rhyming supplement to *mesler,* to mix. Written *mesle-pesle* in Chron. des Ducs de Normandie, 2, 4432."

P. 15, l 7. *Seas of blisse.*] A frequent metaphor in Shakspere. "This great sea of joys," Per. v. 1, 194. "A sea of glory," Hen. VIII. iii. 2, 360 "Sea of troubles," Ham. iii. 1, 59. Lucrece "drenched in a sea of tears," 1100.

P. 15, l. 8. *But what is victorie where no praise is?*] Compare Spenser, Teares of the Muses, 451-6.

> "Or who would ever care to doo brave deed,
> Or strive in vertue others to excell ;
> If none should yeeld him his deservèd meed,
> Due praise, that is the spur of doing well ?
> For if good were not praisèd more than ill,
> None would choose goodnes of his own freewill."

P. 15, l. 15. *Pestering.*] By the older etymologists, pester was connected with pestis, with the sense of infecting, corrupting; as in French, empester, and Italian, impestare, which would suit this passage, and one in Shakspere, Macbeth v. 2, 23, "Who then shall blame his pester'd senses?" But the more general meaning is to encumber, and this is traced by modern Philologists, who deny any connection with pestis, to empetrer, to hobble a horse while he feeds afield, from the medieval Latin, pastorium, a clog for horses. See Skeat, Wedgwood, and Brachet, sub voce. Also, Trench, Select Glossary.

P. 15, l. 18.] Compare Shakspere, Macbeth, iv. 3, 209-10.
"Give sorrow words: the grief that does not speak
Whispers the o'erfraught heart and bids it break."
Tit. And. ii. 4, 36:
"Sorrow concealèd, like an oven stopp'd,
Doth burn the heart to cinders where it is."
V. and A. 329, 330; and the stanza that follows:
"For lovers say the heart hath treble wrong
When it is barr'd the aidance of the tongue."
"An oven that is stopp'd, or river stay'd,
Burneth more hotly, swelleth with more rage :
So of concealèd sorrow may be said :
Free vent of words love's fire doth assuage ;
But when the heart's attorney once is mute
The client breaks, as desperate in his suit."

The coincidence of the comparison of "concealed sorrow" to "an oven stopp'd," in these two passages, does not seem to have been pointed out, and may be an argument in favor of Shakspere having had at least a hand in the composition of the play.

P. 15, l. 26. *Gag-toothed.*] Having projecting teeth, or tusks. Wedgwood has "ON. gagr, prominent." The epithet was applied to Tom Nash by Gabriel Harvey in Pierce's Supererogation, Lond. 1593, p. xiii. " I'le lead the gag-tooth'd fopp a newfounde daunce," and on p. 142, "Take heede of the man whom Nature hath marked with a gag-tooth ; Art furnished with a gag-tongue; and Exercise armed with a gag-penne; as cruell and murderous weapons as ever drewe bloud." Nares in v. quotes instances from Nash. Pierce Penilesse (p. 31, ed. 1842), and from The Return from Parnassus, i. 2 (vol. iii. 217, Hawkins' Drama, Oxf. 1773). It is mentioned in the life of Dr. Peter Heylyn § 7. (p. xxxiii. ed. 1849, by Eccl. Hist. Soc.) "that in his family one of them ever had a gag-tooth, and the same was a notable omen of good fortune." So among the heroes of Romance the sixth son of Melusine was marked by such a tooth. Melusine par Jean d'Arras, p. 117, ed. Paris, 1854: "Melusine enfanta le siziesme enfant qui fut ung fils, il eut nommé Geaffroy, et au naistre il apporta sur terre ung grand dent qui lui sailloit de la bouche plus d'ung pouce, nommé Geaffroy au grand dent." In the Romance of Parthenay (E. E. T. S. 1866, p. 49) it is thus described;

"Gaffrey with great toth Afterwarde she bare,
Which growyn in mouth A wonder toth hade,
Which without issued pasing gret and square."

P. 15, l. 28. *Rave.*] Rage, from rabies madness. The lion's raving is accompanied by his roaring which "duld the heavens."

P. 15, l. 29. *Lizard.*] Apparently a misreading for Libbard. G. Harvey in Pierce's Superogation, 1593, p. 169, "The Oxe and the Asse are good fellowes; the Libbard and the Foxe queint wisardes." Shakspere L. L. L. v. 2, 551, "With libbards head on knee." See especially Harrison's England in Shakspere's Youth, New Sh. Soc. ed. Book iii. chap. iv. p. 27, of Savage Beasts and Vermin: "King Henrie the first of England, who disdaining (as he termed them) to follow or pursue cowardes, cherished of set purpose sundrie kinds of wild beasts (as bears, libards, ounces, lions) at Woodstocke and one or two other places in England, which he walled about with hard stone, and where he would often fight with some one of them hand to hand, when they did turne againe and make any raise upon him."

P. 16, l. 1.] Compare Willobie's Avisa, Cant. lii. 6, p. 104, ed. Grosart 1880:

"Besides you know I am a wife
Not free but bound by plighted oath."

Shakspere Sonnet, clii. 3, "In act thy bed-vow broke."

P. 16, l. 3. *Her who I honour.*] For, *whom.* On this see Abbot's Shakesperian Grammar, 1875, § 204, "The inflection of *who* is frequently neglected."

"Who I myself struck down." Macbeth, iii. 1, 123.

P. 16, l. 8.] Willobie's Avisa, Cant. lii. "How can you than Love her that yeelds to every man?"

P. 16, l. 18]. Compare Shakspere, Sonnet xli. 7, 8:

> "And when a woman woos, what woman's son
> Will sourly leave her till she have prevailed?"

P. 16, l. 21.] Compare Marlowe, H. and L. p. 15:

> "Then treasure is abus'd
> When misers keep it; being put to loan,
> In time it will return us two for one."

Advantage is profit; Shakspere, Sonnet lxxxviii. 11, 12:

> "The injuries that to myself I do
> Doing thee vantage, double-vantage me."

The word should be written avantage, without the *d*. It is so in the Prompt. Parvulorum. From the Low Lat. *ab ante*.

P. 16, l. 23. *Untewed.*] Nares quotes from Lyly's Endymion, ii. 2, "I will encounter that blacke and cruell enemie that beareth rough and *untew'd* locks, &c." To tew is to dress leather, or comb hemp.

P. 16, l. 26. *Bandes.*] Bonds, written obligations to pay a certain sum, securities. So used in Shaksp. Com. of Errors, iv. 2, 49, "Was he arrested on a band?"

P. 16, l. 27. *Sacred throne.*] Compare Milton, P. L. iv. 29, 30:

> "—— The full-blazing sun
> Which now sat high in his meridian tower."

Lucan, ix. 528, 9, has "nil obstat Phœbo quum cardine summo Stat librata dies."

Spenser, in his Translation of Virgil's Gnat, 156, 7:

> "Hyperion throwing forth his beames full hott,
> Into the highest top of heaven gan shine."

P. 16, l. 32. *Folding billows.*] This is a bold metaphor as applied to curls, the word denoting large swelling waves, as in Pericles iii 145, 6, "But sea room, an the brine and cloudy billow kiss the moon, I care not." In the old lines of the Beggar's Daughter of Bednall Green, the metaphor is expressed by the verb "His reverend lockes In comely curles did wave."

P. 17, l. 8, 9. *Pilgrim - tels his case.*] Lucrece, 790, l.
> " And fellowship in woe doth woe assuage ;
> As palmers chat makes short their pilgrimage."

P. 17, l. 15. *Girted-neately.*] So in p. 22. " She *neatly* covers, and her *ungirt* gowne." Neately here seems closely. Neat is pure, without mixture or flaw, and so, close. In this way Drayton says of Warner (Epistle to Reynolds, p. 399, Ed. Chalmers' Poets):
> " Then Warner tho' his lines were not so trimm'd
> Nor yet his poem so exactly limn'd
> And *neatly* jointed."

P. 17, l. 19. *Faire Cytherea.*] Spenser, Teares of the Muses, Erato, 397:
> " Faire Cytheree, the mother of Delight."

And Chaucer, before him, Assemble of Foules, 113:
> " Thou Citherea, blissfull Ladie swete."

P. 17, l. 22. *And hence it was Jove plucked of his vale.*] This is obscure. Is the meaning of the whole passage as follows: That Love at first had only a veil before his eyes, which Jove plucked off in this instance that Love, seeing how pale Aurora was, might pity her distress, and might also note Jove's wrath at Love's treatment of her; but that when Love scornfully refused help, Jove inflicted perpetual blindness on him, a veil irremovable. See Bacon de Sapientia Veterum xvii. for his interpretation of Love's blindness.

P. 17, l. 29. *Wegg.*] That is, wag. A frequent term in Shakspere and other writers contemporary with Edwards. J. Dickenson, Arisbas, pp. 54, 64, 72. Sylvester Urania, stanza 7.
> " Then (gladly) thought I the Wagg-son to sing Of wanton Venus."

P. 17, l. 31. *One.*] For on, indicating progression as in " say on," " play on," and intimating here that the chat was near its end.

P. 18, l. 3. *Sisiphus.*] See Whitney's Emblems, p. 215.
> " Loe Sisyphus, that roles the restlesse stone
> To toppe of hill, with endlesse toile and paine;
> Which beinge there, it tumbleth donne alone."

234   *Cephalus and Procris.*

P. 18, l. 7. *Misse.*] Used actively here to cause his constancie to fail.
P. 18, l. 10.] Compare Willobie's Avisa, cant. xxi. xxvii. and xxviii.
> " Know you some wives use more then one ?
> Go backe to them for here are none."

P. 18, l. 11. *As now.*] Often used in Chaucer and earlier writers for " as re- regards now," " for the present." Chaucer, Knight's Tale, 27,
> " But at that thing I must as now forbere."

See Abbot, Shaksp. Grammar, 114.

P. 18, l. 12. *Marchant Weede.*] This word is used by Shakspere and Milton in both numbers, but more commonly in the plural. Milton, Comus, 189.
> " Like a sad votarist in palmer's *weed.*"

and in the plural " take the *weeds* and likeness of a swain." Ibid. 84. A.S. wæd, clothing, garment.

P. 18, l. 14. *Plede tediously on love.*] At length, laboriously. *On* is for *of* in the sense of " about."

P. 18, l. 16. *Promise rewardes.*] Shakspere, Two G. of Verona, iii. 1, 89.
> " Win her with gifts, if she respect not words:
> Dumb jewels often in their silent kind
> More than quick words do move a woman's mind."

The Northern Mother's Blessing, p. 166. Sir Plasidas, &c. Roxb. Club. ed.
> " Men with their gifts wemen oregone
> Gif they of herts be herd as stone:
> Bounden is he or shee
> That gifts takis securely,
> My leue dere child."

P. 18, l. 19. *Drowned in a sea.*] Before, p. 17—" bathes himself in seas of bliss."

P. 18, l. 28. *Just Radamanth.*] Homer, Od. xi. 568 ; and Dante, Inferno, v. represent Minos as having the powers here assigned to Radamanthus, after Virgil, Æn. vi. 566,
> " Gnosius hæc Radamanthus habet, durissima regna,
> Castigatque, auditque dolos, snbigitque fateri."

Edwards perhaps was influenced by G. Gascoigne, who in the " Adventures of Master F. J." introduces Radamanthus in council with his senators about some new form of punishment. Vol. i. p. 454, ed. Hazlitt.

P. 18, l. 29. *For Woemen.*] After referring to the punishment of the Danaides "with their bottomlesse tubs," he probably adds to Virgil's "radiisque rotarum districti pendent (Æn. vi. 616), the notion of "tearing off their flesh" from the Martyrdom of S. Catherine. This blending things sacred and profane, without any regard to times, is common enough.

P. 19, l. 9. *Lake.*] This is put for Tartarus, over which Proserpina, "The Queene of Hell" (Spenser, Virgil's Gnat, 462), bears rule. So in the F. Q. i. viii. 46, "Bred in the squalid *lakes* of Tartarie," and in Æn. vi. 393, Charon says

"Nec vero Alciden me sum lœtatus euntem
Accepisso *lacu*."

P. 19, l. 12. *Elysium-plaine.*] Was the word "Elysian" not yet introduced? Massinger's Virgin Martyr, first printed in 1622, is the earliest authority cited for it in Richardson's Dictionary. Shakspere has Elysium several times, but always as a substantive.

P. 19, l. 13. *This Center.*] This term is applied (1) to the earth as being, according to the Ptolemaic system, the centre round which the planets move:

"The heavens themselves, the planets, and this center
Observe degree, priority, and place." Tr. and Cress. i. iii. 84.

"I'll fetch from hel stern words to shake the centre." Nicholson's Acolastus, 257.

(2) Figuratively to the soul, opposed to the body:

"Affection, thy intention stabs the center." Wint. T. i. 2, 138.
"Poor soul, the center of my sinful earth." Sonnet, cxlvi. 1.
"Can I go forward when my heart is here?
Turn back, dull earth, and find thy center out." R. and J. ii. 1, 1.

The meaning of the whole line is not very clear. If "this center" be understood of "this world," may it mean that after his death the world will have no object for its disdain to feed on, being "barren of repast?" or, if "this center" be taken for "his soul, or heart," may it mean that he, having no object (since Procris has slain him by her faithlessness) for his heart to rest on (being "barren of repast"), may now devote himself to Proserpine, and "honor her eternall with his ghost."

In either, or any, case the phrase "barren of repast" may be illustrated by the Shaksperian expression in Hamlet:

> "As if increase of appetite had grown
> By what it fed on"; i. 2, 144.

P. 19, l. 14. *Ghost.*] For the Homeric notion as to the disembodied spirit in the realms of Proserpina, see Od. xi. 218—222.

P. 19. l. 15. *Which said.*] So in Shakspere. "Which perform'd, the choir Together sung 'Te Deum.'" Hen. VIII. iv. 1, 90.
On this construction, see Abbott's Shaksp. Gram. 376.

Banisht.] For the feelings excited by banishment, see Romeo and Juliet, iii. 3, and Weever, in the Life and Death of Sir John Oldcastle—

> "Here Cobham lives, oh do not say he lives,
> But dying lives, or living howerly dies,
> A living death exilement alwaies gives
> A banisht man still on his death-bed lies."
> Sir Plasidas, &c. Roxb. Club ed. p. 231.

Even other creatures are actuated by similar feelings. Du Bartas says that certain kinds of fish—

> "Cannot their countreys tender love wipe out
> Of their remembrance; but they needs will home
> In th' ireful Ocean to go seek their tomb."

Sylvester's Du Bartas, the Fift Day of the First Week, p. 118, ed 4to. 1611; p. 40, ed. fol. 1641.

The whole passage is worth consulting:
There are instances of the exiled braving death to see their own land again. Somewhat of the same kind is the "Maladie du pays," or Nostalgia. See Ovid, Tristia, and Epist. Ex Ponto, passim. Keble, Prælect. Poet. p. 20

P. 19, l. 19. *The tombs.*] Petties Pallace, in Cephalus and Procris, T. i. verso, "as in goodly sumptuous sepulchres rotten bones are rife, even so fairest words are ever fullest of falsehood." Pierce Penilesse, p. 90, ed. 1842, "our English peacockes, that painting themselves with Church spoyles, like mighty mens sepulchers, have nothing but atheisme, schisme, hypocrisie, and vainglory, like rotten bones lurking within them." All derived from St. Matthew, xxiii. 27. It must be noticed that Tyndale's version 1534 and the Geneva 1557 render τάφοι "tombs," Wiclif and others, "sepulchres," so that we may infer that Edwards used one of the former translations.

P. 19, l. 20.] On deceitful lovers see Gower, Conf. Amant, book i. vol. i. pp. 64, 65, ed. Pauli. Lond. 1857.

P. 19, l. 31.] Compare Marlowe, H. and L. p. 22,

—— "She wanting no excuse
To feed him with delays, as women use."

and p. 36,

"Treason was in her thought,
And cunningly to yield herself she sought.
Seeming not won, yet soon she was at length:
In such wars women use but half their strength."

Ovid, Amores, i. v. 15, 16:

"Quumque ita pugnaret tanquam quæ vincere nollet,
Victa est non ægrè proditione suâ."

P. 20, l. 5.] Compare Marlowe, H. and L. p. 33:

"Tis wisdom to give much: a gift prevails
When deep-persuading oratory fails."

Nicholson, Acolastus, 340:

"And womens' hearts with heapes of giftes are wonne."

Willobie's Avisa, Cant.xlvii. p. 96, ed. Grosart, 1880:

"Apply her still with dyvers thinges,
(For giftes the wysest will deceave)
Sometymes with gold, sometymes with ringes,
No tyme nor fit occasion leave,
Though coy at first she seeme, and wielde,
These toyes in tyme will make her yielde."

P. 20, l. 10. *Æsopian Snakes.*] This fable is versified and applied by G. Gascoigne (1572).

> " Amongst olde written tales this one I bear in mind,
> A simple soule much like my selfe dyd once a serpent find ;
> Which (almost dead for colde) lay moyling in the myre,
> When he for pittie tooke it up, and brought it to the fyre.
> No sooner was the snake recurèd of hir griefe,
> But straight shee sought to hurt the man that lent hir such reliefe."
>
> Flowers, p. 94, ed. Hazlitt.

If the dates assigned by Malone and Furnival be correct, Shakspere's allusions to this fable would just precede the publication of Cephalus and Procris, 2 Hen. VI.

> " I fear me you but warm the starvèd snake,
> Who, cherish'd in your breasts, will sting your hearts."—iii. 1, 343.

Rich. II.

> " Snakes in my heart blood warm'd that sting my heart.—iii. 2, 129.

Nicholson, in his *Acolastus* (1600), speaking of England, has,

> " Frost-bitten snakes, the Lord tooke pittie on us," &c.—49.
> " But, Serpent like, we sting his blessed name," &c.—67.

See, also, " Shakspere and the Emblem Writers." by H. Green. Lond. 1870, p. 197-9.

P. 20, l. 17. *Tex.*] For text ; as wan for wand, growne for ground.

P. 20, l. 17. *Middle Earth.*] The terrestrial world, as the middle habitation between heaven and hell ; A. S. middan-eard, and middan-geard. Icel. miðgarðr. Gower Conf. Am. i. 153 : " Adam for pride lost his prise In middel-erth." Once only in Shakspere : " I smell a man of middle earth." M. W. W. v. 5, 84.

Merrymentes.] " A hybrid word, having a French suffix, whether the root be the A.S. mery, merry ; or Celtic mir, to play." It is a favorite word with Spencer, *e.g.* F. Q. ii. 5, 32 : " Their wanton follies and light merriments;" and with Shakspere also. The line here indicates a state of hysterical passion.

P. 70, l. 29. *Remotive.*] A word of the poet's own, of which I find no mention in dictionaries. It expresses the "varium et mutabile semper Fœmina" of Virgil, Æn. iv. 569, whose description of Dido's mental perturbation may be compared with this.

P. 20, l. 30. *Chauntecleere.*] Chaucer C. T. 14855, in Nuns Prests T. 29, seems the first authority for this name. Barnfield, 1595, in his Cassandra, p. 127, ed. Roxb. Club, has

"Now had the poore-mans Clock, shrill Chauntycleare
Twice given notice of the morns approach."

where the same phrase occurs as in Edwards, "gave notice." Had either seen the others poem?

In Sylvester's Du Bartas (Third Day of Second Week, The Vocation, p. 395, ed. 4to 1611, p. 149, ed. fol. 1641)

"Cease, sweete Chante-cleere
To bid good morrow to the morning heer."

In the Fift Day of the First Week (p. 137 4to, p. 46 fol.) he writes—

"The peasants trusty clock,
True morning watch, Auroras trumpeter."

Like Hamlet's

"The cock that is the trumpet to the morn." i. 1, 150.

And like Barnfield's "poore-mans clock" See Whitney's Emblems, 120.

P. 20, l. 31. *Bewray.*] Properly to accuse—but in a more general sense to disclose, discover, as in S. Matth. xxvi. 73, "Thy speech bewrayeth thee," (δῆλον σε ποιεῖ), common from Chaucer, C. T. 6529 onwards. Douce, "Illustrations of Shakspere," ii. 26, notes that it has been confounded with *betray;* as is also indicated in The Bible Word-Book by Eastwood and Wright, 1866.

P. 21, l. 5, 6. *Caves whose sound, &c.*] Compare, Gascoigne i. 116, who has

"And when the stony walls have oft renewed
My piteous plaints with ecchoes of remorse."

and V. and A. 829—831.

The construction is irregular. Perhaps it should be "whose sound—" like the aposiopesis in Virgil, Æn. i. 135; "quos ego—sed motos præstat, &c.", or it has, like many Shaksperian sentences, the construction changed by change of thought; or for clearness; or is an instance of the noun absolute. See for these, Abbott's Shaksp. Gram. 415, 416, 417.

P. 21, l. 9. *Fits the grove with.*] See Schmidt's Shaksp. Lexicon in "fit. verb. 1. f." for instances of this phrase.

P. 21, l. 10. *Uncouth.*] Unknown, strange. A. S. uncuð. from cunnan, to ken, know. See Max Muller, Lectures on Science of Language, Second Series, p. 406, and note, "it became evident that the Sanskrit *náman* stood for *gnáman*, just as *nomen* for *gnomen* (cognomen, ignominia), and was derived from a verb, *gná*, to know;" then in note, "Other words derived from gnâ are, notus, nobilis, gnarus, ignarus, ignoro, narrare (gnarigare), gnomon, I ken, I know, uncouth."

P. 21, l. 16. *Autentic.*] As of acknowledged authority. Schmidt Sh. Lex.

P. 21, l. 19. *Unprophane.*] Not in dictionary. Dryden has unprofaned.

P. 21, l. 26. *Debonary.*] This form of the adjective is unknown to lexicographers. Marlowe, H. and L. p. 17, has "So young, so gentle, and so debonair."

P. 21, l. 27. *A Saint.*] This word was applied indiscriminately to divers characters. Shaksp. L. L. L. iv. 3, 366; v. 2, 87, "Saint Cupid." Du Bartas, Miracles of Peace, Sonnet 5, "Saint Hermes shin'd," and Nicholson, in his Acolastus, 821, has "These sinful saints." R. H. Horne, Introduction to Chaucer, modernised 1841, p. xcv., "The reader will be *wisely* pleased on his first introduction to Mars the *knight*, *Saint* Venus, Phœbus the *chivalrous bachelor*, &c." It seems to be used for any object of affection, religious or passionate.

P. 21, l. 29, 30. Marlowe H. and L. p. 6, of Hero:

"She ware no gloves: for neither sun nor wind
Would burn or parch her handes—they were so white."

If Edwards had the notion entertained about the Elle-maids, that they are "hollow behind, like dough-troughs" (Keightley F. M. i. 140), and that they "sometimes offer the breast to those whom they would ensnare" (i. 153), there is more reason for this description.

P. 21, l. 31. *Each so officious*] Dutiful: fulfilling their purpose. Used in good sense, as in Bacon's Essays, xlii. 33, xlviii. 20, and in Par. Reg. ii. 302, "With granted leave officious I return."

The word is noticed by Trench in his "Select Glossary of English Words formerly used in senses different from their present." Here "Her breasts, like ivory globes circled with blue, a pair of maiden worlds unconquered" (Lucr. 407), those "hills of snow which her bosom bare," were for an increase of her charms, and, each of them, so fulfilled their duty and "became her so," as the swans on the rivers set off their natural beauty.

P. 21, l. 12. *Lamie.*] "Lamie be women, which beholding children, or giving to them giftes, doe alter the fourme of them; whiche children be afterwarde called Elfes, or taken with the fayrie. And some such women will sucke the bloud from children. They be also those, which be called Ladyes of the fayrie, which doe allure yong men to companie carnally with them; and after that they be consumed in the act of lecherie, they covet to devour them." Cooper's Thesaurus, Dict. Historic. From this passage Edwards probably took the name "Lamie" for the supernatural being whom he found it necessary to introduce in order to enlighten Procris as to the fraud practised on her by Cephalus at the instigation of Aurora. The name Lamia is Greek, from the root ΛΑΒ, as in λαμβάνω, and would mean one that seizes or takes hold of, and this is appropriately applied to the bugbear with which children were frightened, "terriculæ Lamiæ." It is, however, in the character under which they were regarded in later times that one is here introduced, and with this we have been made familiar by Keats in his poem entitled "Lamia," embodying the story told by Philostratus in his Life of Apollonius of Tyana (iv. 25), condensed and translated by Robert Burton in his Anatomy of Melancholy (Part 3, sec. 2, Memb. 1, subsec. 1), and quoted by Keats at the end of his Lamia. The characteristic features of the Lamia, as described by Edwards, belong not to Greek but to northern and mediæval popular belief; *e.g.* he calls her one of the "fairie elves," "good Faierie Lady," "elvish wanton," "Lady of those pretie ones;" speaks of "her haire down trailing," "sacred haire," "dancing by moonlight," her being "at such a hight," all of which features are alluded to by Keightley as belonging to the elves and ellemaids of Scandinavia. (See his Fairy Mythology,

Lond. 1833, vol. i. pp. 135-153.) Thomas Erastus (whose views on Church discipline have made his name a bye-word) wrote a treatise de Lamiis, Basil. 1578, Amberg. 1606; and there is one by Molitor, de Laniis et Phitonicis Mulieribus—the name having been changed to Laniæ, "a laniando pueros." See the Prompt. Parvulor. under " Elfe, spryte, Lamia," and the note. Rider in his Eng. Lat. Dict. 1589, translates " a Fairie" by " Lamia." Pierce Penilesse has a discourse on such Spirits, pp. 74—87.

P. 21, l. 32. *Doth.*] This is the southern plural in *th:* so, "hurteth," p. 25. Shakspere retains it in "doth," and "hath." Abbott, Shaksp. Gram. 332, 334. The comparison is, " Her white breasts became her as much as Swans now adorn *Thames,* or ever did *Po.*" The principle involved in it is analogous to that maintained by Byron against Bowles in the " Letter on his Strictures on Pope," that the poetry of the ship does *not* depend on the waves, &c. on the contrary, the Ship of the Line confers its own poetry upon the Waters and heightens theirs. The poetry is at least reciprocal."

P. 21, l. 32. *As Thames doth Swannes.*] The meaning I take to be "as Swannes doth Thames." Leland in his " Cygnea Cantio," printed in 1546, having a vignette of a "Cygnea Pompa," with verses beginning—

" Aspice quâ pompâ Tamesinis fertur in undis
Isiacâ veniens Cygnus speciosus ab urbe :"

and again in the Præfatio A iii., " Tamesin nemo ignorat cygnorum et altorem et cultorem esse maximum," bears witness to the abundance of swans in the time of Henry VIII. In the reign of Q. Mary, we have the testimony of an eye-witness, Franco Ferretti in his " Diporti Notturni, 1579, p. 134." " Questo regno ha superbe cittadi et in particolare la Metropolitana Londra; la quale è celebre per la negociatione mercantile in lei maravigliosa; per gli edifitii di tempi, di palazzi, di giardini, d'hospitali, di conventi, et finalmente d'un ponte murato di molta grandezza et di artifitio magistrevole: il quale traversa la larga riviera del Tamigi, vaghissima, et tutta piena di bianchi cigni come l'istessa neve. Io vi fui in tempo che'l

Notes. 243

buon Cardinale Polo vivea, quando con tanta religione governando la faceva una seconda Roma con stupore et infinita allegrezza del mondo, hora è perfidamente heretica in tutto, et per tutto."

For the Elizabethan period Drayton may suffice :
" Our floods-Queene, *Thames*, for shyps and Swannes is crowned."

Sonnet to the River Ankor. Ideas Mirrour (1594), Amour 24, ed. Roxb. Club, p. 161. Sonnet xxxii. ed. Chalmers' Poets.
" Range all thy swannes, faire Thames, together on a ranke,
And place them duly, one by one, upon thy stately banke."

Rowland's Song in praise of the fairest Beta. England's Helicon (1600), p. 27.

While later, Tho. Heywood (1637), in his " Pleasant Dialogues and Drammas," writes,—
" O thou, my best lov'd Sister,
Well knowne in *Poe, Meander*, and *Caister*,
But best in *Thamesis*."—p. 245 ; see also p. 243.

From a passage in Sylvester's Du Bartas, where he is describing his voyage to Brabant, it would seem that their chief delight must have been in the waters above London Bridge.
" While toward the sea our (then Swan-poorer) Thames
Bare down my bark upon her ebbing streams."

Fourth Day of First Week ; p. 100, ed. 4to, 1611; p. 34, ed. fol. 1641.

P. 21, l. 32. *Swans did ever Po.*] For the transformation of Cycnus into a swan on the Eridanus, see Ovid, Met. ii. 367-380. Hence the association of swans with that river by poets ; as by Carew in praise of his mistress :
" Whiter than the Silver swan That swims in Poe."—p. 219, ed. 1651.

P. 22, l. 6. *Mock the frozen zone.*] To mock is to imitate. Shakspeare uses it of a painting, and a statue :
" It is a pretty mocking of the life."—Timon, i. 1, 35.
" To see the life as lively mock'd as ever
Still sleep mock'd death."—Winter's Tale, v. 3, 19, 20.

244 Cephalus and Procris.

Here the elves dance is said to be like the creations of frostwork as seen by moonlight. This is true to nature. Du Chaillu, in the "Land of the Midnight Sun," ii. 420, has an engraving of the Elfdans, as the Swedish peasants call it, " caused by the condensed vapour, white and transparent, forming a sort of veil through which objects were visible in shadowy outline. It was like a fairy cloud. I could see through it every flower and blade of grass. People working in the fields looked like phantoms; and, though near, appeared to be far away." There was " a new phase of the phenomenon. Fairy-like figures were apparently intent on stopping my progress. The sight seemed supernatural but lovely; yet these angels were only a group of flaxen-haired maidens partly shadowed by the mist." " It seemed as if I were in another world; the whole was like a vision ; I might have fancied myself in space, surrounded by the disembodied." " Farther on a gentle zephyr came, and the vapour took a thousand fantastic shapes, which at times seemed to represent human figures, and the dance of the elves began." It was in the evening, after sunset.

P. 22, l. 14. *Deaftly.*] Fitly, becomingly. From A.S. dæfe, gedefe, fit ; gedafnian, to be fit, behove. Spenser, " They daunceu deffly." Gloss. " finely and nimbly." Shepherd's Calendar, April, 111. Shakspere writes it deaftly : "thyself and office deaftly show."—Macb. iv. i. 68. G. Harvey, Pierce's Supererogation, 194, " Or transforme himself into all shapes more deftly." In this form it is now generally written.

P. 22, l. 19. *One troubled in his sleepe.*] Compare the account of Lady Macbeth, act v. i. 80:

"Infected minds
To their deaf pillows will discharge their secrets."

P. 22, l. 20. *Nothe.*] Naught, nought, nothing.

P. 22, l. 24. *Wood.*] Mad, frantic. A.S. Wòd. V. and A. 740:

" Life-poisoning pestilence, and frenzies wood."

P. 22, l. 26. *The Building Oake.*] "The builder oak," F. Q. i. 1. 8. "The bilder oke," Chaucer, Assembly of Fowles, 176.

P. 22, l. 27. *Rob from.*] Equivalent to "rob of." Shakspere, Rich. II. ii. 1, 173:
"Which robs my tongue from speaking native breath."

Ceder.] Marston makes a similar application of these two trees in his Scourge of Villanie, Sat. viii. 44—48:
"O, now my ruder hand begins to quake,
To thinke what loftie cedars I must shake;
But if the canker fret the barkes of oakes,
Like humbler shrubs shall equal beare the stroaks
Of my respectlesse rude Satyrick hand."

P. 22, l. 29. *Swanly.*] This word is not in the Dictionaries.

P. 22, l. 32. *Misse.*] Loss, fault, sin. So p. 18, and on pp. 27, 29, "mis." Spenser, Shepherd's Calendar, July, 13:
"In humble dales is footing sure, the trode is not so tickle,
And though one falls through heedless hast, yet is his misse not mickle."

Shakspere, V. and A. has,
"He saith she is immodest, blames her mis." 55.

That this is the correct reading, and not " 'miss," as it is often printed and erroneously explained as "amiss," is evident from the above quotations, and the usage in Middle English, for examples of which see Stratmann in voce, as well as from its etymology, Icel. missa, to miss, lost, for which see Skeat in "miss" and "amiss."

P. 23, l. 1. *Alluded.*] See Narcissus, p. 38, "Of those sweete Joyes which men allude to her." *i. e.* ascribe, impute; this is a peculiar meaning of the verb.

P. 23, l. 4. *Boorded.*] Accosted, wooed. Tw. N. i. 3, 59, "You mistake, knight: 'accost' is front her, *board* her, woo her, assail her." How the word comes to have this meaning is well shown by Sir G. W. Dasent in his "Jest and Earnest," ii. 47. Board is (1) plank, (2) deck, (3) side of a ship, (4) to scale the side of a ship, or to "board"; (5) to force ones company on another, ("to board,") as Falstaff did on the Merry Wives, i. 1, 92, and Petruchio threatens, "For I will board her though she chide as loud as thunder." T. of Sh. i. 2, 92. The verb occurs again, pp. 25, 54.

P. 23, l. 8, *Leasing.*] So in Ps. iv. 2. v. 6. Lying. A. S. Leásing, leásung.

2 K

P. 23, l. 18. *Kno.*] Known.

P. 23, l. 20. *Curs.*] Used here, without a depreciatory meaning, for hounds. Sidney uses the word in both senses in the verses near the end of the Second Book of the Arcadia, ed. 1725, octavo, vol. i.

"I con thee thank to whom thy dogs be dear,
But commonly like curs we them intreat." P. 410.
"Come, come my curs, 'tis late, I will go in." P. 412.

P. 23, l. 23. *Royall.*] This refers to a hart chased by the King or Queen so far from the forest that he is unlikely to return thither of himself; whereupon proclamation is made that no person shall chase or kill him, but that he may safely return to the forest. And then ever after such a Hart is called a "Hart Royal proclaimed." Guillim, Heraldry, Sect. iii. ch. xiv. p. 154, ed. 1724. Cox, Gentleman's Recreation, p. 3, ed. 1721. Manwood, Forest Laws, iv. section 5.

P. 23, l. 26. *At Stand.*] Equivalent to "at bay" or "a bay." The state of a chase when the game is driven to extremity, and turns to face the baying and barking dogs. I have found no other instance of "at stand."

"Make the cowards stand aloof at bay."—1 Hen. VI. iv. 2, 52.
"He stands at bay."—Thomson, Autumn, 451.

P. 23, l. 27, *A.*] For "He," "A' must needs." 2 Hen. VI. iv. 2, 59. Abbott, Shaksp. Gram. 402. Morris, English Accidence, 157.

P. 23, l. 29. *To kill.*] As a huntsman.

"But come the bow: now mercy goes to kill."—L. L. L. iv. 1, 24.

P. 23, l. 32. *Sporting.*] So used in Genesis xxvi. 8. Marlowe, Dido Q. of Carthage, i. 40, ed. Dyce.

"Whilst they were sporting in this darksome cave."

P. 24, l. 11.] See Measure for Measure, i. 5, 80 (4, 80 in older eds.)

"Go to Lord Angelo,
And let him learn to know, when maidens sue,
Men give like gods; but when they weep and kneel,
All their petitions are as freely theirs
As they themselves would owe them."

See also "Sir John Oldcastle," p. 228, Roxburghe Club ed. of Sir Plasidas, &c.

"Low kneeling doune, teares from her eies did shower:
Hard is that hart which beauty cannot soften."

Notes. 247

P. 24, l. 31. *The new-sprung flowers, &c.*] See Keble, Christian Year, 15th Sunday after Trinity; and his Prælectiones Poet. 1844, p. 524: " Veterum fabellarum ea sit summa, ut nemini misero accusandus sit Deus, tanquam iniquus et aversus, cui vel unica præsto sit in arbore vel graminevirente gemma."

P. 25, l. 5. *Thessalian Metra.*] Ovid, who gives the whole story of her Father, Erisicthon, Met. viii. 739 to end, calls her only by her patronymic Triopeis (873.) She had the power from Poseidon of changing her shape, and was thus enabled to obtain repeatedly food for her father, by returning to him after she had been sold into slavery.

" Illi sua reddita forma est.
Ast ubi habere suam transformia corpora sentit,
Sæpe pater dominis Triopeida vendit. At illa
Nunc equa, nunc ales, modo bos, modo cervus, abibat,
Præbebatque suo non justa alimenta parenti." (871-5.)

Palæphatus de Incredibilibus, 24, suggests that her beauty attracting many suitors, who made presents of divers animals to her father, she was said to transform herself into them. Lycophron, 1393, calls her $\beta\alpha\sigma\sigma\acute{\alpha}\rho\alpha$ $\lambda\alpha\mu$-$\pi o \upsilon \rho \acute{\iota} \varsigma$, a firetail vixen, whose gains arose from $\pi o \rho \nu \epsilon \acute{\iota} \alpha$. Tzetzes adds, that she was also a $\phi\alpha\rho\mu\alpha\kappa\acute{\iota}\varsigma$, or sorceress, and received payment for her favours in cattle, whence the legend. He calls her Mestra, as does Lactantius Placidus, Mythogr. Lat. ii. 252, ed. Muncker, Amst. 1681. Palæphatus has both forms. Antoninus Liberalis, 17, calls her Hypermestra. Mestra is adopted in Smith's Dictionary of Biogr. and Mythology.

P. 25, l. 5, 6.] These two lines are to be read parenthetically. " Procris does not intend to slip out of our storie, as if she were a Thessalian Metra escaping from her masters, nor to rob us of our glorie in telling it." The former negative, "neither," is omitted. See for this ellipsis Abbott Shaksp. Gram. 396.

P. 25, l. 8. *Hurteth.*] The southern form of the plural, as on p. 21 " doth."

P. 25, l. 12. *Downe of thistle.*] " All soft as is the falling thistle-down," Hall, Sat. iv. 4, 74. " As thistles wear the softest down," S. Butler Remains, i. 237. Ed. Thyer, 1759. Down is metaphorically applied here, being a

Scandinavian word properly meaning "eider-down," elastic feathers, and thus other substances having similar substance and lightness, " the light and weightless down." 2 Hen. IV. iv. 5, 33.

P. 25, l. 14. *Devoutly.*] Devotedly, earnestly, "Devoutly dotes." M. N. D. i. 1. 109.

P. 25, l. 18. *Conceited.*] A person is said to be self-conceited, vain, hence the term is here applied to deedes.

P. 25, l. 29. *Sacrilegious.*] Does this line mean, " What obsequies sacrilegiously left undone?"

P. 26, l. 1. *Mercenary.*] Slavish. So on p. 27, " 'Tis servile still on sorrow to dilate."

P. 26, l. 7. *Peevish.*] This word is said to come from the cries of fretful children, and to import all that untowardly children are; silly, wayward, cross, &c. See Skeat in v.

P. 26, l. 10. *Made on.*] We now should say " made much of." Shakspere has

" Why, he is so made on here within, as if he were son and heir to Mars."—Cor. iv. 4, 203.
" The bird is dead That we have made so much on."—Cymb. iv. 2, 198.

P. 26, l. 12. *Region.*] A tract ruled over (fr. rego) hence implying inhabitants, and so here opposed to a Hermitage.

P. 26, l. 13. *Exceede.*] Superiority. The verb as a noun. I find no other instance of it thus used.

P. 26, l 25. *Politicke.*] Prudent, wise. Skilled in government.

P. 26, l. 26. *Headlong or to Jove.*] Diis inferis aut superis.

" Hear it not Duncan, for it is the knell
That sends thy soul to heaven, or to hell."—Macb. ii., 1, 63.

P. 26, l. 27. *Dowdy.*] A term of disparagement applied to women, as Mercutio bantering Romeo says " that to his lady Dido was but a dowdy " (ii. 4, 43); and Riche, Farewell to Military Profession, 1581, " If plaine or homely, we saie she is a doudie or a slut."

Here, however, and I know of no other instance of its application to a man, used of the " uncivill swaine," a " base clowne," " rude in action, rough and harsh, Dull, sluggish, heavie, willfull, more than rash," as he is described on p. 25, epithets which illustrate, or perhaps confirm, Wedgwood's view of the origin of the word, that "the fundamental idea is torpor, sloth, while that of carelessness in dress or appearance is an incidental application." Churchill, in his Epistle to Wilkes, has " Landscapes unknown to dowdy nature rise," but nature is generally personified as a female.

P. 26, l. 30. *Hegg.*] " Hegg or hegge, the A.S. hægtesse, from A.S. haga, a hedge, it being supposed that witches were seen in bushes by night." Skeat. *Larva,* in Cooper's Thesaurus, is translated "a spirit appearing by night; an hegge, a goblin, a goast"; and *strix,* "a witch that chaungeth the favour of children, an hegge or fayrie." In the Mirror for Magistrates, Dame Eleanor Cobham, condemned for witchcraft by Cardinal Beaufort, wishes she had been one, that she might have revenged herself upon him:

" The fiery feends with fevers hot and frenzy,
" The Airy hegges with stench and carren savoures,
" The watry ghosts with gowtes and with dropsy,
" The earthly goblines with Aches at all houres,
" Furies and Fairies, with all infernall powers,
" I would have stird from the dark dungeon
" Of hell Centre, as deepe as Demogorgon." P. 323, ed. 1610.

P. 26, l. 32. *Highes.*] Hies, hastens. Its descent from the A.S. higian to hasten, is indicated by the spelling. See Stratmann's Dict. in "higien" for Middle English quotations.

P. 27, l. 3. *Still doth the Morning, &c.*] See the motto on the title-page, " Aurora Musæ Amica," and compare a passage in Polimanteia relative to the Earl of Essex " Daughter Cambridge--slack not, but write: sleepe not, but sing: let your mornings muse like Aurora blushing march her equipage, in her stateliest buskind poetrie." P. 37, 38, ed. Grosart 1881. British Bibliographer, i. 282.

P. 27, l. 5. *Ha' done.*] A common abbreviation for have. Of the many in Shakspere the closest parallel is " Ha' done with words." T. of S. iii. 2, 118. Even " having " is contracted to one syllable. Abbott, Sh. Gram. 466.

P. 27, l. 7. *Blood-dronken.*] This word is not found elsewhere I think. In 1 and 2 Hen. VI. and in Tit. And. Shakspere has " blood-drinking." The last mentioned play may be taken as a specimen of the works here alluded to. See Ward's Hist. of English Dramatic Literature, 1875, i. p. 265, where, speaking of the extravagance in the treatment of heroic subjects by Shakspere's predecessors, he says, " That they saw but half the significance of true tragic effect. They knew how to mark the great conditions of the conflict, how to express with overpowering energy the terror of the catastrophe. Hence the aberration, which needs no exemplification, towards the horrible as a source of effect."

P. 27, l. 8. *Hell-quickeners.*] Another word peculiar to our Author.

Italian-nots.] Is this a misreading for Italian-mots? The phrase occurs in Hall's Satires, Book V. Sat. ii. 45-8.

"When Mævio's first page of his poesy,
Nail'd to a hundred posts for novelty,
With his big title, an Italian mot,
Lays siege unto the backward buyer's groat."

It was then the fashion to have high-sounding titles with Italian mottoes and devices, says Mr. Singer in his note. To this practice Marston alludes in his " Scourge of Villanie," as the Proem to Bk. II. begins, " I cannot quote a motto Italionate."

If, however, the text as printed is correct, *Italian-nots* may be Edwards's mode of writing the word *Italianates*, meaning those who play the Italian, imitate Italian fashions. It was used by his contemporaries, as Marston, Sat. ix. 92, " Clothes Italionate ;" Hall, Sat. i. 3, 25, " termes Italianate." T. Nash in P. Penilesse, p. 17, " all Italionato is his talke;" p. 68, " Italionate conveyances ;" and in the Introduction to Christ's Tears over Jerusalem, " my Italionate coined verbes all in *ize*," quoted in Intr. to P. Pen. p. xxx. Richardson in his Dict. cites examples from Wilson's Rhetorique, p. 164 ; Ascham's Schoolmaster, Bk. 1 ; Drayton's Ep. of Lady Geraldine to E. of Surrey. The first being spelt " Italienated." As to Italy being the source from which these horrors were derived, Nash affirms it in P. Pen. p. 34, " O Italie, the academie of manslaughter, the sporting place of murther, the apothecary-shop of poyson for all nations! how many kind of weapons hast thou invented for malice!"

P. 27, l. 10. *Teat-sucking.*] This seems to be a compound of the author's own.

P. 27, l. 10. *Her mis.*] Her sin, viz. revenge, implied in "Snakey Nemesis," whom he takes to be a Fury as it seems from the line below—"a milder fury." Or perhaps *her* is the Old English form of *their*. Cyril Tourneur's Tragedies may be cited as extreme instances, though not then written; but probably Marlowe and others were in the author's mind."

P. 27, l. 15.] In this passage Pierce Penilesse, p. 91, ed. 1842, seems to be imitated. There is an ellipsis of "have" before graced.

P. 27, l. 18.] Is there a reference here to Pastorals, like Spenser's Shepheards Calendar?

P. 27. l. 20. *White love.*] Fair and propitious. Albus has both meanings. So in the phrase, "Creta an carbone notare." Hor. Sat. ii. 3, 248. Persius, v. 108. In Thomson's Orpheus Caledonius. Edinb. 1733.

" She spake her favour with a look
Which left nae room to doubt her,
He wisely this *white* minute took,
And flang his arms about her."—i. 24.

P. 27, l. 21. *Styll Musicke.*] Edwards uses this phrase in Narcissus, p. 40, " Some with Still musicke." See the stage directions in As you like it, v. 4, 113, " Still Music ;" and M. N. Dream, iv. 1, 88, " Music still." Titania calls for " Music, the music such as charmeth sleep." Afterwards, Oberon says, " Sound music." The stage direction being "horns winded within." G. Gascoigne's Jocasta, Act v. "The order of the last Dumbe Shewe, First the Still pipes sounded a very mournful melody," explained by Hazlitt in the Index as being " wind instruments, for still opposed to loud music." J. Dickinson's Arisbas, p. 81, " And forthwith the faire chorus cast into a ring began their hymne. In the same moment of time, a shril harmony of winde instruments, sounding miraculously in the aire, not drowning with over-loude noise, but consorting with the musicke of those well-agreeing voices in a fit key, made divine melody." Burney, Hist. of

Music, iii. pp. 331-344, "collects and explains such passages as concern or allude to music in the principal dramatic pieces from Gammer Gurton's Needle, 1551, to Shakspere;" and on p. 338 mentions the "Still Music" in As You Like It, but gives no explanation of it.

P. 27, l. 23. *Ransackt.*] Ransack is a Scandinavian word. Icelandic rann-saka, to search a house. It is first found, and in this sense, in works written in the Northumbrian dialect, as might be expected. Story of Genesis and Exodus, about 1250, (E. E. T. S. ed. 1865) where Laban searches Jacob after his flight—" Ðu me ransakes als an Ðef." 1733; and when the Steward searches Joseph's Brethren for the cup; "He gan hem ransaken on and on." 2323. Again in a Metrical Psalter, before 1300, also Northumbrian, published by the Surtees Society 1843: "Ransakand thair hertes clene," vii. 10, and "Thai ransaked wicnesse, and ivel thinge; Thai waned, ransackand. of ransaking." lxiii. 7. A gloss in Reliquiæ Antiquæ i. 8, and Promptor. Parvul. render "ransake" by "scrutor." Lastly, Chaucer C. T. 1007 has, "To ransake in the tas (or cas) of bodies dede." With Gower the notion of plunder comes in, for when describing covetise he says that "he taketh on honde robbery," and "he can the packes well ransake. So prively none bereth about His gold, that he ne fint it out, Or other juell what it be." Book v. Vol. ii. p. 331. The Elizabethan writers continued this usage. Shakspere has, "Robbed and ransacked by injurious theft," Lucrece 838. "My coffers ransacked," M. W. W. ii. 2, 306. "Ransacking the Church," K. J. iii. 4, 172. "To ransack Troy," Troil. Prol. 8, and—" the ransacked Queen," Troil." ii. 2, 150; in reference to the rape of Helen, which word *rape* is also Scandinavian; the substantive derived from the Latin *rapere* being rapine. Rider in his Engl.-Lat. Dict. 1589, has "to ransacke or rifle," and subsequent Lexicographers all give plunder as one meaning of the word. Still, as Professor Skeat says in v. "ransack is not connected with the A. S. and Icel. word *rán*, plunder, which is quite different from Icel. *rann* a house."

P. 27, l. 29—34.] The drift of this rather obscurely worded passage seems to be that his Muse would have sung more profitably of some "white love," blending " *Styll Musicke* " (that of the eye, and whispers low?) sighs, and tears, and so begetting a series of poems (like the Sonnets of Petrarch, Spenser, and others, or Spenser's Prothalamion and Epithalamion, Sidney's Astrophel and Stella,) which would have been substantially rewarded, as " the Muses wanton favorites " were by the happy lovers whose praises they sung.

P. 27, l. 27. *Vast.*] This word here, as in Narcissus, p. 37, "Corycyus, some haue told you let lie vast," is waste. Vastum, in mediæval and law Latin is waste. Ducange. Kelham Domesday Book Illustrated, "vasta, wast ground, uncultivated." And in Classical Latin vastus is properly void, empty (connected with *vac* as in vacuus), and thus without limits, large.

P 27, l. 27, *note. Fauorites.*] This would seem to be "favourers," patrons, see pp. 5, 11.

P. 28, l. 1. *Arcadia and the Fayerie Land.*] We know from Spenser's Letter to Sir W. Raleigh, prefixed to the F. Q., that he intends by "Faery Land" the Queen's kingdom, and perhaps specially the Court. By Arcadia here is designed also England in respect of Poets and Men of Letters, so perpetually called Shepherds, *e. g.* in Colin Clout, and by Sidney in his Arcadia, Book i. " Even the Muses seem to approve their good determination, by chusing this country for their chief repairing place, and by bestowing their perfections so largely here, that the very shepherds have their fancies lifted to so high conceits, as the learned of other nations are content both to borrow their names and imitate their cunning." Vol. i. p. 17. The "Complaints" (1591) has a notice from the Printer to the Reader, "that the F. Q. hath found a favourable passage amongst you."

P. 28, l. 2-4.] A reference to Spenser's residence in Ireland, whither he returned after publishing the first three Cantos of the F. Q. in 1590, though from the Dedication to Daphnaida, "Jan. 1, 1591, London," he must have been then in England. The Sonnets were sent from Ireland for publication, and entered for publication on " the 19th Nov. 1594, to Wm Ponsonbye." The language of Edwards here seems to confirm the opinion of Lord Burleigh's opposition to Spenser, as indicated in Mother Hubbard's Tale, 901, " To have thy Princes grace yet want her Peeres."

2 L

Cephalus and Procris.

P. 28, l. 9.] The word "Affection" is wanted to make up this line, as is indicated in l. 13.

P. 28, l. 10. *Breast-plate.*] Shakspere also, in the only passage where he uses the word, applies it metaphorically, "What stronger breast-plate than a heart untainted?" 2 Hen. VI. iii. 2, 232. The language of St. Paul, Eph. vi. 11—17, had been lately, 1590, referred to by Spenser in his Letter to Sir W. Raleigh, prefixed to the F. Q. "In the end the Lady told him, that unlesse that Armour which she brought would serve him (that is, the armour of a Christian man, specified by St. Paul, v. Ephes.), that he could not succeed in that enterprise; which being forthwith put upon him with dew furnitures thereunto, he seemed the goodliest man in al that company, and was wel liked of the Lady."

P. 28, l. 11. *The Standard.*] This must be the gorget or "*Standard of Mail.*" "Its purpose seems to be to act as a supplementary piece to the gorget of plate, as the latter, without its aid, might admit the point of a lance to penetrate between the gorget and the breast-plate." Hewitt's Ancient Armour, Oxford 1860, iii. 369. "Sometimes the gorget of mail was covered by the plate gorget," *ibid.* 373. "It is also called camail, and was usually made to terminate in a straight edge across the breast," *ibid.* ii. 216. "In order to prevent the lance from passing beneath the camail to the throat of the knight, it was tied down to the body armour by thongs or laces," *ibid.* ii. 219. From the use of the word "*rivet,*" however, in this passage of our poet, it seems that a gorget of plate is here referred to, as "overlapping plates in armour were sometimes held together by sliding rivets (called Almayne rivets), which enabled them to play freely one over another," *ibid.* iii. 570. Plates vi., xx., and xxv. in Meyrick's Illustrations of Ancient Armour, Oxford 1830, contain engravings of the above. The poet's meaning seems to be that he would maintain Spenser's claims against any assailant, both with heart (breast-plate) and voice (standard).

P. 28, l. 11. *Boare.*] An example of this form of the participle for "borne" is mentioned in Schmidt's Shaksp. Lex. from Hamlet, as printed in the quartos: " He hath *bore* me on his back a thousand times," v. 1, 205. In the folios it is "*borne*." There should be no stop after " such."

P. 28, l. 12. *Or.*] This indicates the ellipsis of some antecedent clause, such as " would assail."

P. 28, l. 21. *Anger.*] Feeling, emotion, not ire or wrath.

P. 28, l. 24. *Perfourmances.*] For performers. Compare Spenser's Virgil's Gnat 177.

" Here also playing on the grassy green,
Woodgods, and Satyres, and swift Dryades,
With many Fairies, oft were dancing seen."

P. 28, l. 26. *Honoured as a Starre.*] Does this refer to Aurora ?

P. 29, l. 4. *As Revels, &c.*] Marlowe H. and L. p. 17.

" The rites
In which love's beauteous empress most delights,
Are banquets, Doric music, midnight revel,
Plays, masques, and all that stern age counteth evil."

Shakspere, L. L. L. iv. 3, 379, " Revels, dances, masks."

P. 29, l. 8. *Aurora.*] Procris supposes that Cephalus would take her for Aurora there awaiting him; so Aurora=Procris here, and in line 12 below, " Of Aurora," that is " on Procris."

P. 29, l. 11. *The Dart.*] See Gosson's School of Abuse, ed. 1841, p. 49:—

" A wanton eye is the dart of Cephalus; where it leveleth, there it lighteth, and where it hitts it woundeth deepe."

P. 29, l. 13. *Martialist.*] Follower of Mars. Not in Shakspere. In Two Noble Kinsmen, i. 216. Cyril Tourneur Funeral Poem on Sir F. Vere, p. 191, " Such a Martialist." See Nares in v. and Todd's Johnson.

P. 29, l. 14. *The accent.*] In accord with to give it emphasis. The author of " Polimanteia," reprinted in Brit. Bibliographer, i. 281, uses the verb in this sense when speaking of the death of Sir Chr. Hatton:—

" *Thames* wil become teares; the sweetest perfumes of the Court will bee sad sighes, everie action shall *accent* grief."

Cephalus and Procris.

P. 29, l. 15. *A good.*] "In good earnest."
> "I made her weep a-good." T. G. of V. iv. 4, 170.
> "Then set together all a-good." Drayton, in England's Helicon, 27.
> "I have laugh'd a-good." Marlowe, Jew of Malta, Act ii. vol. i. 277.

P. 29, l. 17. *Pale death.*] Compare Sackvil's Induction, Mirror of Magistrates, 265, ed. 1610:
> "Wherewith a dart we saw how it did light
> Right on her brest, and therewithall pale Death
> Enthrilling it to reave her of her breath."

P. 29, l. 18. *Surquedie.*] Generally written surquedrie. From *sur* and *cuider* (*cogitare*), to think. Overweening presumption, pride. A word in use from Chaucer and Piers Ploughman, till the seventeenth century, but not found in Shakspere. To the many quotations in Nares and Richardson add Bodenham's Belvedere, 195, "Might wanting measure proveth Surquedric." T. Watson, Tears of Fancie, Sonnet, lviii. p. 207, ed. Arber, "Yet still I twit myself of Surcuidrie."

P. 29, l. 21. *Saffron*] Shakspere also uses it as an adjective, where Ceres speaks of
> "Iris with her saffron wings." Temp. iv. 78.

Others compound it with some adjective, as in the following instances:—
> "And so a solemn interview was appointed; but, as the Poets say, Hymen hath not there his saffron-coloured coat." Sir P. Sidney, Arcadia, Bk. ii. vol. i. 382.
> "Hymen put on his saffron-coloured coate." Sir J. Oldcastle. Plasidas, &c. p. 186.

P. 29, l. 24, 25. *And in tragicke song Doest binde my temples.*] It was customary to bestow crowns on poets; so that "to have the temples bound" is equivalent to saying that one is a poet.
> "Insignemque meo capiti petere inde coronam
> Unde prius nulli velarint tempora Musæ."—Lucretius, i. 928.
> "Tempora sacratâ meâ sunt velata coronâ."—Ovid, Epist. Ex Ponto, iv. xiv. 55.
> "Temporibus non est apta corona meis."—Trist. i. vii. 4.

As the song is tragicke, the lament of Statius will be applicable:
> "Sed nec solitæ mihi vertice laurus
> Nec fronti vittatus honos. En taxea marcet
> Sylva comis: hilaresque hederas plorata cupressus
> Excludit ramis."—Sylv. V. v. Epicedion in Puerum Suum, 28.

Notes. 257

P. 29, l. 26. *Encampes.*] Is contained.

P. 29, l. 26. *Allowde.*] Allowde is here, assigned to, granted to. Allow in this sense is from *allocare;* allow, to approve of, is from *allaudare.*

P. 29, l. 27, 28. *Hymen-Hyems.*] Photius, in his Bibliotheca, has an extract from Proclus, in which, rejecting the mythological origin of the ὑμεναῖος or marriage song, he devises a symbolical explanation of it: "ἐγὼ δὲ οἶμαι βίου τινὰ εὐτυχοῦς προαναφώνησιν ὑπάρχειν, καὶ συνεύχεσθαι τοῖς συνιοῦσι πρὸς γάμου κοινωνίαν μετὰ φιλοστοργίας, αἰολικῇ παραπλέκοντα τὴν εὐχὴν διαλέκτῳ, οἷον ὑμεναίειν καὶ ὁμονοεῖν τούτους ἀεὶ ὁμόσε μένοντας, id est ὁμοναίειν καὶ ὁμονοεῖν, una habitare et eadem sentire eos concorditer viventes." p. 987, ed. D. Hoeschelii. Rothomagi, 1653, fol. Where these conditions are violated then Hymen becomes indeed "acris Hyems," "a winter of discontent."

P. 29, l. 30. *Jealousie.*] See Whitney's Emblems, p. 211. Zelotypia. Plate of the death of Procris. Three stanzas on Jealousy, of which the last is:

> "Lo Procris heare, when wounded therwithall
> Did breede her bane, who mighte have bath'de in blisse:
> This corsie sharpe so fedde uppon her gall
> That all to late shee mourn'd, for her amisse:
> For, whilst shee watch'd her husbandes waies to knowe,
> Shee unawares, was praye unto his bowe."

So Bodenham's Belvedere, of Jealousie, p. 47, ed. Spenser Society:

> "Procris was slaine through her owne jealousie
> Hid in a bush to watch her husband's walke."

P. 30, l. 3. *Pherecydes.*] "A famous Philosopher, and wryter of Tragedies, which died of the lousie sicknesse: he was Pythagoras master." Cooper Thesaurus. The only authority for his having written tragedies is a passage in Serenus Samonicus de Medicina, in reference to the disease of which he is said to have died;

> "Sed quis non paveat Pherecydis fata tragœdi,
> Qui nimio sudore fluens animalia tetra,
> Eduxit, turpi miserum quæ morte tulerunt." 62—64.

He was not strictly a Philosopher: some call him Theologus. He was certainly not a writer of Tragedies.

P. 30, l. 3. *Puppius.*] A Roman dramatist whose compositions are characterised by Horace, whether ironically or not we cannot tell, as the "lacrymosa poemata Pupi." Epist. i. 1, 67. All our information about him is derived from the Scholiast on this passage. " Pupius, tragædiographus, ita affectus spectantium movit ut eos flere compelleret. Inde istum versum fecit."

"Flebunt amici et bene noti mortem meam,
Nam populus in me vivo lacrymatu' est satis."

P. 30, l. 3. *Philocles.*] " A Tragical Poet of Athens." Cooper's Thesaurus. He was nephew, sister's son, of Æschylus: said to have written 100 tragedies. Once victorious over Sophocles who exhibited his Ædipus Tyrannus, which proves the merit of Philocles. He was much ridiculed by the Comic Poets. Aristophanes, Thesmophor. 168, alleges that being ugly he made ugly poetry, ταῦτ' ἄρ' ὁ Φιλοκλέης αἰσχρὸς ὤν αἰσχρῶς ποιεῖ. And the Scholiast on the Wasps 462, where he is again mentioned, informs us that he was nicknamed "Χολή, 'Αλμίων, Bile and Brine." Is any allusion intended by Thomas Edwards to contemporary poets under these names? He seems evidently to refer to others in the line below, "and those who take delight in amorous love."

P. 30, l. 5. *Nightes dark cugly stratagems.*] Bodenham, Belvedere, 230, has

"The tragique Scene where death her play begins,
Are acts of night, and deedes of ougly darke."

P. 30, l. 8. *Heraclian wits.*] See Cooper's Thesaurus in v. Heraclius. "Heraclius lapis, qui et Lidius. Plin. (N. H. xxxiii. 43). The lode-stone: the touchstone. One that hath an exact and fine witte."

See the Adagia of Erasmus, under the head " Judicandi recte, secus." "Lydius, sive Heraclius lapis in eos dicitur qui vehementer acri exactoque judicio sunt." Also, Parœmiographi Gr. ed. Gaisford, Oxon. 1836, in 'Ηρακλεία λίθος.

P. 30, l. 12. *Extremes.*] Great sufferings. So Milton:

"Heard so oft In worst extremes." P. L. i. 275.
"Tending to some relief of our extremes." x. 976.

L'ENVOY.

P. 30. *L'Envoy.*] "*L'Envoy* was a sort of postscript, sent with poetical compositions, and serving either to recommend them to the attention of some particular person, or to enforce what we call the *moral* of them. See the stanzas at the end of Chaucer's *Clerkes Tale*, and of the *Complaint of the Black Knight*, and of *Chaucer's Dreme*." Tyrwhitt, Glossary to Chaucer.

P. 30, l. 13. *Extreames.*] Here used for the points at the greatest distance from each other, as in "The golden mean between two extremes." Virtue is a mean between two extremes.

P. 30, l. 15. *Went.*] So, p. 32, 29. "That tread in uncouth wents." Went is a way, a passage, from wenden to turn to go. Virgil by G. Douglas, p. 289, 48, ed. 1710, "To wele beknawin pethis, turnis, and wentis." In the Manipulus Vocabulorum, 1570, "A went, lane, viculus, angiportus," col. 66. "Cross roads are called in Kent, Went-ways." Notes and Queries, 6th Ser. v. 167. Used by Chaucer, Spenser and others, but not by Shakspere. Stratmann in his Dict. of E. English has omitted the word. Compare the Scotch *wynd*, a narrow street.

P. 30, l. 19. *Fenne.*] Fiend. Chaucer writes it "Fend," C. T. 5200, 7030; and Skelton, ii. p. 77, v. 317, "the flingande fende." See Launcelot Gobbo's soliloquy in the M. of V. ii. 2, for his debate between conscience and the fiend.

P. 31, l. 1. *Tway.*] Chaucer has "Shall tellen tales tway." C. T. 724. Spenser, "And the sharpe steele doth rive her hart in tway." F. Q. iii. xi. 11. Once only in Shakspere, Hen. V. iii. 2, 128, "'Tween you tway," and then in the mouth of Jamy, the Scots captain. The word is omitted in Schmidt's Sh. Lexicon.

"Ulysses was a merry Greek, they say,
So Tom is, and the Greeker of the *tway*."

Verses by Hugo Holland, prefixed to Coryat's Crudities (1611), vol. i. f. 3, verso. ed. 1776.

P. 31, l. 2. *Ycleeped.*] Common in earlier writers, but only twice in Shakspere, and then in an early play, L. L. L. i. 1, 242, v. 2, 602.

Cephalus and Procris.

P. 31, l. 3. *Despaire.*] See the description of Despair, F. Q. i. ix. 28-54, said to have been taken notice of by Sir Philip Sidney.

P. 31, l. 3. *Debate.*] Contest, quarrel. Spenser, F. Q. ii. viii. 54, vi. iii. 22, and vi. viii. 13, on which last Upton notes " contest; as the French use *debat*, and the Italians *dibatto*. So Chaucer and G. Douglas. Spencer also uses the verb *debate* in the sense of fight, or contend."

P. 31, l. 4. *Poets say.*] I do not know the passages here referred to.

P 31, l. 5. *Envy.*] For a description of envy, see Gower Conf. Amant. Bk. ii. F. Q. i. iv. 30-32, and v. xii. 28, 32. Bodenham, Belvedere, 117. Whitney, Emblems p. 94. Ovid Met. ii. 760-781. Pierce Penilesse, p. 31, makes " envie the adopted son of Pride; and hence comes it that proud men repine at others prosperity, and grieve that any should be great but themselves." This is from Lucretius iii.

" Macerat invidia: ante oculos ollum esse potentem;
Ollum adspectari claro qui incedit honore."—75, 6.

Bodenham, Belvedere, 117, " The fruites of envie are despite and hate."

P. 31, p. 5. *The fall.*] "The yeaning of lambs, North," Halliwell. The verb "to fall," is twice used by Shakspere in this sense in the Merchant of Venice:

" That all the eanlings that were streak'd and pied Should fall as Jacob's hire."—i. 3, 80, l.
" Who, then conceiving, did in eaning time Fall particoloured lambs."—i. 3, 88, 9.

and in the general sense of bringing forth,

" Let wives with child Pray that their burthens may not fall this day."—K. John, iii. 1, 90.
" Geld bulcalfe and ram-lamb as soone as they fall.—Tusser, Husbandrie, 35, 32."

P. 31, l. 10. *Abroad.*] The *a* in this and other such words is generally said to be equivalent to *on* as in a-foot, on foot. Sir G. W. Dasent, however, in Jest and Earnest ii. argues that *a* is the old Norse preposition a, which governs the accusative with the idea of motion, and the dative with that of rest—and that in the struggle for mastery among the various dialects the Scandinavian element prevailed (p. 44). And on p. 65 he contends that " abroad " has nothing to do with " breadth," but is the Norse " braut," or " bröd " a way, a path, a road. Thence we have " a brauta " on a path, in viâ: and thence the adverb " ábraut, in the sense of one who has quitted his house, or native land, gone abroad."

Notes. 261

P. 31, l. 10. *Jealousie.*] See Sidney's Astrophel and Stella, lxxviii. Bodenham's Belvedere 45. Carew's Foure Songs, by way of chorus, The First of Jealousie.

P. 31, l. 11. *Dispaire.*] Carew in the above song says, " Despayr her issue is." And Shakspere speaking of Jealousy's effects,

> "What doth ensue,
> But moody and dull melancholy,
> Kinsman to grim and comfortless despair."—Errors v. 80.

Bodenham, Belvedere 47.

> "As no content is like the sweetes of love,
> So no despaire can match with jealousie."

P. 31, l. 12. *Yellow coate.*] This is the colour of jealousy. Shakspere,

> "I will possess him with yellowness." M. W. W. i. 3, 110.

Steevens in his note on this passage adds the following quotations. So in Law Tricks, &c. 1608.

> "If you have me you must not put on yellows."

Again, in the Arraignment of Paris, 1584,

> "Flora well, perdie,
> Did paint her yallow for her jealousy."

P. 31, l. 13. *Wysardes.*] Wise men. Spenser calls the antient philosophers, "The antique Wisards." F. Q. iv. xii. 2: And he says that Lucifera's kingdom was upheld by the policy, "And strong advisement of six wisards old." i. iv. 12. Proteus is called by Milton "The Carpathian Wisard," Comus, 872. The wise men are, "The star-led wisards," Ode on Nativ. 23. In Lycidas he applies this epithet to the Dee, "Nor yet where Deva spreads her wisard stream," 55; as Drayton had previously done to the Weever, "And Amphitrite oft this wizard river led Into her secret walks." Polyolb. Song. xi. See Warton's Notes on Milton's Ode and Lycidas.

Troade.] The meaning of the line seems like Pope's,

> "Fools rush in where angels fear to tread." Essay on Criticism, 625.

To *tread* is the technical word for "treading a measure," a stately and solemn dance, to his skill in which Sir Chr. Hatton was indebted for his promotion. See Nares in "Measure." Here a contrast is made between the quiet measures of the wise, and the hasty acts of Cephalus.

P. 31, l. 18. *Monster-mongers.*] A compound of the author's own. A dealer in strange things.

P. 31, l. 19. *Painted cloathes.*] See Nares in v. for passages in illustration. The material was really cloth or canvas painted in oil, with mottos and moral sentences from the mouths of the figures introduced on them, as in Dekker's comedy, "If this is not a good Play the Devil is in't," 1612. "What *says* the prodigal child in the *painted cloth*?"

P. 31, l. 29. *Chorus.*] In Narcissus, p. 58,

"For what with wordes the *Chorus* setteth forth,
Is but t'explaine th' ensuing tragicke scene."

Here "Debate, his *Chorus* being spent, comes in a tragicke more terrible than actors can engage in with applause." Tragic is given as a substantive in Worcester's Dictionary as meaning 1. An author of tragedy, and 2. A Tragedy; a Tragic Drama. Savage is the authority for the former, Prior for the latter.

P. 32, l. 2. *Plausively.*] This adverb is not in the Dictionaries.

P. 32, l. 4. *Nothe.*] In Promp. Parv. "Nowlite (nowth, nowte) nought, nichil." *Tend.*] Is this "to give attention to," "to hearken to," so as to please Aurora; or "to tend (or tent,) to watch, guard against," so as not to be led into the design against Procris?

P. 32, l 12. *Unmercifully.*] Like "cruelly" in Henry V., v. 2, 216, "I love thee cruelly."

P. 32, l. 16. *Bended knee.*] P. 18. "Goe and intreate with knee and cap in hand." So Webster Duchess of Malfy iii. 2, 6,

"I hope in time 'twill grow into a custom,
That noblemen shall come with cap and knee,
To purchase a night's lodging of their wives."

P. 32, l. 28. *Merriment.*] Like "ludibrium" in Horace. "Tu, nisi ventis Debes ludibrium, cave." Od. i. xiv. 15. The laughing stock, the sport of. Marlowe in Dido Q. of Carthage has "laughing-sport." Act i. vol. ii. 366.

P. 33, l. 1. *Learne.*] When this verb means to teach it is used with a double accusative, an accus. and infinitive, or an accus. and subordinate clause. See Schmidt's Shaksp. Lex. This is the Latin usage of doceo. In Psalm xxv., 4, Prayer Bk. Vers. however, it has only the acc. of the person,

Notes.

"Lead me forth in thy truth, and learn me;" though in verse 8; cxix 66; cxxxii. 13 it has the double acc. Probably in the other example the word "*it*" is mentally supplied.

P. 33, l. 11. *Downe-wards creeps.*] So p. 55, "and downwards would have crept:" Marlow H. and L. p. 29, ed. Dyce,

> "And now the Sun, that through th' horizon peeps,
> As pitying these lovers downward creeps."

P. 33, l. 13. *Servitor.*] The proper meaning of this word seems to be "one who serves at meat." P. Langtoft's Chronicle ed. Hearne, i. p. 55, (sometimes quoted as R. Brunne, or Mannyng)

> "In S. Edward tyme ẟe crle suld with him ete,
> A servitour ẟer was ẟat served at ẟe mete."

Marlowe, Dido Queen of Carthage (1594.) Act ii. vol. ii. p. 381, ed. Dyce.

> "See where her Servitors pass through the hall,
> Bearing a banquet."

And in this sense it has continued in use at Oxford, though the menial duties have ceased. Shakspere gives it in general a wider meaning, and so does Milton. "When such a man would speak, his words, like so many nimble and airy *servitors*, trip about him at command, and in well ordered files as he would wish, fall aptly into their own places." Apology for Smectymnuus.

Our Poet seems to use it in a military sense, as we find it applied twice in Shakspere.

> "Signior Montano, Your trusty and most valiant servitor." Oth. i. 3, 40.
> "Here none but soldiers and Rome's servitors Repose in fame." Tit. And. i. 352.

Stratmann, though he frequently quotes fr. R. Brunne, omits this word.

P. 33, l. 20. *Her honor ere begun.*] Is honor here used as equivalent to success?

P. 33, l. 30. *Tinssell.*] Trench on the Study of Words: "Tinsel, from the French étincelle once meant anything that sparkles or glistens: thus 'cloth of tinsel' would be cloth inwrought with gold and silver: but now is used for that which has no reality of sterling worth under the glittering and specious shows which it makes." Étincelle is fr. Lat. scintilla by transposition into "stincilla," a spark, sparkle.

P. 34, l. 15. *So live by others toyle.*] Should the reading be "To live?" The meaning is like Virgil's "sic vos non vobis."

P. 34, l. 20. *Quit.*] Discharged, satisfied. From quietus.

P. 34, l. 22. *Wan.*] "Feeble or weak in colour, wanting in brightness, pale, livid" A. S. wana, wanting.

P. 34, l. 23. *Strength.*] This is used by Chaucer, Gower, Sir T. More and other old writers, quoted in Richardson's Dict. with the same meaning as strengthen. Shakspere does not use it.

P. 34, l. 25. *Faire Cynthia.*] Possibly some allusion is intended to Q. Elizabeth, as in the Preface, p. 4. "Now is the sap of sweet science budding, and the true honor of *Cynthia* under our climate girt in a robe of bright tralucent lawne: Deckt gloriously with bayes, and under her faire raigne honoured with everlasting renowne, fame and Majesty."

P. 33, l. 26. In this L'Euvoy, or moralization, the poet, having stated in the first three stanzas the conflict of duty and desire arising from jealousy on either side, describes the conduct of Cephalus in the next four—the measures taken by Procris in the following three—and appropriates five to Aurora. The last but one is a reflection as to the justice of her punishment: and in the last perhaps the author refers to some failure of encouragement from some one from whom he had expected it, "The Sonne his strength rebates amaine," and implies a looking for patronage to "Cynthia" herself.

INTRODUCTION TO NARCISSUS.

The myth of Narcissus, though probably of remote antiquity, has not been recorded by any of the earlier classical writers, whose silence is thus accounted for by Creuzer, in the "Præparatio" to his edition of Plotinus de Pulcritudine, Heidelberg, 1814, p. lxix. "Nam licet ante Alexandrinos nemo scriptor, quod sciam, ejus fabulæ diserte mentionem faciat: hoc tamen mihi videor commonstrasse, eam non esse commentum posterioris ætatis, neque arcanam illam ejus explicationem a recentioribus demum Platonicis profectam. Hoc nemini dubium fore arbitror, qui et ad Homerici Hymni, Pausaniæ, Cononis, aliorum locos attenderit, et vero ad opera antiquæ artis, vasa præcipue. Neque illud priscorum scriptorum silentium alio trahi debet in hâc fabulâ, quam quo in reconditioribus aliis multis. Nimirum religioni fuisse proloqui."

Notwithstanding this reference to the Alexandrine writers, by whom are usually meant those who flourished under the Ptolemies during the three centuries preceding our era, there is no allusion to the legend of Narcissus in any of them, nor, I believe, in any extant author before the Augustan age.

During this period, however, Ovid wrote his Metamorphoses, in the third book of which he has interwoven the legend with those of Teiresias and the Nymph Echo, as part of the Theban cycle. Secondly, Hyginus, Librarian of the Palatine Library, in his Fabulæ, under the heading "*Qui ephebi formosissimi fuerunt,*" mentions "Narcissus Cephisi fluminis filius, qui se ipsum amavit." (Fab. cclxxi.) Lastly Conon, a grammarian, who dedicated his Διηγήσεις to Archelaus Philopator King of Cappadocia (of whom Horace wrote "Mancipiis locuples eget æris Cappadocum rex," Epist. i. vi., 39) and who states that his work is based on earlier authorities, περιέχεται δὲ αὐτῷ ἐκ πολλῶν ἀρχαίων συνειλεγμένα πεντήκοντα διηγήματα, devotes the xxiv Narration to Narcissus, giving an account very different from that adopted by the Latin poet.

'Εν Θεσπείᾳ τῆς Βοιωτίας (ἔστι δ' ἡ πόλις οὐχ ἑκὰς τοῦ 'Ελικῶνος), παῖς ἔφυ Νάρκισσος πάνυ καλὸς, καὶ ὑπερόπτης ἔρωτός τε καὶ ἐραστῶν· καὶ οἱ μὲν ἄλλοι τῶν ἐραστῶν ἐρῶντες ἀπηγορεύθησαν. 'Αμεινίας δὲ πολὺς ἦν ἐπιμένων

Introduction to Narcissus.

καὶ δεόμενος. Ὡς δ' οὐ προσίετο, ἀλλὰ καὶ ξίφος προσέπεμψεν, ἑαυτὸν πρὸ τῶν θυρῶν Ναρκίσσου διαχειρίζεται, πολλὰ καθικετεύσας τιμωρόν οἱ γενέσθαι τὸν θεόν. Ὁ δὲ Νάρκισσος ἰδὼν αὐτοῦ τὴν ὄψιν, καὶ τὴν μορφὴν ἐπὶ κρήνης ἰνδαλλομένην τῷ ὕδατι, καὶ μόνος καὶ πρῶτος ἑαυτοῦ γίγνεται ἄτοπος ἐραστής. τέλος ἀμηχανῶν, καὶ δίκαια πάσχειν οἰηθείς, ἀνθ' ὧν Ἀμεινίου ἐξύβρισε τοὺς ἔρωτας, ἑαυτὸν διαχρᾶται καὶ ἐξ ἐκείνου Θεσπιεῖς μᾶλλον τιμᾶν καὶ γεραίρειν τὸν ἔρωτα, πρὸς ταῖς κοιναῖς θεραπείαις, καὶ ἰδίᾳ θύειν ἔγνωσαν. Δοκοῦσι δ' οἱ ἐπιχώριοι τὸν Νάρκισσον τὸ ἄνθος ἐξ ἐκείνης πρῶτον τῆς γῆς ἀνασχεῖν, εἰς ἣν ἐξεχύθη τὸ τοῦ Ναρκίσσου αἷμα.—Conon, Narratio xxiv.

For the preservation of this and many other works we are indebted to Photius, Patriarch of Constantinople in the ninth century, who has inserted an epitome of it in his Bibliotheca, Cod. clxxxvi.

Yet another form of the legend has been handed down by Pausanias, the cicerone and tourist (ὁ περιηγητής), and whose work, "The Gazetteer of Hellas" (ἡ περιήγησις τῆς Ἑλλάδος), is our best repertory of information for the topography, local history, religious observances, architecture, and sculpture of the different states of Greece, as gathered by him during his travels in the middle and latter part of the second century, A.D.

Θεσπιέων δὲ ἐν τῇ γῇ ἡ Δονάκων ἐστὶν ὀνομαζομένη. ἐνταῦθά ἐστι Ναρκίσσου πηγή, καὶ τὸν Νάρκισσον ἰδεῖν ἐς τοῦτο τὸ ὕδωρ φασίν, οὐ συνέντα δὲ ὅτι ἑώρα σκιὰν τὴν ἑαυτοῦ, λαθεῖν τε αὐτὸν ἐρασθέντα αὑτοῦ, καὶ ὑπὸ τοῦ ἔρωτος ἐπὶ τῇ πηγῇ οἱ συμβῆναι τὴν τελευτήν. τοῦτο μὲν δὴ παντάπασιν εὔηθες, ἠλιθιότητος ἤδη τινα ἐς τοῦτο ἥκοντα, ὡς ὑπὸ ἔρωτος ἁλίσκεσθαι, μηδὲ ὁποῖόν τι ἄνθρωπος καὶ ὁποῖόν τι ἀνθρώπου σκιὰ διαγνῶναι. Ἔχει δὲ καὶ ἕτερος εἰς αὐτὸν λόγος, ἧσσον μὲν τοῦ προτέρου γνώριμος, λεγόμενος δὲ καὶ οὗτος· ἀδελφὴν γενέσθαι Ναρκίσσῳ δίδυμον, τὰ τε ἄλλα ἐς ἅπαν ὅμοιον τὸ εἶδος, καὶ ἀμφοτέροις ὡσαύτως κόμην εἶναι, καὶ ἐσθῆτα ἐοικυῖαν αὐτοὺς ἐνδύεσθαι, καὶ δὴ καὶ ἐπὶ θήραν ἰέναι μετὰ ἀλλήλων. Νάρκισσον δὲ ἐρασθῆναι τῆς ἀδελφῆς, καὶ ὡς ἀπέθανεν ἡ παῖς, φοιτῶντα ἐπὶ τὴν πηγήν, συνιέναι μὲν ὅτι τὴν ἑαυτοῦ σκιὰν ἑώρα, εἶναι δὲ οἱ καὶ συνιέντι ῥᾳστώνην τοῦ ἔρωτος, ἅτε οὐχ ἑαυτοῦ σκιὰν δοξάζοντι, ἀλλὰ εἰκόνα ὁρᾶν τῆς ἀδελφῆς. νάρκισσον δὲ ἄνθος ἡ γῆ καὶ πρότερον ἔφυεν (ἐμοὶ δοκεῖν) εἰ τοῖς Πάμφω τεκμαίρεσθαι χρή τι ἡμᾶς ἔπεσι. γεγονὼς γὰρ πολλοῖς πρότερον ἔτεσιν ἢ Νάρκισσος ὁ Θεσπιεύς, κόρην τὴν Δήμητρός φησιν ἁρπασθῆναι παίζουσαν καὶ ἄνθη συλλέγουσαν· ἁρπασθεῖσαν δὲ οὐκ ἴοις ἀπατηθεῖσαν, ἀλλὰ ναρκίσσοις·—Pausanias ix. 31.

Introduction to Narcissus.

We are indebted to the compilations of an Empress, c. 1060, A.D., and an Archbishop of Thessalonica, c. 1160, A.D., for two brief notices of the legend in the form in which it is generally current, which correspond so closely as to suggest that one is copied from the other, or that both drew from some common source.

Περὶ τοῦ Ναρκίσσου.

Νάρκισσος, υἱὸς μὲν ἦν Κηφισσοῦ ποταμοῦ Φωκικοῦ, καὶ Λειριοέσσης νύμφης, κάλλος δὲ ἔχων ἀμύθητον, ἐπικύψας πηγῇ τινι, καὶ τῆς ἑαυτοῦ σκιᾶς ἐρασθεὶς, ἔρριψεν ἑαυτὸν ἐκεῖ, καὶ ἐνεπνίγη τῷ ἐνόπτρῳ ὕδατι· καὶ ἡ γῆ ἀνέδωκε φυτὸν ὁμώνυμον τῷ νεανίᾳ.—Eudociæ 'Ιωνιὰ, sive Violarium, p. 304, ed. Villoison, Venet. 1781. 4to.

ἱστορεῖται δὲ Θεσπιέα εἶναι τὸν Νάρκισσον, ὃς ἦν μὲν υἱὸς Κηφισσοῦ τοῦ ποταμοῦ καὶ Λειριοέσσης νύμφης· κάλλος δὲ ἔχων ἀμύθητον, ἐπικύψας πηγῇ τινι καὶ τῆς ἑαυτοῦ σκιᾶς ἐρασθεὶς, ἔρριψεν ἑαυτὸν ἐκεῖ, καὶ ἐναπεπνίγη τῷ ἐνόπτρῳ ὕδατι. καὶ ἡ γῆ ἀνέδωκε φυτὸν ὁμώνυμον τῷ νεανίᾳ.—Eustathius in Homeri Iliad ii. vol. i. p. 266, ed. Romæ, 1542.

Joannes Tzetzes places his birth in Laconia, a mistake into which he was led by Lucian, who, beside mentioning his name in the xviii Dialogue of the Dead, and in the ii Book of the Vera Historia, c. 19, writes in his Charidemus, c. 24, ἐάν θ' 'Υάκινθον τὸν καλόν, ἢ τὸν Λακεδαιμόνιον Νάρκισσον κάλλει νικῶμεν, a passage which is judiciously corrected by Burman on Ov. Met. iii. 342, as follows: "Lucianus in Charidemo, circa finem, Narcissum Lacedæmonium facit, nisi locus ille transpositione sanandus sit hoc modo, ἐανθ' 'Υάκινθον τὸν Λακεδαιμόνιον, ἢ Νάρκισσον τὸν καλὸν κάλλει νικῶμεν, ut Heinsius in Schedis suis notaverat."

Περὶ Ναρκίσσου.

Νάρκισσος, Λάκων, θηρευτής, φιλώραιος ἦν νέος.
"Ωρᾳ θερείᾳ δέ ποτε διψήσας μετὰ θήραν,
'Ως ἐπικύψας πρὸς πηγὴν εἶδεν αὑτὸν ὡραῖον,
'Ερᾷ σκιᾶς τῆς ἑαυτοῦ καθάπερ ἄλλου νέου.
Χρῄζων δὲ ταύτην κατασχεῖν ὑγρὸν ἀντλεῖ τὸν μόρον.
  Joannes Tzetzes. Historiarum Variarum Chiliades, i. 9, 234—238.

Introduction to Narcissus.

Περὶ φιλαλληλίας τῶν κολοίων καὶ ψαρῶν.

Οἱ κολοιοὶ φιλάλληλοι, καὶ τῶν ψαρῶν τὸ γένος,
'Ως εἴπερ χέεις ἔλαιον ἔν τινι λεκανίσκῃ
Ἐν τῇ σκιᾷ τῇ ἑαυτῶν τοὺς κολοιοὺς κρατήσεις,
Ναρκίσσους ἄλλους Λάκωνας φανέντας φιλοσκίους.
Ibid. iv. 119, 46—49.

He refers to him also in his Exegesis in Iliadem, first published by Hermann in 1812, at Leipsic. προσέτι καὶ λίθοι καὶ δένδρα καὶ ἐφευρήματα ἀπὸ τῶν ἀνθρώπων τὰς προσηγορίας ἐσχήκασιν· ὡς μύρρα, δάφνη, καὶ ὁ κυπάρισσος· ἔτι δὲ ὑάκινθος τε καὶ νάρκισσος, p. 11, 10. Again. Ἀπόλλων πόθῳ τῆς κορῆς δάφνην ὠνόμασεν, ὡς Λακεδαιμόνους τὸν Ὑάκινθον, ἔτι δὲ καὶ τὸν Νάρκισσον, καὶ δυστυχῶς τῷ θαλῷ περιστέφεται, p. 75, 15, and lastly, in the Scholia to the Exegesis, he quotes from some poet, whose name is not given:

Νάρκισσος φιλόκαλος ἦν νεανίας·
ἰδὼν δὲ αὐτὸν ἐν σκιᾷ τῶν ὑδάτων,
οὕτω καλὸν μέγιστον εὐειδῆ νέον,
καὶ συσχεθεὶς ἔρωτι καὶ λαβεῖν θέλων,
ἄλλον δοκῶν κάλλιστον εἰσορᾶν νέον,
πίπτει καθ' ὑγρῶν καὶ περᾷ πύλας βίου·
ἡ γῆ δὲ φυτὸν ἀντιδιδοῖ τοῦ νεοῦ. p. 139, 12.

Narcissus is also mentioned by Nonnus in his Dionysiaca:

ἀλλὰ τεὸν λίπε πένθος ἐπεὶ φονίῃ παρὰ πηγῇ
Νηϊάδες στενάχουσι καὶ οὐ Νάρκισσος ἀκούει, Bk. xi. 322,

and,
εἶχε δὲ Ναρκίσσοιο φερώνυμα φύλλα κορύμβων,
ἠιθέου χαρίεντος, ὃς' εὐπετάλῳ παρὰ Λάτμῳ
νυμφίος Ἐνδυμίων κεραῆς ἔσπειρε Σελήνης,
ὃς πάρος ἠπεροπῆος εὔχροος εἰδεῖ κωφῷ
εἰς τύπον αὐτοτέλεστον ἰδὼν μορφούμενον ὕδωρ,
κάτθανε, παπταίνων σκιοειδέα φάσματα μορφῆς, Bk. xlviii. 581.

on which latter passage see Creuzer, Plotinus de Pulcrit. Præparatio, p. xlvi.

In the second line of this extract there are three readings, ὃς, ὃν, ὃσ'. The first does not make sense. The second raises the question of Narcissus being the

Introduction to Narcissus. 269

son of Endymion and Selene, a statement for which there is no other authority; while the last, δσ', refers to the abundance of the flowers called forth by the Hours, as described in the lines immediately preceding the passage quoted.

χαριζόμεναι δὲ Λυαίῳ
δμωΐδες Ἠελίοιο κατέγραφον ἄνθεσιν Ὧραι,
πίδακος ἄκρα μέτωπα, καὶ εὐόδμοισιν ἀήταις
ἀρτιφύτου λειμῶνος ἱμάσσετο νήδυμος ἀήρ.

This reading is supported as to its meaning by Virgil's,

Quam multa in sylvis autumni frigore primo
Lapsa cadunt folia. Æneid. vi. 309.

and Milton's,

Thick as autumnal leaves that strow the brooks
In Vallombrosa. Paradise Lost, i. 302.

Suidas in his Lexicon, vol. iii. p. 142, ed. Kuster, records the following proverb, which is printed also in Gaisford's Parœmiographi Græci, p. 98, No 807 of those " E cod. Bodleiano," πολλοί σε μισήσουσιν ἂν σαυτὸν φιλῇς· τοῦτό φασι Νύμφας πρὸς τὸν Νάρκισσον εἰπεῖν ἀποβλέποντα εἰς τὴν πηγήν, καὶ τὴν οἰκείαν ποθοῦντα μορφήν.

Another of the late Byzantine authors, Nicetas Eugenianus, who lived in the twelfth century, in his Poem on the adventures of Drosilla and Charicles, alludes to the fate of Narcissus in these lines:

Ἆρ' ἦλθες εἰς νοῦν τοῦ πάθους τοῦ Ναρκίσου,
ἀπορριφέντος ἐξ ἔρωτος εἰς φρέαρ ;

iv. 246, 7, ed. Boissonade, Lugd. Bat. 1819.

Nor was it overlooked by some of the Greek Christian Fathers. Clemens Alexandrinus, in his Pædagog, iii. 94, 45 (vol. i. 258, ed. Potter), adduces it in argument:

οὐδὲ γὰρ, ὡς ὁ μῦθος Ἑλλήνων ἔχει, Ναρκίσσῳ προεχώρησεν τῷ καλῷ, τῆς ἑαυτοῦ εἰκόνος γενέσθαι θεατήν.

And Gregory Nazianz. introduces it in his Carmen xxix. Adversus Mulieres se nimis ornantes.

καὶ μορφῆς τις ἑῆς ποτ' ἐράσσατο, καὶ κατὰ πηγῆς
ἥλατ' ἐπ' εἰδώλῳ κάλλεος οὐλομένου. Vol. ii. p. 572, 155, 6.

also in his Carmen Ad Vitellianum.

μορφῆς μέν τις ἑῆς ποτ' ἐράσσατο, καὶ κατὰ πηγῆς
ἥλατο, καὶ μιν ἔσοπτρον ἀπώλεσεν εἴδεος ἐσθλοῦ. Vol. ii. p. 1020. 52, 3.

2 N

Introduction to Narcissus.

Several of the later Latin Poets make mention of Narcissus. Statius, in his Thebaid:

> Tu quoque præclarum formâ Cephisse dedisses
> Narcissum, sed Thespiacis jam pallet in agris
> Trux puer; orbatâ florem pater allinit undâ.—vii. 340.

Claudian De Raptu Proserpinæ:

> Te quoque flebilibus mœrens, Hyacinthe, figuris,
> Narcissumque metunt, nunc inclyta germina veris,
> Præstantes olim pueros : tu natus Amyclis;
> Hunc Helicon genuit : te disci perculit error;
> Hunc fontis decepit amor: te fronte retusâ
> Delius; hunc fractâ Cephissus arundine luget.—ii. 131.

Ausonius, in his 6th Idyll, "Cupido Cruci affixus":

> Quorum per ripas nebuloso lumine marcent
> Fleti olim regum et puerorum nomina flores,
> Mirator Narcissus, et Œbalides Hyacinthus.—8.

and in his Epigrams:

> XCVI.
> Furitis procaces Naiades,
> Amore sævo et irrito.
> Ephebus iste flos erit.
>
> XCVII.
> Si cuperes alium, posses, Narcisse, potiri:
> Nunc tibi amoris adest copia, fructus abest.
>
> XCVIII.
> Quid non ex hujus formâ pateretur amator,
> Ipse suam qui sic deperit effigiem?
>
> XCIX.
> Commoritur, Narcisse, tibi resonabilis Echo,
> Vocis ad extremos exanimata modos.
> Et pereuntis adhuc gemitum resecuta querelis,
> Ultima nunc etiam verba loquentis amat.

Pentadius, in Anthologia Meyeri Lips. 1835, 242, sqq. pp. 96, 97 and others, anonymous, 666, sqq. pp. 223, 224. In the Poetæ Latini Minores, ed. Wernsdorf, Altenburg 1782, vol. iii. pp. 272-275. Burmannus Anthologia Latina, i. n. 139, sqq. and in the Collectio Pisaurensis Pisauri 1766, vol. iv. pp. 439, 440:

> 242. Narcissus.
> Cui pater amnis erat, fontes puer ille colebat,
> Laudabatque undas, cui pater amnis erat.
> Se puer ipse videt, patrem dum quærit in amne,
> Perspicuuoque lacu se puer ipse videt.

Introduction to Narcissus.

Quod Dryas igne calet, puer hunc inridet amorem,
Nec putat esse decus, quod Dryas igne calet.
Stat stupet hæret amat rogat innuit adspicit ardet
Blanditur queritur stat stupet hæret amat,
Quodque amat, ipse facit vultu prece lumine fletu,
Oscula dat fonti, quodque amat, ipse facit.

243. Narcissus.
Invenit proprios mediis in fontibus ignes,
Et sua deceptum torret imago virum.

244. Narcissus.
Hic est ille, suis nimium qui credidit undis,
Narcissus vero dignus amore puer.
Cernis ab irriguo repetentem gramine ripam,
Ut, per quas periit, crescere possit, aquas.

245. Narcissus.
Crede ratem ventis : animum ne crede puellis.
Namque est femineâ tutior unda fide.
Femina nulla bona est, vel si bona contigit una,
Nescio quo fato res mala facta bona.

246. Narcissus.
Se Narcissus amat, captus lenonibus undis :
Cui si tollis aquas, non est ubi sæviat ignis.

666. Narcissus.
Dum putat esse parem vitreis Narcissus in undis,
Solus amore perit, dum putat esse parem.

667. Narcissus.
Ardet amore sui flagrans Narcissus in undis
Cum modo perspicuâ se speculatur aquâ.

668. Narcissus.
Suspirat propriæ Narcissus gaudia formæ,
Quem scrutata suis vultibus unda domat.

669. Narcissus. Cento Virgilianus.
Candida per silvam primævo flore juventus
Adsidue veniebat; ibi hæc cœlestia dona
Et fontes sacros insigni laude ferebat
Insignis facie, longumque bibebat amorem,
Intentos volvens oculos securus Amorum.
Dum stupet atque animum picturâ pascit inani,
Expleri mentem nequit ardescitque tuendo
Egregium formâ juvenem, quem Nympha crearat,

272   *Introduction to Narcissus.*

>Sic oculos, sic ille manus, sic ora ferebat.
>His amor unus erat; dorso dum pendet iniquo,
>Oblitusve sui est, et membra decora juventæ
>Miratur, rerumque ignarus imagine gaudet.
>Ilicet ignis edax secreti ad fluminis undas
>Ipsius in vultu vanâ spe lusit amantem,
>Et præceps animi collo dare brachia circum
>Ter conatus erat, nec quid speraret habebat.

Some of the later Latin mythographers have condensed Ovid's version of the story of Narcissus into brief prose narratives; of whom Lactantius Placidus is printed in the Mythographi Latini, by Muncker, Amst. 1681; and two others were inserted by Angelo Mai in his collection "Classicorum auctorum e Vaticanis Codicibus Editorum," vol. iii. Romæ, 1831. The former of these he thinks may be a second Hyginus, living in the fifth century A.D.; and the other, who was a Christian, copied his predecessor to some extent, but occasionally differs from him entirely. In the account of Narcissus he gives the name of his mother as Alciope instead of Liriope, or Leirioessa as it is in some of the Greek writers.

Isidorus Origines xvii. cap. ix. p. 1254, 16.   Ed. Gothofredi 1622:

>"Narcissus herba fabulosè impositum nomen habet à quodam puero, cujus membra in hunc florem transierunt, qui et nomen Narcissi in appellatione custodit, et decus pulchritudinis in candore retinet florum."

Servius in Virgilii Eclog. ii. 47, 8:

>"Sané Papaver, Narcissus, Anethus, pulcherrimi pueri fuerunt: quique in flores suorum nominum versi sunt: quos ei offerendo, quasi admonet, nequid etiam hic tale aliquid unquam ex amore patiatur."

The following are added from the modern Latin poets:

Andreæ Alciati Emblemata.
Φιλαυτία. 147.

>Quod nimium tua forma tibi Narcisse placebat,
>In florem, et noti est versa stuporis olus.
>Ingenii est marcor, cladesque Philautia; doctos
>Quæ pessum plures datque, deditque viros:
>Qui veterum abjectâ methodo, nova dogmata quærunt,
>Nilque suas præter tradere phantasias.
>   Delitiæ Poetar. Italor. 1608, vol. i. p. 44.

Joannis Francisci Apostolii Poemata.
Ad Narcissum.

>Das meritò, Narcisse puer pulcherrime, pœnas,
>Das meritò, et facies te tua jure capit.

Introduction to Narcissus. 273

Jactabat frustra voces resonabilis Echo ;
Nunc frustra vultus expetis ipse tuos.
    Carmina Illustrium Poetarum Italorum,
      Florentiæ, MDCCXIX. Tom. i. p. 310.
   Delitiæ Poetarum Italorum, 1608. Vol. i. p. 242.
    De Narcisso.
Narcissum in claris Narcissus viderat undis:
 Dum putat esse alium, quem videt, ardet amans.
Miratur, loquitur, blanditur; ut omnia cernit
 Irrita, in ingratas se jaculatur aquas.
Et propriâ ardentem deceptus imagine flammam
 Extinxit gelidis quam sibi fecit aquis.
    Faustus Sabæus, Delit. Poet. Ital. ii. 554.
    De Narcisso.
Hic est ille puer, qui dum fallacibus undis
 Crederet, est vano lusus amore sui.
Et nunc adserpit languenti gramine ripæ;
 Ut quibus aruerit, jam revirescat aquis.—Ibid. p. 570.
    De Narcisso.
Ardebat proprii Narcissus imagine vultus,
 Fontis et ad ripas hæc moriturus ait:
Forma in amore juvat: extinguitur ignis in undâ:
 Me miserum, nostri est utraque causa mali.
    Jo. Bapt. Scaphenatius, Del. Poet. Ital. ii. 921.
   Ad Echo de Morte Narcissi.
Funera Narcissi Nymphæ lacrymentur, at Echo
 Gaude, rivalis dum perit ille tuus.
    Henrici Harderi Epigr. Lib. ii. 38, in Delitiæ
      Poetarum Danorum, ii. 255.
    Narcissus.
Nymphas despexi; Narcissi unius amore
 Flagravi, atque amor hic, corporis umbra fuit.
Flos tandem factus: miraris? nempe brevis flos.
 Quin umbra est quicquid vanus ineptit Amor.
    Paschasii Icones, Del. Poet. Gallor. ii. 847.
    Narcissi.
Hei mihi quid prodest vanæ ostentatio formæ
 Quæ peritura fugit, quæ fugitiva perit ?
En ego flos, olim nostri tam stultus amator,
 Objicior pecori pastus et esca levis.
Quod commune aliis, mihi cur natura negavit,
 Umbram ut qui colui, mortuus umbra forem ?
Nempe quod, et vivum, et morientem, pendere pœnas
 Invisi fastus me voluere Dei.
    Paschasii Epitaph. Ibid. p. 1019.

Introduction to Narcissus.

Narcissus.

Dum vitreo se fonte videt Narcissus, et ardet
Protinus adspectâ florentis imagine formæ.
Quæ res exitio fuit illi, atque omnibus olim
Semper erit, similis quoscunque agitaverit error.
Michael Hospitalius Epistolar. iv. 1. Del. Poet. Gallor, ii. p. 186.

The myth of Narcissus was well-suited to meet the notions of the Neo-Platonists, whence Plotinus (ob. 270 A.D.) in his disputation περὶ τοῦ καλοῦ (Ennead. i. vi. 8, p. 112, ed. Creuzer, Oxon. 1835, 4to, and p. 56, ed. Heidelberg, 1814), introduces it in illustration of his argument, that the soul must penetrate through the outward to discover the inward beauty. τίς οὖν ὁ τρόπος; τίς μηχανή; πῶς τις θεάσηται κάλλος ἀμήχανον, οἷον ἔνδον ἐν ἁγίοις ἱεροῖς μένον, οὐδὲ προϊὸν εἰς τὸ ἔξω, ἵνα τις καὶ βέβηλος ἴδῃ. ἴτω δὴ καὶ συνεπέσθω εἰς τὸ εἴσω ὁ δυνάμενος, ἔξω καταλιπὼν ὄψιν ὀμμάτων, μηδ' ἐπιστρέφων αὐτὸν εἰς τὰς προτέρας ἀγλαΐας σωμάτων· ἰδόντα γὰρ δεῖ τὰ ἐν σώμασι καλά, μήτι προστρέχειν, ἀλλὰ γνόντας ὡς εἰσὶν εἰκόνες καὶ ἴχνη καὶ σκιαὶ, φεύγειν πρὸς ἐκεῖνο, οὗ ταῦτα εἰκόνες. εἰ γάρ τις ἐπιδράμοι λαβεῖν βουλόμενος ὡς ἀληθινόν, οἷα εἰδώλου καλοῦ ἐφ' ὕδατος ὀχουμένου, οὗ λαβεῖν βουληθεὶς ὥς που τὶς μῦθος, δοκῶ μοι, αἰνέττεται, δὺς εἰς τὸ κάτω τοῦ ῥεύματος, ἀφανὴς ἐγένετο· τὸν αὐτὸν δὴ τρόπον ὁ ἐχόμενος τῶν καλῶν σωμάτων, καὶ μὴ ἀφιεὶς, οὐ τῷ σώματι, τῇ δὲ ψυχῇ καταδύσεται εἰς σκοτεινὰ καὶ ἀτερπῆ τῷ νῷ βάθη, ἔνθα τυφλὸς ἐν ᾅδου μένων, καὶ ἐνταῦθα κἀκεῖ σύνεστι. See Creuzer's edition, 1814, and his Præparatio, prefixed to it, of which pp. xlv. to lxx. treat *De Narcisso.*

Another writer published by Gale in his Opuscula Mythologica, Amst. 1688, under the title of "Anonymus de Incredibilibus," and who cannot have lived before the latter part of the fifth century, (as he quotes Proclus, who died in 485 A.D.,) and would thus be at least two centuries later than Plotinus, moralises the story, as follows, in the ix. chapter, περὶ Ναρκίσσου.

Λέγεται περὶ αὐτοῦ, ὡς ἐν ὕδατι τὴν ἑαυτοῦ σκιὰν ἰδὼν, καὶ ἐρασθεὶς ἥλατο εἰς τὸ ὕδωρ, ἐφ' ᾧ τὴν αὐτοῦ σκιὰν περιπτύξασθαι, καὶ οὕτως ἀπεπνίγη. οὐκ ἀληθὲς δὲ τοῦτο. οὐ γὰρ εἰς ὕδωρ ἀπεπνίγη, ἀλλ' ἐν τῇ ῥευστῇ τοῦ ἐνύλου σώματος φύσει τὴν ἑαυτοῦ θεασάμενος σκιὰν, ἤτοι τὴν ἐν τῷ σώματι ζωὴν, ἥτις ἐστὶ τὸ ἔσχατον εἴδωλον τῆς ὄντως ψυχῆς, καὶ ταύτην ὡς οἰκείαν περιπτύξασθαι σπουδάσας, τουτέστι τὴν κατ' αὐτὴν ζωὴν ἀγαπήσας, ἀπεπνίγη, γεγονὼς ὑποβρύχιος, ὡς φθείρας τὴν ὄντως ψυχήν· ταὐτὸν δὲ εἰπεῖν τὸν ὄντως ἑαυτῷ προσήκοντα βίον. ὅθεν καὶ παροιμία τις φάσκει, Δεδιὼς τὴν σαυτοῦ σκιὰν,

Introduction to Narcissus. 275

διδάσκει δὲ δεδιέναι τὴν περὶ τὰ ἔσχατα ὡς πρῶτα σπουδὴν, ὄλεθρον ἡμῖν ἐνάγουσαν τῆς ψυχῆς, ἤτοι ἀφανισμὸν τῆς ἀληθοῦς τῶν πραγμάτων γνώσεως, καὶ τῆς προσηκούσης αὐτῇ κατ' οὐσίαν τελειότητος. οὕτως ὁ εἰς τὰς παρὰ Πλάτωνι Παροιμίας γράψας.

From Severus, a Sophist who taught at Alexandria about the end of the fifth century, we have this short narrative:

τὸ κάτα Νάρκισσον διήγημα.

παραλόγου πάθους ὁ λόγος ὑπῆρξε παραλογώτερος· Νάρκισσος γὰρ ἦν ἐρῶν οἴκοθεν καὶ φθειρόμενος οἴκοθεν· ὥρᾳ μὲν γὰρ διέφερε σώματος· ὅθεν δὲ τὴν ὥραν καὶ τὸν πόνον ἐκτήσατο· καταλαμβάνει γὰρ πηγὴν ὁ πιόμενος. θεατὴς δὲ τῆς οἰκείας μορφῆς καταστὰς, ἐραστὴς ὁ αὐτὸς καὶ θεατὴς κατεφαίνετο. ἤρα δὲ, ὅθεν αὐτὸς ἐξ αὐτοῦ καταφθείρεται· ἐρώμενος ἦν ἐραστὴν οὐ κτησάμενος· ἀλλ' ἐπὶ πηγὴν ἑαυτὸν ἐπαφεὶς, ἔστεργε μὲν τὴν σκιὰν ὡς ἐρώμενος· ἑαυτοῦ δὲ λαβόμενος, ἑαυτὸν ἐναφῆκε τοῖς ὕδασι· καὶ παραψύχην τοῦ πάθους ζητῶν βίου στέρησιν εὕρατο, τοσοῦτον τῆς τελευτῆς ὀνησάμενος, ὅσον εἰς τέλος μεταπεσεῖν· καὶ δηλοῖ τὴν μνήμην ὁμωνύμῳ βλαστήματι.— Severi Narrationes et Ethopoeiae. Narr. 3, ed. Walz. in Rhetores Graeci, Stuttgartiae 1832, oct. vol. i. p. 538.

Nicolaus, a Rhetor, also living about the end of the fifth century, and perhaps at Constantinople, makes Narcissus the subject of one of his Progymnasmata:

κατασκευὴ ὅτι εἰκότα τὰ κατὰ Νάρκισσον.

φθέγγονται μὲν οἱ ποιηταὶ τὰ Μουσῶν, καὶ παρ' ἐκείνων ὅ τι ἂν διεξέλθωσι φέρουσι· καὶ δεῖ βουλὰς οἰκείας νομίσαι Μουσῶν, ἃ ποιηταὶ κατεμέτρησαν, ὥστε τοῖς ἀπιστοῦσι καταλείπεται κίνδυνος· οὐ γὰρ ποιηταῖς ἀντερεῖν, ἀλλ' αὐταῖς ἀναγκάζονται Μούσαις· καὶ πολλῶν μὲν πάρεστι τοὺς ποιητὰς ἄγασθαι, μάλιστα δὲ ὧν φιλοσοφοῦσιν εἰς Νάρκισσον. οἷα γὰρ εἰπόντων ἀντερεῖν τινες τετολμήκασι· Νάρκισσος, φασὶ, μειράκιον γέγονε. τί τούτου πρὸς θεῶν ἄπιστον; οὐ πρεσβυτάτη τῶν ἀνθρώπων γένεσις, ᾗ τὰ ἀνθῶν προῆλθε βλαστήματα, πρὸς ἀνθρώπων τῇ γᾷ τὰ δι' ἀνθρώπους γενόμενα. δι' ὧν τοίνυν ἡ γῆ πάντα βλαστήματα πρὸς τὴν ἀνθρώπων προενήνοχεν ὄνησιν, πειράκιόν τι νενόμισται Νάρκισσος, ἐξ οὗ προῆλθεν ἄνθος ὁμώνυμον, καὶ τὸ παρασχὸν τὴν γονὴν καταβάλλει τὴν ὄνησιν· γεγονὼς τοίνυν ὁ νέος διαπρεπὴς τὴν ὄψιν, εἰς τὸν οἰκεῖον προελήλυθε πόθον. ᾧ γὰρ ἄνθρωποι ποθεῖν ἑτέρους ἐπαίρονται, τούτῳ Νάρκισσος ποθεῖν ἑαυτὸν ἠναγκάζετο, καὶ κάλλος οἰκεῖον ἤγαγεν ἔρωτα, ὡς ἑτέρους

276 Introduction to Narcissus.

κεκίνηκε, καὶ τοιοῦτο μᾶλλον οἰκείας ὄψεως ἐρᾶν πιθανώτερον, ὅσον τὰ μὲν ἑαυτῶν ἀκριβέστερον ἔγνωμεν, ἃ δὲ μὴ πρόσεστι μόνον εἰκάζομεν· ὥστε εἰ τὸ μᾶλλον εἰδέναι πλέον παρασκευάζει ποθεῖν, οἰκείας ὄψεως ἑτοιμότερον ἔρως ἐγγίνεται, καὶ μᾶλλον παράλογον ἐραστὴς ἑτέρου φανεὶς, ἢ μορφῆς οἰκείας ἑαλωκὼς, ὥστε ἢ τὴν ὥραν ἀναιρητέον τοῦ νέου, ἢ τιθεμένου συγχωρητέον τῷ πόθῳ· ἐρῶν δὲ ἑαυτοῦ καὶ τὴν οἰκείαν ὥραν πόθου δεξάμενος εὕρεσιν, ὅθεν ἐπόθει, παρὰ τοῦτον ἠπείγετο· τῆς γοῦν ἐν ὕδασιν ἰδέας ἁλοὺς, ἐπὶ τῶν ὑδάτων τὸ φαινόμενον ἔστεργεν. Οἶδα τοίνυν, ὅτι τινὲς ἀντεροῦσιν, ὡς οὐχ οἷόν τε εἶναι, σκιᾶς ἐρασθῆναι τὸν νέον, ἐγὼ δὲ, ὅσον ἐρᾶν τις αὐτὸν συγχωρήσειε, τοσοῦτον ἄν φαίην ἁμαρτάνειν εἰς κρίσιν. ἔρως γὰρ περὶ ὃ ποθεῖ κρίνειν οὐκ ἔγνωκεν· αἱ γὰρ ὁπωσοῦν ἐπιθυμίαι τὸ κρίνειν τοῖς ἐπιθυμοῦσιν οὐ καταλείπουσιν· τοσούτῳ δὲ μᾶλλον ἀφαιρεῖται τὴν κρίσιν ὅσῳ καὶ μεῖζον παντὸς γέγονεν ἔρωτος· ἤδη δὲ καὶ πολλοὶ σωμάτων αἰσχρῶν ἐρασταὶ καθεστήκασι· κάλλους μὲν ἔρως προέρχεται, ὃ δὲ μὴ καλὸν εἰδέ τις, τοῦτο δι' ἔρωτος ἔκρινεν ἄριστον. ὅθεν οὐδὲν ἀπεικὸς, οὐδὲ Νάρκισσον ἐμπεσόντα εἰς ἔρωτα τὴν σκιὰν τιμᾶν ὡς ἐρώμενον· ἀεὶ γὰρ τι μεῖζον ὁ πόθος οἷς ποθεῖ περιτίθησιν· οὐκοῦν οὐδὲ ἀπεικὸς, οὐδὲ Νάρκισσον ποθεῖν τὸ τῆς οἰκείας ὄψεως εἴδωλον· σφαλεὶς δὲ τὰ πρῶτα τὴν δόξαν, εἰκότως ἁμαρτάνει τὰ δεύτερα, καὶ τοῖς ὕδασιν ἐπαφῆκεν αὑτὸν, ὥσπερ τι ληψόμενον· πεσόντα δὲ διαδέχεται θάνατος· οὐ γὰρ ἐστιν, οὐκ ἔστιν παραλόγου πόθου πέρας ἔξω κινδύνων εὑρεῖν· πεσόντος δὲ τοῦ νέου παρὰ τὰ νάματα προῆλθεν ἄνθος, ὃ τὴν ἐκ τοῦ νέου δέχεται κλῆσιν· καὶ ταῦτα ποιητῶν ἄγαμαι μάλιστα, προσηγορίας εἶναι τῶν ἀνθρώπων φιλοσοφούντων τοῖς ἄνθεσιν; ὧν γὰρ αἱ κλήσεις, τούτων αἱ γενέσεις νομίζονται· ταῦτα καὶ τὰ τοιαῦτα καὶ λέγειν ἔδει τοὺς ποιητὰς καὶ εἰποῦσι προστίθεσθαι.—Nicolai Progymnasmata, cap. vi. 2, ed. Walz. in Rhetores Græci, Stuttgartiæ 1832, oct. vol. i. p. 294.

Lastly, Nicephorus, another Rhetor towards the end of the twelfth century, under Alexius Comnenus at Constantinople, displays his skill in another but similar exercise:

τὸ κατὰ τὸν Νάρκισσον.

Νάρκισσος ὁ νῦν διαπρέπων ἐν ἄνθεσιν ἐν μειρακίοις πάλαι διέλαμπεν. εὐανθὴς ἦν τὸν τοῦ προσώπου λειμῶνα, καλὸς τὴν μορφὴν, ἄμαχος τὴν θέαν, τὸ κάλλος ἀνίκητος. ἐφείλκετο καὶ τοὺς τῶν ἄλλων ὀφθαλμούς. ἀλλ' εἶχεν αὐτὸς ἕτερον ἔρωτα, κύνας ἐπισύρεσθαι, καὶ πρὸς θήρας ἱππάζεσθαι, καὶ ποτε πολλοὺς τοὺς ἐκ τῆς θήρας ἀποστάζων ἱδρῶτας περιΐσταταί τινα πηγήν, διαφανῆ

Introduction to Narcissus. 277

μὲν ἰδεῖν, ποτιμωτάτην δὲ πιεῖν, ἡ δὲ τὴν μὲν τῆς δίψης φλόγα μαραίνει τῷ μειρακίῳ, ἕτερον δὲ πῦρ ἀνάπτει τὸν ἔρωτα. καὶ διψῶντα μὲν ὕδατος παύει, κάλλους δὲ διψᾶν αὖθις βιάζεται. γίνεται τῆς ὥρας κάτοπτρον· ὡς ἐν πίνακι τῷ ῥεύματι γράφει τὸν Νάρκισσον. καὶ τοῖς αὐτοῦ κάλλεσι βάλλεται Νάρκισσος. καὶ ὃ πολλοὺς πρότερον ἔδρασε, τοῦτο τηνικαῦτα παθὼν αὐτὸς ἔλαθε. Νάρκισσος ἐκ πηγῆς τὸ κάλλος ἀνέβλυζε, καὶ Νάρκισσος διψῶν οὐκ ἐμπίπλαται. Νάρκισσος ὑπερίσταται τῶν ναμάτων, καὶ Νάρκισσος ἕτερος ὑπὸ τὴν πηγὴν διεφαίνετο· ἐμειδία Νάρκισσος ἄνωθεν, καὶ κάτωθεν αὖθις ἀντεμειδία τὸ κάλλος. ταῦτα ἦν ἀμφοῖν πάντα ὡς ἐν κατόπτρῳ διαφανεῖ τῇ πηγῇ. ἀλλ' εἶχε τι καὶ θαύματος, οἷς διήλλαττε τὸ φαινόμενον. ὀφθαλμοὶ πρὸς τὴν ὄψιν ἐπεπήγεσαν, καὶ τὸ κάλλος ἐναπέσταζε τῇ πηγῇ· ἡ τῶν ὑδάτων φύσις θᾶσσον ἀπέρρει, καὶ τὸ ῥεῦσαν ἐκ τῶν ὀφθαλμῶν ἐν οὐκ εἰδόσι μένειν ἐπεπήγει τοῖς ὕδασιν. ἐντεῦθεν ὁ ἔρως θερμότερον ἐπέζεσεν τῷ Ναρκίσσῳ, ὁ δὲ μὴ φέρων τὸ πῦρ ἐπαφῆκεν ἑαυτὸν τοῖς ῥεύμασιν, ὡς ἂν καὶ τὸν δοκοῦντα περιπτύξαιτο Νάρκισσον, καὶ τὴν ἔρωτος πυρκαϊὰν ἀποσβέσειεν. ἀλλ' ἡ τῶν ὑδάτων φύσις αὐτῷ κάλλει τὸν ἔρωτα ξυναπέσβεσε, τῷ ζῶντι Ναρκίσσῳ καὶ τὸν δοκοῦντα συναποκρύψασα. οὐ μιμεῖται τὴν πηγὴν ἡ γῆ, ἀλλ' οἰκτείρει τὴν συμφοράν, καὶ σοφίζεται τὴν μνήμην τοῦ πάθους, καὶ τοῦ καλοῦ μειρακίου καλὸν ἄνθος ἀντιχαρίζεται Ναρκίσσῳ καὶ ἔρωτι. οὕτω καὶ μετὰ τελευτὴν περίεστι Νάρκισσος, καὶ αὖθις οὐδὲν ἧττον ἢ πρότερον εἰς κάλλος ἀνθεῖ.— Nicephori Progymnasmata, cap. ii. 14, ed. Walz. in Rhetores Græci, Stuttgartiæ, 1832, oct. vol. i. p. 440.

Such a story as that of Narcissus could not fail to be attractive to artists. The elder Philostratus (c. 200 A.D.), in his Εἰκόνες, ch. xxiii. and Callistratus (an author of uncertain date, but in the opinion of his editor, F. Jacobs, "ad seriora tempora detrudendus"), in his ἐκφράσεις ἀγαλμάτων, ch. v. have described respectively a painting and a statue of which he was the subject. Nor are we without original specimens of these ancient works. At Herculaneum were four pictures representing the whole myth, which are engraved in Ant. Herc. vii. tab. 28-31, though, according to Welcker, their order has been inverted, and tab. 28 should be the last of the series, which will then exhibit Narcissus "just returned from hunting (29), as having noticed his image reflected in the fountain, but yet unaffected by it (30), as totally absorbed in gazing on it, with Love standing near, holding an inverted torch (31), and, lastly, as worn out with his hopeless passion, Love still near him with his torch quite extinguished (28). Several statues have also been preserved and engraved. One, formerly in the Barberini collection, representing him as a young man standing with his eyes fixed on the shadow in the fountain and insensible to any other object, is engraved in " Causci Museum Romanum, Romæ, 1746, fol. vol. i. § 2, pl. liii." Another at Florence, which exhibits him rather younger, and kneeling by the fountain, " stupens ac se in fonte prospiciens, vultuque ipso amoris excestuantis vim, suæque pulchritudinis admirationem gestu pariter suspensi brachii et manus expansæ perbellè declarans," is engraved in Gorii Mus. Florent. Flor. 1734, vol. iii. tab. lxxi. A third is in Guattani Mon. Ined. 1805, pl. 7, 8, and a fourth in the Vatican, in the Museo Pio-Clementino, by Visconti. This is mentioned in Tales of the Classics, 1830, i. p. 142, with this criticism by Sir J. E. Smith, " He has a very foolish face, as perhaps he ought."

With regard to these statues, however, the following cautions must be noticed. Creuzer, Præparatio ad Plotinum, p. lxv. says, " Sunt et alia opera artis antiquæ quæ Narcissum vel exhibeant, vel exhibere sint judicata. Neque enim singuli pro Narcisso habendi, qui vulgo ita dictitantur, sive in signis, sive in anaglyphis alioque opere. Vide de his doctè disputantem Ennium Quirinum Viscontium in Museo Pio-Clementino," tom. ii. p. 60 seqq. Similarly Welcker, in his note on Philostratus, xxiii. p. 344, says, " Sculptas Narcissi imagines duas tantum sibi notas esse scripsit Zoega, quas statuas fuisse suspicor unam in Guattani Mon. Ined. et in Museo Florentino alterum. Sed in hâc Niobes filium ex dorso vulnerato nuper agnovit Danorum decus, Albertus Thorwaldsen." v. Zannonii Gal. di Firenze, Statue, tom. ii. tab. 74.

Engravings from ancient gems are in the Mus. Florent. ii. pl. xxxvi. No. 2; Winckelmann's Monument. Ant. Inedit. Roma, 1767, fol. No. xxiv. with an explanation on p. 29 of text; and in Worlidge's Engraved Gems, Lond. 1768, No. 13.

C. O. Muller, Hist. of Ancient Art, Lond. 1850, 8vo. p. 568, says that Narcissus was the device on the Thespian coins, and gives references to the following works, in addition to those already quoted. Museo Borbonico, i. 4, ii. 18; Lippert, i. ii. 63; Impr. d. Inst. i. 73; Bronze figure in the Royal Library at Paris, Clarac, pl. 590, No. 1281.

In the year 1797 a marble " puteal " was dug up near Ostia, on which the stories of Hylas and Narcissus were represented in combination, of which Zoega, a learned Dane, wrote an account in his own language.

Creuzer, in his Præparatio ad Plotinum, p. lxvi. calls attention to another class of ancient works of art, the paintings on Greek vases. These, he states, often relate to the Mysteries, and sometimes to the fable of Narcissus. " Quam in rem non inepta est conjectura *Millini*, Francogalli, qui in opere cui titulus Peint. d. Vases, antiqq. tom. ii. p. 50, ubi de vase illo Poniatowskii Principis, Proserpinæ raptum exhibente, exponit, in alterâ ejus vasis parte florem Narcissum adumbratum suspicatur, in alterius partis orâ caput juvenis Narcissi, lepidè comans, venustum, atque ex calyce floris lætè virescentis prominens."

There is a copperplate engraving by Ægidius Sadeler (1570-1629), from his own design, of Narcissus admiring himself in a fountain, which is reckoned by Bryan, Dict. of Engravers, among his best productions. Another, by A. Diepenbeck, is No. xxxvi. of the " Tableaux du Temple des Muses tirez du cabinet de feu M. Favereau," Paris, 1655, fol. p. 283, with a description, and learned notes by M. de Marolles. Bryan speaks highly of Diepenbeck's powers.

The ancient expositions of the myth tended either towards the ethical side, and regarded Narcissus as a warning against self-love, or were metaphysical as in Plotinus and his followers. Modern interpreters, incline, however, towards the physical, either like the following French writer interpreting it of the phænomena of the world, or like Sir George Cox connecting it with the cycle of solar legends.

L'amour et la mort de Narcisse ont inspiré à Ovide un des Episodes les plus Spirituels des Metamorphoses. Dumoustier, *Lettres sur La Mythologie*, a heureusement imité et quelquefois embelli ce morceau, qui est a coup sûr le plus agréable de son ouvrage. Le mythe de Narcisse tient à la religion des Thespies, où sans cesse on voit reparaître les eaux, lacs, sources, fleuves, dieux-fleuves, nymphes, et les fleurs: les fleurs se mirent dans les eaux, et d'autre part, les fleurs jaunes sont des symboles de deuil. Ce n'est rien encore; à toute minute des éphèbes, de jeunes braves, des vierges s'identifient aux fleurs: Clytie, Ajax, Hyacinthe, Abder, Daphné, en sont les charmants et tristes temoins. Ces existences qui s'effacent de plus en plus, ces héros, ces vierges qui deviennent des fleurs, ces fleuves qui se resolvent en images, ces images qui ne sont que le néant, symbolisent la vanité non pas des choses humaines, c'est dire trop peu, mais de l'univers entier. Qu'est ce que le Monde? Maïa, Maïa, beauté mais illusion. Sans doute il est beau, cet univers, avec ses astres, sa lumiere, ses couleurs, son harmonie et sa population d'animaux et de fleurs; mais tout cela dans les dogmes du spiritualisme, est-ce ou n'est-ce pas? Voila la question. Et la réponse, la voici: cela n'est pas. Qu'arrive-t-il donc? L'univers tout illusionnel qu'il est, ne s'imagine pas que tout soit illusion: il s'aime, il se mire, il s'admire, il aspire a la possession de quelque partie de lui-même. Il soupire pour des illusions. Il tend les bras à des images, il trouble l'eau paisible, condition du phénomène: et alors adieu le spectacle dans lequel il s'est complu! Narcisse est donc le monde. En un sens moins haut, Narcisse est l'ame qui, avide de positif, prend la fantasmagorie physique pour une réalité, et tantôt sur les ailes du plaisir la poursuit, l'embrasse, l'etreint, et s'apperçoit qui elle n'étreint qu'une ombre, tantôt se livrant aux speculations de la metaphysique, scrute le phénomène, cherche un critérium, et ne trouve à la place de la certitude que de désolantes raisons de tout revoquer en doute. Les idées que nous esquissons ont été variees de plus d'une manière par d'habiles mythographes. Nous ne pouvons les suivre dans tous les détails aux quels ils se livrent. Le phénomène si fameux du mirage, qui a donné lieu à la creation de la fée Morgane et à la Melusine etc. se lie de loin aux fables de Narcisse. L'eau est la grande magicienne. Qui pénétré de cette idée, on parcoure les fables de Circé, de Calypso, d'Addirdaga, de Neith, on sera étonné de la richesse de ces mythes en eux-mêmes, et des rapports qu'ils offrent avec Narcisse, et tout d'autres. Comp. aussi le mythe des Nymphes Ascanides enlevant Hylas, ainsi que celui des Sirenes attirant à elles quiconque passe et le gardant à tous jamais dans leur eaux. La plus celebre representation figurée de Narcisse est celle qu'on trouve dans le *Musée Florentin*, iii. 71. Voy. aussi Winckelman, *Monum. Ant. Ined.* xxiv.; et les remarques de Visconti, *Musee Pio-Clementin.* ii. p. 60 etc.

Biographie Universelle. Partie Mythologique. Paris 1832. Art. Narcisse.

"Of the story of Narkissos, Pausanias* gives two versions. The former, which describes him as wasting away and dying through love of his own face and form reflected in a fountain, he rejects, on account of the utter absurdity of supposing that Narkissos could not distinguish between a man and his shadow. Hence he prefers the other, but less known, legend, that Narkissos loved his own twin sister, and that on her death he found a melancholy comfort in noting the likeness of his own form and countenance to that of his lost love. But the more common tale, that Narkissos was deaf to the entreaties of the nymph Echo, is nearer to the spirit of the old phrase, which spoke of the sleep of the tired sun.

---

* ix. 31, 6. "He rejects also the notion that the flower was so named after Narkissos, the former having certainly existed before his time, inasmuch as Persephonê, who belongs to an earlier period, was caught while plucking a narcissus from its stem "—Note, ii. p. 32.

"The stupefying narcissus, with its hundred flowers springing from a single stem, . . must be a narcotic which lulls to sleep the vegetation of nature in the bright yet sad autumn days when heaven and earth smile with the beauty of the dying year, and the myth necessarily chose the flower whose name denoted this dreamy lethargy."—Cox. Mythology of the Aryan Nations, ii. 299.

Introduction to Narcissus. 281

His very name denotes the deadly lethargy (νάρκη) which makes the pleadings of Selênê fall unheeded on the ear of Endymiôn; and hence it is that when Persephonê is to be taken at the close of summer to the land of darkness, the narcissus is made the instrument of her capture. It is the narcotic which plunges Brynhild into her profound slumber on the Glistening Heath, and drowns Briar Rose and her fellows in a sleep as still as death."—Cox, G. W., Mythology of the Aryan Nations, ii. 32, 33, section x. "Hellenic Sun-Gods and Heroes."

A poem entitled Narcissus, in Latin verse, was published by John Clapham, Lond. 1521, 4to., a copy of which is in the British Museum. The full title of this poem is, Narcissus, sive Amoris Juvenilis et præcipuè Philautiæ Brevis atque Moralis Descriptio, Londini, excudebat Thomas Scarlet, 1591. It comprises, Dedication to the Earl of Southampton A, 2. The poem itself, *Narcissus*, in Latin Hexameters, printed in Italic Type, six leaves, A 3, to B. 4. On B. 2 are 31 lines of Echo Verses. His end is thus stated:

"Deficit, et pronus de ripâ decidit, et sic
Ipse suæ periit deceptus imaginis umbrâ."

Venus procures his metamorphosis into the flower:

"Flos erit, atque suo sumet de nomine nomen.
Flosque. Juventuti sacer est, bene notus in arvis.
Ultima sors hæc est nimium infelicis amantis."

The story of Narcissus is introduced by Warner (1586-1592) into his Albions England, chap. xlvi. Richard Brathwaite wrote "The Golden Fleece, whereto bee annexed Two Elegies entitled Narcissus Change and Æsons Dotage," London, 1611, 8vo. See Collectanea Anglo-Poetica ii. 336 (Chetham Society), 1861. Henry Reynolds appended one in English to his Mythomystes London [c. 1630], 4to., entitled "The Tale of Narcissvs briefly Mythologised." It is in stanzas of eight lines each, being "Ovids story paraphrastically Englisht after the authors owne way." It occupies pp. 87-105, and is followed by six pages of Observations upon the Tale. There is a notice of it with extracts in Collier's Bibliographical Account of Rare Books, 1865, vol. i. pp. 553-555. James Shirley, the Dramatist, wrote Narcissus or the Self Lover, London, 1646, 12mo. In Dyce's edition, London, 1833, vol. vi. pp. 463-489; and in 1873 a volume was issued by E. Carpenter,— Narcissus, and other poems,—the former occupying nineteen pages. It may be noted that Narcissus was the subject of a "Classic Carol" in the "Comic Offering for 1834, the fair editress, Miss L. H. Sheridan, perhaps avenging her sex by allowing one who had despised their beauty to be held up to laughter in a burlesque. The French have a poem by Malfilatre, entitled "Narcisse en l'isle de Venus, en quatre Chants;" (based chiefly on Ovid), Paris, n.d., but the Approbation dated 1766, and stating justly, "Il y a dans cet Ouvrage de la Poesie, et de la facilité: c'est une fiction agréable où la Fable est ingénieusement mise en œuvre." Also a comedy by Rousseau, "Narcisse ou L'Amant de Lui Même, 1752." There is in Italian, "L'Alterazza di Narciso," Ven. 1611, 12mo. a dramatic piece by Francis Andreini.

Bacon, in his book "De Sapientia Veterum," inserts Narcissus as an example of self-love, chapter iv. being headed "Narcissus sive Philautia." In Shaw's English version the Fables are classified as Physical, Moral, and Political Mythology; and Narcissus is the third of the Moral Fables. Allusions to Narcissus are frequent in our own literature, and no doubt in that of other peoples, but it may be as well to cite those in Shakspere, as the two from his poems may have had some influence on our author, and led him to select this story as a subject for his own work. In Antony and Cleopatra, ii. 5, 96, Cleopatra says to Charmian:

"Hadst thou Narcissus in thy face, to me
Thou wouldst appear most ugly."

In Venus and Adonis the goddess urges:

"Is thine own heart to thine own face affected?
Can thy right hand seize love upon thy left?
Then woo thyself, be of thyself rejected,
Steal thine own freedom and complain of theft.
  Narcissus so himself himself forsook,
  And died to kiss his shadow in the brook." 157-162.

While lastly in Lucrece Tarquin soliloquizes:

"And how her hand, in my hand being lock'd,
Forced it to tremble with her loyal fear!
Which struck her sad, and then it faster rock'd,
Until her husband's welfare she did hear:
  Whereat she smiled with so sweet a cheer,
  That had Narcissus seen her as she stood
  Self-love had never drown'd him in the flood." 260-267

NOTES TO NARCISSUS.

P. 37, l. 2. *Nice.*] "Nice is from 'nescius,' meaning first, 'ignorant,' then 'foolish,' then 'foolishly hard to please,' then 'judiciously hard to please,' then 'refined,' 'agreeable.'" Dr. Abbott on Bacon's Essay, 2, 30. Professor Skeat adds, that "the remarkable changes in the sense may have been due to confusion with E. *nesh*, which sometimes meant 'delicate' as well as 'soft.'" It is properly applied to persons, as on p. 39, "I stood as nice as any she alive ;" and p. 44, "nice dames so quaint." Marlowe, H. and L. iii. 18, "Fair fools delight to be accounted nice." But is also used of things as here, and on p. 39, "I not regarded plaintes, or nice smiles speaking." See also the article "Nice" in Wedgwood.

P. 37, l. 3. *Delians.*] Followers of Apollo, Poets. Marston Sat. iii. Proem 3, "I invocate no *Delian* Deitie."

P. 37, l. 4. This line seems to mean, "You that instead of one poore thing, like my poem, make such as give enjoyment to thousands." Or it may refer to the pleasure afforded by stage-plays to great numbers. T. Nash, in "Pierce Penilesse," p. 60, writes, "How would it have joy'd braue Talbot (the terror of the French) to thinke that after he had layne two hundred yeare in his tomb he should triumph againe on the stage, and haue his bones new embalmed with the teares of ten thousand spectators at least (at seuerall times), who, in the tragedian that represents his person, imagine they behold him fresh bleeding ?"

P. 37, l. 5. *Curuate.*] Lat. "curvare." O. Ital. corvare, "to bend, make crooked, stoope." Florio. Here, with Mercutio and Romeo, "to bow in the hams. Meaning to court'sy." R. and J. ii. 4, 57. Curvate as a verb is not in the Dictionaries.

P. 37, l. 7. *Prickt.*] P. 59, "each sharp prickt noate." The old way of setting down a tune or song. Coryat, vol. i. p. 2, "Also there is this tune added to the verses, and pricked according to the forme of Musicke to be sung by those who are so disposed."

P. 37, l. 10. *Plaine-song.*] Skelton's "Phyllyp Sparowe 426-8, "But with a large and a longe, To kepe iust playne songe, Our chaünters shalbe the cuckoue." So Shakspere M. N. D. "The plain-song cuckoo gray," iii. 1, 135. Brewer. Lingua:

> *Audi.* "Lingua thou strikest too much upon one string,
> Thy tedious *plain-song* grates my tender ears.
> *Lin.* 'Tis *plain*, indeed, for truth no discant needs." i. 1.

"By *plain-song* the uniform modulation or simplicity of the *chaunt* was anciently distinguished, in opposition to *prick-song*, or variegated music sung by note." T. Warton, note on M. N. D.

P. 37, l. 11. *Cynicke beauties visor.*] The visor is a moveable part of the helmet with holes through which the wearer can see. See Douce Ill. to Shakspere, i. 438-443. Also that which covers the face or visage, a mask, L. L. L. v. ii. 227, 242, etc. Hence applied to the face, as in Sidney's Arcadia, vol. i. p. 19. "This lowtish clown is such that you never saw so ill-favoured a vizor." Cynicke beauty that which Cynick-like despises others. For a similar combination of these words see Marston's Scourge of Villanie, Sat. vii. a Cynicke Satyre, 160 :

> "Her maske so hinders me
> I cannot see her beauties deitie.
> Now that is off, she is so vizarded,
> So steeptt in lemons juyce, so surphuled
> I cannot see her face."

P. 37, l. 20. *Corycyus.*] Du Bartas, by Sylvester,. The Colonies, p. 344 :

> "And the delicious strange Corycian cave
> Which warbling sounds of cymballs seems to have."

Corycyus being an adjective should not have been used as it is here without its substantive for the Corycian Cave, so called from the nymph Corycia, as Pausanias, x. 6, and the Scholiast on Apollonius Rhodius, ii. 711, state. It is mentioned by Æschylus, Eumenides, 22:

> σέβω δὲ Νύμφας ἔνθα Κωρυκὶς πέτρα
> κοίλη, φίλορνις, δαιμόνων ἀναστροφή.

Herodotus, viii. 36, tells us that the inhabitants of Phocis, on the approach of the army of Xerxes, withdrew to the summit of Parnassus, καὶ ἐς τὸ κωρύκιον ἄντρον ἀνηνείκαντο. Strabo says that Parnassus is altogether sacred, having many caves held in honour and reverence, ὧν ἐστὶ γνωριμώτατον καὶ κάλλιστον τὸ Κωρύκιον Νυμφῶν ἄντρον ὁμώνυμον τῷ Κιλικίῳ. Pausanias gives a full description of the cave, x. 32, which is corroborated by modern travellers: Mr. Raikes in Walpole's Memoirs of Turkey, Lond. 1818, vol. i. pp. 311-315; Col. Leake, Northern Greece, ii. whose account is printed in Smith's Dict. of Geogr. i. 768, under "Delphi." Dodwell (Greece, i. 189) was prevented from visiting it by a heavy fall of snow. The Nymphs having the name *Coryciæ*, as Apollon. Rh. ii. 713, Ovid Heroid. xx. 221, or *Corycides* as Ovid Met. i. 320, are apparently the Muses. In Sophocles Antigone 1127, they are Βακχίδες.

P. 37, l. 20. *You let lie vast.*] Compare Claudian Præf. in lib. iii. de Rapt. Proserpinæ:

" Antraque Musarum longo torpentia somno
Excutis." 51.

Where "longo torpentia somno"="you let lie vast," *i. e.* waste, unoccupied, as before on p. 27.

P. 38, l. 4. *Sit downe.*] Perhaps the reading should be "set downe," as Shakspere, Lucrece, "What wit sets down is blotted straight with will," 1299.

P. 38. l. 10. *Imbracing clowdie sighes.*] "Imbracing" is here welcoming, entertaining, so as to have a sufficient store of sighs for the "leaden tale" he has to tell. The word is used by Shakspere of things, as Lucrece, "Yet strive I to embrace mine infamy," 504. Edwards has the same phrase again, p. 60, 13, "Imbracing sighs," where see note for explanation of "clowdie."

P. 38, l. 16. *Allude.*] As on p. 23, ascribe.

P. 38, l. 19. *Organing.*] Not in the Dictionary. Organization. Compare Acts xvii. 28, "as certain also of your own poets have said, For we are also his offspring."

P. 38, l. 22. *Dalliance.*] A Shaksperian word. Wedgwood connects it with *talus* the ankle-bone, then a die to play with. Skeat with the "M. E. *dwelien*, to err, to be foolish." Edwards makes it a dissyllable, as Shakspere does in four out of the seven passages in which he uses the word.

P. 38, l. 25. *They as the shot.*] A tavern-reckoning, unpleasing when the banquet is past. Shaksp. Two Gent. ii. 5, 7. Cymb. v. 4, 158. Nicholson Acolastus, 321, "Golde—thou art sought to pay fond Pleasures shot."

2 P

P. 39, l. 5. *Of, &c.*] Shakspere in Sonnet lxvii. 6, "and steal dead seeing of his living hue," and in Sonn. xcix. 10, "a third nor red nor white had stol'n of both," uses "*of*" after "steal" as equivalent to "*from*," which seems to be its force here.

P. 39, l. 7. *There to.*] Thereto.

P. 39, l. 11. *Abjectes.*] Psalm xxxv. 15, "Yea the very abjects came together against me unawares." Shakspere, Rich. III. "We are the queen's abjects and must obey," i. 1, 106.

P. 39. l. 12.] Compare Shakspere, "He jests at scars that never felt a wound." R. and J. ii. 2, 1. If this play be rightly dated, 1591-3, this is an early reference to it.

P. 40, l. 1. *Massacred.*] To massacre is to slaughter indiscriminately: so here had injured in any way and to any extent. I find no instance of the word being applied as it is in this line.

P. 40, l. 11. *The people runne.*] Compare Marlowe, H. and L. p. 10,

"So ran the people forth to gaze upon her,
And all that view'd her were enamour'd on her."

Fenelon, Histoire de Florise, Fable VI. "Tout le pais qui acouroit en foule pour la voire, lui fit encore connôitre ses charmes."

P. 40, l. 22. *Still Music.*] See Cephalus and Procris, p. 27. Add this from T. Carew,

"The gentle blasts of Western winds shall move
The trembling leaves, and through their close bows breath
Still Musick." A Rapture, p. 66, ed. 1651.

P. 40, l. 24. *Alluring tounges.*] "Frame snares of looks, trains of alluring speech." Fairfax, Tasso, iv. 25, and Milton, Samson Agon. 402.

"Yet the fourth time, when mustering all her wiles,
With blandished parlies, feminine assaults,
Tongue-batteries, she surceased not day nor night."

P. 40, l. 27. *Approve on.*] To approve themselves to one? to persuade one?

P. 40, l. 28. *Wenches.*] Very common in Shakspere, and explained in Schmidt's Shaksp. Lexicon, "A female person, a woman: not always in a bad sense, as at present, but used as a general familiar expression, in any variation of tone between tenderness and contempt." Horne Tooke, Part II. ch. iv. takes it in a bad sense, Warton on Spenser F. Q. Bk. II. c. vi. 8, shows that if generally in a depreciatory, it is sometimes used in an honorable meaning, for Douglas in his Virgil renders "audetque viris concurrere virgo" (Æneid. i. 493) "This wensche stoutlye rencounter durst with men." But a still more convincing instance may be quoted from Piers Plowman, Text C, " The Whitaker Text," Pass. xix. 134,

<blockquote>
" And in the wombe of that wenche he was fourty wokes,
And man by-cam of pat mayde to saue mankynde."—(P. 336, E. E. T. ed.)
</blockquote>

The same line occurs in Text B, "The Crowley Text": Pass. xvi. 100. (P. 293, E. E. T. ed.) I have frequently heard the word used in Middleton Cheney, Northamptonshire, by the poor as a familiar term for the female members of their families, married or unmarried.

P. 41, l. 4. *Who.*] For whom. So pp. 16, 3, 45, 25, 49, 12. See Abbott Shaksp. Gram. 274. "The inflection of *who* is frequently neglected."

P. 41, l. 7. *Low-lou'de.*] Such play on words is quite in accordance with the practice of the age. See Note on p. 4, l. 28. Notes, p. 199 supra. P. 49, 20, "And made this well my ill."

P. 41, l. 11. *I perceive a cheere.*] "Cheer," says Richardson, "is now applied to that which has an effect on the countenance, which inspires with mirth, courage, &c.; to the food or entertainment;" so here it seems to be applied to the sport or amusement referred to in the previous line. " As I wont to sport away the time so now (" well now ") I perceive, an amusement for us (" a cheere ").

P. 41, l. 12. *You pricke a cast.*] These words are spoken by the Lady. To prick is " to aim at a point, mark, place," according to Worcester from Hawkins—presumably J. Hawkins, who in 1724 published Cocker's English Dictionary, enlarged and altered. " A cast " is the technical term in bowling in leading jack, and is used also for each throw, or bowling, as appears by the next stanza, " The *cast* is mine," " the *thro.*"

P. 41, l. 12. *Mistres.*] This was a term applied to the jack in bowling. Shaksp. Troilus, " Rub on and kiss the mistress," iii. 2, 52. Beaumont and Fletcher, Wit at Several Weapons, " Follow your mistress there." " A Woman Never Vexed," Dodsley's Old Plays, vol. xii. ed. Hazlitt, act ii. sc. i. p. 120 : " Stephen. ' Who's in the bowling alley, mine host?' Host. ' Honest traders, thrifty lads, they are rubbing on't; towardly boys, every one strives to lie nearest the mistress.' " P. 165. " Robert. ' My sweet mistress!' Lambskin. 'Zounds! Sir knight, we have stood beating the bush, and the bird's flown away; this city bowler has kissed the mistress at first cast.'" See Nares in vv. "Mistress," and "Short."

P. 41, l. 13. *Ah short in faith.*] Should this be printed Ah! short, in faith; being the Lady's comment on Narcissus's cast which fell short of the mark she was wishing him to aim at, viz. herself? There is an obvious double sense all through the two stanzas.

P. 41, l. 14. *Marie.*] Used, as Gill used to be, as a generic name for a woman.

P. 41, l. 17. *Standing measure.*] A standard measure. "If at any end there shall be any bowls so near the jack as that *a standing measure* cannot decide in favour of either of them it shall be deemed a void end." Rules of the Edgehill Archery and Bowling Society, 1859, p. 28.

P. 41, l. 21. *Rubs.*] Another technical term at Bowls. "Inequality of ground that hinders the motion of a bowl." Halliwell quotes "Like a bowle that runneth in a smooth allie without any *rub.*" Stanihurst, p. 18. Add Strype in his Life of Bp. Aylmer, cxiv. (p. 193, ed. Oxon. 1821), "The recreation he delighted in was bowling: which he used for the diversion of his cares, and preservation of his health at Fulham, according as he had leisure. This exercise he used on Sundays, in the afternoon, after evening prayer. And herein he would be so eager, that he sometimes had such expressions in his game as exposed him to the censure of many, especially of his enemies. Hence Martin Marprelate spake of his running after his bowl and crying *Rub, Rub, Rub;* and then, *The Devil go with it,* when he followed himself." T. Freeman in 1614 published " Rubbe, and a great Cast."

P. 41, l. 23. *Onely.*] Unique, singular, very, utter. Milton uses "single" in a similar way.

"Yet naught but single darkness do I find."—Comus, 204.

Simplicitie.] Simpleness: artlessness, opposed to duplicity, doublefacedness, dissimulation, hiding one's real feelings.

P. 41, l. 27. *By this booke.*] Narcissus himself.

P. 42, l. 5. *Not soes.*] These short exclamations used as substantives are frequently introduced. Shakspere, "His flattering ' Holla,'" or his " Stand I say"? V. and A. 284. So "Had-I-wist," for instances of which see Nares's Glossary. "Aye me," as in Marston, Sat. viii. 51.

"To view Mavortius metamorphos'd quite
To puling sighes, or into ' Aye mee's ' state."

Notes. 289

P. 42, l. 12. *Ruinous.*] In ruins, decayed, powerless. Shakspere, Tit. And. V. i. 21, " A ruinous monastery." Com. Err. iii. 2, 4, " Shall love in building grow so ruinous?" Two G. of Ver. v. 4, 9 " Lest, growing ruinous, the building fall." Tim. iv. 3, 465. " Is yond despised and ruinous man my lord?"

P. 42, l. 12. *Content.*] This means both capacity to contain and that which is contained. The power which the potion contained in itself, its efficacy, disappears when nature recovers her full powers.

P. 42, l. 18. *Put in ure.*] The Stanley Poem in Halliwell's Palatine Anthology,
" And when he perceived the Duke was gonne sure,
He thought good to put this commission in ure." 240.

P. 42, l. 19. *Beauty, &c.*] So Shakspere,
" Beauty itself doth of itself persuade
The eyes of men without an orator."—Lucrece, 29.

P. 42, l. 22. *Faire Adonis.*] Venus addresses him as " Thrice fairer than myself." V. and A. 7. And Edwards, p. 43, 2, adopts this, " Thrice fair Adonis."

P. 42, l. 23. *Purple haire.*] A very dark-red colour. Spenser applies these words to the dawn. " The morrow next appeared with *purple haire*." F. Q. v. x. 16. Shakspere, I Hen. IV. ii. 1, 83, " These mad mustachio-purple-hued malt-worms." Mid. N. D. i. 2, 97. " Your purple-in-grain beard." It is in several places used as epithet of blood, as V. and A. " With purple tears that his wound wept." 1054. So of the morn: Spenser F. Q. i. ii. 7. " The rosy-fingred morning faire Had spread her purple robe through deawy aire." Gray imitating Virgil, " Vere rubenti " Georg. II. 319, has " Wake the purple year." Ode on the Spring; and again in the Progress of Poesy, after Virgil's " Lumenque juventæ Purpureum," Æn. i. 590, " the purple light of Love."

P. 42, l. 24. *Dove-drawn.*] Shakspere, V. and A. " Two strengthless doves will draw me through the sky." 153.

P. 42, l. 25. *Love sole commander.*] Perhaps we should read, "Love's sole commander," *i. e.* Venus his mother.

P. 42, l. 26. *Yew.*] The emblem of death, as in the song in Twelfth Night." ii. 4, 56.
" My shroud of white stuck all with yew, O prepare it !"

And in a similar song by Matthew Arnold,
" Strew her with roses, roses, But never a spray of yew."

Narcissus.

P. 42, l. 28. *Coate.*] See Marlowe, Ed. Dyce, iii. 315. Appendix. " He sayeth moreover that he hath *coated* a number of contrarieties out of the Scriptures." *i. e.* quoted, noted down. The origin of the word is thus given by Skeat: " Low Latin *Quotare*, to mark off into chapters and verses; thus the real sense of *quote* is to give a reference. The literal sense of *quotare* is ' to say how many ' with reference to the numbering of chapters (or the price of a thing, Brachet). Lat. *quotus* how much, how many." Shakspere uses cote, or quote, several times as to note, or set down in writing. So Hall Sat. Bk ii. 1, 32—" in every margent *coted*." See p. 62 for another sense of this word.

P. 43, l. 3. *Branches.*] Shakspere in Tit. And. " Speak, gentle niece, what stern ungentle hands Have lopp'd and hew'd and made thy body bare Of her two *branches*," *i. e.* arms. ii. 4, 16. So here *branches* is put for the lower limbs, reminding one of Falstaff's description of Justice Shallow, " when a' was naked he was, for all the world, like a forked radish." 2 Hen. IV. iii. 2, 333. Branch is connected with Latin *Brachium*, an arm, and also with a Low Latin word *Branca* the claw of a bird, or beast of prey, and so may fairly be applied to arms or legs. See Skeat in v. and Ducange in *Branca*. I never met with the word used as it is here.

P. 43, l. 4. *Plains to meads, these meades to plaine tears.*] Another instance of his playing on words. Meads, meadows, are lands that are mowed; especially lands by rivers liable to be overflowed, or that are irrigated, water meadows; like the Latin *prata* of which Varro de Re Rusticâ, viii. 1, says, " Pratum si irriguum habebis, fenum non deficiet." Propertius, i. 20, 37, " Et circum irriguo surgebant lilia prato." Virgil, Æn. vi. 674, " prata recentia rivis." These are opposed by Columella, i. 2, 3, to other divisions, " campus in prata et arva, salictaque, et arundineta digestus." Campus is the *plain*, fit for many sorts of produce, but needing irrigation to become a *mead*, (and Valpy in his Etymological Dict. of Latin connects pratum with περάω to penetrate with moisture) so that here Narcissus professes to shed tears enough to make the plains into meadows by overflowing them, and then when the first outburst of sorrow is over, the flood of tears subsided, to come back to "*plain* tears," *i. e.* common ordinary usual sorrowing, which will then afford them pleasure, " the luxury of woe"; on the principle " quod fuit durum pati meminisse dulce est," or with Æneas, " forsan et hæc olim meminisse juvabit." Æn. i. 203.

Notes. 291

P. 43, l. 7. *Venus-sparrows.*] Marlowe, H. and L.

"And there, God knows, I play
With Venus' swans and sparrowes all the day." p. 19.

Drayton, Ode to his Valentine, p. 408, Roxburghe Club ed.

"The Sparrow, Swanne, the Dove,
Though Venus birds they be."

And Ben Jonson Poetaster, iv. 1, vol. ii. 472, says of Love and his mother,

"He hath plucked her doves and sparrows,
To feather his sharp arrows."

The only classical authority seems to be Sappho, who in her Ode to Aphrodite speaks of her coming in her chariot

κάλοι δὲ σ' ἆγον
ὠκέες στροῦθοι. 10.

The reason for dedicating this bird to her, is given by Athenæus, Bk. ix. 46, p. 392. καὶ οἱ στρουθοὶ δὲ εἰσιν ὀχευτικοί· μήποτε οὖν καὶ ἡ Σαπφὼ ἀπὸ τῆς ἱστορίας τὴν 'Αφροδίτην ἐπ' αὐτῶν φησιν ὀχεῖσθαι· καὶ γὰρ ὀχευτικὸν τὸ ζῶον καὶ πολύγονον· Eustathius on Il. ii. 311. (Vol. i. p. 228, ed. Rom. 1542.) ἡ δὲ στρουθὸς εἶδος μικροῦ ὀρνέου ἀνειμένου τῇ 'Αφροδίτῃ, διά τε τὸ ὡς ἐν μεγέθει οὐ μεγάλῳ πολύγονον ὡς ἐρρέθη, καὶ διὰ τὸ χαίρειν τῇ μίξει. Horus Apollo, Hieroglyphic ii. 115. "Ἄνθρωπον γόνιμον βουλόμενοι σημῆναι, στρουθίον πυργίτην ζωγραφοῦσιν. Οὗτος γὰρ ὑπὸ ὀργῆς ἀμέτρου καὶ πολυσπερμίας ὀχλούμενος, ἑπτάκις μίγνυται τῇ θηλείᾳ ἐν μιᾷ ὥρᾳ, ἀθρόως σπερμαίνων. The curious may consult Sterne's Sentimental Journey, vol. ii. p. 80, ed. 1, in the last of the chapters headed "Versailles The Passport," for an illustration of this passage.

P. 43, l. 7. *Ingling.*] To ingle is to caress, fondle, toy with; it is used with reference to children by Donne, Elegy IV. (or in Grosart's Ed. V) "The Perfume;"

"Thy little brethren, which like feary sprightes
Oft skipt into our chamber, those sweet nightes;
And kyst and ingled on thy fathers knee,
Were bryb'd next day to tell what they did see." 37—40.

A later ed. in 1669 reads "dandled" for "ingled," thus explaining its meaning. The word was, however, perverted to a less innocent sense, as in " Micro-cynicon, or Six Snarling Satyres 1599," printed in fifth vol. of T. Middleton's Works by Dyce, though it is doubtful whether he is the author. The fifth Sat. is entitled " Ingling Pyander," and on p. 499 is a line " Ingling Pyander's damnèd villany." See Nares Glossary in v. and Gifford's notes to Ben Jonson, ii. 429, iii. 344. Ingle is a fire or fire-place (Lat. ignis. Gaelic Aingeall. Jamieson Sc. Dict.), and is so used by Burns, Shirreff, and also in some parts of England, hence a fireside companion, an inmate of a house, an intimate in divers senses; and thus " to ingle " to treat as an intimate, to caress. Some connect it with the Spanish ingle, inguen; but though this might account for the worst sense of the word, it does not so well accord with such use of it as in the passage from Donne.

P. 43, l. 16. *The Map of Sorrow.*] Probably Chr. Marlowe must be credited with the first use of this metaphor. He was slain on June 1, 1593, as is entered in the burial register of St. Nicholas Deptford. It occurs in his play Dido Queen of Carthege, act i. p. 372, Ed. Dyce.

" Though we be now in extreme misery,
And rest the map of weatherbeaten woe."

The date of the representation of the play has not been ascertained, but it was printed in 1594, as written by Christopher Marlowe and Thomas Nash. It is found also in Titus Andronicus, iii. 2, 12.

" Thou map of woe, that thus dost talk in signs."

This play is entered in the Stationers' Books, Feb. 6, 1594, and is by some e. g. J. Boswell (Shakspere, xxi. p. 261) attributed to Marlowe. Both these plays preceded Lucrece, in which Shakspere uses the same expression —

" Showing life's triumph in the map of death." 402.

and again,

" The face, that map, which deep impression bears
Of hard misfortune carv'd in it with tears." 1712.

Next to these, and not in any way inferior, is the line in Narcissus.

" 'Tis one that hath the map of sorrow drawn."

Shakspere, Sonnet lxviii. 1, again uses it,

" Thus is his cheek the map of days out-worn."

A. Scoloker (1604) in his Daiphantus, p. 39,

" The Ladies all who late from hunting came
Untimely came to view this map of sorrow."

Shakspere more than once has " the map of honour."

P. 43, l. 18. *Pawne.*] As in Cephalus and Procris, p. 16, 24, "upon pawne of mine."

P. 43, l. 19. *Vale of lawne.*] Hero and Leander.
"Her veil was artificial flowers and leaves." p. 6.
"The outside of her garments was of lawne." p. 6.

P. 43, l. 20. *Buskins, &c.*] H. and L.
"Buskins of shells all silvered used she
And branched with blushing coral to the knee." p. 6.

So Milton, Arcades 33,
"Fair silver-buskined nymphs."

P. 43, l. 21. *Packs.*] This word is often used by Shakspere. Poems, xv. Globe ed. xii. p. 255, Aldine ed. Passionate Pilgrim, 209,
"Pack night, peep day."

M. W. W. "Trudge, plod away o' the hoof; seek shelter, pack." i. 3, 91. Willobies Avisa, p. 48.
"Now fortune packe." p. 137.
"You may be walking when you list
Look ther's the doore, and ther's the way." p. 48, 13, 14.

See Richardson's Dict. and Wedgwood in v. for good accounts of this word.

P. 43, l. 25. *It skils not.*] "It makes no difference, it matters not." Schmidt. Shaksp. Lex. Thrice in Shakspere. In Icelandic *skilja*. The original sense, to *cut*, Lat. *secare*, appears in Goth. *skilja*, a butcher: A. S. *scylan*, to separate. See Cleasby's Dictionary. Nares in v. "generally with a negative."

P. 44, l. 2. *Sport.*] As on p. 23 before. Shakspere, "Be bold to play, our sport is not in sight." V. and A. 124 and elsewhere. See Schmidt. Sh. Lex. in v. 1. d.

P 44, l. 4. *Musæus.*] Marlowe, H. and L. "Whose tragedy divine Musæus sung," p. 7. Some, especially the elder Scaliger, and Edwards as it would seem from the epithet "divine," attributed the poem on Hero and Leander to the ancient Musæus mentioned by Virgil, Æn. vi. 667. But it is now admitted to be the composition of a grammarian named Musæus, who lived not earlier than the fifth century of our æra. There are many editions of the Greek original, and versions in most European languages.

P. 44, l. 5. *Dandling.*] H. and L. " His dangling tresses that were never shorn, p. 7. V. R. " dandling."
Fair Hero.] H. and L. " Hero the fair," p. 6. " So lovely fair was Hero," p. 7. " But you are fair, aye me! so wondrous fair," p. 17.

P. 44, l. 7. *For without men, &c.*] H. and L.:

" One is no number; maids are nothing, then,
Without the sweet society of men." p. 15.

P 44, l. 9. *Tempe.*] Spenser, in his translation of Virgil's Gnat:

" O Flocks, O Faunes, and O ye pleasaunt Springs
Of Tempe, where the countrey Nymphs are rife." 145, 6.

The original of which is:

"O pecudes, O Panes, et O gratissima Tempe
Fontis Hamadryadum." Culex, 93.

P. 44, l. 13. *Thought.*] Either for though or though't.
P. 44, l. 14. *Abydos.*] H. and L.:

" Amorous Leander, beautiful and young,
Dwelt at Abydos." p. 7.

P. 44, l. 16. *Furie.*] Madness, frenzy. Shakspere twice in this sense, Errors, v. 1, 147. Timon, iii. 6, 118, " Know you the quality of Lord Timon's fury? "

P. 44. l. 18. *Ghosts afrighting.*] This may be some reference to the old play of Hamlet. " In a tract entitled ' Wits Miserie ' or ' The World's Madnesse,' discovering the incarnate Devils of the Age, by Thomas Lodge, 1596, 4to. (reprinted by the Hunterian Society at Glasgow), one of the devils (as Dr. Farmer has observed) is said to be 'a foule lubber, and looks as pale as the vizard of the *Ghost*, who cried so miserably at the theatre, *Hamlet, revenge.*' " Boswell's Shakspere, ii. 373. The passage from Lodge will be found at p. 56 of the original, p. 62 of the Hunterian edition.

P. 44, l. 21. *He, him.*] If these pronouns refer, as they seem to do, to night, this is a special instance of making night masculine. So far as I know night is always feminine.

P 44, l. 22. *Sable winged messenger of Jove.*] Shakspere, Lucrece, " Till sable night, mother of dread and fear," 117. Euripides, Orestes, 176, calls night κατάπτερος. Aristophanes, Birds 695, μελανόπτερος. So Virgil, Nox ruit, et fuscis tellurem amplectitur alis, Æn. viii. 369, and Manilius,

"Nigras Nox contrahit alas," v. 62. G. Cuperus in his Apotheosis Homeri, Amst. 1683, on the Dii Alati, at p. 179, says of Nox, "Illi alæ tribuuntur, quia celerrime fluit, et vix homines dormientes eam præteriisse sentiunt." In the old cosmogonies Nox is one of the very first created beings, for she is the daughter of Chaos (Hes. Theog. 123), and Homer, Il. xiv. 259, relates that Zeus himself stood in awe of her. How then is Night his messenger? She is not like Hermes or Iris, an ἄγγελος, and in the Odyssey, xiv. 93, where day and night are mentioned together as proceeding from Jove, "Ὅσσαι γὰρ νύκτες τε καὶ ἡμέραι ἐκ Διός εἰσιν, the regular succession of nights and days is only meant. Messenger, from *missus*, one sent, must be understood in this simple sense, as sent by Jove.

P. 44, l. 23.] Compare Milton, The Passion, v. "Befriend me Night, best patroness of grief."

P. 44, l. 26.] Psalm vi. 6, "Every night wash I my bed: and water my couch with my tears."

P. 44. l. 28. *Like the cock.*] Milton, L'Allegro:

"While the cock with lively din
Scatters the rear of darkness thin." 49, 50.

Sound alarm.] Shakspere, 1 Hen. VI. "Sound, sound alarum," i. 2, 18. 2 Hen. VI. "Now when the angry trumpet sounds alarum." v. 2, 3. "Alarm is simply *all' arme*, and was borrowed from the Italian, and may very well have become known at the time of the Crusades." Skeat. See Puttenham, Poesie 201. "Alarme, Alarme he gan to call."

P. 45, l. 7. *Ges.*] Note the old spelling. Chaucer, C. T. "Of twenty yeer he was of age I gesse," 82. "The insertion of *u* was merely for the purpose of preserving the *g* as hard. It is highly probable that *guess* meant originally to 'try to get,' being a secondary (desiderative) verb formed from *get*." Skeat in v.

P. 45, l. 12. *Thought wandering night.*] Compare Sophocles, Œdipus Tyrannus:

ὥστ᾽ οὐχ ὕπνῳ γ᾽ εὕδοντα μ᾽ ἐξεγείρετε,
ἀλλ᾽ ἴστε πολλὰ μέν με δακρύσαντα δή,
πολλὰς δ᾽ ὁδοὺς ἐλθόντα φροντίδος πλάνοις. 65-67.

P. 45, l. 15. *I, I.*] For "aye, aye." So p. 59, "she answeres I, I." See Drayton Idea Sonnet 4, p. 443, Roxburghe Club ed. of which "No and I" is the subject. Shakspere, R. and J. iii. 2, 45-50.

Narcissus.

P. 45, l. 16. *Where the serpents lie.*] Shakspere, R. and J. " Or bid me lurk where serpents are." iv. 1, 79.

P. 45, l. 22. *I, there's the sore.*] Hamlet, iii. 1, 65, "Aye, there's the rub."

P. 45, l. 25. *Who.*] For "whom" as before, p. 41.

P. 46, l. 4. *Tragic massacre made knowen.*] Does he here allude to plays such as Titus Andronicus, Marlowe's Tragedies, Romeo and Juliet, and others?

P. 46, l. 5. *Poets imping them now perfect growen.*] May this refer to Shakspere's Lucrece, and if so, that T. Edwards considered the Lucrece to be an improvement on the Venus and Adonis and his other previous works? The Lucrece was first printed in 1594, in which year also came out Willobies Avisa, prefixed to which are some lines containing a mention of that poem, which had apparently been circulated for some time in MS. :

> " Though *Collatine* haue deerely bought
> To high renowne a lasting life,
> And found that most in vaine haue sought
> To haue a Faire and Constant wife.
> Yet Tarquyne pluckt his glistering grape
> And Shake-speare paints poor Lucreece rape." P. 15, ed. Grosart, 1880.

P. 46, l. 18. *Descant.*] To make division or variation in music on the plainsong or ground. Then generally, to enlarge upon any subject. T. Nash, " Have with you to Saffron Walden," p. 117. " And so I wind up his thrid of life, which I feare I have drawne out too large, although in three quarters of it (of purpose to curtall it) I have left *descant*, and taskt mee to *plaine song.*" See Nares' Glossary.

P. 46, l. 24. *Inserted.*] Is this like the middle voice in Greek "inserted himself" as the subject for the Muse?

P. 47, l. 15. *Fouling's Queene.*] Venus. Fowling is properly taking or catching birds, but here it is used for the birds themselves, or it may be a diminutive from fowl. See Morris, English Accidence, sect 321, " Ling = 1 + ing (diminutive)," so that fowl + l + ing = fowling, one *l* being dropped. In this sense it is not in dictionaries. Above, p. 43, mention is made of Venus and her sparrows.

P. 47, l. 17. *To talent out.*] To weigh out, to reckon up the value; from the Greek τάλαντον. This verb is not in the dictionaries, and *talented* is said to be formed from the noun, like *gifted, turreted*, &c. This is a term borrowed from the Mint. Ruding in his Annals of the Coinage says, " In the

Saxon Mints the weight used differed from that applied to commercial purposes. It has been conjectured that the Saxons derived this weight, and its application to money, from the Greeks . . . . . . The Talent was common to both people as a weight, and continues to be so used in the Mint to this day, for the journey of silver, or the quantity which is weighed off at one time, is sixty pounds, and the journey of gold one fourth of that weight." Vol. i. 205, ed. 1817.

P. 47, l. 20. *A flaming blast.*] Virgil, Æneid, ii. 694, "de cœlo lapsa per umbras Stella facem ducens multâ cum luce cucurrit." Rendered by the Earl of Surrey, 915, p. 147, Aldine ed. :

> "Out of the sky, by the dark night there fell
> A blasing star, dragging a brand of flame."

Blast is the Anglo-Saxon *blæst*, a flame, a burning. If the writer be not speaking of a meteor, but of a flame quickly kindled and as quickly burnt out, compare Psalm cxviii. 12, "They are quenched as the fire of thorns." Ps. lviii. 9, "Or ever your pots be made hot with thorns."

P. 47, l. 25.] An instance of the omission of the relative pronoun. See Abbott's Shakspere Grammar, 244. The meaning of the two lines seems to be, "The general who by fortunes aide doth ken fatal death, sad messenger, who detains (*i.e.* prevents the attainment of) his hoped wish, viz. safety or victory."

P. 48, l. 15. *Life obtaining fields.*] Sophocles, Philoctetes, 1162, has βιόδωρος åια. The Homeric Hymn xxx. 9, ἄρουρα φερέσβιος. The more frequent word in Homer and Hesiod is ζείδωρος, always an epithet of earth, and usually ζείδωρος ἄρουρα, which though probably zea-giving (zea being a sort of grain) is no doubt by implication *life-giving*, as stated by Liddell and Scott in v.

P. 48, l. 16. *To sport each other.*] Sport is sometimes used as a reflective verb. V. and A. 154, "Where I list to sport me." Puttenham's Arte of English Poesie, p. 202, ed. Haslewood 1811, "to sport them in the fire." Here it is similarly employed.

P. 48, l. 18. *Sonetto's.*] He preserves the Italian word, as on p. 8, banditos. "Sonetto, genus carminis quod ad citharæ sonum caneretur." Ferrario Origines Ling. Ital. Patavii, 1676, p. 282. "Vulgariter poetantes sua Poemata multimodis protulerunt. Quidam per cantiones, quidam per Ballatas, quidam per Sonitus." Dante de Vulgari Eloquentia, ii. 3. In the

Italian version by Trissino, "alcuni per Canzoni, altri per Ballate, altri per Sonetti." So Menage, Dict. Etymol. de la Lang. Franc. "Sonnet, sorte de Poesie. De *Sonettus*, diminutif de *sonus*, qui a signifie une chanson. F. Ubaldini, Come abbiamo da motto motteto, cosi sonetto e diminutivo di suono." Crescimbeni in his Comentari Poetici devotes chapters xiv. to xxi. of the second book to the sonnet. Capel Lofft, in his " Laura, or an Anthology of Sonnets " (1000), Lond. 1814, five vols, shows its analogy with the Grecian Ode, and with Music, in the Preface which is a digest of every thing relating to this species of poem. More recent works are, "The Sonnet, by Charles Tomlinson," Lond. 1874; "The Treasury of English Sonnets," by D. M. Main; and " Sonnets of Three Centuries," by T. Hall Caine. Essays on the Sonnet are in Drake's " Literary Hours," 4th ed. 1820, vol. i. No. vi., and in H. Kirke White's "Melancholy Hours," No. v., in which he suggests that the name may come from the French *sonnette*, a little bell. Capel Lofft adduces Chaucer as the earliest English writer of a sonnet; but this is hardly borne out by the instance quoted, which is a translation of Petrarch's cii. sonnet, introduced in Troilus and Cressida, a poem written in stanzas of seven lines, two of which are put together to make the sonnet. The Earl of Surrey is generally allowed to have introduced the sonnet. Dr. Nott, in the Dissertation prefixed to his edition of Surrey's and Wyatt's Poems, Lond. 1815, quarto, 2 vols., says, " Those who are conversant with Italian literature, and know the nice conduct which is required in a sonnet, and the rules on which it should be formed, will be best able to appreciate Surrey's merit in this particular branch of composition. It adds greatly to his merit to know that Surrey's sonnets are the first that appeared in our language," p. ccxxix. At first our English authors seem to have spelt the word *sonets*. It occurs in John Vander Noodt's " Theatre," &c. printed in 1569, a volume containing poems, viz. Spenser's Six Visions of Petrarch. Then the remaining poems, all entitled *sonets*. See Todd's Spenser, vii. 525. George Gascoigne has it in both forms, but generally as *sonets*. See his " Certayn Notes of Instruction concerning the making verse or ryme in English." " Then have you sonnets: some thinke that all poems being short may be called *sonets*, as indeed it is a diminutive worde derived of *sonare*, but yet I can best allowe to call those *sonets* which are of fouretene lynes, every lyne conteyning ten syllables," p. 10, ed. Haslewood. And in his Dan Bartholomew of Bathe, p. 130, ed. Hazlitt, "To take this *sonet* for my last farewell." Again in his Advertisement to the Reader (Hazlitt's ed. i. p. 15), "Well though my folly bee greater than my fortune, yet overgreat were mine unconstancie if (in my owne behalfe) I shoulde compyle so many sundrie songs or *sonets.*" So in the letter of G. T. dated 1572, printed in Hazlitt's Gascoigne, p. xl. "I have thought good to present you with this written booke, wherein you shall find a number of *sonets*, layes, letters, ballades, rondlets, verlayes, and verses." J. Dickenson (1594), Arisbas, p. 62, "He loved him for his passionate grace in pleasing *sonets.*" On the title, however, of Barnabe Barne's Parthenophil, 1593, it is "*sonnettes*"; in Percy's Cælia, 1594, "*sonnets*"; in 1598 F. Meres in his Palladis Tamia refers to "Shakspeare's sugred sonnets among his private friends," and this spelling was adopted when they were printed in 1609 in the mysterious dedication, "To the only begetter of these insuing sonnets," and has since prevailed.

P. 48, l. 25. *Once.*] Seems to be used like *aliquando*, at some time or other, or, as Bishop Hall has it, at a future time. "The wisdom of God thought fit to acquaint David with that court which we shall *once* govern," quoted in Worcester's Dictionary.

P. 49, l. 12, *Who.*] For "whom."

Misse.] For "mistress." As Master was colloquially abbreviated into "*Mas*," (see Nares in v. and quotations from Ben Jonson,) so Mistress was similarly shortened into "Miss," both as a title, and in the other sense of the word. This passage seems to be the first instance of its use, at least Richardson, and after him Skeat, says, "the earliest example appears to be the following. 'In this acted the faire and famous comedian, call'd Roxolana, from the part she performed: and I think it was the last, she being taken to be the Earl of Oxford's *misse* (as at this time they began to call lewd women).'" Evelyn, Diary, 9th Jan. 1662. Congreve in his "Love for Love" is supposed to be about the first to have introduced the term into Dramatic Writing.

"*Miss Prue.* Mother, mother, mother, look you here.
Mrs. Foresight. Fie, miss, how you bawl." Act iii.

Shakspere always uses Mistress. Gifford in his Notes to Massinger, i. 185, ii. 244, ed. 1805, says, "that in the language of Massinger's time *servant* and *mistress* signified a lover and the object of his affections."

P. 49, l. 13. *Fire him.*] So Shirley in his Poem on Narcissus (Vol. vi. p. 483, ed. Gifford and Dyce),

> "Thon fatal looking-glass that doth present
> Myself to me, mine own incendiary."

P. 49, l. 14. *Did desire him.*] The relative is omitted here. The meaning of the couplet is, " his own conceit fired him with the notion that his shadow in the water burned with love for him, while the actual love of the nymphs who did desire him cooled all feeling in him of love towards them."

P. 49, l. 15. *Syren-singing.*] Marlowe, H. and L.

> "For like sea-nymphs invcigling harmony." p. 9.

P. 49, l. 17. *Shelf.*] Compare Daniel, The Complaint of Rosamond, 97, 98, p. 40, ed. 1718.

> "Ah me ! (poor Wench) on this unhappy shelf
> I grounded me, and cast away my self."

P. 49, l. 19. *Authoritie.*] This seems to mean the actualization of those which were absent, *i. e.* non-existent—that his shadow should become a real substance.

P. 49, l. 20. *Well my ill.*] Another example of his playing on words. The Earl of Surrey in his Faithful Lover, 24 (p. 54 Aldine ed. 1831, p. 10, ed. Nott.), plays on the same word,

> "There do my flowing eyes shew forth my melting heart;
> So that the streams of those two wells right well declare my smart."

On which Dr. Nott is very severe; "This play on words in this line is wholly unworthy of Surrey's pen and is not in his general manner."

P. 49, l. 22. *Close downe I lay.*] Ovid, Met. iii. 420 " humi positus."

P. 49, l. 24. *Azured.*] Again, p. 55, " azured brooke." This seems to have been the form of the word commonly used by the Elizabethan writers. Marlowe, Dido Q. of Carthage, act i. (vol. ii. 369), has " azur'd gates." N. Breton, " A solemne Passion of the Soules Loue," p. 6, 2, l. 29 (ed. Grosart) " Compare—The pibble stone unto the azurde skie." W. Smith, Chloris, 1596, Sonnet 47, 6. " Nor of thine azurde vaines which are so cleere." Shakspere, Tempest, v. 43, " And 'twixt the green sea and the azured vault "; and in Cymbeline, iv. 2, 222, " The azured harebell like thy veins," which seems to be a reminiscence of W. Smith's Chloris. We now generally use the form azure, as was the case in Middle English, as Chaucer, Queen Anelida, 333, "Clad in asure." Joseph of Arimathea, 195, 198. E. E. T. S. "Gold and Seluer he seis and Asur forsothe," this form being adopted from the French, " in which language it can be traced back to the 11th century" (Brachet). The best account of the word is contained in an article contributed to Notes and Queries, 5th Series, xi. p. 189, by Sir J. A. Picton. "Marco Polo mentions a mountain in which *azure* is found, on which Col. Yule notes, that the mines of *Lajwurd* whence *l'azur*, and *lazuli*, lie in the upper valley of the Kokcha. Proceeding westward this name *lojwurd* became *lazur*, and in Italian and French, the initial *l* being taken for the article, it was written *l'azur*, whence English *azure*. It was Latinized into *lazulus*, whence *lapis lazuli*." Azure is given in Worcester's Dictionary as noun, adjective, and verb. Perhaps Edwards is simply translating Ovid, who has " *Cærula Liriope*," Met. iii. 342, the fabled mother of Narcissus, but in reality a fountain or well-head, as mentioned by Vibius Sequester. If *lajwurd* be the source of the term the form *azured* is nearer the original as it retains the final *d*.

P. 50, l. 10.] Compare Horace Sat i. 3, 107. " Nam fuit ante Helenam mulier teterrima belli Causa."

P. 50, l. 13. *Vile.*] For vilely. But adjectives were freely used as adverbs, as Abbott, Shakspere Gram. 1, shows by many instances.

P. 50, l. 14. *Narciss.*] Such abbreviations of names are common, p. 52, Polyp. p. 59, Tythons. p. 62, Adon. They are very numerous in the Poems of King James VI. *e. g.* Parnass, Esculap, Erostrat, &c. Was this from the influence of the French writers?

P. 50, l. 17. *Allusions.*] Apparently used for "illusions."

P. 50, l. 18. *Defact.*] For defect or default, in M. E. defaute. I find no other instance of this form of the word.

P. 51, l. 2. *Coyne-imbracing fathers.*] See " Tell-Trothes New Yeares Gift," 1593, New Shakspere Soc. ed. p. 5. " The first cause of Jelosy is a constrained love, when as parentes do by compulsion coople two bodies, neither respectinge the joyning of their hartes, nor hauinge any care of the continuance of their wellfare, but more regarding the linkinge of wealth and money together then of loue with honesty: will force affection without liking, and cause loue with Jelosie." Also The Prologue to Daniel's

Hymen's Triumph: aud Burton's Anatomy of Melancholy, Part 3, Sec. 2, Mem. 6, Subs. 5.

P. 51, l. 3. *Yld.*] That is make their children a source of profit. Yelde, yield, is to pay, to produce, to give. Spenser F. Q. iii. xi. 17.

"Because to *yield* him love she doth deny,
Once to me *yold*, not to be *yold* again."

'*ild*, in the phrase "God 'ild," God yield, or bless, Ant. and Cleop. iv. 2, 33, "and the Gods yield you for 't," is used by Shakspere in As You Like It, iii. 3, 76. v. 4, 56. Macbeth, i. 6, 13. Haml. iv. 5, 41, and is well illustrated by Nares.

P. 51, l. 4 *Chopping them to Church.*] "To chop was used somewhat in the sense of our word to *pop*. 'As flise at libertee in and out might chop.' Heywood's Spider and Flie, 1567. f. 122." Nares. So in the True Tragedie of Richard III. p. 31, or p. 84 ed. Hazlitt. "*Chopt* up in prison." And in the quarto edition of Rich. III 1597, i. 4, 160, "and then we will chop him in the malmsey butt in the next room:" and again, 277, "I'll *chop* you in the malmsey-butt within," where the folios 1, and 2, have "throw" and "drown." The word means to strike in or out, suddenly, with the quickness of a blow or stroke. Alexander Scott's "Counsale to Lustic Ladyis," Sibbald's Chronicle of Scotch Poetry, iii. 151. "Sum mone-brunt maidynis myld, At none-tyde of the nicht, Ar chapit up with chyld, Bot coil or candle-licht." Also in Ramsay's Evergreen, i. p. 126, ed. 1761. And in the Bannatyne MS. printed by the Hunterian Society, p. 361; under another title. There is another combination of these two words with a different meaning, and origin. Burton, Anat. of Melan. Part i. 2, 3, 15, speaks of "Simoniacal Church-chopping patrons," and Kennet, in his Parochial Antiquities, of "Chop-churches," explained in his Glossary; "those secular priests who made an advantage by exchanging their benefices," this being from ccapan to buy, or cheapen.

P. 51, l. 8. *The English globe-incompasser.*] Sir Francis Drake. "He was the first Englishman that sailed round the world; and the first commander in chief: for Magellan (1519, 1520), whose ship executed the same adventure, perished on the passage." (At the Molucca Islands.) Hume, Hist. of England, ch. xli. In the Life of Drake in the Biographia Britannica, note (F.) there is a detailed account of the unsuccessful attempts to follow

Magellan. Drake was obliged to keep his design secret. He sailed from Plymouth Nov. 15, and from Falmouth Dec. 13, 1577, and returned to Plymouth Sep. 26, 1580, according to Prince in his Worthies of Devon, but on Nov. 3 according to Holland, and Fuller, Holy State. After this voyage Drake gave for his device " The globe of the world " with this motto " Tu primus circumdedisti me," but without excluding his former motto " Divino auxilio." The Queen knighted him, and gave him a new coat of arms, " Sable, a fess wavy, between the two pole-stars, Argent. And for a Crest: On a helmet, a ship under Ruff [or Reef] drawn round a Globe with a Cable-rope by a Hand out of the Clouds, with this motto over it, '*Auxilio Divino*'; and under it, ' *Sic parvis magna.*'" Wotton's Baronetage, i. 532. Edmondson, Heraldry, ii. under Drake, blazons it somewhat differently. This Crest is introduced by Whitney in his Choice of Emblemes, Leyden 1586, at p. 203. To the reprint of Whitney in 1866 by the Rev. H. Green are added notes from which the following extract is taken. "An account of the Voyage was published by the nephew of the circumnavigator, with the significant title of "THE WORLD ENCOMPASSED," and doubtless gave origin to Whitney's device and stanzas." This conjecture, however, is erroneous, for although the narrator (Master Francis Fletcher, Preacher in this employment) speaks of " overcoming difficulties in this our *encompassing* of this nether globe," there was no edition under this title until that printed in quarto in 1628. I venture to make this correction of Mr. Green's note on the authority of my friend Mr. Madan, Under Librarian of the Bodleian, who very kindly looked at the early editions of Drake's Voyages and Hakluyt's Collection, and informs me that he has not found any such Title as " *The World Encompassed*" in any of them. In 1596 Charles Fitzgeffrey published his " Sir Francis Drake," (reprinted by Sir S. E. Brydges in 1819, and by Dr. Grosart in 1881,) and calls him " the pilgrime of the world," stanza 266, p. 101, ed. Grosart, and celebrates his ship " The Pelican," whose name he changed to " The Hind " on reaching the South Seas:

> " A Golden-Hynde, led by his art and might
> Bare him about the earth's sea-walled round,
> With unresisted Roe-out-running flight,
> While Fame (the harbinger) a trumpe did sound." Stanza 139, p. 59.

This was laid up at Deptford, and is mentioned by Marston in his Eastward Hoe, " Wee'll have our provided supper brought a bord Sir Francis Drake's ship that hath compast the world." Act iii. 2, p. 55, ed. 1856. The chair made out of its timbers is still to be seen in the Picture Gallery at Oxford. Drake's Portrait is in Holland's Heroologia, p. 106. In The Mirror for Magistrates 1610, England's Eliza, p. 793.

"To add more fame to this for future time,
Great Drake to quell their pride that had sat downe,
Their *Ne plus ultra* in the farthest clime
By seas, sands, rocks, and many a sea-sieg'd towne,
Did compasse earth in spight of Neptune's frowne;
For which his name with fame for aye is crown'd,
Whose barke still sailes about the worlds whole round. "

P. 51, l. 9. *Found another land.*] While engaged in the attempt to find a passage about the N. of America from the South Sea into our Ocean, Drake discovered a land which he called Nova Albion, a fact which is alluded to by Sylvester in his Du Bartas;

" While (famous Drake-like) coasting every strand,
I do discover many a New-found-land."
The Colonies. iii^d Part of ii^d Day of ii^d Week, 3, 4.

P. 51, l. 10. *Richards err.*] An apocopated form for error, as in Davison's Poet. Rhapsody, " Eclogue entitled Cuddy," i. p. 62, ed. Nicolas.

" A little herdgroom, for he was no bett'."

Such abbreviations seems more frequent in Scottish poets, *e. g.* Montgomery's Poems, Edinb. 1821. p. 195 " deput," for deputy." 201 " determe," for determine. 210 " alabast," for alabaster. The phrase may be like the classical βίη Ἡρακληείη, sapientia Læli, a periphrasis for Richard III. whose whole career, with all deference to Horace Walpole, was a mistake, culminating in the defeat and death at Bosworth Field, where, as C. Aleyn says, " He fought as bravely as he justly fell."

P. 51, l. 11. *Done to disgrace.*] On p. 11 " done to shame," and " put into disgrace." Here equivalent to having ended in defeat.

P. 51, l 11. *A taske nere tooke in hand.*] In the Mirror for Magistrates, King Richard the Third, p. 767, ed. 1610:

" For in my cheefest hope to winne the day,
Appointed by the heauens most iust decree,
My souldiers in the forefront shranke away,
Which heauie newes declared was to mee
By one that counsel'd mee away to flee."

P. 51, l. 12. *By Hercules.*] As the words stand this must be a mere interjection, "Mehercule." But bearing in mind the lines fixed on Drake's ship at Deptford when Q. Elizabeth visited him on board,

"*Plus ultra*, Herculeis inscribas Drake Columnis,
Et magno, dicas, Hercule major ero."

The words "a tasko nere tooke in hand By Hercules," would aptly describe Drake's adventure, if the structure of the stanza would allow of the trajection.

P. 51, l. 19. *Loosing of the maine.*] A term at hazard. Hall, Satire, ii. 5, 86.

"Or the red hat that cries the lucklesse mayne."

Shakspere.

"To set so rich a mayne
On the nice hazard of one doubtfull houre." 1 Hen. IV. iv. 1, 47.

"And not unlike the use of foul gamesters who having lost the maine by true judgment thinke to face it out with a false oath." Lylie's Euphues and his England, in Nares.

P. 51, l. 18. *Stroke blinde.*] Marlowe, H. and L. p. 7:

"Some say, for her the fairest Cupid pin'd
And, looking in her face, was strooken blind."

P. 51, l. 23. *None-age.*] Infancy, or minority (in law). Once only in Shakspere, Rich III. "in his nonage," ii. 3, 13. Though Narcissus was young his passion was too deep-seated to yield to threats.

P. 51, l. 24. *Set up their rest.*] Abode. Pericles, Prologue to act ii. 25, 26:

"And that in Tarsus was not best
Longer for him to make his rest."

For another sense see Ford, 'Tis pity she's a whore, v. 3. "I have set up my rest," *i. e.* made my determination, a metaphor from fixing the musket rest. Gifford's Ben Johnson, i. 62; ii. 142.

P. 51, l. 28. *Lost their mold.*] See "Raleigh and Courtly Poets," by Dr. Hannah, 1875, p. 127, in "A Description of a most noble Lady," from Tottell's "Songs and Sonnets," 1557:

"I think Nature hath lost the mould
Where she her shape did take;
Or else I doubt if Nature could
So fair a creature make."

The Poems of Alexander Montgomery (1570-1600), Edinburgh, 1821, p. 210:

> "The mold is lost whairin wes maid
> This *A per se* of all."

A similar thought differently expressed is in Marlowe, H. and L. p. 7:

> "So lovely fair was Hero, Venus' nnn,
> As Nature wept, thinking she was undone,
> Because she took more from her than she left,
> And of such wondrous beauty her bereft."

P. 52, l. 1. *Sad and drier thoughts.*] Sad is grave, serious, as often in Shakspere, *e.g.* Lucrece 277, "Sad pause, and deep regard beseem the sage." For "dry" see Bacon, Essay 27, 170, "Heraclitus saith well, in one of his enigmas, *Dry light is ever the best*. And certain it is, that the light that a man receiveth by counsel from another is drier and purer than that which cometh from his own understanding and judgment; which is ever infused and drenched in his affections and customs." See Dr. Abbott's note on this passage.

P. 52, l. 3. *Sepulchrizing.*] Laying his body at full length like a corpse in a grave. In Simon Graham's Anatomie of Humors, Edinb. 1609, "wishing that your Honours discretion may sepulchrise this boldnesse," A. 3 recto; and in the prefatory sonnet to the Countesse of Errol:

> "If quicknes of thy wit find any crime,
> In thy discretion sepulchrize my wrong." A. 4, verso.

I have met with no other instance. The word is not in the Dictionaries. *Him.*] For it.

P. 52, l. 6. *Treating.*] Entreating. Again p. 56, "And I am treating but to be her shep-heard." Worcester cites *Berners* by name only as his authority for this meaning.

P. 52, l. 10. *Talke Sun-go-downe.*] Virgil, Eclog. ix. "Sæpe ego longos Cantando puerum memini me condere soles," 51, 2. Callimachus, Epigram, ii. 2,

$$\text{———} \;\; \dot{\epsilon}\mu\nu\dot{\eta}\sigma\theta\eta\nu \;\; \delta' \;\; \dot{o}\sigma\sigma\acute{a}\kappa\iota\varsigma \;\; \dot{a}\mu\phi\acute{o}\tau\epsilon\rho o\iota$$
$$\ddot{\eta}\lambda\iota o\nu \;\; \dot{\epsilon}\nu \;\; \lambda\acute{\epsilon}\sigma\chi\eta \;\; \kappa a\tau\epsilon\delta\acute{v}\sigma a\mu\epsilon\nu.$$

Ovid. Tristia, v. 13, 27:

> "Utque solebamus consumere longa loquendo
> Tempora sermonem deficiente die."

Ovid. Met. i. 682 :

"Sedit Atlantiades, et euntem multa loquendo
Detinuit sermone diem."

Similarly Shakspere in Lucrece :

"Long he questioned
With modest Lucrece and wore out the night." 122, 3.

And Milton in Lycidas :

"Battening our flocks with the fresh dews of night,
Oft till the star that rose, at evening, bright,
Toward heaven's descent had slop'd his westering wheel." 29.

For a very full collection of passages in illustration see Boissonade's note on Aristænetus, i. Epist. 24, p. 109, ed. Lutetiæ 1822.

P. 52, l. 24. *Polyp turning.*] R. Greene, Mamillia, 1583, ed. Grosart 1881, p. 17, " as there is a chāgable *Polipe*, so there is a sted fast *Emerauld*." P. 61, " Though the Polipe chaungeth colour euery houre; yet the Saphyre will cracke before it consent to disloyaltie." P. 77, " Comparing them [women] to the *Polipe* stone, that chaungeth colours every houre." In these passages he seems to confound the polyp with the opal. There is no stone bearing the name polyp. Again in his Anatomie of Fortune, 1584, p. 184, " The picture whiche thou seest heere, is the perfect counterparte of her inconstant conditions, for she, like the Polipe fishe, turneth himselfe into the likenesse of everie object." Henry Crosse, Vertues Commonwealth, 1603, p. 56, ed. Grosart, " The fish *Polipus* (as some write) hath this propertie, that it can turne itselfe into the likenesse of a stone, or seeme to be that which is next it, and so under colour of not seeming as it is, doeth rauen upon other fishes." Ovid, Halieuticon, 30-33 :

"At contra scopulis crinali corpore segnis
Polypus hæret, et hâc eludit retia fraude,
Et sub lege loci sumit mutatque colores
Semper ei similis quem contigit."

Plin. Nat. Hist. ix. 46, " Colorem mutat polypus ad similitudinem loci, et maximè in metu."

P. 52, l. 24. Several Greek Poets have noticed this characteristic of the Polypus:

Theognis. πουλύπου ὀργὴν ἴσχε πολυπλόκου, ὃς ποτὶ πέτρῃ,
τῇ προσομιλήσει, τοῖος ἰδεῖν ἐφάνη. 215.

308   *Narcissus.*

Sophocles.   νοῦν δεῖ πρὸς ἀνδρὶ, σῶμα πουλύπους ὅπως
             πέτρᾳ, τραπέσθαι γνησίου φρονήματος.
                  Iphigeniæ Fragment. apud Athenæum, xii. 7, p. 513, d.

Oppian.   πουλυπόδων δ' οὔπω τιν' ὄιομαι ἔμμεν' ἄπυστον
             τέχνης, οἳ πέτρῃσιν ὁμοίιοι ἰνδάλλονται,
             τήν κε ποτιπτύξωσι, περὶ σπείρης τε βάλωνται.
                                        Halieuticon, ii. 233.

Phocylides. μηδ' ἕτερον κεύθης κραδίῃ νόον, ἀλλ' ἀγορεύων·
             μηδ' ὡς πετροφυὴς πολύπους, κατὰ χώρον ἀμείβου.   44. 5.

The writers on Natural History repeat the fact, and assign reasons for it. Aristotle, Hist. Anim. lx. 37, "καὶ θηρεύει τοὺς ἰχθῦς, τὸ χρῶμα μεταβάλλων, καὶ ποιῶν ὅμοιον οἷς ἂν πλησιάσῃ λίθοις· τὸ δ' αὐτὸ τοῦτο ποιεῖ καὶ φοβηθείς." So Theophrastus also according to Athenæus, vii. 104, Θεόφραστος δὲ, ἐν τῷ περὶ τῶν Μεταβαλλόντων τὰς χρόας, τὸν πολύποδα, φησὶ, τοῖς πετρώδεσι μάλιστα τόποις συνεξομοιοῦσθαι, τοῦτο ποιοῦντα φόβῳ." Plutarch, Quæst. Nat. p. 916, b. "μεταβάλλει οὕτως ὥστε τὴν χροιὰν αἷς ἂν πλησιάζῃ πέτραις ὁμοιοῦν." And Ælian, V. Hist. i. 1, "πολύποδες ὑπὸ ταῖς πέτραις κάθηνται, καὶ ἑαυτοὺς εἰς τὴν ἐκείνων μεταμορφοῦσι χροιάν."

P. 53, l. 3, *Top-gallant.*] The top-gallant sail above the topsail. Once in Shakspere, and there used metaphorically, "The high top-gallant of my joy." R. and J. ii. 4, 202. In Whitney's Choice of Emblemes, p. 11, "The gallante ship—with streamers, flagges, topgallantes, pendantes braue."

Hoist.] "The verb is properly *hoise* with pp. *hoist* = *hoised*, '*Hoised* up the mainsail,' Acts xxvii. 40. Shakspere has both *hoise* and *hoist*. (The *t* is excrescent, and due to confusion with the pp.) Root unknown. Quite distinct from Fr. *hausser* to exalt, which is from Lat. altus, high." Skeat.

P. 53, l. 4. *Fer.*] Fir, must.

P. 53, l. 6. *The sea prefer'd our vintage.*] Prefer is here used in a peculiar and uncommon sense, to take before hand, to anticipate, as præfero is also, though rarely, used in Latin. The sea, that is the water of the spring, anticipated and carried off what would have been the fruit for the vintage, before it had time to form. For the general idea of the stanza, the ship

Notes.

making out in full sail, yet with a fatal issue, compare Whitney's Emblemes, xi. 1586. Spenser, Visions of Petrarch, ii. printed in 1591. Shakspere, M. of V. ii. 6, 14-19, circa 1596. Giles Fletcher, Christ's Victorie, ii. stanza 35, 1610. Gray's Bard, 71-6.

P. 53, l. 8. *Downe stouping.*] Marlowe, H. and L.:

> "With that Leander stooped to have embraced her,
> But from his spreading arms away she cast her." P. 19.

P. 53, l. 11. *Who so, &c.*] For the construction see Abbott's Shaksp. Gram. 248, 249, "of the Relative with Supplementary Pronoun." This repetition was common in Anglo-Saxon. In the same way in Elizabethan authors we find *who his* for *whose*, &c. Here "who" may be explained "with regard to whom."

P. 53, l. 17. *Monsters of time.*] Monster is here used as the Latin monstrum (fr. moneo), lit. that which teaches or points out; quia ostendunt, portendunt, monstrant, prædicunt, ostenta, portenta, monstra, prodigia dicuntur. Cicero, De Div. i. 42. Narcissus had previously called in Adonis and Leander (pp. 42, 43), and refers to them here as examples "that beautie hath small good for men to owe (own) it."

P. 53, l. 22. *What but time perfection gives.*] See The Essayes of a Prentise in the Divine Art of Poesie, Edinb. 1585, by K. James VI. p. 74, at the end of the Poeme of Tyme:

> "Hæc quoque perficiat, quod perficit omnia, Tempus."

Shakspere:
> "Time is the nurse and breeder of all good." Two G. of V. iii. 1, 243.
> "I have a young conception in my brain,
> Be you my time to bring it to some shape." Troil. i. 3, 313.

Tennyson, Love and Duty, 25:
> "My faith is large in time
> And that which brings it to its perfect end."

P. 53, l. 27. *Slanderous men, &c.*] See N. Breton's Praise of Virtuous Ladies (1606), p. 15, "Some will say, Women are unconstant, But I say not all, for Penelope and Cleopatra, Lucretia, with divers more too long to rehearse, shall stand for examples of such constancy as no man ever more constant."

P. 54, l. 15. *Closet up.*] Perhaps the earliest instance of the use of this word as a verb. Johnson quotes it from Herbert's Temple (1633), see lxxv. Decay:

"Thy great love once spread, as in an urn Doth closet up itself."

P. 55, l. 7. *Maine.*] Properly the great or open sea, as opposed to minor divisions, such as bays, gulfs. Here used for water.

P. 55, l. 8. *The Heavens.*] The Gods. See Marston's Scourge of Villanie (1599), Sat. ii. 23-26:

"Walk but in duskie night
With Lynceus' eyes, and to thy piercing sight
Disguised Gods will showe, in peasant shape
Prest to commit some execrable rape."

and afterwards Sat. viii. 169-164.

Ovid, Metam. viii. 626, in the story of Philemon and Baucis:

"Jupiter huc, specie mortali, cumque parente
Venit Atlantiades positis caducifer alis."

P. 55, l. 9. *Misconceited.*] There is a noun misconceit, a false notion, but no adjective given in the Dictionaries. Misconceited = calculated to give a false notion of the wearer.

P. 55, l. 12. *Playes with Saints.*] To play, as in Latin, ludere. Catullus, lxi. 204, "Ludite ut lubet." Propertius, ii. 6, 4, "in quâ populus lusit Ericthonius." Horace, Ep. ii. 2, 214, "Lusisti satis, edisti satis, atque bibisti." When the Saint was a Vestal, not only was she buried alive, but the paramour was scourged to death. Festus, "Probrum virginis Vestalis, ut capite puniretur: vir qui eam incestavisset verberibus necaretur," in v. Probrum. For instances see Liv. xxii. 57, Suetonii Domitianus viii., and Plin. Epist. iv. 11. Both the Secular and the Ecclesiastical Laws appointed penalties for similar offences with those who had taken vows of celibacy. See the Indexes to the Anglo-Saxon Laws, Record Commission, 1840, under "Nun."

Welkin.] The late Mr. Corser, whose acquaintance with the Elizabethan authors was most extensive, remarks on this word, "Welkin was a poet's word, and if we may judge from the clown's observation upon it in *Twelfth Night*, came into fashion towards the end of the sixteenth century." Collectanea Anglo-Poetica, viii. p. 333 (Chetham Society, No. cii. 1878). The clown says, "I will construe to them whence you come;

who you are and what you would are out of my welkin, I might say element, but the word is overworn." Tw. Night, iii. 1, 64. Welkin, however, was used continuously from the Saxon period to the time of Chaucer, Gower, and possibly later writers. It is found in Lord Surrey's Poems, after him it became fashionable, as stated above.

P. 55, l. 17. *The lesser planets.*] Compare:

"Looke how the suns approach doth overshade
The lesser stars from entercourse of sight."

Seeme to die.] Pontanus in his Urania, sive de Stellis, i. p. 10, ed. Ald. 1513, says of the stars by night:

"Collucent: sed mox Phœbo exoriente perempta,
Torpent luce novâ, et candenti lampade victa
Emoriuntur, et obscuro condnntur Olympo."

Nicholson in his Acolastus (1600) applies these words to the Marigold:

"But when the sunne his glory doth infold,
This prettie creature shuts and *seemes to die.*" 891, 2.

P. 55, l. 23. *Gooddest.*] I find no other instance of this form. Chaucer has "badder" from bad. Gooddest=goodliest, or best.

P. 55, l 24. *A womanning.*] Shakspere, Alls Well, iii. 2, 51-3, uses this verb:

"I have felt so many quirks of joy and grief,
That the first face of neither, on the start,
Can *woman* me unto 't."

"*i. e.* can affect me suddenly and deeply as my sex are usually affected." Steevens. The sense of the verb is expressed by "play the woman," as Wolsey uses the phrase:

"Cromwell, I did not think to shed a tear
In all my miseries; but thou hast forced me,
Out of thy honest truth, to play the woman." H. VIII. iii. 2, 436.

And Laertes in Hamlet:

"When these are gone
The woman will be out." iv. 7, 189.

Other nouns are similarly used as verbs, p. 7, "to *godd* it." Hall, Satires, "But had I *maiden'd* it as many use," iii. 3, 5. *Lady*=to lady it. N. Breton, "Pasquil's Madcap," p. 10:

"But if a Jacke will be a gentleman
And mistress Needens *lady it* at will."

So Shakspere has *lover*, "who, young and simple, would not be so *lover'd?*" Complaint, 319.

P. 56, l. 3. *Loftly bent.*] Inclined or desirous of rising aloft, the adverb indicating that which is purposed. So Shakspere, 2 Hen. VI. "a sort of naughty persons *lewdly bent.*" ii. 1, 167. Also in Sir John Harington's Papers, in Nichols's Progresses of Q. Elizabeth. " 1599. The Queene did once aske my wife in merrie sorte ' how she kepe my good wyll and love, which I did alwayes mayntaine to be trulye good towardes her and my childrene?' My Mal, in wise and discrete manner, told her Highnesse ' she had confidence in her husbands understandinge and courage, well founded on her own stedfastness not to offend or thwart, but to cherishe and obey; hereby did she persuade her husbande of her own affections, and in so doinge did commande his.' ' Go to, go to, mistresse,' saithe the Queene, ' you are *wisely bente* I finde; after such sorte do I keepe the good wyll of all my husbandes, my good people: for if they did not reste assurede of some special love towarde them, they would not readilie yielde me suche goode obedience.' This deservethe notinge, as beinge both wise and pleasaunte." Vol. ii. p. 443, ed. 1823.

P. 56, l. 4. *Tottering.*] Wavering, unsteady. " The radical element by itself signifies a slight sound, in N. *tot* a murmur. It. *ni totto ni motto*, not a syllable. Then, as in so many other cases, the syllables representing sound are transferred to the sense of bodily action and bodily substance. Hence Buv. *tattern* to tremble. E. *totter* to move unsteadily." Wedgwood in v. To *hover* has something of the same sense as *totter* in this line, as in the name of the kestrel, the *wind-hover.*

P 56, l. 16. *Nuns.*] Marlowe.

"So lovely fair was Hero Venus' nun." H. and L. p. 7.
" You exceed her far—whose nun you are." Ibid. p. 14.
"Then shall you most resemble Venus' nun." Ibid. p. 18.

Nash has, " Cytherea's nuns." Lenten Stuffe, p. 68. Gosson, " Like Venus nunnes." School of Abuse, p. 26.

Surrey in his Translation of Virgil, Æneid iv., " like Bacchus' nun." 389. In this he followed the translation of Gawin Douglas, " Sic wise as when the nunnys of Bachus." p. 110, l. 10.

Drayton with more propriety applies the term to the Virgin followers of Diana.

"Where Dians nuns their Goddess do adore." Eclogue V. stanza 18.

P. 56, l. 17. *Chast votaries for Gods to chase th' aire.*] Another instance of play on words. The line is not very intelligible, and wants a syllable. Is *in* left out? " To chase in th' aire " meaning to chase in the heavens, referring to the last line of the preceding stanza, " heavenly saints "—who will be able to turn Arcadian nymphs from hating to love, by telling them that Gods are their lovers. Arcadia was a favourite haunt of Diana, to whose service its nymphs were devoted. Syrinx for instance " Ortygiam studiis ipsâque colebat Virginitate Deam." Ovid Met. i. 694; and Callisto " Miles erat Phœbes." Id. ii. 415, Jove's triumph over the latter is hinted at in the words " never yet wun."

P. 56, l. 19. *Godhood.*] A rare word. It is found in Warner, Albion's England, iii. 16. " Accept my simple legacie, O godhood most deuyne," p. 543. ed. Chalmers' Poets: and earlier (c. 1200) in the Ancren Riwle, 112, as quoted by Stratmann. No other instances are recorded. Yet it is the right form. " The termination—*hood* was an independent substantive in Saxon literature, in the form of *hâd*. This word signified office, degree, faculty, quality. An altered form is—*head,* as in *Godhead,* an alteration which makes it difficult for many to see that it is the analogue of *manhood,* and as if *God-hood.*" Earle, Philology of English, p. 274, who does not seem to have met with the word. In the Athanasian Creed the two words come together, " not by conversion of the Godhead into flesh, but by taking the manhood into God;" and God-hood, for God-head, would mark the distinction more obviously.

P. 56, l. 22. *Fortune.*] Adverbially, as in Latin " forte," and as in the word " chance:" *e.g.* Gray,

"If chance, by lonely contemplation led,
Some kindred spirit shall enquire thy fate." Elegy, 95.

Shakspere several times has " by fortune " in this sense—but I have not met with any parallel example of " fortune " as an adverb.

P. 56, l. 24. *Diu'd downe to yonger method.*] In Richard III. Gloucester says,

"But gentle Lady Anne,
To leave this keen encounter of our wits
And fall somewhat into *a slower method.*" i. 2, 114.

314 *Narcissus.*

What is young is not complete in growth, is yet at its beginning, and is therefore imperfect. So his love for a shadow is a childish method or plan of loving, and as it can never come to anything, it must leave him for ever among the forsaken and forlorne lovers.

P. 56, l. 26.] As the term bastard is applied to the fruit of illicit, irregular, love, so through his passion, which is irregularly begotten, he is brought into the class to which that name is properly applicable. The line and its connection with the context is not very clear.

P. 56, l. 27.] Should this line be read, "Why? are not princes subject to report?" so as to be more in accordance with the next?

P. 56, l. 27. *Report.*] Report is fame. Chaucer, Prologue to The House of Fame. "In this Book is shewed how the Deeds of all Men and Women, be they good or bad, are carried by Report to Posterity." Nash in Pierce Penilesse says, "Report, which our moderners clepe flundering fame." Edwards seems to have had in memory some lines of Daniel in the Complaint of Rosamond,

> "And this is ever proper unto Courts,
> That nothing can be done, but Fame reports.
> Fame doth explore what lies most secret hidden,
> Entring the Closet of the Palace-Dweller;
> Abroad revealing what is most forbidden,
> Of Truth and Falsehood both an equal Teller,
> 'Tis not a Guard can serve for to expel her:
> The Sword of Justice cannot cut her Wings,
> Nor stop her Mouth from uttering secret Things." i. p. 18, ed. 1718.

P. 57, l. 1. *Livia's rich statues.*] According to an apophthegm of Livia recorded by Dion Cassius these statues were naked men. "καὶ αὐτῆς ἄλλα τε καλῶς εἰρημένα ἀποφθέγματα φέρεται, καὶ ὅτι γυμνούς ποτε ἄνδρας ἀπαντήσαντας αὐτῇ, καὶ μέλλοντας διὰ τοῦτο θανατωθήσεσθαι, ἔσωσεν, εἰποῦσα ὅτι οὐδὲν ἀνδριάντων ταῖς σωφρονούσαις οἱ τοιοῦτοι διαφέρουσι." Hist. Rom. lviii. 2. This passage is thus expressed in Heywood's Gunaikeion, "Dion in Tiberio says that Livia, the wife of Augustus Cæsar, beholding men naked said to the rest about her 'that to continent women and chast matrons such objects differed nothing from statues or images,' for the modest heart with immodest sights ought not to be corrupted." p. 284. The law, under which these men were liable to the penalty of death, originated from the wish of the Romans to conciliate the Sabines

Notes. 315

by showing respect to their daughters whom they had seized. "Igitur Romanis hoc moribus sub pœna capitali constitutum præsente fœminâ abstinere obscœnis dictis, et μηδένα ὀφθῆναι γυμνόν, nudum neminem conspiciendum se dare, teste Plutarcho in Romulo, p. 30 (i. p. 63, ed. Bryan 1729)." Reimar. in Dion. Cass.

P. 57, l. 1. *In his gallery*] Among the "cloistered ills that fame beares from Courts" those relating to Tiberius at Capreæ are notorious. The solitude and inaccessibility of the island, for which indeed it was chosen, " præcipuè delectatus insulâ quod uno parvoque litore adiretur, septa undique præruptis immensæ altitudinis rupibus, et profundo maris," (Suetonii Tiberius 40) could not prevent the imperial profligacy from becoming known. "Secessu Capreensi etiam *sellariam* excogitavit," which may perhaps be intended by our author's "*gallery*," as it is simply a room furnished with seats, wherein these "statues of Livia, portraide by lyfe," that is actually, such scenes as are enumerated in the rest of the stanza. See the Life of Tiberius by Suetonius, 43, and Tacitus, Hist. vi. 1.

P. 57, l. 3. *Mask't through the cloudie stitched canapie.*] Moved through like characters in masked balls, as in Romeo and Juliet, i. 5, sustaining their several parts; which may be supposed to have been represented also by needlework in the tapestry, and "canapie" or curtain stretched across the ceiling. Ovid describes all these "scapes" of the Gods as wrought by Arachne in her web. Met. vi. 103—128, a passage imitated by Spenser F. Q. iii. xi. 28, *sqq*. Shakspere also introduces the arras and its story in Cymbeline, ii. 4, 68—76. Lucrece, 1366, *sqq*. See also Warton on Spenser F. Q. vii. 7, 10.

A pavement representing similar subjects is described by Marlowe, Hero and Leander, p. 11, the wording of which was probably in the mind of Edwards when writing this stanza.

"There might you see the Gods in sundry shapes
Committing heady riots, incest, scapes."

P. 57, l. 20. *Women doo yeeld.*] Somewhat like Marlowe's lines in H. and L. p. 36.

"Treason was in her thought
And cunningly to yield herself she sought,
Seeming not won; yet won she was at length,
In such wars Women use but half their strength."

P. 57, l. 22. *Romane actors.*] The most celebrated in tragedy was Æsopus—called by Horace, Epist. ii. 1, 82, "gravis," pathetic—and by Quintilian "gravior." Inst. Orat. xi. 3, 111. By Cicero, with whom he was intimate ("noster Æsopus"), he is said to have been "summus artifex" (Pro Sext. 56) and to have excelled in power of looks and fire of expression ("tantum ardorem vultuum atque motuum"). De Div. i. 37. From the passage in Cicero and the anecdotes related of him his acting would seem to have been characterised chiefly by strong emphasis and vehemence. During Cicero's exile, having to act the part of Telamon banished, in one of Accius's plays, by his manner and skilful emphasis, and an occasional change of a word, he led the audience to apply the whole to the case of Cicero, and so did him essential service—and was immensely applauded. (Dict. of Biography.) From this we may see that there is no exaggeration in our poets words, " Charged the hearts and eyes of the spectators."

P. 57, l. 23. *Prætextati seamed robes.*] Toga Prætextata, or Prætexta, was a toga bordered with purple, or with a stripe of purple sewn on, and was worn by magistrates of high rank; hence " fabula prætexta " or " prætextata " was a tragedy; so that when Roman actors appeared in plays taken from their own history (for which Horace praises his countrymen

"Nil intentatum nostri liquere poetæ;
Nec minimum meruere decus, vestigia Græca
Ausi deserere, et celebrare domestica facta;
Vel qui prætextas, vel qui docuere togatas." De A. P. 285.)

they naturally adopted the Roman dress. It is strange that, though even the titles of most Tragedies on Roman subjects have perished, some few fragments have been preserved of the " Paulus " of Pacuvius, and of the " Brutus " and " Decius " of Accius. Of the ten tragedies ascribed to Seneca one only, the Octavia, is taken from Roman history.

P. 57, l. 24. *Charged.*] Shakspere, Macbeth,

"What a sigh is there ! The heart is sorely *charged.*" v. 1, 60.

Tennyson, Dream of Fair Women,

" *Charged* both mine eyes with tears." iv.

P. 57, l. 25. *Flintie Niobes.*] To emphasize the phrase, " still continuing sorrow," he adds the illustration of Niobe, who

"fixa cacumine montis
Liquitur, et lacrymis etiamnum marmora manant." Ov. Met. vi. 311.

or as given by Whitney in his Choice of Emblems, 1586, p. 13,

> "Of Niobe behould the ruthefull plighte;
> And while herselfe with trickling teares did pine,
> Shee was transformde into a marble stone,
> Which yet with teares doth seeme to waile and mone."

Hamlet's "like Niobe all tears" is familiar to all, but the other passage in which Shakspere introduces her name may be cited as an authority for its being pronounced as a dissyllable, as it must be in Edwards's poem where it rhymes to "robes" and "globes." It is in Troilus and Cressida,

> "Make wells and Niobes of the maids and wives." v. 10, 19.

which, if a ten-syllable line, requires Niobes to be read as a dissyllable.

P. 57, l. 26. *And of each circled eie framed thousand globes.*] There is here a play not on words but things. The "circled eie," that is the eye-ball or globe of the eye, is multiplied into a thousand other "globes," that is "tears." In his lines "On a Tear" Sam. Rogers writes

> "That very law * which moulds a tear
> And bids it trickle from its sonrce,
> That law preserves the earth a sphere
> And guides the planets in their course."

Shakspere with a different sort of globe in view writes

> "O were mine eyeballs into bullets turned,
> That I in rage might shoot them at your faces." 1 Hen. VI. iv. 7, 79.

P. 57, l. 27. *Flat images not men.*] Flat is downright, absolute, as used several times in Shakspere, "flat blasphemy." Meas. ii. 2, 131. "flat perjury," Much Ado. iv. 2, 44, and generally in common conversation. The word "images" must be intended to denote some effect of the actors' skill on the spectators or hearers. Perhaps the words of Marcus in Titus Andronicus come as near as any to illustrate it:

> "See thy two sons' heads,
> Thy warlike hand, thy mangled daughter here;
> Thy other banished son with this dear sight
> Struck pale and bloodless; and thy brother, I,
> Even like *a stony image, cold and numb.*" iii. 1, 255.

---

* The Law of Gravitation.

G. Gascoigne in his Dan Bartholomew of Bathe has the same idea to express the intensity of his feelings on discovering the faithlessness of his mistress—

> "from all company him selfe he kept:
> Wherby so farre in stormes of strife he stept,
> That now he seemed an *Image not a man,*
> His eyes so dead, his colour waxt so wan." i. p. 109.

Sylvester also in his Version of Du Bartas uses it to indicate ignorance,

> "And sith a dull dunce which no knowledge can
> Is a *dead Image,* and *no living man."*
> "Eden." First Part of First Day of Second Week. p. 87, ed. 1641.

The word occurred before in Cephalus and Procris, p. 10, where it is said of Poets,

> "And had not *Jove* been fauorable then,
> They never should haue been accounted men,
> But liu'd as pesants, shaddowes, *imagies."*

Both "images" and "shadows" are often used by Shakspere for what is unreal; like the corresponding words in Latin, "imago" and "umbra."

P. 58, l. 1. *The Chorus.*] The office of the Chorus in a Greek Tragedy is here well set forth, and accords with the precept of Horace in his Art of Poetry,

> "Actoris partes Chorus, officiumque virile
> Defendat: neu quid medios intercinat actus
> Quod non proposito conducat et hæreat apte." 193.

And in the last chorus especially the audience are prepared for the coming catastrophe, which ought to happen off the stage and be narrated by one of the actors, or by a messenger, as Horace says:

> "Aut agitur res in scenis, aut acta refertur,
> Segnius irritant animos demissa per aures
> Quam quæ sunt oculis subjecta fidelibus, et quæ
> Ipse sibi tradit spectator: non tamen intus
> Digna geri, promes in *scenam."* De A. P. 179.

P. 58, l. 4. *'Tis I the siege must countenance.*] None of the meanings of *siege* seem to give any probable sense to this clause, and the word is probably a misprint for *"stage."* Narcissus in contravention of the usual rules of tragedy is about to enact the last " tragicke scene " " *coram populo* " so to

Notes. 319

say. The words of the Chorus he tells us are "of little worth," and he himself must give effect to the catastrophe, "'*tis I the stage must countenance*," and bring forward "*in scenam*" what would in general be done out of sight. (Horace De A. P. 183-5.)

P. 58, l. 10. *Though they have past.*] They, viz. the persons celebrated in these stories. To pass is to die. The Passing Bell preserves the meaning. The word occurs three times in Shakspere in this sense,

"Let him pass peaceably." 2 Hen. VI. iii. 3, 25.
"Thus might he pass indeed." Lear, iv. 6, 47.
"Let him pass." v. 3, 313.

and has now been revived and made current in Literature by the Laureate's poem, "The Passing of Arthur,"

"He passes to be King among the dead."

And got the golden vale.] Golden, as in the "*golden* age" both of the World, and of Latinity, is the best the purest; the Laureate uses it in the same sense in his "Golden Year:"

"'Tis like the second world to us that live,
'Twere all as one to fix our hopes on Heaven
As on this vision of the *golden* year."

The "*vale*" is from Virgil's account in the 6th Æneid:

"At pater Anchises penitus *convalle* virenti." 679.

And

"Interea videt Æneas in *valle* reducta." 703.

The more general term is the Elysian *plain*, or *fields*, 'Ηλύσιον πέδιον, Od. iv. 563.

"Devenere locos lætos et amœna vireta
Fortunatorum nemorum, sedesque beatas.
Largior hic *campos* æther et lumine vestit
Purpureo." Æn. vi. 638.

Pindar, Olymp. 2, in a splendid passage, has, "ἔνθα μακάρων νᾶσον ὠκεανίδες αὖραι περιπνέουσιν· ἄνθεμα δὲ χρυσοῦ φλέγει," κ. τ. λ. which Tennyson puts into the mouth of his Ulysses,

"It may be we shall touch the Happy Isles
And see the great Achilles, whom we knew."

2 T 2

But in the Lotos Eaters (8, near the end,) another reproduction of Greek imagination, he reverts to the notion of the "*vale*,"

"Others in Elysian *valleys* dwell."

And again in the Morte d'Arthur:

"I am going a long way
To the *island-valley* of Avilion;
Where falls not hail, or rain, or any snow,
Nor ever wind blows loudly; but it lies
Deep-meadow'd, happy, fair with orchard lawns
And bowery hollows crown'd with summer sea,
Where I will heal me of my grievous wound."

An exquisite blending of some of the choicest lines of the Odyssey, descriptive of the Elysian plain, with his own;

οὐ νιφετὸς, οὔτ' ἄρ χείμων πολὺς, οὔτέ ποτ' ὄμβρος,
ἀλλ' αἰεὶ Ζεφύροιο λιγυπνείοντας ἀήτας
Ὠκεανὸς ἀνίησιν, ἀναψύχειν ἀνθώπους. iv. 566.

And again of Olympus—

οὔτ' ἀνέμοισι τινάσσεται, οὔτέ ποτ' ὄμβρῳ
δεύεται, οὔτε χιὼν ἐπιπίλναται· ἀλλὰ μάλ' αἴθρη
πέπταται ἀνέφελος, λευκὴ δ' ἐπιδέδρομεν αἴγλη·
τῇ ἐνὶ τέρπονται μάκαρες θεοὶ ἤματα πάντα. vi. 43.

P. 58, l. 11. *From Artes bright eie.*] If the preceding lines be read as parenthetical, these words would be connected with the end of the second line, "Sweet persuasive stories," derived from the poets, whose art is referred to throughout the stanza. "Artes bright eie" suggests the kindred passage:

"The poet's eye, in a fine frenzy rolling,
Doth glance from heaven to earth, from earth to heaven." M. N. D. v. 1, 12.

If, however, the third line be not parenthetical the occupants of "the golden vale" will be intended as having been indebted to the poets, who have sung of them, "for their local habitation, and a name."

P. 58, l. 11. *Ascraes gentle vallies.*] The mention of *vallies* may make the second of the above interpretations the more probable. The actual vallies of Ascra, however, seem to have been anything but gentle, as we learn from Ovid:

" Esset perpetuo sua quam vitabilis Ascra,
Ausa est agricolæ Musa docere senis:
At fuerat terrâ genitus, qui scripsit, in illâ,
Intumuit vati nec tamen Ascra suo." De Ponto, iv. xiv. 31.

Hesiod, who is meant, thus honestly describes his fatherland, for having mentioned his father, who was a merchant of Cume in Æolia, and settled at Ascra; he adds:

Νάσσατο δ' ἄγχ' Ἑλικῶνος ὀϊζυρῇ ἐνὶ κώμῃ,
"Ἀσκρῃ, χεῖμα κακῇ, θέρει ἀργαλέῃ, οὐδέ ποτ' ἐσθλῇ.
Opera et Dies. 639, 40.

Hesiod is the "Ascræus senex" of Virgil's sixth eclogue, where, speaking of Gallus, he says:

" Hos tibi dant calamos (en accipe), Musæ,
Ascræo quos ante seni." 69, 70.

Both Ovid in other passages and Propertius speak of him under the name "Ascræus." Ascra is on Mount Helicon, and in the territory of Thespiæ (the birth-place of Narcissus), from which it was 40 stadia distant.

P. 59, l. 12. *Tottering rockes.*] Tottering is here used in the sense of dizzy, "causing giddiness," as in Lear, iv. 6, 12, "How fearful and dizzy 'tis to cast one's eye so low"; and hence equivalent to high.

P. 59, l. 17. *To send the time away.*] The Latin equivalent is "fallere," as Ovid:

" Interea medius fallunt sermonibus horas,
Sentirique moram prohibent." Met. viii. 651.

" Nec mihi, quærenti spatiosam fallere noctem,
Lassaret viduas pendula tela manus." Heroid. Epist. i. 9.

Shakspere uses the verbs "beguile" and "wear away" for the same thought in M. N. Dream:

" How shall we *beguile*
The lazy time, if not with some delight?" v. 1, 40.

" Come now, what masques, what dances shall we have,
To *wear away* this long age of three hours." v. 1, 32.

It is expressed differently in L. L. L., "We will with some strange *pastime* solace them," iv. 3, 337. On which word see Trench on the Study of Words, Lect. i. p. 9.

P. 59, l. 18. *Nimble Throate.*] He uses the expression again, p. 62:
> "Blessed be your *nimble throates*
> That so amorously could sing."

King James VI. in his Translation of Du Bartas, L'Uranie, p. 25:
> "The tone is pleasaunt of my sisters deir:
> Yet though *their throts* make heaven and earth admire,
> They yeld to me." *

Nimble is from A.-S. *nim-an*, to take, seize, catch, and is applied by Shakspere to spirit, thought, wit, and in the Tempest to the *lungs*, "these gentlemen who are of such sensible and *nimble lungs* that they always use to laugh at nothing," ii. 1, 174.

P. 59, l. 22. *Thus while the lark, &c.*] The song in Cymbeline—a play written in 1609, but not printed till 1623 in the first folio — may perhaps be indebted to this stanza for the introduction of "*the steeds*" of Phœbus, of which there is no mention in the passages quoted in the Variorum ed. of 1821. There can be no doubt that Lyly's Alexander and Campaspe supplied Shakspere with the expressions "*Hark! Hark!*" and "*Heaven's gate.*" Gifford, in a note on Ford's The Sun's Darling, ii. 1, p. 390, ed. 1827, says, "The lark is justly a favourite with our old poets; and I should imagine, from my own observations, that a greater number of descriptive passages might be found respecting him than the nightingale. A judicious collection of both would furnish not a few pages of surpassing taste and beauty." See Papers of Manchester Literary Club, vol. iii. 1877, for article on Shelley and the Skylark.

Her mounted tale.] V. and A. 853, 4:
> "Lo, here the gentle lark, weary of rest,
> From his moist cabinet *mounts up on high.*"

and previously, Skelton in his "Garlande of Laurell," 533:
> "Lyke as the larke
> *Mountith on hy* with her melodious lay."

---

* The original has "leur gosier."

Notes. 323

P. 59, l. 24. *Her noates sweet orizons.*] Prayers, through French *orison*, later *oraison*, from Lat. *orationem, orare. Or* is stem of *os*, the mouth, so properly "utterance." While most of our poets describe the lark's song, or carol, it is here made also a religious service, and in this Shakspere again agrees, for in Sonnet xxix, 11, 12, he writes:

> "Like to the larke at break of day arising
> From sullen earth sings hymns at heaven's gate."

P. 59, l. 25. *Jove's high court.*] Marlow, H. and L., " To Jove's high court," p. 17, and the early translation of Du Bartas in 1593 renders " Vers la voute du ciel," " Up to the court of Jove."

P. 60, l. 8. *Amaine unto the spring I made.*] So Shakspere in V. and A.:

> "Sick-thoughted Venus *makes amain unto* him," 5.

P. 60, l. 9. *Finding beautie culling nakedness.*] Whether we read these words separately, or as " beautie-culling nakedness," they seem to be intended to express "obtaining a clear view of his own beautie." Nakedness in Shakspere, Much Ado, " That which appears in proper nakedness," iv. 1, 177, is explained " openness to view," in Schmidt's Lex.

P. 60, l. 10 *Sweet love reviving.*] That is, making good in his imagination all that he had lost while pining away by the fountain, a change which Ovid thus notices:

> "Attenuatus amore—
> Et neque jam color est misto candore rubori
> Nec corpus remanet, quondam quod amaverat Echo." Met. iii. 487.

P. 60, l. 13. *Imbracing sighs.*] A line in Lord Surrey's Sonnet at Windsor may illustrate this expression. He says:

> "The heavy charge of care
> Heaped in my breast, breaks forth against my will
> In *smoky sighs* that overcast the air." p. 50.

On this Dr. Nott observes "that the hyperbole is extravagant." Surrey suffered himself to be betrayed into the use of the latter by his partiality to his master Petrarch (Son. 247, Part 2):

> "I'ho pien di sospir quest' aer tutto."

As Surrey copied Petrarch so did Sackville copy Surrey:

"With *smoke of sighs* sometimes I might behold
The place all dim'd, like to the morning mist."
Mirror for Magistrates, fol. 222.

In a subsequent passage he borrows the very expression:

"So strove he thus awhile as with the death,
Now pale as lead, and cold as any stone;
Now still as calm, now storming forth a breath
Of *smoky sighs*."

Both here, and before, p. 43, "Imbrace thou sighs, with teares I'll fil the aire," there may be some imitation of this hyperbolical language—and they embraced the smoke of sighs as Æneas would have embraced the shade of Anchises:

"Ter conatus ibi collo dare brachia circum;
Ter frustra comprensa manus effugit imago
Par levibus ventis volncriqne simillima somno." Æn. vi. 700.

P. 60, l. 14. *Amidst the spring I leapt.*] Marlowe, H. and L.:

"Let it suffice
That my slack muse sings of Leanders eyes:
Those orient cheeks and lips, exceeding his
That *leapt into the water* for a kiss
Of his own shadow, and despising many
Died ere he could enjoy the love of any."

P. 60, l. 16. *Shaddowes wanting appetite and sence.*] Compare the language of Venus to Adonis.

"Fie, lifeless picture, cold and senseless stone,
Well-painted idol, image dull and dead,
Statue contenting but the eye alone,
Thing like a man, but of no woman bred." 211.

P. 60, l. 20. *Cephisus.*] The author inserts here a marginal note, "Ovid 3. Met. Narcissus fuit Cephisi fluvii ex Liriope nympha filius." Why? It seems not improbable that instead of *Cephisus* in the text of the poem the reading should be *Cephisius*, a name once applied to Narcissus by Ovid,

"Jamque ter ad quinos unum Cephisius annum
Addiderat." Met. iii. 351:

and that the note was added to explain and justify this introduction of the name. In the preceding line Narcissus speaks, "Pardon *my* tale, for *I* am going hence," and in the following one, "And thus *my* candle flam'd, and here burnt out," so that it would seem more in keeping to take "*Cephisus now freezed*" to be descriptive of his death rather than of the effect produced on his father by that event. The words also that complete the line, "*Whereat the Sea-nymphs shout*," confirm this view, as they are evidently a rendering of Ovid's lines,

> "Planxere *sorores*
> Naides, et sectos *fratri* posuere capillos."

"Freez'd" imports both the dying, "froze the genial current of the soul," in a sense different from Gray, and then "death's eternal cold," as in Shakspere's Sonnet, xiii. 12. If, however, "Cephisus" must be retained in the text, and understood of the river, it may be noted that Statius has the phrase, "Cephissi glaciale caput." Thebaid. vii. 349; an icy coldness which we must suppose to have been suddenly intensified through horror at his son's untimely end.

Sea-nymphs.] The Oceanides are properly the sea-nymphs—but as "sea" is used for the element of water in general

> "Whether in sea or fire, in earth or air,
> The extravagant and erring spirit hies,
> To his confine." Hamlet, i. 1, 153.

so sea-nymphs is here an allowable translation of "Naiades," who are properly Water-nymphs, as in the Tempest:

> "You Nymphs, call'd Naiads, of the windring brooks
> With your sedged crowns, and ever-harmless looks,
> Leave your crisp channels." iv. 128.

P. 60, l. 21. *And thus my candle flam'd, and here burnt out.*] A Shaksperian phrase, candle being used as a symbol of life.

> "Here burns my candle out; ay, here it dies,
> Which, whiles it lasted, gave King Henry light." 3 Hen. VI. 6. 1.

> "Out, out, brief candle." Macbeth, v. 5, 23.

The former of these two plays was probably known to our author, as it is supposed to have been written about 1592-4.

Narcissus.

P. 61, l. 1. *Scarring*.] Wounding, "and leaving a permanent mark behind." See Wyatt's Poems. "*The Lover describeth his restless state*."

"The wound, alas! hap in some other place,
From whence no tool away the scar can raze." P. 16. (Aldine 16.)

To his unkind Love.

"In deep wide wound the deadly stroke doth turn
To cured scar, that never shall return." P. 45. (Aldine 53.)

The sense evidently is "The stroke made a wound which though cured leaves a scar that never can be removed." Nott.

He has the same expression in an epigram, "*Wyatt being in prison to Bryan*."

"Sure I am, Bryan, this wound shall heal again,
But yet, alas! the scar shall still remain." P. 72. (Ald. 176.)

And introduced it into his "*Oration to the Judges after the Indictment and the Evidence*." "These men thinketh it enough to accuse; and, as all these slanderers use for a general rule, whom thou lovest not, accuse; for though he heal the wound, yet the scar shall remain." p. 291. (Ald. lxiii.) It received the imprimatur of Lord Surrey, in his "*Exhortation to learn by others troubles*." p. 51. (Ald. 68.)

"Yet Solomon said, the wronged shall recure:
But Wyatt said true; 'The scar doth aye endure.'"

Such passages doubtless influenced Shakspere in Lucrece

"Bearing away the wound that nothing healeth
The scar that will despite of cure remain." 732.

And intensify the depth of meaning in Romeo's reply to Mercutio

"He jests at scars, that never felt a wound." ii. 2, 43.

P. 61, l. 1. *Bewitching*.] R. and J. "Alike bewitched by the charm of looks." Lovers Complaint, "Consents bewitch'd, ere he desire, have granted." 131.

P 61, l. 2. *Tell*.] Should this be *tels* as in lines 3 and 5 of the stanza?

To hurt it selfe.] Nash in Pierce Peniless (1592) says, that Cornelius Agrippa wrote against learning, "against which he could neuer have lifted his penne if herself had not helpt him *to hurt herselfe*." p. 39.

P. 61, l. 5. *Womens shewes are pelfe*.] This seems more appropriate to Procris than to anything in the poem of Narcissus. There is a curious passage in Strype's Life of Aylmer Bp. of London (d. 1594), "Speaking of the pride of women and of their excess when the nation wanted necessary defence, he thus accosted them: 'Oh! ye English ladies learn rather to wear Roman hearts than Spanish knacks: rather to help your country, than hinder your husbands; to make your Queen rich for your defence, than your husbands poor for your gearish gayness. If every one of you would employ your rings and chains, or the price of your superfluous ruffs, furs, fringes, and such other trinkets, upon the necessary defence of your country, I think you should make the Queen much richer, and abler to meet with your enemies, and yourselves much the honester." Chap. xiii. p. 180, ed. Oxford, 1821.

P. 61, l. 6. *Constancies as flowers.*] In 1575 was published "A small Handfull of Fragrant Flowers, &c. by N. B" (often assigned to Nicholas Breton, but disavowed by Dr. Grosart, Memorial-Introduction to Breton, p. lxxiii., and attributed by him rather to Nathl. Baxter) in which the author begins

"Dear Dames, your sences to revive
Accept these flowers in order here:
The first resembleth Constancie
A worthy budde of passing fame."

Our author, however, likens Women's Constancies to flowers as being so evanescent; like St. James, "because as the flower of the grass he shall pass away. For the sun is no sooner risen with a burning heat, but it withereth the grass, and the flower thereof falleth, and the grace of the fashion of it perisheth." i. 10, 11, and Isaiah, xl. 6, 7, 8, "All flesh is grass, and the goodliness thereof is as the flower of the field. The grass withereth, the flower fadeth, because the Spirit of the Lord bloweth upon it: surely the people is grass. The grass withereth, the flower fadeth; but the word of our God shall stand for ever." So Psalm ciii. 15, 16. Compare Cymbeline, ii. 4, 110–113, and ii. 5, 29–32.

P. 61, l. 13. *Divinely dreampt.*] The Poet according to Horace (Sat. i. 4, 43) is one "Cui mens *divinior*," as well as the "Os magna sonaturum," has been given. To dream is often used for to imagine, to think, with *of*, or *on*. "The verb is formed from the noun, A.-S. *dream*, (1) a sweet sound, music. (2) joy, glee. The sense of vision arose from that of happiness: we still talk of a dream of bliss." Skeat in v.

P. 61, l. 14. *Visedly.*] For advisedly. The Dictionaries do not give "visedly."

P. 61, l. 15. *Slow Muse.*] Marlowe, H. and L. has "my slack muse." p. 8.

P. 61, l. 15. *Benempt.*] Taken away. Beniman (Sax.) to take away, Benimen Mid. English; and "to nimm or take as late as by Fuller." Trench, English Past and Present. Lect. iii. p. 102.

P. 61, l. 16. *Skonce.*] The head. In the Comedy of Errors, ii. 2, 34–38, there is a play on the different meanings of this word: "*Sconce* call you it, so you would leave battering I would rather have it a *head;* an you use these blows long I must get a *sconce* for my head and *insconce* it too." " In the sense of head *sconce* is now comic or ignoble." Trench, English Past and Present, Lect. iii. p. 130. It is derived from the Latin *absconsa, sconsa, consa*=lanterna, and from the semicircular form of these, like the skull or pate, has come to be used for the head. See Ducange, Glossar. in Absconsa. Lee's Glossary of Liturgical Terms under " Mortar," and the illustration from an old English mortar or sconce in Magdalen College Chapel at Oxford. An "*absconsa*" was a dark lantern used by the monks in going round the dormitories—from *abscondere*, which has *absconsum*, as well as *absconditum*. The meaning of the word (says Wedgwood in v.) is something to conceal or cover one from the enemy—a sconce being a small fort or block house—esconsail a screen or shelter—and "absconsa candela" a light hidden—and hence that which holds a light, without the notion of concealing it.

Aslackt.] The form "slakt" occurred on p. 4. Aslake is used by Chaucer, Surrey and Spenser.

P 61, l. 21. *Equipage.*] Spenser, Shepheard's Calendar, October, 112-114, the Eclogue being on Poetry,

> "How I could rear the Muse on stately stage
> And teach her tread aloft in buskin fine,
> With queint Bellona in her *equipage*."

Where the glosse explains *equipage*, as *order*. Equip, Fr. *equiper*, to fit out, Icelandic *skipa* to arrange, set in order; closely related to Icel. *skapa* to shape. Skeat in v. Verstegan in his "Restoration of Decayed Intelligence," 1605, chap. 7 has a story about this word. "A principall Courtier writing from London to a personage of authority in the North willed him among other things to *equippe* his horses. This word proving unintelligible to all whom he consulted, at last a Messenger was sent to London to the Court to learne the meaninge thereof of the Writer of the Letter."

Notes.

It seems to have been thought an affected word. John Davies of Hereford writes

> " And though I grieve, yet cannot choose but smile
> To see some modern Poets seed my soile
> With mighty words that yeald a monstrous crop,
> Which they do spur-gall in a false-gallop.
> *Embellish, Blandishment,* and *Equipage,*
> Such Furies flie from their Muse' holy rage.
> And if perchance one hit on *Surquedry,*
> O he writes rarely in sweet Poesy!
> But, he that (*point-blank*) hits *Enveloped,*
> Hee, (Lord receave his Soule) strikes Poetry dead."
> Papers Complaint 113—122, in his Scourge of Folly, p. 233.

He adds in a marginal note " These words are good: but ill us'd: in overmuch vse savouring of witlesse affectation."

P. 62, l. 1—3. These lines are obscure, et " Davus sum non Œdipus." May it be that the two former refer to himself; "*eies*" meaning "images" (as above " I cannot cunningly make an image to awake "), my imaginations are broken, imperfect, hazy (" light blearing "), my pen cannot " turn them to shape " as the true " poet's pen " does—while such as I have just spoken of, and whom I am now about to enumerate, " devize magick-spels " that charm and delight by their perfect realization of the poet's imaginings."

P. 62, l. 4. *Collyn.*] On p. 28 there is the marginal note " He thinks it the duetie of every one that sailes to strike maine-top before that great and mighty Poet COLLYN." He referred to him also on p. 12. The first Eclogue of the Shepheard's Calendar is by Colin Clout, on which E. K. has this Glosse: " Colin Clout is a name not greatly used and yet have I seen a poesie of M. Skelton's under that title. But in deede the worde Colin is French, and used of the French Poet Marot (if hee be Worthie of the name of a poet) in a certaine Æglogue. Under which name this poet secretly shadoweth himselfe." See the Commendatory Poems in Todd's edition— to which add N. Breton's Melancholike Humours, p. 15, 16, ed. Grosart, pp. 69-72, ed. Brydges, Lee Priory. Return from Parnassus, i. 2, p. 211, and Sir J. Oldcastle, p. 194. Roxb. Club. ed.

> " O grief that Spensers gone !
> With whose life heavens a while enricht us more,
> That by his death wee might be ever pore."

Narcissus.

P. 62, l. 8. *Nourish.*] The verb is here used intransitively, as in Bacon's Essay, xix. 149, " For their merchants; they are *vena porta*, and if they flourish not, a kingdom may have good limbs, but will have empty veins, and *nourish* little." Dr. Abbott notes, "Here used intransitively, to gain flesh," Lat. " empty veins, and *a lean habit of body*." In the last line of this poem " *nourish* " is an active verb.

P. 62, l. 10. *Albion's glorie.*] " In That Faery Queene I meane *glory* in my generall intention, but in my particular I conceive the most excellent and glorious person of our soveraine *the Queene*, and her kingdom in *Faery Land*." Spenser's letter to Sir W. Raleigh prefixed to the F. Q. Barnabe Barnes in his *Parthenophil*, 1593, thus alludes to the same:

" Here Colin sittes beneath that oken tree
Eliza singing in his layes." Canzon 2, p. 106.

P. 62, l. 11. *Sidney's honor.*] " The Shepheard's Calendar—entitled to the noble and vertuous Gentleman, most worthie of all titles both of learning and chivalry, Maister Philip Sidney. To his Booke:

"Goe little Booke! thy selfe present,
As childe whose parent is unkent,
To him that is the President
Of Noblenesse and chevalree."

The first edition was in 1579, others in 1581, 1586, 1591. It was not till 1595 that Spenser published his Colin Clout, and with it Astrophel and the subsequent Elegies on Sir Philip Sidney.

P. 62, l. 12. *Stories.*] This refers to the F. Q., and the Eglogue two lines below to the Shepheard's Calendar, the fourth Eglogue in which is specially in praise of Q. Elizabeth. Drayton, " To the Reader of his Pastorals," says. " Spenser is the prime Pastoralist of England," p. 431, ed. Chalmer's Poets.

P 62, l. 16. *Deale we not with Rosamond.*] He refers here to Samuel Daniel, whose " Delia, contayning certayne Sonnets, with the Complaint of Rosamond," was printed three times in 1592, and twice in 1594. Does the word " deale " involve a punning allusion to *Delia?* Nash, Pierce Penilesse (1592), p. 40, " You shall finde there goes more exquisite paynes and purity of wit to the writing of one such rare poem as Rosamond, than to a hundred of your dunsticall sermons." Gabriel Harvey, in Pierce's Supercrogation (1593), p. 191, " In Kiffin, Warner, and Daniell, in an hundred such vulgar writers, many things are commendable, divers things notable, some things excellent." John Dickinson in his Shepheard's Complaint (c. 1594), p. 4, alludes to Rosamond:

> "Nec placuere minus viridi dignissima lauro
> Aurifluis fœcunda metris Sidnœia scripta,
> Et laudes Rosamunda tuœ."

Like our author, Richard Barnfield, at the beginning of his Prayse of Lady Pecunia, 1598, says:

> "I sing not of *Angellica* the faire,
> Nor of sweet *Rosamond* old *Clifford's* heire."

P. 62, l. 15.] In the Return from Parnassus, acted at St. John's, Cambridge, 1606, we find:

> "Sweet honey-dropping *Daniel* doth wage
> War with the proudest big *Italian*,
> That melts his heart in sugar'd sonetting;
> Only let him more sparingly make use
> Of others' wit, and use his own the more,
> That well may scorn base imitation." i. 2, p. 213, ed. 1773.

P. 62, l. 16. *Our sawe will coate.*] This implies high praise of Daniel's poem, for our author declares that if he were himself to write on that subject the world would disregard his work. To *coate* is to pass by, to pass the side of another, from *costoyer*, O. Fr. It is used by Shakspere, Hamlet, ii. 2, 230, " We *coted* them on the way, and hither they are coming." L. L. L. iv 3, 87, " Her amber hair for foul hath amber *coted*," i.e, hath so far passed amber as to make it seem foul. It is a term borrowed from sporting, both in buck hunting, for which see Return from Parnassus (Origin of Drama, iii. p. 238), and coursing. This latter is fully described in Drayton's Polyolbion, song xxiii. p. 353, ed. Chalmer's Poets:

> "When each man runs his horse, with fixed eyes and notes
> Which dog first turns the hare, which first the other *coats*."

There is a noun of the same meaning. Drayton, *ibid.* :

> "But when he cannot reach her
> This giving him a *coat*, about again doth fetch her."

From Nares's Glossary in v.

P. 62, l. 17. *Amintas.*] Thomas Watson, "a notable Poet," as Gabriel Harvey styles him in "Pierce's Supercrogation," p. 39, wrote "Amyntas" in 1585, in consequence of which his contemporaries applied that name to him. He died in 1592. Barnfield thus commemorates him, in 1596:

> "And thou my sweete *Amintas*, vertuous minde,
> Should I forget thy Learning or thy Love,
> Well might I be accounted but vnkinde,
> Whose pure affection I so oft did prove:
> Might my poore Plaints hard stones to Pitty move,
> His losse should be lamented of each creature,
> So great his Name, so gentle was his nature."
>
> The Shepheard's Content, xix. In Affectionate Shepheard, p. 42.

and again in the same poem:

> "By thee great *Collin* lost his libertie,
> By thee sweet *Astrophell* forewent his ioy;
> By thee *Amyntas* wept incessantly,
> By thee good *Rowland* liu'd in great annoy." *Ibid.* xxxiii. p. 47.

John Dickenson also, perhaps a little earlier, in "The Shepheard's Complaint," n. d., but about 1593 or 4, p. 4, ed. Grosart, 1878:

> "Vidit Amor, visos legit, lectosque probavit,
> Anglia quos de se libros musæque Britannæ
> Composnêre: Deo placuit mutatus Amintas
> Veste nitens propria, et Romana veste decorus."

A passage in Spenser's "Colin Clout," 432-443, published in 1595, may refer to him under the name *Amyntas*, though Todd understands it of Ferdinando, Earl of Derby, who is so called by T. Nash in Pierce Penilesse, p. 91. For full particulars of Thomas Watson see Arber's edition, in "English Reprints," with the account prefixed of his writings.

P. 62, l. 17. *Leander.*] Christopher Marlowe, who died in 1593. His works have been well edited by Dyce in 3 vols. Lond. 1850, with an excellent account of his Life and Writings. Our author was evidently much indebted to the study of his Hero and Leander, from which Shakspere quotes, "Who ever lov'd that lov'd not at first sight?" in As You Like It, iii. 5, 82.

P. 62, l. 18. *Deere sonnes of stately kings.*] True and worthy descendants of former great poets. King is often used for one pre-eminent. Two Gent. of Verona, iv. i. 37, of outlaws, "This fellow were a king for our wild faction," and so 67. Burns in Willie brew'd a peck o' maut, " Wha last beside his chair shall fa' Shall be the king amang us three."

P. 62, l. 21. *Adon.*] This shortened form is used by Shakspere in Venus and Adonis:

"Nay then, quoth *Adon*, you will fall again." 769.
"And yet, quoth she, behold two *Adons* dead." 1070.

and in the Passionate Pilgrim:

"A brook where *Adon* used to cool his spleen." 76.
"For *Adon's* sake a youngster proud and wilde." 120.

It stands here no doubt for the great Poet himself.

P. 62, l. 21. *Deafly masking.*] "Maskt" was used before, p. 57, for acting, so it may here indicate both his acting, and the skill with which he makes his characters move through his plays with appropriate sentiments, "rich conceited." Deafly is also written "deffly" and "deftly." "Deft-deff, neat, skilful, trim. A.-S. *dæfe, dæfte, gedefe*, fit, convenient; *gedafan, gedafnian*, to become, behove, befit; *gedæftan*, to do a thing in time, take the opportunity, to be fit, ready." Wedgwood in v.

P. 62, l. 25. *And had not loue herself intreated.*] This seems to refer to his poems Venus and Adonis, and Lucrece, and possibly others circulated in MS. according to the then practice, whereby he gained "baies," though if he had chosen subjects of a different character he would have been equally successful, "other nymphs would have sent him baies."

P. 63, l. 1. The first two stanzas present considerable difficulties, both as to the person alluded to, and in the terms by which he is indicated, which are so vague as to make identification a mere matter of conjecture.

P. 63, l. 1. *Purple.*] This is defined to be a colour produced by the union of blue and red, the red predominating. Or as given by Littré in his French Dictionary, under Pourpre, "Matière colorante d'un rouge foncé et éclatant. (2.) Par extension, rouge. (3.) Couleur d'un beau rouge foncé qui tire sur le violet. Adjectivement. Qui est de la couleur de la pourpre." Thus, like the Latin *purpureus,* it includes divers shades of colour, violet, rose-red, other shades of red, and is diversly applied. Spenser uses it of the "hues of the rich unfolding morn," "soone as the

2 X

morrowe fayre with *purple* beames," F. Q. ii. 3, 1, to which his contemporary, Barnabe Barnes, applies the epithet *scarlette*:

"Before bright Titan rais'de his teame,
Or lonely morne with *rosie* cheeke
With *scarlette* did'e the easterne streame."
Parthenophil and Parthenophe, Ode 16, p. 130, ed. Grosart.

In the present passage, therefore, it probably means some shade of red, and would be applicable to the robes of peers, judges, and perhaps to the law as a profession. *Purpura* was thus used in Latin, as in the Consolatio ad Liviam:

"Jura silent, mutæque tacent sine vindice leges,
Adspicitur toto *purpura* nulla foro." 185, 6.

and in England, as in an epigram on the sudden death of a Law Knight (perhaps Sir John Davies):

"How durst thou sawcie death intrapp
This *purple* gowne, this golden capp?"
Farmer, MS. Chetham Society, vol. xc. 1873, p. 193.

P. 63, l. 1. *Roabes.*] These may be the robes of the Knights of the Garter. Ashmole, in his History of that Order, p. 209, says " The *Colour* of these *Mantles* is appointed by the Statutes to be *Blue;* and of this coloured Cloth was the first *Robe* made for the *Founder*, by which, as by the ground-work of the Royal *Garter* it is not unlike, he alluded (in this no less than that) to the Colour of the *Field* in the *French* Arms, which a few years before he had assumed in *Quarter* with those of his kingdom of *England*." This continued to be the colour till the reign of Philip and Mary, as Ashmole proves by references. "But in Queen *Elizabeth's* reign (upon what ground is no where mentioned) the Colour of Foreign *Princes' Mantles* was changed from *Blue* to *Purple*" (for proof divers instances are cited). "Thus the *Purple* Colour came in, and continued till about the 12th year of King *Charles* the First, when that *Soveraign* (having determined to restore the Colour of the *Mantle* to the primitive Institution, namely, a rich *Celestial Blue*) gave directions to *Mr. Peter Richaut*, Merchant (afterwards knighted by him), to furnish himself with a parcel of Velvets of that Colour from *Genoa* . . . . for new Robes against the following *St. George's* day," p. 210.

Notes.

P. 63, l. 1. *Distaind.*] The verb *distain* (Old French, desteindre) is (1) to take the colour out of a stuff, to sully, to dishonour, which force it has in Shakspere; but (2) it means to tinge with another colour, and is so used by Dryden (see Worcester's Dictionary), and, I think, in the present line.

P. 63, l. 2. *Amid'st the center of this clime.*] Geographically this would be somewhere about Leicester, according to Shakspere in Richard III.:

> *Richmond.* "This foul swine
> Lies now even in the center of this isle,
> Near to the town of Leicester, as we learne." v. 2, 10-12.

and to Sir John Beaumont, in his Bosworth Field:

> "Now strength no longer Fortune can withstand,
> I perish in the center of my land." (Six lines from end of the Poem.)

There may, however, be a reference to the Midland Counties generally. But politically, socially, and as connected with literature, London would be the centre then as now. T. Nash, in Pierce Penilesse, implies this when he says of poets, "That they have cleansed our language from barbarisme, and made the vulgar sort here in *London* (which is the fountaine whose rivers flowe round about England) to aspire to a richer puritie of speech than is communicated with the comminaltie of anie nation under heaven," p. 41. And again he speaks of " our countrymen, that lyve out of the echo of the courte " (p. 92), as if that were the heart of the kingdom; and "center" is used for the soul or heart, see pp. 13, 19, and note at p. 235.

P. 63, l. 8. *Done.*] The auxiliary verb, *have*, is here omitted.

P. 63, l. 10. *Tilting under Frieries.*] A Friary is a Monastery or Convent of Friars, and after the suppression of the several Orders the name remained, when Theatres had taken the places of the buildings previously set apart for the Religious Life. At any rate this had happened with the Black Friars, where was one of the theatres of the company to which Shakspere belonged. Hence "tilting under Fricries" may refer to acting, as in plays there are opposing forces, a Richard and a Richmond in array one against the other, or may include writers for the stage, who bring about mock combats and spectacles, just as tilting is an imitation of the encounters in warfare.

After the above explanations of some of the more difficult phrases, a conjecture must be hazarded as to the person meant. He must be (1) "in purple robes distained;" (2) "one whose power floweth far;" (3) one of "a bewitching pen;" (4) of a "golden art;" (5) one that "differs much from men tilting under Frieries;" (6) one who is "amidst the center of this clime;" (7) one that "ought to have been the onely object and the star of our rime." Whoever then he was, he must have been a person of noble birth—not like actors, clothed for a few hours with the trappings of royalty and rank, yet all the while simply personating the great—and of high natural and acquired mental endowments. To this he must have added influence and power—and this perhaps gained by the practice of the law. There must have been some reason why he ought to have been the only object and star of the poet's rime, and some reason also why he could not be openly designated by any poetical title, as others were by *Collin, Rosamond, Amintas, Leander, Adon;* while he must be looked for "*amidst*" the center of this clime, not *in* or *at* merely but "*amidst*," as if one of a body or company such as the frequenters of a court would be. The poem having been entered (probably) in the Stationors' Register in 1593 and published in 1595, all the above requisites must be found concentrated in some personage about that time.

I. Altogether most of the conditions laid down in these two stanzas, if not all, are satisfied by Thomas Sackville, Lord Buckhurst, afterwards Earl of Dorset. His pen might well be called "bewitching," and "his art golden," from the excellence of the "Induction" which he prefixed to the Legend of Henry Stafford, Duke of Buckingham, in the Mirror for Magistrates, and of that Legend itself; as well as from his having written the first genuine English Tragedy, "Gorboduc," or, as it was afterwards entitled, "Ferrex and Porrex," of which Warton says "that the language has great purity and perspicuity, and is entirely free from tumid phraseology." Hist. of Eng. Poetry, sect. lvi. vol. iv. p. 186.

Further, as a writer of tragedy he differed much from those who followed "men tilting under Frieries," of whom Warton goes on to say "that when play-writing had become a trade, our poets found it their interest to captivate the multitude by the false sublime, and by those exaggerated imageries and pedantic metaphors, which are the chief blemishes of the scenes of Shakespeare, and which are at this day mistaken for his capital beauties by too many readers." Ibid. p. 186. From a line at the end of the next stanza, "*Hath alike the Muses staide*," applied to Sylvester, we see that the person here alluded to had given up writing poetry, which was the case with Sackville; whose "Induction" and "Legend" were first published in the second edition of the Myrrour for Magistrates in 1563; and his Tragedy of Gorboduc (exhibited in the Hall of the Inner Temple in 1561) was printed in 1565, and again in 1571. Meanwhile, his "eminent accomplishments and abilities having acquired the confidence and esteem of Queen Elizabeth, the poet was soon lost in the statesman, and negotiations and embassies extinguished the milder ambitions of the ingenuous Muse." "Nor is it foreign to our purpose to remark that his original elegance and brilliancy of mind sometimes broke forth in the exercise of his more formal political functions." He was frequently disgusted at the pedantry and official barbarity of style with which the public letters and instruments were usually framed, and Naunton relates that "his secretarie had difficulty to please him, he was so *facete* and choice in his style." Even in the decisions and pleadings of the Star Chamber, that rigid tribunal, which was never esteemed the school of rhetoric, he practised and encouraged an unaccustomed strain of eloquent and graceful oratory, on which account, says Lloyd, "so flowing was his invention, that he was called the Star Chamber bell." Warton, iv. 34, 35. He was made a peer by the title of Lord Buckhurst in 1567, a Knight of the Garter in 1589, and succeeded Sir Christopher Hatton in the Chancellorship of the University of Oxford in 1591, when the Queen condescended to solicit the University in his favour, and in opposition to his competitor the Earl of Essex.

Now if Thomas Edwards were an Oxford man, as is not improbable, he might fairly say that such a Chancellor "Should have bene of our rime The onely object and the star;" and if he were at this time a resident in the University he might use such a phrase as "*I haue heard saie doth remaine* Amidst the center of this clime, One whose power floweth far, Eke in purple roabes distain'd;" this great personage being a Knight of the Garter, a Lord of the Privy Council, a Commissioner for divers purposes, and Magn. Pincerna Angliæ, high in the favour of the Queen, and destined shortly to succeed Lord Burleigh as Lord High Treasurer of England. Yet be it said to the credit of Thomas Edwards that he "would have honored him with baies," not for all these high distinctions, but for his skill as a poet, of "bewitching pen," and "golden art," "who could (if he would) have done the Muses objects" to the world.

If it be asked why he did not name him directly, or by some nom de plume, I can only suggest that the poet's modesty and sense of respect would not allow him to take any liberty with one so high in rank and station, and especially with the chief officer of his own University, if indeed Edwards were an Oxford man. The others whom he does name are poets, men of his own station and pursuits, with whom he considered himself to be on equal terms socially, though acknowledging their superiority to himself as votaries of the Muses. "Poets that divinely dreampt, Telling wonders visedly, My slow Muse have quite benempt;" and afterwards, "Yourselves know your lines have warrant, I will talk of *Robin Hood.*"

If the phrase "*Eke in purple roabes distain'd*" limits the competitors to those who were Knights of the Garter, no one remains but the Earl of Essex, as no other members of that order in the reign of Elizabeth have any pretensions to literary distinction.

In some, but only in a few respects, viz. as a Knight of the Garter, a man of power at Court, and of general ability, these two stanzas may refer to the Earl of Essex, allowance being made for the flattering language then customary. Warton, in his History of English Poetry, section lviii. writes, "Coxeter says that he had seen one of Ovid's Epistles translated by Robert Earl of Essex. This I have never seen; and, if it could be recovered, I trust it would be valued as a curiosity. A few of his sonnets are in the Ashmolean Museum, which have no marks of poetic genius. He is a vigorous and elegant writer of prose. But if Essex was no poet, few noblemen of his age were more courted by poets. From Spenser to the lowest rhymer he was the subject of numerous sonnets or popular ballads. I will not except Sydney. I could produce evidence to prove that he scarce ever went out of England, or even left London, on the most frivolous enterprise, without a pastoral in his praise, or a panegyric in metre, which were sold and sung in the streets. Having interested himself in the fashionable poetry of the times, he was placed high in the ideal Arcadia now just established; and among other instances which might be brought, on his return from Portugal in 1589 he was complimented with a poem, called 'An Egloge gratulatorie entituled to the right honourable and

Notes. 339

renowned shepherd of Albion's Arcadie, Robert Earl of Essex, and for his returne lately into England.' This is a light in which Lord Essex is seldom viewed. I know not if the Queen's fatal partiality, or his own inherent attractions, his love of literature, his heroism, integrity, and generosity, qualities which abundantly overbalance his presumption, his vanity and impetuosity, had the greater share in dictating these praises. If adulation were anywhere justifiable, it must be when paid to the man who endeavoured to save Spenser from starving in the streets of Dublin, and who buried him in Westminster Abbey with becoming solemnity. Spenser was persecuted by Burleigh because he was patronised by Essex." (iv. 248, ed. 1824.) The few poems of this unfortunate nobleman that have come down to us have been printed by Dr. Grosart in The Fuller's Worthies Library, Miscellanies, vol. iv. and some of them by Archdeacon Hannah in his Courtly Poets, 1875. But they would hardly justify such terms of praise as Edwards bestows on the unnamed personage for a "bewitching pen," "golden art," and general poetic ability. So the claim of Essex must be dismissed.

The conjecture that Sackville, Lord Buckhurst, was alluded to by Edwards in these two stanzas may receive some confirmation from the terms in which he is spoken of by Richard Niccols in his Notice "To the Reader" in the 1610 edition of the "Mirour for Magistrates" (reprinted by Hazlewood in his Introduction, p. xxx), where on A. 4, verso, he speaks of "that *golden* Preface called M. Sackuil's Induction;" and again in a subsequent Notice "To the Reader," at p. 253 (reprinted by Hazlewood, vol. ii. p. 11), he writes, "I purpose only to follow the intended scope of that most honorable personage, who, by how much he did surpass the rest in the eminence of his noble condition, by so much he hath exceeded them all in the excellencie of his heroicall stile, which with a golden pen he hath limned out to posteritie in that worthy object of his minde the Tragedie of the Duke of Buckingham, and in his preface then intituled Master Sackuil's Induction. This worthie President of learning, intending to perfect all this storie himselfe from the Conquest, being called to a more serious expense of his time in the great State-affairs of his most royall Ladie and Soueraigne, left the dispose thereof to M. Baldwine, M. Ferrers, and others." This passage is almost a prose rendering of Edwards's lines. Another early testimony to his poetic ability is in

340   *Narcissus.*

Cooper's Muses Library, 1738, supposed to be the work of Oldys: "The Induction by Mr. Sackville is indeed a Master-Piece; and if the whole could have been completed with the same Spirit, it wou'd have been an Honour to the Nation at this Day; nor could have sunk under the Ruins of Time. But the *Courtier* put an end to the *Poet*, and he has left just enough to eclipse all the Writers that succeeded Him in the same Task; and makes us wish that his Preferment had been at least a little longer delay'd. The Reader, in this Performance, will see that *Allegory* was brought to great Perfection before *Spencer* appear'd, and that, if Mr. Sackville did not surpass him, 'twas because he had the Disadvantage of Writing first. Agreeable to what *Tasso* exclaim'd on seeing *Guarini's Pastor-Fido*, '*If he had not seen my* Aminta *He had not excell'd it!*'" Mr. Hazlewood speaks of "his unrivalled genius," Intro. p. xl. and prints at p. xiv. a letter from Sir Egerton Brydges, who attributes to him "high fancy, vigorous talents, conscious grandeur of genius." While after entering into public life "his vigorous and inspired hand might no longer possess either the impulse, or the skill, or the strength, to strike the lyre, which formerly returned to his touch alternate strains of sublime morality and glowing description." See also his remarks in his edition of Collins's Peerage, vol. ii. 119-145. The Works of Thomas Sackville, Lord Buckhurst, were printed at the Chiswick Press by C. Whittingham for J. Russell Smith in his "Library of Old Authors," 1859, 12mo. under the editorial care of his descendant, the Hon. and Rev. Reginald W. Sackville-West, M.A. who has since succeeded to the Earldom of De La Warr.

II. If "*purple roabes*" may mean a Nobleman's robes, it gives some colour to the conjecture of Professor Dowden, that Vere, Earl of Oxford, may have been intended, "as his reputation stood high as a Poet, and Patron of Poets." Puttenham names him first among the crew of courtly makers: his poems are almost all amorous (? not *tilting under Frieries*). Spenser has a Sonnet to him, in which he speaks of "the love that thou didst bear To th' Heliconian Nymphs, and they to thee." His "power flowed far," as he was Lord High Chamberlain of England. He had contributed to the Paradyse of Dainty Devyses, signing E. O. or E. Ox., and to the Phœnix Nest in 1593. One of his Poems is a Vision of a Fair Maid ("clad all in coulor of a Nun and coverèd with a Vaylle") who complains of love, and gets Echo answers of " Vere." Another (? referred to by Edwards) represents himself as " *wearing black and tawny* " and " *no bays*, because he is a rejected lover, and as leading an *ankers life*." He was said (by Coxeter) to have translated Ovid, which would connect him with Narcissus, but no one has ever seen his Ovid. He died in 1604. (From a letter addressed to Mr. Furnivall by Professor Dowden.)

Mr. Arber writes: " I do not know who was meant by Edwards. I do not know whether Lord Henry Howard wrote verse. He was a voluminous writer of unprinted books. Evidently the person intended is such a nobleman, who did not print." (Letter to Mr. Furnivall.)

The Rev. Richard Hooper writes: " There is a hint, ' *amidst the center of this clime*,' which points to Warwickshire. Query whether Kenilworth and the younger Robert Dudley, who had the reputation of being one of the finest gentlemen in England, and wrote several works, before and after he left England. He appears to me a very probable person for Edwards to allude to." (From a letter to myself.)

Mr. Furnivall writes: " To me the verses point to a man of high rank, or high birth, who was an orator or writer. I expect that ' *men* ' should be read without the , that follows it, and ' *tilting* ' is like Warner's ' *tilt*,' show in writing. Can it be Essex? or Raleigh? But none of us can suggest a man for this center hero." (From letters addressed to myself and Mr. Gibbs.)

Our lamented friend the late Rev. H. O. Coxe, Bodleian Librarian, thought that from the mention of " purple roabes " some K.G., perhaps Essex, was meant; but with his keen insight could not see how the particulars in the following stanza could justly be understood as relating to him.

III. On the hypothesis that " *purple roabes distained* " must be interpreted of the robes of Knights of the Garter, or Noblemen, Sackville, Essex, and others, have been contemplated as likely to be the poet intended by Edwards, and the verdict has been given in favour of Sackville, as fulfilling most completely the several conditions specified. But if " *purple roabes* " may be applied to a member of the Legal Profession, then Francis Bacon may have strong claims for consideration. He had a " *bewitching pen* " and " *golden art* "—he lived " *amidst the center of this clime* "—as a speaker in the Law Courts and in Parliament he might be said to differ much from

2 Y

men speaking on the stage, that is "*tilting under Frieries.*" A question might be raised as to his being one "*whose power floweth far.*" But first his birth, of which Ben Jonson " on Lord Bacon's Birthday," in his Underwoods, lxx. writes:

> " England's high Chancellor: the destin'd heir
> In his soft cradle of his father's Chair;"

and then his relationship to the Cecils made him a prominent and influential man at his outset in public life; and secondly, he had attached himself to, and was very closely connected with, the Earl of Essex, who since 1589 had become the Queen's favourite. Thus he may have been thought to exercise great power through this political union; and must have been felt to be the rising man in the world of politics, law, literature, and philosophy on his own merits, as well as from being the mouthpiece of Essex. Again it may be asked why does not the poet name him? To which there is this reply: that at the time (1593) he was in temporary disgrace, and forbidden the Court, owing to his speech in the House of Commons opposing a grant of three subsidies to the Queen. Thus it might have been impolitic to introduce his name, as being detrimental both to him, and also to the poet's hopes of patronage. Hence a special force in the words, "*I have heard say doth remaine,*" as a star of that magnitude would be sure to reappear more brightly. Why again should he have been "*the only object and star of this rime*"? If Edwards were a Cambridge man (as is not impossible) he might wish to honour the greatest living genius of his University. Further, as the Poems are dedicated to Master Thomas Argall, who was, it seems, a lawyer, there may thus have been something to bring the poet and the most rising barrister of the day together, in however humble a way, in the office, or chambers, of Master Argall, and in the ordinary way of legal business. Then could he "*have done the Muses objects to us*"? Who can doubt it? He had in 1592 composed a device for the Earl of Essex on the Queen's day, entitled a "Conference of Pleasure," (edited by James Spedding in 1870,) which though not in verse is highly poetical in conception and language. Besides he had, it seems, written and circulated in MS. some poems, for there is a letter of Bacon to Mr. Davies, dated Gray's Inn, 28th March, 1603, which ends with the remarkable words, " So desiring you to be good to *concealed poets*, I continue your assured friend, Fr. Bacon." Now

Davies himself was a poet, and appears to have been aware of some writings of his friend's to which his name for prudential reasons was not attached. So Thomas Edwards may have been in the secret also, perhaps having copied the poems for the press, or having been in some way professionally engaged. In describing himself Bacon says he possessed especially the faculty of "*recognising similarities.*" And on this Dr. Abbott remarks, " It is curiously characteristic of Bacon that he lays more stress upon *that most important object, the recognition of similarities,*" than upon the *observation of subtile shades of difference.* Yet the latter is preeminently the philosopher's faculty, while the former is the poet's. But Bacon was a poet, the Poet of Science. His eye like the poet's—

" In a fine frenzy rolling
Doth glance from heaven to earth, from earth to heaven."

Catching at similarities and analogies invisible to uninspired eyes, giving them names and shapes, investing them with substantial reality, and mapping out the whole realm of knowledge in ordered beauty." Bacon's Essays, 1876, Introduction, p. xxiii. It is not necessary, however, that Bacon should have written poetry in order to make the words of our author applicable to him. It is enough that he had, and was known to have, the power. In fact the words almost imply that he had not been strictly a votary of the Muses. They state that "his bewitching pen" and "golden art" *could* have presented the Muses' objects to the world. Ben Jonson says of his eloquence, "There happened in my time one noble speaker who was full of gravity in his speaking; his language where he could spare or pass by a jest was nobly censorious. No man ever spake more neatly, more pressly, more weightily, or suffered less emptiness, less idleness in what he uttered; no member of his speech but consisted of his own graces. His hearers could not cough or look aside from him without loss; he commanded when he spoke, and had his judges angry and pleased at his devotion. No man had their affections more in his power; the fear of every man that heard him was lest he should make an end." Discoveries, "*Dominus Verulamius.*" And in the next article, "*Scriptorum Catalogus,*" after many wits have been commended, he adds, "But his learned and able (though unfortunate) successor is he who hath filled up all numbers, and performed that in our tongue, which may be compared or preferred either to insolent Greece or haughty Rome. In short, within his view and about his times were all the wits born that could honour a language or help study."

I am indebted to Dr. Grosart for the hint that Bacon was intended, and I have endeavoured by the above arguments to substantiate his conjecture. But it must be taken as a conjecture only—and as one out of many.

IV. To descend from men of high birth and rank, Nobles and Knights of the Garter, to men of poetic celebrity only, there are three conjectures to be recorded which suggest respectively Drayton, Southwell, and Shakspere.

Professor Henry Morley says, " I take the reference on the top of p. 63 to be to Michael Drayton, who was born in Warwickshire, '*amidst the center of this clime,*' and among whose verses are some of the most delightful of the fairy fancies upon which there was a run for a little time, Shakspere's Queen Mab being a contribution to the stock. I think there was no publication of *Nymphidia* so early as 1595, but it may have been written early, and the allusion seems to be to that with a misprint of *Frieries* for *Faeries*. There is Pigwiggen mounted on an earwig with his knightly armour playfully devised from small things of the world, and then his tilting with Oberon:

> 'Their shields were into pieces cleft,
> Their helmets from their heads were reft,
> And to defend them nothing left,
> These Champions would not budge yet.'

Allusion to such writing might well take the form of a suggestion that Drayton '*differs much from Men*' when he paints deeds of arms under the guise of a tilt of faeries. I am away from books, and can make no references in aid of the suggestion." (Letter to Mr. Furnivall.)

Mr. P. A. Daniel writes: " I am not good at recognizing men under the disguises which were so fashionable with the poetlings of the sixteenth century. I don't in fact recognize Shakspere under the name of *Adon*, though you appear—no doubt on good grounds—to have settled that point * * * Qy. would Southwell fit this '*center man*.' The Jesuit in the livery of the scarlet whore ('*in purple robes*') confined from 1592 to 1595 in the Tower of London (? '*the center of this clime*'), '*tilting under Frieries,*' *i.e.* poetising under the influence of his order. Poor

Notes. 345

Southwell was hanged 21 Feb. 1595. Ben Jonson so esteemed his work that he is reported by Drummond to have said that 'so he had written that piece of his, *The Burning Babe*, he would have been content to destroy many of his, *i. e.* his own.' It's a long time since I read Southwell, but the impression I retain of him is, that he ranks high among the minor poets of his age." (From letter to Mr. Furnivall.)

My friend Archdeacon Hannah, whose editions of Raleigh, Wotton, and King are so scholarlike, regretted that "graver pursuits had withdrawn him so long from his earlier studies among Elizabethan poets, that he was unable to solve the question proposed, and could only venture a suggestion that it was one of the greater writers of the Elizabethan period who had withdrawn from literature."

Lastly, Dr. B. Nicholson is of opinion that these two stanzas must be connected with the preceding one in which *Adon*, that is Shakspere, is described. "I cannot doubt but that the three stanzas from ' Adon ' to ' with baies ' refer to him. My reasons are: 1. No one else wrote any thing of note about Adonis till he did. His poem was published in 1593. 2. The poem is distinctly dealing with living English Poets, both before and after these stanzas. 3. He is in London, '*the center of this clime.*' 4. To me he alludes to his station as a player and dramatic author (a) by allusion to his social state thereby lowered, '*Eke in purple roabes distained,*' and same stanza, l. 5, ' *Should have been of our rime The only object and the star.*' (b) '*Although he differs much from men,*' *i. e.* from men of repute, honourable men like Spencer, &c. (c) For I am inclined to read ' *men ;* ' not ' *men,*' *Tilting under Frieries*, '*Yet his golden art might woo us, To have honored him with baies.*' I can give no sense to '*Frieries,*' unless he mean Black-friars (Theatre), and this interpretation is supported by ' *Yet might have honored.*' This is written very hurriedly, close to bed time, but I think I have culled all the points, and don't think I could put them more clearly, though I could in better language. See as corroboration of my reading of '*the center of this clime,*' the last line, ' *As Thames may nourish as did Po,*' and for my interpretation of ' *Eke in purple roabes distained* ' (though like ' center ' they do not want corroboration), '*And I not much unlike the Romane actors That girt in Prætextati seamed robes,*' p. 57, last stanza. As to the punctuation, I suggest the punctuation of the original is bad, cf. p. 58, st. 1, l. 5, ' men.'

where clearly there ought to be none, or at most a comma." (From letter to Mr. Furnivall.)

There is one other name to be suggested, that of Fulke Greville, afterwards Lord Brooke, the friend of Sir Philip Sidney. In " Cephalus and Procris," p. 12, as well as in this " Envoy " to " Narcissus," Edwards has intimated his admiration of that illustrious Knight and writer, and may thus have wished to compliment his friend and biographer; but in other respects Greville does not seem to satisfy the required conditions, which Sackville and Bacon appear to do more completely than any others.

P. 63, l. 13. *He that gan, &c.*] That is Joshua Sylvester, who was for many years engaged in translating the works of Du Bartas. In 1591 he published The Battail of Yvry. In 1592 The Triumph of Faith, and some portions of the Divine Weekes, viz. The Sacrifice of Isaac (afterwards entitled The Fathers, Part of the 2nd Part of the Third Day of the ii Week), and The Shipwracke of Jonas (a portion of The Schisme, the Third Booke of the Fourth Day of the ii Week). In 1593 " There came out a Collection of such pieces as had been so far translated, each with separate Titles." Hazlitt. No perfect copy of this is known, but it must have included the two pieces mentioned by J. Edwards, which he calls " The World's Wracke," and " Babel," for these were the first parts that were translated, as Sylvester records in two Dedications to Mr. Anthonie Bacon, prefixed to the Second Week:

> " Bound by thy Bounty, and mine own Desire,
> To tender still new Tribute of my Zeal
> To Thee, whose favour did the first repeal
> My *proto Bartas* from Self-doomed Fire.
> Having new tuned to du Bartas Lyre
> These tragic murmurs of his Furies fell,
> To whom but thee should I present the same? "

In the second he says:

> " Thy friendly censure of my first *Essay*
> (*Du Bartas Furies*, and his *Babylon*),
> My faint Endevours hath so cheered on
> That both *His Weeks* are also *Ours* to-day."

" *The Furies*," previously translated by King James VI. contains " *The World's Wracke*," and " *Babylon* " is " *Babel.*" No addition to these

Notes.

seems to have been made till 1598, and Edwards here alludes to this cessation of Sylvester's labours in the lines, " *He that gan—Hath alike the Muses staide.*" But alike to whom ? To the poet alluded to in the two previous stanzas.

P. 63, l. 25. *Audacious.*] This is among the words which Puttenham in his Art of English Poesy, 1589, (reprinted by Haslewood 1811, and by Arber 1869,) states to have been recently introduced. (See Book iii. ch. iv. near the end.) It occurs, and very probably for the first time, at the end of the prose Introduction to Shore's Wife in the Mirror for Magistrates, ed. 1587, " But since without blushing I have so long been a talkative Wench (whose words a world hath delighted in), I will now goe on boldly with my *audacious* manner." Although Puttenham disallowed it, yet it has maintained its ground, perhaps from Shakspere's use of it. See Trench, English Past and Present, Lect. ii. p. 50. It is in this place used adverbially, as in Lear, iv. 6, 3, " Horrible steep," and in Tw. N. iii. 4, 196, " swear horrible." " In the West of England 'terrible' is still used in this adverbial sense." Abbott, Shakspere Gram. 2. " Cruel," " dreadful," are also used in this way, and so is " audacious " at the present day. This passage presents, probably, the earliest instance of its adverbial use.

P. 63, l. 26. *Devises are of Currant.*] In Polimanteia, 1595, England tells the Universities and Inns of Court, " take the course to canonize your owne writers, that not every bald ballader to the prejudice of art may passe *currant* with a poet's name, but they onely may bee reputed Hon. by that tearme that shall live privileged under your pennes." Brit. Bibliogr. i. 281. Dickinson's Arisbas, " But take them as he wrote them, wherein if all be not *currant*, impute it to his thoughts which were not clearde," p. 67. Perhaps Edwards had in mind the words of Puttenham, iii. 4, p. 157, Arber: " Our maker therfore at these dayes shall not follow *Piers plowman* nor *Gower* nor *Lydgate* nor yet *Chaucer*, for their language is now out of vse with vs: neither shall he take the termes of Northern-men, such as they vse in dayly talke, whether they be noble men or gentlemen, or of their best clarkes all is a matter: nor in effect any speach vsed beyond the river of Trent, though no man can deny but that theirs is the purer English Saxon at this day, yet 'tis not so Courtly nor so *currant* as our Southerne English is, no more is the far Westerne mans Speach." The metaphor is taken from the circulation of money, as Bishop Aylmer, speaking against covetous men, says, "Your gold and your angels are called *current* not *sleepant.*" Strype's Life, 180, ed. Oxon. 1821.

P. 63, l. 27. *Everie stampe is not allowed.*] This shows that the reference is to coin, or rather to tokens in lieu of coins. Erasmus calls them " Plumbeos Angliæ" in his Adagia, p. 130, so that they must have been in use at the latter end of Hen. VII. or in first three years of Hen. VIII. when Erasmus was in England." Ruding, Annals of Coinage, ii. 69, 70. In 1574 the use of private tokens for money had grown to great excess. " They were *stamped* by inferior tradesmen, and made of Lead, Tin, Latten, and even Leather. Hence a proclamation was drawn up to make *current* copper pledges for farthings and halfpence, for which Her Majesty had received divers *devices.* It is supposed that this never proceeded further than sinking a die and striking off some pieces as patterns." See Ruding, pp. 62–64. From p. 175, anno 1591, " It would seem that the Plumbei Angliæ were still circulated." See again temp. James I. pp. 209, 210.

P. 64, l. 3. *I will talk of Robin Hood.*] This must be on the principles laid down by Horace in his Art of Poetry,

"Publica materies privati juris erit;" (131), and

"Sumite materiam vestris qui scribitis æquam
Viribus." Ibid 38.

The words also seem to imply some consciousness on Edwards's part of failure in dealing with the classical subjects he had chosen. " Robin Hood" had become a popular phrase: Skelton, ' Why come ye not to Courte?'

' He sayth, how saye ye my Lordes?
Is not my reason good?
Good evyn, good *Robyn Hood.*' " 194.

"This," Ritson observes, "had become a proverbial expression." Dyce's note. In G. Gascoigne's " Dulce Bellum Inexpertis," 152; " Yea! *Robyn Hood!* our foes came downe apace." i. p. 183, ed. Hazlitt. In Love Poems, printed by the Ballad Society, 1874, p. 7 :

" O Love whose power and mighte, None ever yet withstoode,
Thou makest me to write—Come, turne about, *Robbin Hoode.*"

N. Breton, Pasquils Fooles-Cappe, p. 20, col. 2, l. 50 :

" Hee that doth love to talke of *Robin Hoode*
Yet never drew an arrow in his Bowe."

The meaning is that these greater poets "*have warrant,*" and will be read on account of their own reputation as authors, whatever they may choose to write about—while he himself will be read for the sake of the popular hero alone, being thought nothing of personally. How popular that hero then was may be estimated by the following remarks of Ritson (Robin Hood 1795), "That poems and stories on the subject of Robin Hood were extraordinarily popular and common before and during the sixteenth century is evident from the testimony of divers writers." p. lxxvii. "That some of these pieces, or others of like nature were great favourites with the common people in the time of Queen Elizabeth, though not much esteemed, it would seem, by the refined critic, may be inferred from a passage in Webbes *Discourse of English Poetrie* printed in 1586." " If I lette passe the unaccountable rabble of ryming ballet-makers, and compylers of sencelesse sonets, I trust I shall with the best sort be excused. For though many such can frame an *alehouse-song* of five or sixe score verses, hobbling uppon some tune of a *northern jugge*, or ROBYN HOODE, &c. yet if these might be accounted poets (as it is sayde some of them make meanes to be promoted to the lawrell) surely we shall shortly have whole swarmes of poets." Ibid. lxxxii.—lxxxiv. Percy, Ritson, and Gutch have collected all the Ballads and Songs connected with Robin Hood—and John Keats has sung regretfully of him.

P. 64, l. 5. *Narcissus in another Sort.*] Did he intend a play? These phrases, "*in another sort*," "*in gaier clothes*," "*shall be pla'st*," seem to imply some work designed for the stage. Nothing further was ever written by Edwards so far as can be ascertained.

P. 64, l. 11. *Due honor and the Praise That longs to Poets.*] Mirror for Magistrates—England's Eliza:

"O how the wreath of Phœbus flowring bay,
The victors due desert, and learnings need,
Did flourish in her time without decay." p. 787, ed. 1610.

P. 64, l. 17. *As Thames may nourish as did Po.*] Poets are swans, for which Po is renowned:

"Nor Po, nor Tyburs Swans so much renowned." Spenser, Colin Clout, 412.

"A sweeter Swan than ever sung in Po."
Return from Parnassus, i. 2, p. 211 (of Spenser).

"Sidney, sweet Cignet, pride of Thamesis."
B. Barnes, Sonet in G. Harvey's Pierce's Supererogation.

To these lines may be appended a striking passage in John Dickenson's Arisbas (1594) where commenting on the worth of Poesie he writes, "But in *Albion* the wonder of Ilands louely *Thamesis*, fairest of the faire *Nereides* loues sea-borne Queene adoring, vaunts the glory of her maiden streames, happy harbour of so maney Swans, *Apollos* musicall birds, which warble wonders of worth, and chaunt pleasures choise in seuerall sounds of sweetnesse, pleasant, loftie, louely, whose matchlesse notes, the faire Nymph keeping tyme with the billowing of her Chrystall waues, carrying to the *Ocean* with her ebbe, doth there echo them to her astonisht sisters which assemble in those vast flouds by timely confluence. *Bœtis* grac'd with many bounties, *Po* and *Arno*, garnish'd with many pleasures, *Rhone* and *Araris*, enriched with many royalties, yet none of these may vaunt more heauens of happinesse then *Thamesis*, in harbouring such Swans, such sweetness." p. 79, ed. Grosart 1878. One of the final stanzas of Daniel's "Complaint of Rosamond" was probably in our Author's mind when finishing his own poem, and will therefore be an appropriate conclusion to our remarks:

> "Then when Confusion in her Course shall bring
> Sad Desolation on the Times to come:
> When mirthless *Thames* shall have no Swan to sing,
> All Musick silent, and the Muses dumb;
> And yet even then it must be known to some,
>   That once they flourish'd, tho' not cherish'd so.
>   And *Thames* had Swans as well as ever *Po*.
> But here an End."

FINIS.

INDEX

TO

CEPHALUS AND PROCRIS AND NARCISSUS.

[*Proper Names, and some words so printed in the Text, are in Italics.*]

A (-he) 23
Abhorre 49
Ahjectes 30
Aboune 40
Abownes 48
Abydos 44
Accent 29
Acheron 20, 29
Actor 29
Actors 32, 57
Adamantine 4
Adon 62
Adonis 42, 43
Adultus 51
Aduantage 16
Æsopian 20
Æthiopian 12
Affection 28
Afoote 31, 52
Afrighting 44
Aie me 14, 22, 26, 29, 32, 34, 38, 61
A good 29
Alacke 43, 53, 56
Alarme 44
Albion 28, 64
Albions 62, 63
Allowde 29
Allude 38
Alluded 23
Allusions 50
Amaine 6, 9, 13, 30, 34, 47, 53, 60
Amazed, 40
Amber-coloured 12
Ambitious 55
Ambrosia 5
Amintas 4, 62
Amoretta 25
Amorons 33, 42
Amorously 23, 32, 62
Angellike 12
Angels 11

Anger 11, 28
Anguish 57
Annoy 61
Anon 14, 59
Anone 41, 59
Aoris 14
Apes 11, 12
Apollo 9, 12
Appetite 60
Apples 52
Appointed 59
Approue 28, 29, 38, 40
Arcadia 28
Arcadian 12, 13, 56
Argall 3
Arguments 58
Arte 3, 34, 50
Artists 50
Ascraes 58
Aslackt 61
As now 18
Assault 58
Assent 56
Atlas 7
Attent 33
Attire 48
Attractiue 49
Audacious 63
Aulter 12
Aurora 6, 7, 9, 10, 11, 12, 14, 15, 17, 27, 29, 32, 33, 34, 59
Antenticke 21
Author 29, 43
Authoritie 49
Azured 49, 55

Babels 63
Backt 11
Badge 11
Baies 62, 63, 64
Baites 42

Balefull 14
Bandes 16
Banditos 8
Bane 48, 49
Banquet 5, 38
Barbarisme 3
Bare-foot 28
Base 46
Bastardie 56
Bastardy 4
Bayes 4
Bearded 56
Beat backe 23, 24
Beckens 54
Beckning 52
Beguiled 32
Benempt 61
Bent 44, 56
Benum 52
Bereane 6
Bereauen 38
Beset 49
Betooke 50
Betrapt 11
Bewitching 61, 63
Bewray 20, 25
Bid 11
Billowes 16
Blasted 53
Blearing 62
Bleeding-ripe 15
Blinde 51
Blisseful 45
Blith 59
Blood-dronken 27
Bloome 53
Blush 54
Boare 12, 13, 15
Boare (verb) 28
Bod 10, 11
Bode 4

Index.

Bones 19
Bonnie 49
Booke 41
Boord 25, 54
Boorded 23
Bosworth 51
Bottomlesse 18
Bowre 49
Brain-sick 47
Braine-sick 26
Branches 43
Brauely 59
Breste-plate 28
Bride 55
Bright-seeming 49
Brinke 49
Broathes 31
Brooke 22, 55
Burne 5
Buskin 5, 43
Bussome 12
Buzze 30

Cabin 28
Cage 45
Canapie 6, 57
Candle 60
Care-swallowing 39
Cast 41
Catalogues 63
Cane 37, 45
Ceder 22
Center 19, 63
Cephalian 27
Cephalus 10, 12, 14, 15, 17, 18, 20, 21, 22, 23, 27, 30, 32
Cephisus 60
Chaos 19, 50
Chaps 15
Charyat 7
Chase 7, 12, 14
Chaste (verb) 15
Chat 17
Chaunt 48, 59
Chaunteclcere 20
Checke 7
Checkt 11
Cheere 30, 41
Chim'bde 11
Chopping 51

Chorus 31, 58
Christall 55
Chrystaline 7
Circled 57
Clad 32
Clapt 59
Clime 27, 63
Cloakt 42
Cloistred 25, 56
Closet 54
Cloudes 29
Clownes 25
Clymate 5, 34
Coape 7
Coats 42, 62
Coates 12
Cock 44
Cocytus 29
Coie 46 48
Coine 51 64
Colchos 9
Colde 49
Collyn 62
Comfort 44
Commander 42
Commets 15
Compare 10, 42, 58
Compasse 21
Complaining 46, 47
Complaints 44
Complementes 4
Complot 23
Conceited 25, 62
Conceites 37, 38, 52
Condigne 28
Confines 63
Congealed 56
Consort 45
Constancies 61
Constancy 7
Content 33, 42, 44
Contentious 57
Contrarieties 13
Coole-spring 49
Cooling 43
Coronet 8
Corycyus 37
Couched 52
Counterfeite 18, 20
Course 23, 24

Coye 33, 40
Coyne-imbracing 51
Craggie 21
Creepes 33
Cristall 10
Crouched 52
Culling 12, 60
Cunningly 61
Cupid 14, 20, 29, 30
Cur 23
Curl'd 39
Curled 16
Currant 53, 63
Curtesie 52
Curuate 37
Cynicke 37
Cytherea 17
Cythereas 60
Cynthia 4, 6, 20, 34

Dalliance 38, 39, 56
Dame 37, 48
Damned 19
Danae 9
Dandled 53
Dandleth 22
Dandling 44
Dashing 55
Dasht 40
Deadfully 14
Deafely 22
Deafly 62
Deale 62
Debate 31
Debonary 21
Decaide 60
Deem 45
Deepe-searching 47
Defact 50
Degree 39
Delians 37
Derogated 55
Descant 46
Desolations 42
Despaire 10, 11
Despight 9, 17, 31
Denises 63
Denising 6
Denize 62
Denontly 25

Index.

Dingeth 7
Dion 8
Disastrous 48
Discord 37
Discourteous 20
Disdayning 47
Disease 7
Disgorg'd 44
Disgrace 11, 26, 30, 40, 50, 51, 59
Disgrast 37, 45
Disloyall 18
Disloyally 19
Disloyaltie 33
Dispaire 12, 31
Dispatch't 59
Disport 38, 48
Disquietnesse 13
Distaind 63
Distill 5
Distilling 27
Distract 50
Distressfull 25
Din'd 56
Dininely 61
Doating 58
Dogged 14
Done 11, 40, 51, 63
Done on 55
Dotage 58
Done-drawn 42
Dones 9
Dowdy 26
Down-soft 13
Downe-soft 59
Downe-ward 33
Downwards 55
Dreampt 61
Driades 25, 28
Drier 52
Droncke 13
Duetie 5, 8, 13, 28, 39
Duld 15, 30
Dum 46
Dumme 12
Dungeon 45

Eccho 10, 17
Eccho 28, 60
Eft-soone 29
Eglogue 62

Eke, 63, 64
Elizium 10, 44
Elues 21
Eluish 24
Emperours 5
Emprize 8
Enact 50
Enamoured 33, 48, 51
Encampes 29
Encountred 15
English 51
Entrals 15
Equipage 61
Err 27, 51
Erst 34
Esops 51
Essence 38, 49
Eternize 5
Eterniz'd 11, 56, 63
Eumenydes 30
Extasie 7
Extreames 30 43
Extremitie 58
Fairie 12, 21
Fairies 28
Faulkon 56
Fall (subs) 31, 34
Fame 33, 51
Famish 33
Fashioned 51
Fathers 51
Faunes 22
Fauorites 4
Fauonr 21
Fauourites 5, 11, 27
Fayerie 28
Featcs 9
Feathers 9
Fenne 30
Fennes 21
Fiends 11
Filius 60
Fire 49
Fits 21
Flat 57
Flax 20
Fleece, golden 9
Flic-like 13
Flintie 57
Flowers 8, 61

Fluuii 60 (side-note)
Footing 24
Forbare 52
Forbeare 13
Forbeares 7
Foredone 40
Forgone 51
Forlorne 6, 47, 56, 57
Forsaken 56
Fortunatly 51
Fortune 5, 56
Foulings 47
Fount 49
Fountalne 49
Freez'd 60
Frieries 63
Frontier 33
Frostie 61
Frozen 8, 22
Fruitles 59
Fume 8
Fuming 56
Furie 22, 44

Gag-tooth'd 15
Gaier 64
Gallants 21
Gallery 57
Garded 12
Gashly 15
Gay 49
Gemme 13
Gentlemen,
Ges 45
Ghoastes 28
Ghost 19, 44, 45
Ghosts 57
Giddie 20
Girted 17
Glee 34
Globe-encompasser 51
Globes 57
Glory 38
Gloses 3
Gnats 38
Goate-bleeding 4
Goatheardes 10
Godd 7
Goddesse 25
Godhood 56

Index.

Golden 4, 9, 10, 12
Golden vained 55
Gooddest 55
Greedie 24, 52
Groome 10
Groueling 51
Growen 46
Growne 13, 22
Guise 5
Guize 28

Ha (have) 27
Hal'd 53
Handes 8
Harbour 28
Harrould 9
Hartes-soule 3
Hatch 61
Hazard 5
Headlong 26
Headstrong 7
Heauens-gloryfier 27
Hector 27
Hegg 26
Heisell 11
Helicon, 4 10
Hell 52
Hell houndes 30
Hell quickeners 27
Hem (him) 13
Heraclian 30
Herbe 21
Hercules 51
Hermes 10
Hermitage 26
Hero 44
Heroes 43
Hesperides 9
Hew 42
High-court 59
Highes 26, 47
Hight 21, 27
Hits 32
Hoist 53
Hollow 24, 59
Holly 41
Homely 27
Homer 4, 27
Honor 4, 8
Horizon 8

Houle 39
Houer 38, 44
Hugges 12
Humilitie 8
Hunting 10
Hyems 29
Hymen 20, 29
Hymni 30

I (aye, yes) 45, 59
Iarre 50
Idalian 9
Image 61
Images 57
Imagies 10
Imbrace 43
Imbraced, 50 51
Imbracing 38
Immortall 16, 24, 27
Imperfection 49
Imping 46
Inamored 11, 16
Inamoured 47
Incestuous 57
Indiaes 55
Ingling 43
Inlarg'd 62
Intemperance 5
Intercession 57
Inur'd 3
Io 13, 41
Irus 4
Italian-nots 27
Itis 9

Jealousie 31, 33
Jems 43
Jewels 28, 48
Joue 6, 7, 9, 10, 11, 13, 17, 26, 38, 41, 44, 50, 55, 56, 59
Judge 45
Judiciall 4
Jupiter 4, 22

Keepe 22
Ken 47
Kenn'st 61
Kill 23
Kisse 41
Knight 12
Knightes 9, 10, 11

Knightes of *Rhodes* 10
Knightes of the *Garter* 10
Knightes of the *Sonne* 9
Kno 23
Knowen 46

Ladies 50
Læda 22
Lake 8
Lake 19
Lamie 21, 22
Lampe 14
Languish 46
Languishment 21
Lapwincke 9
Larke 59
Lasciuiously 44
Lawlesse 53
Lawne 4, 33, 43
Leaden 38
Leander 43, 44
Leander's 62
Leapt 60
Learne 33
Leasing 23
Leisure 38
Liceuse 44
Licurgus 8
Life-obtaining 48
Lion 15
Liriope 60 (side-note)
Liuely 52
Liuia's 57
Lizard 15
Locke 39
Loose-borne 53
Loue-mates 44
Louer 56
Low 41
Luke-warme 12
Luld 40
Lure 42
Lute 25

Madrigals 14
Magick-spels 62
Maiden-head 19
Maiden-likenes 60
Maidens 7
Maine 51, 55

Index.

Mainly 10, 14
Majestie 5
Making-out 53
Map 43
Marchants 18
Margining 3
Marie 41
Mars-like 11
Martialist 29
Maskes 29
Masking 62
Mask't 57
Massacred 40
Massacres 27, 46
Master 3, 52
Mate 32
Matron 58
Meudes 43
Measure 41
Melancholy 26, 28, 38, 44
Melodiouslie 45
Mercenary 26
Mercury 4, 9
Meritorions 3
Mermaid 54
Merriment 23, 32, 44
Merrymentes 20, 38
Messenger 44, 47
Metamorphosis 7
Metra 25
Mickle 61
Middle earth 20
Million 7, 47
Minion 50
Mirtle 3
Mis 27, 29
Misconceited 55
Mis-lead 44, 47
Misse 18, 22, 49
Mistres 59
Mistrusting 29, 49
Mittigate 52
Mo 28
Mocke 22, 60
Mocking 28
Moe 32
Mold 51
Monster-mongers 31
Monsters 31, 53
Moorie 21
Morpheus 25

Morralize 5
Morrow 60
Mounted 59
Mourning 21
Murmuring 58
Murmyring 10
Musæus 44
Muse 21, 27
Muses 37
Musicke 27, 29, 40, 45

Naked 12
Nakedness 60
Narciss 50
Narcissus 37, 38, 40, 41, 42, 44, 45, 46, 47, 49, 59, 60, 64
Nations 63
Nature 49
Ne 61
Neat 42
Neatly 17, 22
Neut-heard 56
Neatest 41
Necessitie 4, 9
Nemesis 27
Neptune 8, 9, 20, 54
Nice 37, 39, 44
Nightingale 9
Nimble 59, 62
Nimphe 13, 27
Niobes 57
Nipt 59
Noate 42, 43
None-age 51
Note 17
Not soes 42
Nothe, Noth 5, 17, 22, 32, 43
Nourish 62, 64
Nuns 56
Nurse 33
Nymph 45, 48, 55, 59
Nympha 60
Nymphes 28
Nymphs 46, 48, 62

Oaks 22
Oberon's 22
Obsequies 25
Ocean 10
Oceans 53
Oceanus 6

Odes 48
Officious 21
On 30, 37
One 17
Ope 44
Oppose 28
Or 28
Orchard 9
Oregone 15
Organ 56
Organing 38
Orient 10, 51
Orizons 14, 24, 59
Orpheus 52
Otomie 8
Ougly 5, 12, 27, 30
Out-coates 8
Out-cries 21, 30
Ouergonne 4, 7
Ouer-lauishly 54
Ouerpries 56
Ouer-ripe 43
Ouerswelling 18
Ouerthrew 41
Ouerthrow 45
Ow 50
Owe 53

Pack 43
Painted cloathes 31
Pallace 59
Pan 13
Paradise 55
Paraphrase 5
Parenthesis 28
Parnassus 37
Parramore 12, 22
Partner 45
Pash 11
Pastime 23
Patterne 41
Pawne 16, 43
Peeres 18, 41
Peerlesse 63
Peeuish 26
Pegasus 9
Pelfe 61
Pel mel 15
Pent 26
Perfect 46
Perfourmances 28

Index.

Perfume 52
Pernitious 26
Pesants 10
Pestering 15
Phaeton 7
Pheasant 9
Phebe 7
Phebus 6, 7, 10, 14, 16, 55, 56, 59
Pherecydes 30
Philocles 30
Philomela 9
Phlegyton 29
Pilate 53
Pilgrim 17
Pip'd 59
Pitchie 45
Plaine-song 37
Plaints 44
Plaintes 39
Planets 55
Plausiue 5
Plausinely 32
Playning, Playn'd 38, 39
Pleasance 51
Pleiades 8, note
Pliant 5, 24
Plodding 37
Plums 9
Po 21, 64
Poast 59
Poasted 58
Poetry 37
Poets 8, 10, 46
Pole 8
Politicke 26
Polyp 52
Pompe 56
Portraide 57
Postes 6, 7, 10
Potion 42
Pretextati 57
Prancke 22
Prest 5
Presumptuous 50
Pretie 46, 48, 49
Prettie 11, 13
Priapus 24, 40
Pricke 41
Prickt 13, 23, 37, 59
Pride 11, 42
Pries 55

Priuce 27
Princes 56
Procris 11, 18, 19, 20, 21, 22, 23, 24, 26, 28, 31, 32
Prodigious 27
Progne 9
Proserpina 19
Proportion 50
Puppius 30
Purple 42, 63
Purpled 8
Purueying 51

Quaint 27, 44, 62
Queen 56, 59
Queene 47
Queintly 12, 41
Quel 55
Quench 5, 10
Quick 28
Quicke 15
Quicke-listed 14
Quickener 27
Quill, 12, 28, 46
Quintessence, 27
Quit 34
Quoth 15, 18

Radomanth 18
Rag 43
Ransackt 27
Rape 22
Rapes 57
Raue 15
Rauishment 9
Rauisht 9, 25
Reakst 41
Rebate 29, 34
Receipte 8
Receit 52
Red-boat 9
Redoune 43
Redresse 60
Reckoning 34
Region 26
Registred 9
Reigne 12
Reliefe 15, 16, 45
Relique 47, 53
Remembrance 63

Remotiue 20
Repast 19, 20
Report 56
Reproache 37
Requitall 18
Resyant 3
Retreit 50
Reuels 29
Reuiuing 60
Reuying 13
Richards 51
Rich-dew-Summoning 55
Rime 27, 63
Riotouse 13, 27
Rioteously 17
Rinet 28
Roabes 63
Robes, 57
Robin Hood 64
Romane 57
Rondelaies 10, 59
Rosamond 62
Rose 39
Rose-ycoloured 29
Roundelaies 59
Royall 23
Rubs 41
Ruffe 13
Ruffe-beard 13
Ruinous 42
Ruth 18, 24
Ruthelesse 17

Sable 29
Sable-winged 44
Sacrilegious 25
Saffron 29, 56
Saint 21, 49, 52, 54, 55, 56
Sample 32
Sans 8
Satyres 10, 13, 28
Satyricke 3
Sauour 52
Sawe 62
Scales 59
Scape 20, 22, 55, 58
Scapes 55, 57
Scarring 61
Scene 58
Schollers 4, 5, 10, 11, 34
Sconce 61

Index.

Scoured 6
Seamed 57
Sea-nymphs 60
Seeming 3, 52
Self-love 48
Semblance 63
Semele 13
Sepulchrizing 52
Sequel 25
Serpents 45
Scruile 27
Seruitor 33
Seuered 49
Shaddo 59
Shaddow 57, 59
Shaddowed 60
Shaddowes 10, 51, 60
Shallow 49
Shame 12, 34, 40
Shelfe 49
Shels 43
Shepheard 56, 59, 62
Shepheardes 10
Sheuering 24
Shewen 46
Shewes 61
Shipwracke 13
Shooting 47
Shot 38
Shout 60
Show 64
Shro'dly 5
Shrouded 58
Shrowded 28
Sidney 62
Siege 58
Sighs 43, 45, 47
Siluan 10
Siluans 11
Siluer 59
Similies 10
Simplicitic 41
Sing 37
Sinke 47
Sire 61
Sisiphus 18
Sisterhood 41
Skils 43, 44
Skoure 33
Skoures 8
Skymes 8

Slak't 4
Slanderous 53
Sluggard 34
Smooth-cut 28
Snakes 20
Snaky 27
Soft-stealing 28
Sollace 28
Sommer 11, 15
Sonettoes 48
Sonne-beames 9, 10
Sore 45
Sort 11
Sound 50
Soueraigne 22, 48, 59
Soueranize 10
Sowzed 4
Sparrows 43
Spiced 31
Spider 13
Spightfull 49
Spilt 63
Sport 48, 49
Sprite 28
Spued 30
Staide 63
Staine 3
Stained 33
Stampe 63
Stand 23
Standard 28
Starre 8
Statelesse 3
Stately 5, 9, 12, 27, 34
Statues 57
Steads 59
Steepe 4
Stem 53
Stitched 57
Stoope 4
Stoupe 4, 9
Stratagems 30
Streake 28, 55
Streking 39
Strength 34
Strengthlesse 23
Stripling 40
Stroke 51
Styll, still, musicke 27, 40
Styx 29
Substance 49, 51

Subtilly 31
Suites 48
Sun-go-downe 52
Sunne-shining 45
Sun-shine 51
Sun-shine-shadow 49
Supposes 3
Surquedie 29
Swaine 25, 27, 28, 62
Swanly 22
Swannes 21
Swarme 38
Swim 28
Syluans 60
Sympathy 7
Syren, Syrens 54
Syren-singing 49
Syrinx 13

Taint 13
Talent 47
Tantalus 52
Tatlest 5
Tauntes 18
Taunts 50
Teared 4
Teares 4, 27
Teate-sucking 27
Tediously 18
Tempe 44
Temples 29
Temporize 5
Tend 32
Tereus 9
Tex 20
Thames 21, 64
Theater 30
Thessalian 25
Thicket 29
Thissels 25
Thought-wandering 45
Threates 12
Thro 41
Throate 59, 62
Throughly 60
Thunder 40
Thwarting 37
Tide 24, 55
Tilt 3, 63
Tilted 51
Tilting 63

Index.

Tinsell 33
Titan 8
Toies, Toy 48, 49, 50
Tombe 19
Too too 12, 17, 18
Top-gallant 53
Torture 18
Tosse 5
Tottering 56, 59
Touch 10
Tourne 34
Tower 9
Toyde 33, 40
Tragicke 12, 29, 30, 31, 39, 47, 58
Tralucent 4
Trauailing 21
Traunce 39
Tread 61
Treason 20
Treasure 61
Treating 14, 52
Treble 15, 16, 21, 47 (subs.), 46
Tresses 12, 44, 53
Trice 8
Trips 59
Triumphes 10
Troade 31
Troupe 47, 51
Troupes 62
Tubs 18
Tune 37, 42
Tup 27
Turning 52
Tut 23
Twaine 16, 28
Tway 31
Twisting 3
Tyger 15
Type 33
Tyrannize 47
Tyres 57
Tythons 59

Ugly 45
Ulysses 4, 27
Unarm'd 58
Unciuill 25
Uncorrected 7
Uncounceld 17

Uncouth 21, 32, 61
Undoe 40
Unlockt 62
Unmaskt 23
Unmercifully 32
Unprophane 21
Untewed 16
Untrain'd 56
Unwoldie 51
Ure 27, 42

Vaine 52
Vale 8, 17, 19, 43 58
Vallies 58
Vapor 55, 56
Vast 27, 37
Vaulted 21
Venus 8, 9, 11, 22, 43, 57
Venum'd 14
Vesper 8
Vicious 49
Vintage 53
Virayon-like 28
Visedly 61
Visor 37
Voice 60
Votarie 54, 56

Wan 18, 34
Wan(wand, 11
Wane 49
Wanton (adj.) 8, 27, 12, 49, 50
Wanton (subs.) 24
Wantonnes 44
Ware 32
Warrant 64
Wauers 53
Waues 29
Weale 31
Weather 38
Weau'd 33
Wedded 32, 34
Weede 18
Weeds 55, 59
Weene 59
Weening 51
Wegg 17
Welkin 55
Wemen 14, 15

Wenches 40, 49
Went (subs.) 30, 32
Wheeles 19
Whelpes 31
White 27
Widow-hood 17
Wilfull 59
Willow 25
Winnings 64
Wit 34
Witlesse 47
Wittie 39
Woemen 15, 18, 19, 26
Woer 49
Womanning 55
Wonder-breeder 40
Wonderment 30
Wood 22
Worlds-wracke 63
Wot 25, 26
Wotting 16
Woxen 12
Woxt 17
Wrangl'de 41
Wrangle 13, 41
Wrought 11
Wysardes 31

Yalpe 14
Ycleeped 31
Yclept 9
Ycoucht 12
Ydone 9, 23
Yellow 31
Yew 42
Yld, yeld 51
Yode 10
Yongster 26
Yore 10, 45
Ypaint 27
Ysiluered 43
Yspoken 27
Yssyckles 11
Ytasked 27
Yuorie 11, 14

Zephirus 11
Zone 8, 22

www.ingramcontent.com/pod-product-compliance
Lightning Source LLC
Chambersburg PA
CBHW051722300426
44115CB00007B/427